NEOPLATONISM AND CHRISTIAN THOUGHT

Studies in Neoplatonism:
  Ancient and Modern

Volume III

R. BAINE HARRIS, GENERAL EDITOR

NEOPLATONISM AND CHRISTIAN THOUGHT

Edited by

Dominic J. O'Meara
THE CATHOLIC UNIVERSITY OF AMERICA

INTERNATIONAL SOCIETY FOR NEOPLATONIC STUDIES
NORFOLK, VIRGINIA

Published by
State University of New York Press, Albany

For information, address State University of New York
Press, State University Plaza, Albany, N.Y., 12246

Library of Congress Cataloging in Publication Data

Main entry under title:

Neoplatonism and Christian thought.

(Studies in Neoplatonism; v. 3)
Includes papers delivered at the Conference on
"Neoplatonism and Christian Thought," held Oct. 1978 at
Catholic University of America, Washington, D.C.
Includes index.
Contents: Introduction / Dominic J. O'Meara —
The Platonic and Christian Ulysses / Jean Pépin —
Origen's doctrine of the Trinity and some later
Neoplatonic theories / John Dillon — [etc.]
1. Neoplatonism—Congresses. 2. Theology—Congresses.
3. Christianity—Philosophy—Congresses. I. O'Meara,
Dominic J. II. Conference on "Neoplatonism and
Christian Thought" (1978: Catholic University of
America) III. Series.
B645.N46   230'.01   81-5272
ISBN O-87395-492-0   AACR2
ISBN O-87395-493-9 (pbk.)

Contents

INTRODUCTION, *Dominic J. O'Meara*   ix

PART I: PATRISTIC THOUGHT

1. THE PLATONIC AND CHRISTIAN ULYSSES
   Jean Pépin, ECOLE PRATIQUE DES HAUTES ETUDES (PARIS)   3
2. ORIGEN'S DOCTRINE OF THE TRINITY AND
   SOME LATER NEOPLATONIC THEORIES
   John Dillon, TRINITY COLLEGE, DUBLIN   19
3. A NEOPLATONIC COMMENTARY ON THE
   CHRISTIAN TRINITY: MARIUS VICTORINUS
   Mary T. Clark, MANHATTENVILLE COLLEGE   24
4. THE NEOPLATONISM OF SAINT AUGUSTINE
   John J. O'Meara, UNIVERSITY COLLEGE, DUBLIN   34

PART II: LATER GREEK AND BYZANTINE THOUGHT

5. SOME LATER NEOPLATONIC VIEWS ON DIVINE
CREATION AND THE ETERNITY OF THE WORLD
Gérard Verbeke, UNIVERSITÉ CATHOLIQUE DE LOUVAIN   45
6. JOHN PHILOPONUS AND STEPHANUS OF ALEXANDRIA:
TWO NEOPLATONIC CHRISTIAN COMMENTATORS
ON ARISTOTLE?
Henry Blumenthal, UNIVERSITY OF LIVERPOOL   54
7. NEW OBJECTIVE LINKS BETWEEN THE
PSEUDO-DIONYSIUS AND PROCLUS
Henri-Dominique Saffrey,
CENTRE NATIONAL DE LA RECHERCHE SCIENTIFIQUE (PARIS)   64
8. THE PROBLEM OF GENERAL CONCEPTS IN
NEOPLATONISM AND BYZANTINE THOUGHT
Linos Benakis, UNIVERSITY OF ATHENS   75

PART III: MEDIEVAL LATIN THOUGHT

9. THE PRIMACY OF EXISTENCE IN
THE THOUGHT OF ERIUGENA
G.-H. Allard, UNIVERSITÉ DE MONTRÉAL   89
10. THE OVERCOMING OF THE NEOPLATONIC TRIAD OF
BEING, LIFE AND INTELLECT BY THOMAS AQUINAS
Cornelio Fabro, UNIVERSITÀ DI PERUGIA   97
11. THE PROBLEM OF THE REALITY AND MULTIPLICITY
OF DIVINE IDEAS IN CHRISTIAN NEOPLATONISM
Norris Clarke, FORDHAM UNIVERSITY   109
12. MEISTER ECKHART ON GOD AS ABSOLUTE UNITY
Bernard McGinn, UNIVERSITY OF CHICAGO   128

PART IV: RENAISSANCE THOUGHT

13. NEOPLATONISM AND CHRISTIAN THOUGHT
IN THE FIFTEENTH CENTURY
(NICHOLAS OF CUSA AND MARSILIO FICINO)
Maurice de Gandillac, UNIVERSITÉ DE PARIS-I   143
14. NEOPLATONISM, THE GREEK COMMENTATORS
AND RENAISSANCE ARISTOTELIANISM
Edward P. Mahoney, DUKE UNIVERSITY   169
15. ANDREAS CAMUTIUS ON THE CONCORD OF PLATO
AND ARISTOTLE WITH SCRIPTURE
Charles B. Schmitt, THE WARBURG INSTITUTE   178

PART V: MODERN THOUGHT

16. TRIADS AND TRINITY IN
    THE POETRY OF ROBERT BROWNING
    Elizabeth Bieman, WESTERN ONTARIO UNIVERSITY   187
17. THE CHRISTIAN PLATONISM OF C.S.LEWIS,
    J.R.R.TOLKIEN AND CHARLES WILLIAMS
    Mary Carman Rose, GOUCHER COLLEGE   203
18. NEGATIVE THEOLOGY, MYTH AND INCARNATION
    A. Hilary Armstrong, DALHOUSIE UNIVERSITY   213
19. WHY CHRISTIANS SHOULD BE PLATONISTS
    John N. Findlay, BOSTON UNIVERSITY   223

NOTES   233

INDEX OF NAMES AND SUBJECTS   293

Introduction

Ever since Christians began to reflect on their faith, to express and explain it both to themselves and to others, they have availed themselves of the intellectual means which appeared to be suitable for this and which had been developed by the philosophical movements of their time. The use made of Stoic, Cynic, and Platonic conceptions in Saint John and Saint Paul is well known. Even a writer such as Tertullian, who vigorously condemned philosophy, can be found to be articulating the Christian message with the help of pagan philosophical concepts, and those Christians who favored taking advantage of philosophical ideas had no difficulty in elaborating a scripturally based justification of their practice.[1]

The intellectual system that many influential early Christian thinkers made most use of was Platonic philosophy in the eclectic (Aristotelianizing and Stoicizing) form in which this philosophy was understood and widely taught in the early centuries of the Christian era[2] and in particular in the coherent and inspiring structure given this eclectic Platonism by Plotinus (ca. A.D. 204–270) and by his many no less influential followers, Porphyry (ca. A.D. 232–305), Iamblichus (ca. A.D. 245–326), and Proclus (ca. A.D. 412–485), to name but a few.[3] The interest of early Christians in Platonism had to do not merely with the fact that it was the dominant and by far the most lively philosophical movement of late antiquity. As a philosophy, it also seemed to have more in common with Christian belief than did other philosophies. Saint Augustine, for example, tells us in his *Confessions* that "when I recorded how I had read certain books of the Platonists, . . . he [Simplicianus, who succeeded Saint Ambrose as Bishop of Milan] congratulated me because I had not fallen in with the writings of other philosophers, full of fallacies and deceits according to the elements of this world, whereas in the works of the Platonists God and his Word are introduced in all manners" (VIII. 2. 3, trans. Ryan).

Although it might appear that Aristotelianism displaced Platonism in the later Middle Ages as a privileged philosophy in Christian thought, it did so as a philosophy enriched with fundamental Neoplatonic insights.[4] Indirectly, through the works of Gregory of Nyssa, Ambrose, Augustine, Pseudo-Dionysius and others, Neoplatonism exerted great influence not only on medieval Christianity but also on all Christians who ever since, consciously or not, have been indebted to these thinkers. Since the revival of interest in Plotinus and his school in the Renaissance, direct access to the original Neoplatonic texts has strengthened the presence of Neoplatonic ideas in Christian thought. This presence in recent times is perhaps less easily discerned on a surface troubled by the swift waves driven in rapid succession by contemporary movements in philosophy and the social sciences, but, as several papers in this volume indicate, it is far from losing its living appeal to Christian thinkers.

The relationship between Neoplatonism and Christianity, as indeed the relationship between any philosophy and a religion, raises many questions of different kinds, not the least of which challenges such a relationship. From the point of view of the historian, the presence of Neoplatonic ideas in Christian thought is undeniable. But how should we go about identifying precisely and measuring this presence? To what extent did particular Christian writers actually read and make use of particular Neoplatonic texts? To what extent and in what ways were Neoplatonic conceptions influential in a Christian writer's reflection on his faith? Did those conceptions contribute significantly or only superficially to the development of theology? If significantly, should they, from a theologian's point of view, be discarded or should they be preserved, and if so, on what basis? Since a relation between a philosophy and a religion is in question, is there subversion of the philosophy in a religious appropriation of its theories, or is there subversion of the faith in a philosophical interpretation of revealed truths, so that both from a philosophical and from a religious standpoint, the relation can only be either superficial or undesirable? Since both philosophy and religion make truth-claims, might there not be some structure of harmonization?

Modern approaches to dealing with these and other relevant questions have tended to become increasingly fragmented and complex as a result of considerable expansion in the study both of Christian thought and of Neoplatonic philosophy in a variety of different disciplines and as a result of advances in critical method in these disciplines, which make superficial answers no longer acceptable.[5] It was therefore decided by the International Society for Neoplatonic Studies and The Catholic University of America to cosponsor a Conference on "Neoplatonism and Christian Thought" in 1978 which would serve to bring together scholars in different disciplines who could thus review in common the results of contemporary research in the field, discuss remaining problems, and identify new lines of investigation. The present volume includes papers delivered at this conference. Of course not every area could be covered by the participating scholars, nor could final solutions be presented for all the relevant problems. However, the papers of this volume constitute a conspectus of contemporary studies in this rich field, present advances in the field, and, it is hoped, will provide a focus and stimulus for further discussion and research. In what follows I will attempt to note briefly some of the points made in these papers, organizing my account roughly with reference to the sequence of questions presented above as likely to arise with respect to the relationship between Neoplatonism and Christianity.

*   *   *

There have been several accurate studies of the knowledge and use of specific Neoplatonic texts in the great Christian writers of the fourth century—Basil, Gregory of Nyssa, Marius Victorinus, Ambrose, and Augustine.[6] In his paper Father Henri-Dominique Saffrey continues his earlier work providing *precise* evidence of the debt of the influential sixth-century Christian writer known as (Pseudo-) Dionysius the Areopagite to the philosophy of Proclus. He presents a critique of the sorts of doctrinal rapprochements between Pseudo-Dionysius and Neoplatonism that are, in terms of historical method, inadequate[7] and then characterizes what can count as an "objective link" between Pseudo-Dionysius and a Neoplatonic source: links in vocabulary, in intellectual structures, and especially those links betrayed by the earliest commentator on Pseudo-Dionysius, John of Scythopolis, in his attempts to explain unusual (Neoplatonic) expressions in the Dionysian writings. One such expression which Saffrey shows as deriving from Proclus is that referring to divine names as "statues." Saffrey also uncovers two quotations from Proclus in Pseudo-Dionysius and suggests that much more remains to be done in establishing objective links between Pseudo-Dionysius and Proclus.

If in some cases precise links can be established between Neoplatonic and Christian texts, in others large gaps in the surviving evidence necessitate a more tentative treatment. Professor John Dillon's paper takes up a doctrine in Origen (ca. A.D. 185–254) concerning the Trinity, which represents God the Father's power as extending to all that exists, God the Son's as extending only to living beings, and the Holy Spirit's extending only to the "saved." He finds a similar doctrine concerning the range of activity of causal principles in Proclus' *Elements of Theology,* a much later (fifth century) Neoplatonic text, but suggests grounds for assuming, nevertheless, that Origen's doctrine must be an adaptation of an originally Platonic doctrine, evidence for the existence of which in Origen's time is lacking but which may well have been part of a Middle Platonic system.

In considering Origen's doctrine to be an adaptation of a Platonic doctrine, one is not only referring to the Platonic sources, but one is also raising the issue as to how this Platonic doctrine was made use of by Origen in a Christian context. Professor Jean Pépin considers the question of the adaptation of Middle and Neoplatonic ideas in relation to a wide range of early Christian writers and with respect to the similarities between their interpretation of the figure of Ulysses and the interpretation of Ulysses in Platonic texts. He shows that in its emphasis on the Ulysses of the *Odyssey* and in its "metaphysical," and thus more allegorical exegesis, the Platonic interpretation resembles Christian interpretations and constitutes a new approach in comparison to the moralistic interpretation of the figure of Ulysses in Cynic and Stoic philosophy. However, if indebted to Platonism in its interpretation, for example, of the sea of the *Odyssey* as the tempting world, of Ithaca as the fatherland of the soul, Christian interpretation also introduces specifically Christian features: Ulysses' ship is seen for instance as the image of the Church, the mast as a symbol of the cross.

Mother Mary T. Clark also considers the question of the Christian use of Neoplatonic ideas in her study of Marius Victorinus' Platonic-inspired interpretation of the Trinity. She argues that Victorinus' understanding of the Trinity was fundamentally scriptural and that he made use of the philosophy "best adapted to convey the possibility of a triune God," that is, Porphyrian rather than Plotinian Platonism, in the context in particular of dealing with the philosophically deficient Trinitarian formulations of Arians and Neo-Arians. Porphyry's philosophy thus had the limited role for Victorinus of providing a philosophical defense of the coherence of a doctrine, itself, however, based on interpretation of Scripture.

In relation to a personality as subtle and complex as that of Saint Augustine, discussion of the Christian use of Neoplatonism must take account of several different levels of use and a variety of different interests guiding this use. Professor John O'Meara reviews scholarship on some of the problems concerning Augustine's Neoplatonism and draws attention in particular to the moral and emotional importance to Augustine of Plotinus' account of the *conversio*, or turning, of the soul to God, the interest for Augustine of Porphyry's search for a "universal path to the liberation of the soul," and the little-recognized use made by Augustine of Plotinian negative theology. O'Meara concludes that the complex and sometimes conflicting tendencies of Augustine are reflected in Augustine's attitude toward Neoplatonism, which he rejected in its opposition to the doctrines of the Incarnation and Resurrection but which also provided him with a "rational understanding of the problems and mysteries of Christian theology."

Professor Guy Allard's study of the lexicographical, gnoseological, and ontological primacy of existence in the thought of the ninth century philosopher John Scottus Eriugena (or John the Scot) shows how, in his commentary on Pseudo-Dionysius, Eriugena reinterprets and modifies the Dionysian texts, replacing Neoplatonic essentialism with a metaphysics in which God is understood as existence, pure activity, the creator (not a Platonic demiurge) of the existence of essences in which these essences become knowable. In this radical modification Allard sees the philosopher and theologian in Eriugena working as one, bringing out what was to be a major theme in Thomas Aquinas.

Another case of reinterpretation or modification of Neoplatonic ideas, this time in relation to Aquinas, is examined by Father Cornelio Fabro. He discusses Aquinas' commentary on the *Liber de causis* (a medieval Arabic work based on Proclus' *Elements of Theology*) and the late incomplete work *De substantiis separatis* with a view to analyzing Aquinas' absorption and critical reshaping of Neoplatonic metaphysics, in particular of the Neoplatonic metaphysical triad Being-Life-Intellect.[8] He shows how Aquinas, using Proclus' *Elements of Theology* and Pseudo-Dionysius, brings out the absolute dominion and unique creative act of Being, as *ipsum esse subsistens* (God), and how he gives to the principles of life and intellect a formative (noncreative) causality, thus reshaping the Neoplatonic triad on metaphysical grounds in support of which he could refer to his Neoplatonic sources.

Professor Bernard McGinn's paper on Meister Eckhart (ca. 1260–1327) is a study of Christian use of Neoplatonic dialectic. Three problems in the interpretation of Eckhart's doctrine of God are taken: the priority of understanding to existence in reference to God in some texts and the priority of existence to understanding in others; the distinction between God and the Godhead and the separation this appears to introduce in the divine nature; the meaning of Eckhart's conception of the birth of the Word in the soul. Predication, analogy, and dialectic are then explored as three levels of "increasing depth" in Eckhart's presentation of God and as a way of approaching a resolution of the first of these problems. Finally McGinn discusses aspects of the Christian use of Neoplatonism as this relates to the potential value of Neoplatonic dialectic to Christian reflections on the transcendence and immanence of God.

Discussing a much more recent writer in relation to a broad conception of Neoplatonic ideas and their role in serving to structure Christian beliefs, Professor Elizabeth Bieman traces Robert Browning's "lifelong quest for God and truth" as expressed in his poetry and as this quest develops in three phases, beginning in a search for the absolute truth denied to fallen man, passing through a theological expression of the Incarnation, and ending in an awareness of man's epistemological limitations and of the rewards of the search for truth. She brings out in these phases of Browning's quest the role played by the triad of Power, Love, and Knowledge (the third term linking the first two, opposed, terms) which she suggests can be associated in Browning with the persons of the Trinity.

Finally, Professor Mary Rose examines in her paper how Christian Platonism informs the literary activity of C. S. Lewis, J. R. R. Tolkien, and Charles Williams. She provides evidence that all three writers can be considered orthodox Christians and then brings out the use made in their works of three Platonic themes: the reality of supersensory aspects of creation; the means of acquiring knowledge of these aspects; and, the ideal copresence of Truth, Beauty, and Goodness in all parts of creation. Other Platonic conceptions in these three authors are discussed: psychophysical dualism, otherworldliness, and the hierarchy of being.

If there were many Neoplatonic conceptions that could be used and adapted in a wide variety of ways by Christian thinkers, there were, however, some elements of Neoplatonism that were of doubtful assimilability for a Christian, just as there were Christian doctines (e.g., the Incarnation of Christ, the resurrection of the body) which pagan Neoplatonists rejected. Father Norris Clarke examines one Neoplatonic conception which he believes resists coherent assimilation into Christian thought—the conception of a multiplicity of really existent Forms or Ideas as objects of divine thought. In a survey of the treatment of this conception in the Latin West, from Saint Augustine to the fourteenth century, he argues that the conception could not be satisfactorily reconciled by Christian thinkers with the Christian denial of a "plurality in God outside that of the three divine Persons." He suggests that a resolution to the conflict of these two positions was provided by Aquinas who saw the divine ideas, not as the true being of creatures, but as possessing "intentional" being. The divine intelligence "thinks them up . . . as possible limited modes of participation in his own infinite act of *esse subsistens*."

Whether or not there are such things as separately existing Forms or Ideas was itself the subject of the great debate about "universals" in Western medieval philosophy. Professor Linos Benakis examines this debate in the form it took in Byzantine philosophy. He characterizes the dominant Byzantine attitude to this question as "conceptual realism" (universals understood as concepts produced through conceptual apprehension of the common characteristics of things). This approach he shows to be indebted to the works of the Neoplatonic school of Alexandria of the fifth and sixth centuries (Ammonius, John Philoponus, and others) that also appears to have influenced Boethius and the Arabic writers who formed the background to Western discussions of the subject. He concludes by pointing to the need for investigation into what contacts there might have been between Byzantine thinkers and the thinkers of the Latin West.

Another conception (both Aristotelian and Neoplatonic) whose consistency with Christian belief was a matter of doubt was the idea that the world never began but exists from eternity. The acceptability of this position was discussed with great vigor and subtlety in the West in the thirteenth century, but many of the arguments, as can be seen from Father Gérard Verbeke's paper, had already been developed in the Neoplatonic school of Alexandria. Verbeke notes that numerous Christian members of the school did not reject the doctrine of the eternity of the world and that Philoponus, a Christian, attacked the doctrine, not on religious grounds, but on the basis of philosophical arguments drawn from Aristotle. In his reply to Philoponus, Simplicius (an Athenian contemporary of Philoponus) stressed the compatibility in his view of the idea of creation from nothing (an idea found in pagan as well as Christian Neoplatonism) with the doctrine of the eternity of the world. The subject was thus (as it would be later) a matter of philosophical debate within Neoplatonism, irrespective of any problem of theological acceptability that an eternal world might raise.

Professor Henry Blumenthal's study of the commentaries on the crucial third book of Aristotle's *De anima* by Philoponus and Stephanus of Alexandria comes to similar conclusions about the extent to which the Christianity of these two commentators affected the positions they took in their reading of Aristotle. Blumenthal shows that the positions they take are explicable in terms of the Neoplatonic tradition, need not be seen as reflecting their Christianity and, in fact, may appear to be at variance on some points with Christian doctrine. He establishes that the commentaries are two separate works (and not merely different versions of a standard Alexandrian lecture course) and points out that they are really Neoplatonic interpretations of Aristotle and not merely expositions, free of philosophical "bias," of the text.

If there are aspects of Neoplatonic philosophy and Christian doctrine that appear to be in conflict, a case might still be made for the existence of a common ground and indeed the extreme position could be taken that not only is there no genuine fundamental conflict, but, on the contrary, there is a harmony between Neoplatonism and Christian thought. This last position is found most extensively (if not exclusively) in the Renaissance. Professor Maurice de Gandillac examines two leading Renaissance champions of harmony, Nicholas of Cusa (1401–1464) and Marsilio Ficino (1433–1499). For each author de Gandillac indicates his knowledge of Greek sources and the development of his views concerning the nature of this harmony. In Nicholas of Cusa all religions and philosophies are seen as a spectrum of different insights which can be reconciled in a consistent structure fundamental to which are the doctrines of the Trinity and the Incarnation. Ficino, it is suggested, is concerned less with these doctrines than with proving in philosophy truths (the immortality of the soul, in particular) that prepare the way for religion. However, Christian religion and philosophy (conceived along Neoplatonic lines as an ascent to God) are found to blend into each other in Ficino's mind.

Professor Charles Schmitt extends our knowledge of the influence of Ficino's harmonization of Neoplatonism and Christianity in his study of a little-known Renaissance thinker, Andrea Camuzio (ca. 1512–1587). Schmitt discusses Camuzio's attempt to demonstrate the harmony of Scripture with Plato and Aristotle on the basis of a Neoplatonic conception of philosophy as directed to an end (God) which is also the goal of religion. Camuzio was also however an Aristotelian in certain respects and thus exemplifies two points made by Schmitt—that, contrary to common conceptions, Aristotelianism is the dominant philosophy of the Renaissance and that this Aristotelianism embodies Neoplatonic ideas to a greater degree than is usually realized.

Professor Edward Mahoney examines two ways in which Neoplatonism came to have a special impact on Renaissance Aristotelianism. He shows how the Greek commentators, especially Themistius and Simplicius, were studied by and had influence on the psychology of Nicoletto Vernia (d. 1499) and of his pupil Agostino Nifo (1470–1535), the latter using Ficino's commentaries on Plotinus to understand Simplicius and seeing in Neoplatonism support for Christian belief. After Nifo, the use of the Greek commentators became widespread in Renaissance Aristotelianism. Mahoney also discusses the continuous debate that took place in Renaissance Aristotelianism about the Neoplatonic conceptual scheme of a hierarchy of being in which God and matter constitute the termini.

It may appear that the attempt to harmonize Neoplatonism and Christian belief is possible only at the price of ignoring certain difficulties and even of abandoning elements that may be thought to be essential either by a Neoplatonist or by a Christian. Professor John Findlay suggests in his paper that both Christianity and

Platonism contribute to "Absolute theory." To the Absolute he ascribes seven "demarcating characteristics": it exists in an unqualified sense, exists of necessity, is unique, is unitary, is capable of having an inner distinction of the essential and inessential, is all-comprehensive, and has room in it for Mind and its guiding values. This Absolute he finds in both Christianity and Neoplatonism. However, he suggests that Platonism's concept of the Absolute is preferable to the Christian concept in that it does not attribute to the Absolute the individuality, contingency, and arbitrariness he finds in the Christian Absolute. The adoption of a (Neo-) Platonic Absolute which he recommends to Christians may be felt by them, however, to entail abandoning central elements of their religion.

However, it must be noted that as there is room within Neoplatonism for different interpretations and positions, so is there a diversity in the ways Christians view their religion and attempt to understand its mysteries.[9] Professor A. Hilary Armstrong argues that certain Neoplatonic ways of thinking are of value to a Christian's attempt to interpret his or her religion in the context of a contemporary religious crisis, which Armstrong describes as a breakdown in the acceptability of claims made for certain "forms of words and ways of thinking about God as timelessly and universally true." In such a context, negative theology is useful in allowing both for the use of language about God and for preservation of a "distance" with respect to such language.[10] He also recommends "mythical" interpretation of systematic theology ("mythical" understood in a Neoplatonic sense as taking account of the "image" status of the ways through which the Unknowable God communicates) and provides as an example a Pseudo-Dionysian view of the Incarnation that emphasizes the cosmic and universal outgoing and return of the Godhead.

*   *   *

In conclusion, I may be permitted to draw attention to some ideas, primarily methodological in character, which I believe to emerge from the papers of this volume and which may be of use to further inquiries in the field. It is clear, first of all, that the relation between Neoplatonic philosophy and Christian thought, as viewed today by the historian, the philosopher, or the theologian, is hardly a simple one of concord or confrontation between two uniform entities. Christian thought is constituted, as is Neoplatonic philosophy, of many different thinkers with different interests and different approaches in relation to a unity of inspiration. In order then to reach a sound assessment of the historical influence of Neoplatonic philosophy on the development of Christian thought, much work must be done that will bring out specific "objective links" between individual Neoplatonic and Christian thinkers and texts. The critical standards to be met in such work are indicated in Saffrey's paper. In cases such as that discussed by Dillon, lack of evidence may force us to hypothesize. Yet there is hope that such hypotheses may be verified as further advances are made in our knowledge both of the history of Neoplatonism and of the history of Christian thought. Detailed work concentrating on specific texts can be expected to provide a solid basis for historical generalization and has already helped undermine some untested assumptions, a case in point being the demonstration by Schmitt and Mahoney of the unsuspected importance of Neoplatonic ideas to Renaissance Aristotelians and to their interpretation of their beliefs.

In adopting Neoplatonic ideas, a Christian author is as likely as not to use them selectively (as shown, for example, in Pépin's paper) or even to modify them. The motives guiding such adoption, selection, and modification may not always be easily uncovered, nor the same in every instance. One may need to take account (as is done in O'Meara's paper) of the particular complexity of a personality such as that of Saint Augustine's, of an intellectual and spiritual development such as that traced by Bieman. In the case examined by Mother Clark, it appears that Victorinus selected the Neoplatonic theory that seemed most consonant with Scripture. However, the situation with respect to scriptural and theological motives for selecting or adapting Neoplatonic ideas is sometimes far from simple. As Verbeke and Blumenthal show, a Christian writer might espouse positions for reasons that we would assume are theological but which in fact turn out to be purely philosophical. Indeed, in the cases analyzed by Allard and Fabro, it becomes difficult clearly to distinguish theological from philosophical reasons for the adoption or modification of a Neoplatonic theory by a Christian thinker.

These difficulties in separating theological from philosophical motives serve as a useful reminder that theology and philosophy converge (as the Renaissance well knew) as attempts to reach true understanding of fundamental issues in life. The way in which a Christian thinker makes use of Neoplatonic philosophy represents a position taken in relation to such issues, which means that one must be sensitive to these issues in order to appreciate adequately the position taken by the Christian Neoplatonist in relation to them. Such a position can even present itself as a challenge to one's own possible or actual exploration of these issues.

The meeting of philosophy and theology may also remind us that each of these, as an attempt at understanding, is bound by canons of rational interpretation. If a philosophical theory is selected by a Christian as suitable in a particular religious context, it does not cease for all that to be subject to philosophical critique; and if such a theory is found to be theologically unsuitable, it can only be replaced by another theory which is itself philosophically defensible, as is shown, for example, in Mother Clark's paper. The theologies of today also make use in various ways of contemporary philosophical ideas that may or may not prove philosophically adequate. A perception of inadequacies in these has led some indeed to call for reflection on an older philosophy from which, Armstrong and McGinn suggest, the Christian thinker may derive a better interpretation of his religion.

*　　*　　*

ACKNOWLEDGMENTS

For their generous assistance I would like to thank the members of the International Society for Neoplatonic Studies Executive Committee and the members of the Conference Planning Committee; Edward P. Mahoney, who translated Fabro's paper from the Italian (making use of an earlier incomplete translation by

Margaret Calderon); John F. Wippel, who checked my translations of the sections of Aquinas' commentary on the *De causis* quoted in Fabro; and especially Mary Brennan, who translated from the French the papers by Allard, de Gandillac, and Saffrey. I have prepared the translation from the French of Pépin's paper. French versions of the papers by Armstrong and Saffrey have appeared respectively in *Mélanges Trouillard* ed. S. Breton (Paris, 1981), and *Revue des sciences philosophiques et théologiques* 63 (1979); permission to reprint these papers here in English is gratefully acknowledged. Bieman's paper is reprinted with permission from *Cithara* 19 (1980). This volume owes much to Mary Ann Ellery, who prepared the Index, Peter Manchester, and Owen Sadlier. The Conference was supported by a grant from the National Endowment for the Humanities. Translation costs were met with grants from The Catholic University of America and from the International Society for Neoplatonic Studies.

I

PATRISTIC
THOUGHT

1

The Platonic and Christian Ulysses

JEAN PÉPIN

I
PHILOSOPHOS ODYSSEUS[1]

Several philosophical schools in antiquity made use of the figure of Ulysses. Take the case of the Cynics, to begin with, who put him forward as an *exemplum*. The idea is already suggested in the fifth century B.C. by the founder of the Cynic movement, Antisthenes. Ulysses is for him a sage who knows life, the gods and men—and women!—and who knows how to adapt his speech in relation to different interlocutors.[2] The same kind of evaluation of Ulysses is found two centuries later in Bion.[3] It becomes a literary cliche in the apocryphal letters of the Cynics, which date from the imperial period and which see in Ulysses, notably in his clothes (that is, his rags), the incarnation of the kind of life advocated by Cynicism.[4] It was to be expected that the Stoics, who admitted to being under Cynic influence in their ethics, would in turn choose Ulysses as a model of morality. In fact, no trace of this is found in the documents relating to the founders of Stoicism, but it is a well-established idea in the Stoics of the imperial period: Seneca, then Epictetus, and in two texts influenced by Stoicism that probably date from the first or second century A.D., the *De vita et poesi Homeri* of Pseudo-Plutarch and the *Quaestiones homericae* of Heraclitus. In these texts we find a Ulysses extolled because of his endurance, his indifference to pain, his contempt for pleasure.[5]

Parallel to this Cynic and Stoic tendency, there developed another philosophical use of Ulysses, of which I would like to give a representative sample. The reader must forgive the length of this passage in view of the fact that I will use it in the following pages as a point of comparison. It concerns the episode of the Sirens, which Plutarch prides himself in using to show that there is no conflict between Homer and Plato (*Republic* X, 517B):

> Now Homer's Sirens, it is true, frighten us, inconsistently with the Platonic myth; but the poet too conveyed a truth symbolically, namely that the power of their music is not inhuman or destructive; as souls depart from this world to the next, so it seems, and drift uncertainly after death, it creates in them a passionate love for the heavenly and divine, and forgetfulness of mortality; it possesses them and enchants them with its spell, so that in joyfulness they follow the Sirens and join them in their circuits. Here on earth a kind of faint echo of that music reaches us, and appealing to our souls through the medium of words, reminds them of what they experienced in an earlier existence. The ears of most souls, however, are plastered over and blocked up, not with wax, but with carnal obstructions and affections. But any soul that through innate gifts is aware of this echo, and remembers that other world, suffers what falls in no way short of the very maddest passions of love, longing and yearning to break the tie with the body, but unable to do so. (Trans. Sandbach)[6]

Although Plutarch puts this passage in the mouth of the Platonic speaker in his dialogue, the exegesis thus presented is not specifically Platonic, but is Pythagorean, as can be seen from some comparisons.[7] There were, therefore, at a time which is hard to determine, Pythagoreans for whom the song of the Homeric Sirens represented the planetary music that enthralls souls after death and agitates them already in this life, on the condition that their ears are not sealed by carnal passions as wax blocked the ears of Ulysses' companions.[8] This exegesis must also have been a very significant part of a larger whole that is only partially known, that is, the allegorical interpretation of the figure of Ulysses in the Pythagorean tradition.[9] It is likely that this Pythagorean Ulysses influenced the image that the later followers of Plato would have of the Homeric hero, an image some aspects of which will be traced in the following pages.

In looking back over what has been noted about the way in which the Cynics, Stoics, and Pythagoreans saw the figure of Ulysses, and anticipating what will be seen about its meaning in Neoplatonism, we see a clear difference that, from different angles, separates these four philosophical movements into two groups of two. First, while the Cynics and the Stoics also take into account Ulysses' actions in the *Iliad*,[10] the Neoplatonists and, as far as we can tell, the Pythagoreans concern themselves exclusively with the figure of the *Odyssey*, that is, with his maritime adventures.[11] Further, as we have quickly seen in the case of the former group and as we will see in more detail concerning the latter group, Pythagoreans and Neoplatonists agree to confer on Ulysses a metaphysical dimension—to discover in his legend the history of the soul—whereas the other group confines itself to extolling him as a moral ideal. Hence the former are forced to make use of an allegorical exegesis which goes far beyond the immediate meaning of the poem,[12] contrary to the Cynics and Stoics who could be satisfied with an almost literal reading.[13]

II
THE NEOPLATONIC EXEGESIS

1. Three Stages in a Long Tradition

Ulysses freeing himself from Circe and Calypso, despite their charms, so as to escape to his fatherland, Ithaca, which he loves is Homer's reminder to us to return to our fatherland on high, tearing ourselves away from the beauties of the sensible world. Such is Plotinus' interpretation in his famous treatise *On Beauty*:

> This would be truer advice, "Let us fly to our dear country." What then is our way of escape, and how are we to find it? We shall put out to sea, as Ulysses did, from the witch Circe or Calypso—as the poet [Homer] says (I think with a hidden meaning) (αἰνιττόμενος)—and was not content to stay though he had delights of the eyes and lived among much beauty of sense. Our country from which we came is there, our Father is there. (Trans. Armstrong)[14]

Proclus, in turn, sees in Ithaca "that mystical port of the soul (μυστικὸς ὅρμος τῆς ψυχῆς) to which the poet brings back Ulysses after the long wanderings of his life, and to which we rather must return, that is, if we wish to be saved."[15] As to the wandering in which the soul is commonly caught and the ascent which will deliver it, these Proclus discerns in the order of knowledge; throughout this epistemological odyssey, the soul will transcend successively sensations, images, opinions, sciences, discursive reason itself, to reach a "life according to the intellect, which alone possesses stability."[16] Here the progressive return of Ulysses is used as an illustration and guarantee of the hierarchy of knowledge defined in Books VI and VII of the *Republic*. Elsewhere, the same Proclus finds in the sea in which Ulysses struggles the symbol of the world of coming-to-be, whose temptations are embodied by the Sirens. Hence Plato's advice (*Phaedrus* 259A) to avoid the Sirens:

> As to souls, who live in the world of coming-to-be, they should "sail past them," imitating Homer's Ulysses—if it is true that the sea also is the image of coming-to-be (θάλασσα γενέσεως εἰκών)—so as not to allow themselves to be bewitched (θέλγωνται) by coming-to-be.[17]

Eustathius of Thessalonica, a Byzantine scholar of the twelfth century, has preserved many Neoplatonic allegories concerning the Homeric poems. One of these, on Ulysses and Calypso, coincides substantially with Plotinus' exegesis, but weighs it down with plays on etymology and by establishing detailed correspondences; Calypso, meaning she who "envelops" (συγκαλύπτουσαν), stands for our body, envelope of the soul; she held back Ulysses as the flesh fetters man; if her island is said to be "encircled by currents of water" and "planted with trees," it is because the body on the one hand is traversed, as Plato says, by a liquid flux, and, on the other hand, consists of a matter similar to wood and dense as a forest; but, Ulysses returns to his beloved fatherland, which, according to the Platonists,[18] denotes the intelligible world, the true fatherland of souls.

2. Two Important Texts

(a) HERMIAS, *In Phaedrum* 259A

Eustathius is a witness to the fact that, nine centuries after Plotinus, there were still readers interested in his interpretation of Ulysses. Of this long history, for which we have just picked out three witnesses who expressly name the Homeric hero, one can find many other traces which are more vague and more limited. At any rate, I have not yet discussed the texts which are most instructive. I must present them now.

One of these texts is found in the commentary on Plato's *Phaedrus* which has been transmitted under the name of Hermias (second half of the fifth century A.D.), but which is inspired by Syrianus, the teacher of Proclus. The passage of Plato commented on is the beginning of the myth of the crickets (*Phaedrus* 259AB), which, paraphrased, follows: At noon the crickets are singing in the trees above Socrates and Phaedrus. Socrates imagines that the crickets are watching them, and that if they saw the two men give in to sleep, as if enchanted by their magic (κηλουμένους), they would mock them; if, on the contrary, Socrates says, they see us "sailing past them as if they were Sirens, resisting their spells, then perhaps they would give us the gift they have from the gods to give to men,"[19] that is, as what follows shows (259C), the privilege of singing until death and then becoming the couriers of the Muses.

This is how Hermias comments on this text:

> Just as those, [Plato] says, who are attracted and bewitched (κατακηλούμενοι) by the Sirens forget their own fatherland, so also we, if we give in to the magic of these sights and these crickets and are plunged into sleep, forget our fatherland and our ascent to the intelligible (τῆς εἰς τὸ νοητὸν ἀναγωγῆς). But if we awaken in ourselves discernment and vigilance, if we refuse the attraction of the sweetness of life, we sail past (παραπλέομεν) like Ulysses, we avoid life here below (τὸν ἐνταῦθα βίον), we become worthy of our own fatherland and of our ascent toward the intelligible. "The gift that they have from the gods";—if, then, it were to happen, [Plato] says, that we would be able to sail past the Sirens (παραπλεῦσαι), the Sirens who are in the sensible world (ἐν τῷ αἰσθητῷ κόσμῳ), which is to say the demons who hold back souls in the proximity of coming-to-be (περὶ τὴν γένεσιν), then at that moment the crickets, that is, the divine souls and the gods, seeing us revolting against coming-to-be (γενέσεως) and living like gods, would give us the greatest gift for men, which is to treat us as companions. For as the gods are vigilant in their own activity, so we also should awaken ourselves as far as possible, and it is then that we awaken ourselves, if we reactivate the reason (λόγον) which is in us. The most speculative of the exegetes of the *Iliad* and the *Odyssey* [have said that it is] also the ascent (ἄνοδον) [of the soul which Homer has portrayed]; they understand the *Iliad*

thus: it is because the soul fights [so as to leave] matter that [the poet] represented battles, wars and suchlike; as to the *Odyssey*, it is [Ulysses] sailing past the Sirens (παραπλέοντα), escaping Circe, the Cyclops, Calypso, and all the obstacles in the way of the ascent (ἀναγωγήν) of the soul, leaving them for his fatherland, that is, for the intelligible (νοητόν).[20]

It is clearly the comparison—incidental, fleeting, and, it seems, purely literary—made by Plato ὥσπερ Σειρῆνας that led Hermias to have recourse to Ulysses and to his interpretation in Neoplatonism. The weakness of this starting point makes the commentator, especially at the beginning, attribute to Plato much more than he actually says, not indeed without some arbitrariness, since the Sirens and the crickets, united first in that their magic produces in their respective victims forgetfulness of the fatherland, are immediately afterwards set in opposition as maleficent demons and helping divinities. The Homeric exegesis itself appears to conform, as more complete and systematic, to the elements which we found in Plotinus, Proclus, and Eustathius: the difficult return of Ulysses to his fatherland represents the ascent of the soul to the intelligible; the soul is blocked by obstacles corresponding to those which Ulysses had to overcome; among these obstacles, the Sirens represent the lure of life here below, the sensible world, or better, the demons which imprison the soul in coming-to-be. The end of the commentary adds an important piece of information: the Neoplatonists (it is certainly these, or some of these, that are indicated by "the most speculative of the exegetes") apply this framework not only, as one might expect, to the *Odyssey*, but also to the battles of the *Iliad*.

If the allegory developed by Hermias goes far beyond the tiny reference in Plato to the Sirens and imputes to him some adventurous assumptions, nevertheless the passage of the *Phaedrus* has influence on the interpretation of the figure of Ulysses by introducing elements which do not normally appear there; this is the case of the ideas of sleep (to which is related the idea, which is absent from Homer's account of the Sirens, of a forgetting of the homeland), of the awakening of the soul (conceived as a reactivation of the λόγος), of vigilance, of the divine aid assured for souls which imitate the gods and rebel against genesis.

But the principal interest of this page of Hermias is that it establishes a connection between the exegesis of Ulysses and that of *Phaedrus* 259A. Hermias is not the only witness to this connection, which has been pointed out already here in relation to two texts in Proclus,[21] and which might probably be found in many other places. There is one indicator that the source of this connection is earlier in date. For after Hermias, but already before him, many pagan and Christian authors, of whom we will see some examples, wishing (outside all visible reference to the passage of the *Phaedrus*) to make clear that Ulysses avoided the rock of the Sirens and "sailed past," use the verb παραπλέειν.[22] But if one is to believe the concordances,[23] this verb is absent from the passages of the *Odyssey* dealing with the Sirens, and if it appears in the poem, and then only once,[24] it is in another episode. It therefore cannot have been suggested to these authors by a reading of Homer. For those, such as Hermias and Proclus after him, who refer explicitly to the *Phaedrus,* it is clear that it is from there that they derive παραπλέοντάς σφας ὥσπεϱ Σειϱῆνας. But one must suppose that all their predecessors, who have recourse to the same verb when commenting on the Homeric passage from which it is absent, witness in turn to a certain dependence, immediate or at a distance, in relation to the Platonic dialogue. The initiative, illustrated by Hermias and Proclus, of having recourse to *Phaedrus* 259A in order to interpret the Homeric episode of the Sirens should thus be viewed as anterior to the earliest use of παϱαπλέειν in this context. We will see presently how far back this hypothesis will allow us to go. One should note also that Hermias and Proclus agree in discerning in the Sirens the evil demons who hold back souls caught in coming-to-be, whereas there is nothing pejorative in the brief mention of them in Plato. If it is true, as I have said above, that the Pythagoreans and Neoplatonists agreed in reading into the navigation of Ulysses the history of the soul, the latter did not keep the imagery that seemed essential to the former and which had the Sirens appearing as soul-guiding and helping musicians.

(b) PORPHYRY, *De antro* 34–35

The other Neoplatonic text which should be studied carefully was written about two centuries earlier than Hermias. It is part of Porphyry's little treatise *De antro nympharum*:

> For it is my opinion that Numenius and his school were correct in thinking that for Homer in the *Odyssey*, Odysseus bears a symbol of one who passes through the stages of genesis (γενέσεως) and, in doing so, returns (ἀποκαθισταμένου) to those beyond every wave (κλύδωνος) who have no knowledge of the sea,
>
> > "Until you come to those who are unacquainted with the sea,
> > men who do not eat food mixed with salt."
>
> The deep, the sea, and the sea-swell are, according to Plato as well, material substance. (πόντος δὲ καὶ θάλασσα καὶ κλύδων καὶ παϱὰ Πλάτωνι ἡ ὑλικὴ σύστασις). (Trans. Westerink)[25]

The same exegesis continues a few lines further on:

> But rather, the man [Ulysses] who had dared these things was pursued by the wrath of the gods of the sea and of matter. (ἁλίων καὶ ὑλικῶν θεῶν) . . . But he will be past all toil when, entirely removed from the sea, he finds himself among souls so ignorant of everything that has to do with the sea, that is to say, with matter (θαλασσίων καὶ ἐνύλων ἔϱγων), that his oar is thought to be a winnowing-fan, because of the utter ignorance of nautical instruments and activities.[26]

This interpretation of the figure of Ulysses is substantially similar to that found before Porphyry and especially after him. The distinctive character of Porphyry's exegesis is to find in the sea the symbol, not only of the world of coming-to-be, but more widely of matter, doubtless because of the fluid and disorganized nature they share in common. This symbolism is referred back to Plato. Various Platonic texts, all quite distant, might be invoked in relation to this.[27] The nearest text is without doubt the famous myth in the *Politicus* 272D–273E, where the universe, at certain moments of its existence and in consequence of its corporeal constitution, is compared to a boat buffeted by the storm and very near to sinking "in the bottomless ocean of unlikeness."[28] In fact, the Neoplatonists saw in this ocean the image of matter,[29] and it is therefore this that Porphyry must have in mind. At any rate, Plato is not the source of the idea of personifying the hostile forces of the sea-matter by the gods of that element (Poseidon) bent on destroying Ulysses; however, he (that is, the soul of which he is the image) will triumph in overcoming one by one the degrees of coming-to-be and will be restored to his pristine state.[30] Finally, another aspect peculiar to Porphyry is the skillful reading of the return of the soul to its first condition, not only in the return to Ithaca, but also in the prophecy of Teiresias, whose shade is called forth by Ulysses, that the hero will not receive from Poseidon complete rest until he goes to the people who know nothing of the sea (*Od.* xi. 121–129), in other words, the souls who have not had experience of coming-to-be.

But the important thing in Porphyry is clearly the attribution of this exegesis to Numenius. One may doubt if the reference to Numenius in chapter 34 of the *De antro* extends, as the editors of the fragment believe, to include the reference to Plato. But one is reassured in this regard by another fragment of Numenius that is independent of this one and in which matter, held from on high by the Demiurge, is assimilated (certainly in relation to *Politicus* 272Dff.) in some detail to the sea which the pilot masters from his ship.[31] Thus we are brought back for this exegesis of Ulysses to a period prior to Plotinus—to the first half of the second century A.D.

There might be, perhaps,[32] another indicator of the pre-Plotinian character of this interpretation in a contemporary of Numenius, the Platonic rhetor Maximus of Tyre. The episode of the *Odyssey* concerned is no longer that of the Sirens, as in the majority of the texts we have seen, but the passage in the poem (v. 333–353) where the goddess Leucothea takes pity on Ulysses against whom the elements rage, and gives him a veil which, stretched under his chest, will serve as a life belt. Maximus finds in this scene the image of the philosophy which saves the human soul plunged into the tempest of the sensible world and ready to succumb:

> Thrown into the tumult here below and abandoning itself to the irresistible waves which carry it, the soul swims in an adverse sea, until philosophy itself takes it under its protection by slipping under it[33] its arguments, just as Leucothea did for Ulysses with her veil.[34]

This interpretation of Ulysses as the symbol of the soul which is not resigned to its fall is very similar, despite the differences, to Neoplatonic exegesis, and could thus be its earliest formulation.

III
CHRISTIAN EXEGESIS

1. Main Features

Parallel to the Platonic tradition, appearing almost at the same time as it and also lasting for several centuries, there evolves a Christian reading of the figure of

Ulysses, of his navigation and especially of his victory over the Sirens. One will not be surprised to find that Christian exegesis made use here of pagan materials, just as did the Christian art of the time.[35] It even goes beyond the pagan sources in that it systematically confers an allegorical meaning on all of the details of the Homeric episode, whereas the Platonists left some details in the shadow. Here are the principal elements of this new exegesis.

The sea in which Ulysses struggles represents the world in the Johannine sense of that word, the hostile *saeculum* whose pleasures are represented by the Sirens. The rock to which the latter lure the sailors symbolizes the body on which is broken the discernment of spiritual intelligence. Ithaca is the celestial fatherland (paradise) to which we must return, escaping from here and living the true life; the means of return is the Church, a traditional image of which is a ship.

Up to this point, with the exception, obviously, of the last idea, the exegesis of Christian authors is not specifically Christian. But it becomes so with the meaning it gives to the figure of Ulysses. Certainly, as before, he embodies the human condition, but also much more: tied to his mast which symbolizes the Cross, he represents the crucified, and, with less emphasis, the Christian saved by the wood, and even all of humanity. His companions are to be understood as the more distant adherents to whom, however, the shadow of the Cross reaches, such as the good thief. Finally, even the wax stopping up their ears is given meaning; that is, it represents Scripture.

2. The Main Texts

This detailed description corresponds to the final complete stage of Christian exegesis, as it is found in the fifth century A.D., and where a place is found for almost all the elements of the Homeric story relative to the Sirens. But this fairly late stage was naturally preceded by attempts that were less complete.[36]

One of the earliest attempts was that of Clement of Alexandria (late second to early third centuries A.D.). For him the Sirens represent the misdeeds of habit and the lures of pleasure, and Ulysses who fools them by tying himself to his mast is the image of the Christian who triumphs over perdition by clinging to the wood of the Cross.

> Let us flee (Φύγωμεν), then, habit (συνήθειαν); let us flee it as we would a dangerous promontory, the menace of Charybdis, or of the Sirens of legend. Habit strangles man, turns him away from the truth and from life, is a trap, an abyss, a ditch, it is a keen evil.
>
> > "Far from this smoke, far from these waves take
> > Your ship."
>
> Let us flee (Φεύγωμεν), then, my sailor companions, let us flee these waves, they vomit forth fire; there, there is an accursed island on which are piled bones and corpses; in that place a bold courtesan (that is, pleasure) sings, delighting in vulgar music:

"Come here, famous Ulysses, supreme glory of the Achaians!
Halt your ship to hear a more divine voice."

She praises you, sailor, speaking your great fame, and she seeks, this prostitute, to capture him who is the glory of the Greeks. Leave her to feed on her corpses; a heavenly wind (πνεῦμα οὐράνιον) comes to your aid. Sail past pleasure (πάριθι τὴν ἡδονήν), it is a deceiver:

"Neither let a lewd woman make you lose your mind;
Her flattering chatter is only interested in your barn."

Sail past (παράπλει) this song, it produces death. Just want it (ἐὰν ἐθέλῃς) and you will conquer perdition. Chained to the Wood, you will be delivered from all corruption; you will have for pilot the Word (λόγος) of God; you will reach the port of the heavens, thanks to the Holy Spirit (τοῖς λιμέσι καθορμίσει τῶν οὐρανῶν τὸ πνεῦμα τὸ ἅγιον). Then you will contemplate my God; you will be initiated into these sacred mysteries; you will enjoy these realities hidden in the heavens and which I keep, "which no ear hath heard and which have not risen to the heart" of anyone.[37]

The first point that strikes one in this text is the attack on habit, συνήθεια, which seems unduly vehement. In fact, Clement indicates by this word the weight of pagan traditions which chain the Greeks to their religious practices, notably to the cult of divine images, and which prevent them from adhering to the Christian truth, which is something new: "One pushes one to the abyss, that is habit; the other raises one to heaven, that is truth."[38] It should be noted too that the denunciation of habit, nurse of vice, belonged to the literary genre of protreptics,[39] among which figures, even in its title, Clement's work. These two circumstances make less surprising the offensive he mounts against συνήθεια, to the point of making it the main subject of the allegory of the Sirens (and also of Charybdis). As to the other danger which the Sirens represent, it is pleasure; especially, it seems sexual pleasure, since the Sirens are given the traits of a tempting prostitute who solicits by means of song and flattery. Ulysses is exhorted to flee this song of death in terms that seal his transposition into Christianity: the wood to which he chains himself prefigures that of the Cross; the divine Word is at his rudder; the Holy Spirit which is at first a puff of wind, πνεῦμα οὐράνιον, fills his sails and pushes him to the port of salvation.

We can see that Clement picks out here the positive aspects of the figure of Ulysses. It is quite different some pages earlier where the same author, opposing to the believers in love with eternal salvation the others who mock it, places the latter under the patronage of the Greek hero:

But the others, stuck to the world like seaweed stuck to the rocks in the sea, make little of immortality, and, in the manner of the old man of Ithaca (καθάπερ ὁ Ἰθακήσιος γέρων), take as object of their desire, not the truth nor the heavenly fatherland, nor further the true light, but . . . smoke.[40]

The portrait of Ulysses on which this text is based is the product of bringing together some verses taken from the first books of the *Odyssey*: i. 57–59 (held back by Calypso, Ulysses, who wants only to see again the smoke of Ithaca, calls for death); v. 135–136 and vii. 256–257 (Calypso in vain makes an offer to Ulysses to keep him from death and old age, ἀθάνατον καὶ ἀγήραον); and v. 203–209 (Ulysses wants to return to his terrestrial homeland, ἐς πατρίδα γαῖαν, instead of becoming immortal). Ulysses' refusal to escape old age explains in part the curious circumlocution which Clement uses in referring to him as "the old man of Ithaca," but this formula must also have the purpose of emphasizing, as expressed in one of its major heroes, the oldness of paganism whose inertia blocks the arrival of the newness of Christianity. In other words, Ulysses is enrolled here in the camp of perverse "habit," whereas, on the contrary, in the text cited earlier, he escapes from its grasp under the cover of his flight far from the Sirens. We can see that Clement is a master of allegorical practice, of which one of the axioms is that the same mythical figure can produce many different, even opposed, interpretations. Besides, we might note that Clement's stern evaluation of Ulysses' sacrifice of immortality in order to return to Ithaca and to see its smoke again takes the opposite tack to the praises conferred on him in the Stoic tradition, which sees in this same behavior the proof of the hero's moderation and of his love for his fatherland.[41]

As for the Sirens, another interpretation can also be found in Clement, who sees them as the image of pagan Greek culture in its relation to Christian catechesis: the converts registered to receive baptism fear lest the melodious pagan knowledge, like the Sirens, block their way to the faith, and they prefer, like Ulysses' sailors, to stop their ears with corks of ignorance. But their instructor will not imitate them in their summary refusal; he will know how to select from pagan culture elements of use to catechesis, on condition that he does not dally with it and does not compromise his return to the Christian philosophy which is his fatherland. It is understood that he will profit by the song of the Sirens without losing himself in it; he will take Ulysses as his model. These preliminaries prepare us for reading Clement's own text:

> But it appears that most of those who register themselves, just like Ulysses' companions, hold to the word like peasants. They pass by, not the Sirens, but their harmony and their music; it is from ignorant prejudice that they stop their ears, knowing well that if they listen only once to the teaching of the Greeks, they will never be able to return. But he who selects from it, on behalf of the catechumens, what is useful, especially if they themselves are Greeks ("the earth belongs to the Lord and all which fills it"), he does not have to abstain, as do irrational animals, from the love of knowledge. He should rather collect from it as much help as possible for his flock. This is on condition, however, that he does not become attached to it, only for the use that can be made of it, so as to be able, once the borrowing is done and becomes his property, to return in himself to the true philosophy, in possession of that solid conviction of the soul which is security guaranteed by all means.[42]

There is a noteworthy appreciation of the song of the Sirens in this praise of Ulysses who listened to it without succumbing to it and in this reproval of those who did not wish to (in reality, who could not) hear anything. Other Christian authors would again see in the song the image of the seduction of pagan culture and philosophy, but most often only to reject these entirely,[43] or to reduce them to the vanity of fine speech.[44] Clement was less original when the call of the Sirens evoked for him the call of the pleasures of the senses. One might note again, at any rate, that in the case of the Sirens, as before in the case of Ulysses, he does not neglect to subject the same mythical figure to different allegorical interpretations.

We will spend less time with the Fathers of the Church who, in various ways, took up and extended the great exegesis in *Protrepticus* XII. They do not in any case require as much attention on this point. A few years after Clement, Hippolytus of Rome, in his account of Basilides the Gnostic, reminds us of the episode of the Sirens, after he had named quickly the mythical monsters of the sea around Sicily—the Cyclops, Charybdis, and Scylla. The sea-crossing full of obstacles is now that of the Christians in the midst of the doctrines of the heretics. Let the Christians use as a model the cunning Ulysses, who fills the ears of his companions with wax, whereas he himself, tied to the mast, "sails past the Sirens without obstacle" (παραπλεῦσα ἀκινδύνως τὰς Σειρῆνας) while clearly hearing their song. The weaker will not listen to the heresies, which are quite able to drag them where they wish; but the man of faith will hear them without being disturbed as long as he is chained to the wood of Christ.[45] This last phrase (ἑαυτὸν τῷ ξύλῳ Χριστοῦ προσδήσαντα), which assimilates the mast of Ulysses to the Cross of Christ, is taken almost word-for-word from Clement (τῷ ξύλῳ προσδεδεμένος) despite the fact that the two authors give the Sirens a quite different meaning. One will note also that Hippolytus gives value to a detail in the story in the *Odyssey* (the wax in the ears of the sailors) that his predecessor, at least in the *Protrepticus,* did not single out.

The debt to Clement is admitted from the start, near the end of the third century, by Bishop Methodius of Olympus, who indeed calls Ulysses ὁ Ἰθακήσιος γέρων,[46] and explains the latter's behavior by the fact that he wished neither to deny himself the uncontrolled pleasure of hearing the song of the Sirens, nor to expose himself to the death which followed this song. But Methodius uses the Homeric episode mainly as a foil: to the mortal song of the Sirens he opposes the divine and saving voices of the choir of the Prophets and of their interpreters, the Apostles; to hear this song which produces, not death, but a better life, there is no need to block the ears of our companions or to tie ourselves.[47] Besides this completely negative approach, and indeed because of it, we may note that this author, quite different in this from his two predecessors, avoids assimilating Ulysses' mast to the wood of the Cross.

A century later Saint Ambrose takes up the tradition, making himself its first important representative in Latin Christianity. For him the sea is the deceiving world, the *saeculum* (*Quod autem mare abruptius quam saeculum tam infidum?*); the Sirens are the pleasures of the senses which ensnare the mind and sap its strength; the rocks on which they live are the body that softens spiritual keenness; far from blocking our ears, let us open them to the voice of Christ; let us bind ourselves, not like Ulysses hurrying back to his fatherland (*Ulixem illum . . . festinantem ad patriam*), with corporeal bindings to the mast, but spiritually with the knots of the soul to the wood of the Cross.[48] This entire allegory is in its substance found already in the Greek Fathers, with the exception, perhaps, of the assimilation of the rock of the Sirens to the human body. Ambrose also introduces some innovations in some minor details: among the circumstances delaying Ulysses' return he cites, besides the Sirens, the sweet fruits of the Lotus-Eaters and the gardens of Alcinous (*Od.* vii. 112–132; ix. 82–104). As is natural for a Latin author, he mixes into his memory of Homer allusions to Aeneas' navigation according to Virgil (*Aeneid* I. 536 and II. 23). Finally he notes that the prophet also named the Sirens,[49] one of the several mythological allusions he believes are to be found in Scripture.

The Christian exegesis of the victory of Ulysses over the Sirens in a sense reaches perfection in the fifth century in a homily by Bishop Maximus of Turin.[50] Several expressions taken word-for-word from Ambrose show his debt to Ambrose. But he contributes much to this exegesis: the item-to-item correspondence between the episode of the *Odyssey* and its Christian application is now pushed to the limit. In his detailed parallels, Maximus capitalizes on nearly all the contributions of his predecessors and his weakness for rhetorical amplification helps him orchestrate these with ingenuity. The prolixity of these passages makes quotation difficult. In any case, we already know their substance, since my account of the "main features" of patristic exegesis as sketched above is drawn almost exclusively from him. It remains that this last stage in the exegesis represents the completion of some parallels that were only suggested before. Thus Maximus finalizes the correspondence between Ithaca and the *patria paradysi, de qua primus homo exierat*. More important, Ulysses chained to his mast becomes for Maximus the image, no longer only, as before, of the incorruptible Christian, but of Christ Himself on the Cross: to *de Ulixe illo refert fabula quod eum arboris religatio de periculo liberarit* the response is given *Christus dominus religatus in cruce est*.

3. The Relation to Platonism

This Christian tradition, which lasts from the third to the fifth century, is approximately contemporaneous with the exegesis of Ulysses that we traced from Numenius to Proclus. The differences between these two parallel developments are evident. The most fundamental difference consists naturally in the fact that the Christian truth which is supposed to be found in the myth, or which is at least illustrated by it, is without equivalent in the exegesis of the Platonists. This is clear. But there are also other differences, even if we limit ourselves to the episode of the Sirens.

Christian exegesis, from the beginning, seems to be more complete in that it integrates, and even views as essential, aspects of the legend not picked out by the Platonists. This is the case in relation to Ulysses tied to the mast, the ears of his companions stopped up by wax (we have seen, however, that this last aspect is given meaning when, by amalgamating the Sirens of Homer and of Plato, Plutarch gives an eschatological interpretation of the Sirens with reference to the harmony of the spheres; but this is, it seems, a Pythagorean and not strictly a Platonic exegesis).

On the other hand, several meanings which Platonic exegesis was fond of introducing are not echoed by the Christians. This is the case for the notion of genesis whose identification with the hostile sea of the *Odyssey* is a constant theme in Platonic exegesis from Numenius to Proclus. Another case is that of the practice, which continues from Hermias to Eustathius, of discerning in the father-land Ithaca the intelligible world. One should note, however, that these ideas do not fail to evoke fairly close substitutes in Christian exegesis. The deceiving world (*saeculum*) of Ambrose, more merciless than the sea, is not without affinities to the world of coming-to-be from which the Neoplatonists wish to rescue the soul. As for the intelligible world, we know that some later Christians had begun to assimilate it to the Kingdom of God of Scripture, only to blame themselves for this later on.[51] This suggests that the distance can be shortened between the Platonic notion and the "heavens" of Clement of Alexandria, or the "Paradise" of Maximus of Turin.

In saying this we cannot fail to recognize in Clement and his successors the presence of elements found in the Platonic tradition. We can begin with some aspects of vocabularly. We saw above the important clues that are yielded by the use in Hermias and Proclus of the verb παραπλέειν in order to express Ulysses' giving a wide berth to the Sirens. Unless I am mistaken, this word is the sign that the Sirens of the *Odyssey* were interpreted in the light of the Sirens of the *Phaedrus*. But here we find, about two centuries before these pagan authors, the same word παραπλέειν used several times in the same fashion, as we have seen, by Clement[52] and by Hippolytus—a fact that suggests that the contamination I have pointed out (between the *Odyssey* and the *Phaedrus*) originated at the beginning of the third century at the latest. It does not appear that we can push the date back further than this, or at least not further back than Lucian of Samosata, twenty or thirty years earlier.[53]

Another word to note is the present imperative φεύγωμεν used twice by Clement as a sort of retraction, since he used, some lines earlier, also twice, the aorist φύγωμεν. But we found the same word in Plotinus where it is part of a short quotation from the *Iliad*, having as its background a memory of the famous "flight" of Plato's *Theaetetus* 176A: χρὴ ἐνθένδε ἐκεῖσε φεύγειν.[54] It is therefore possible to assume the same literary and doctrinal context for Clement's φεύγωμεν, who would again, therefore, have anticipated the Neoplatonists. One can probably find further signs of a vocabulary shared in common. Thus, the same verb παρέρχεσθαι is used both by Clement and by Hermias to indicate that we must avoid worldly pleasures.[55]

Other similarities go beyond the level of words and have to do with doctrine. The grandiose symbolism that Christian authors progressively confer on the figure of Ulysses is grafted on an exegetical foundation which is substantially the same as that of the Platonists. For both, the hero embodies man in love with salvation and fighting against the hostile forces that are part of the sensible world. In this perspective salvation is conceived of as a return to the fatherland. As Numenius strikingly expresses it in a clever use of the very verses of the *Odyssey*, the fatherland's essential characteristic is to be irreducible to the actual world. Furthermore, if this fatherland is so "dear" to us, it is because it was the point of departure before being the point of arrival; πατρὶς . . . ὅθεν παρήλθομεν in Plotinus (I 6,8,21) harmonizes in this respect with Maximus of Turin's *patria paradysi, de qua primus homo exierat*. Reestablishment in a place or previous state is what is well expressed by Numenius (or Porphyry) by the use of a word that reminds us of that eschatological reestablishment which is Origen's "apocatastasis." Finally, since the world here below has as its mythical image the ocean, the place of salvation will naturally be represented by a port: when Proclus discovers in Ithaca the μυστικὸς ὅρμος τῆς ψυχῆς, he takes up the allegory in Clement which has Ulysses arrive at τοῖς λιμέσι . . . τῶν οὐρανῶν.[56]

The pilot whom Clement credits with steering towards salvation is none other than the divine Logos; the reactivation of the immanent logos is for Hermias the condition of our awakening, by means of which we approach the vigilance that constitutes the gods. Another fundamental idea common to the two traditions is that the necessary condition for salvation is the desire to be saved; on this point Clement's ἐὰν ἐθέλῃς μόνον is an exact anticipation of Proclus' ἐὰν ἄρα σώζεσθαι θελῶμεν.[57] I will end with a comparison that requires attention, even though it relates only to Origen and not to any of the Christian authors quoted above. The Platonists I have examined above introduce a kind of "demonization of the cosmos:"[58] for Hermias the domain of coming-to-be has its demons who imprison captive souls in it. These demons are what the Sirens are. Porphyry previously made note in a similar way of the gods of the sea, that is, of matter, who vengefully pursued Ulysses. We know, on the other hand, that in the cosmogonies of the ancient Near East, including Jewish cosmogony, the apparition of the organized world was conceived as a victory of God over a primordial hostile ocean populated with sea monsters.[59] Early Christianity preserves a trace of this archaic image when it gives the devil the features of a monstrous fish. This is the case notably in Origen and in Ambrose in whom we find expressions such as *cetus, diabolus scilicet*.[60] Why then would not the Sirens, who are also sea monsters, have featured in the *pompa diaboli*? This connection has not left as many traces as one would expect. However, H. Rahner found one[61] in an exegetical fragment of Origen on the Lamentations of Jeremiah, in which one finds the Sirens of the pagan myth identified with corrupting demons, πονηρὰ πνεύματα.[62] How can one avoid comparing this interpretation to that of Porphyry and especially that of Hermias?

These many literary and doctrinal resemblances suggest that these two traditions of exegesis of the figure of Ulysses are not two completely independent totalities. There is nothing to suggest that the Platonists were acquainted with Christian interpretation. It is reasonable, then, to suppose that the latter, especially at the beginning, borrowed from the Platonists elements to which I have drawn attention. This must be the case in particular in relation to Clement of Alexandria: all of the aspects he shares in common with Hermias, Proclus, and so on, show that the Platonic exegesis predates Neoplatonism and that he was familiar with its main lines. Added to what we have seen earlier about Numenius, Maximus of

Tyre, and Lucian, this indicates that the Platonic Ulysses was composed in the second century A.D. The Middle Platonist Numenius, in particular, is very likely to have been one of Clement's sources. Clement knew his work well and is even used as the nearest *terminus ante quem* for the dating of Numenius. Concerning what might be specific to the Middle Platonic Ulysses, we have only the few texts and fragments studied above to go on. Might not Clement provide some supplementary information? In particular, at that place in *Protrepticus* IX where the "old man of Ithaca" is blamed for not having had any desire for the truth, for the celestial fatherland, or for the true light, does Clement have in mind, as has been thought,[63] interpreters for whom Ulysses embodied man striving for these three things? This attractive idea loses its probability when we see that Clement is attacking the Stoic glorification of Ulysses, and not the meaning of Ulysses for Platonists.

4. The Gnostic Ulysses

Without doubt Christian exegesis of Ulysses begins at a period earlier than Clement. We know that the Gnostics were very interested in Homeric myths and their interest in the navigation of the *Odyssey* has left some traces in Hippolytus. Thus, Simon the Mage seems to have referred to the "moly" plant, a magic herb which Hermes gave as a gift to Ulysses in order to counter the evil deeds of Circe.[64] Again, for the Naasenes, Penelope's suitors whose souls are called forth by Hermes stand, in fact, for men whom the action of the Logos brings back from sleep and makes remember (ἐξυπνισμένων καὶ ἀνεμνησμένων) the dignity which they have lost.[65] This Gnostic exegesis is all the more interesting in that the same episode of the *Odyssey* will be given a similar meaning in Neoplatonism, a meaning preserved in Proclus: when Homer speaks of sleep and of awakening, we must understand by this the descent of the souls into coming-to-be and their ascent from it by means of the recollection of true realities.[66] But sleep and forgetting, awakening through the action of the Logos, the fall of souls into coming-to-be and their ascent out of it—these are also the themes thanks to which Hermias interprets the episode of the Sirens in the light of the *Phaedrus*. To come back to the Naasenes, one might remember also that J. Carcopino attributed to them the construction and decoration of a famous grave in the Viale Manzoni, on whose walls are represented, according to him, the return of Ulysses to Ithaca, with Penelope, her loom, and her suitors.[67]

There is indeed a Nag Hammadi treatise (II 6), *The Exegesis on the Soul,* which gives a firsthand example of a Valentinian author of the end of the second century[68] referring to Ulysses' symbolic meaning:

> For no one is worthy of salvation who still loves the place of erring (πλάνη). Therefore it is written in the poet: "Ulysses sat on the island weeping and grieving and turning his face from the words of Calypso and from her tricks, longing to see his fatherland and smoke (καπνός) coming forth from it. And had he not [received] help from heaven, [he would] not [have been able to] return to his fatherland." (Trans. Robinson, modified)[69]

There is no doubt but that these lines contain themes which have been met throughout this article. The Gnostic author anticipates Plotinus who also made the break with the same symbolic Calypso the condition of Ulysses' return to his fatherland on high. Furthermore, the definition of the conditions of salvation by means of the union of will (the hate of wandering) and of celestial aid has its equivalent in Clement and in Hermias. As to the traits chosen in the composition of the Gnostic image of Ulysses, notably the homesick desire for the smoke of Ithaca, we have found several of these also in Clement. It is even possible that the immortality that is denied by Ulysses is understood here in the "words of Calypso." All that would be lacking in this sympathetic account is Clement's attack on "the old man of Ithaca." It is true that we have not yet met the striking image of Ulysses sitting on the shore in tears. But this image is not unknown to the philosophers, to Epictetus, for example, who even provides a severe evaluation of it, along the lines used by Clement.[70] In any case, from the fact that the Valentinian treatise's general theme is the fall and the ascent of the soul,[71] there can be no doubt that the allegory of Ulysses in it is controlled by the same inspiration as that which governs the allegory in the contemporaneous Middle Platonists. This glance at Gnostic literature harmonizes with our earlier inquiry into the Ulysses allegory. It is probably the most noteworthy example of a Greek myth for which the Christians were able, at the beginning, to make use of Platonic exegesis, and yet to reach finally a result in which the myth seems made expressly to receive a Christian meaning.

2

Origen's Doctrine of the Trinity and Some Later Neoplatonic Theories

JOHN DILLON

In Chapter 3 of Book I of his *Peri Archon,* Origen advances a remarkable doctrine concerning the varying extent of the influences of the three persons of the Trinity. It is one of the doctrines that involved him in some posthumous trouble, a fortunate consequence of which is that we have a statement of it by Justinian, in his *Letter to Menas,*[1] as well as an accurate Latin version by Jerome in his *Letter to Avitus,*[2] a circumstance which frees us from reliance upon the circumlocutions and prevarications of the loyal but cautious Rufinus.

From a Platonist perspective, this doctrine is of great interest, but poses something of a puzzle, as will become apparent presently. First, however, I should like to set out the doctrine as it is presented to us by Justinian who, though hostile, is sufficiently bald and factual to inspire in one the confidence that he is truer to Origen than is Rufinus:

> "[Origen declares] that God the Father, in holding together all things, extends his power to every level of being, imparting to each from His own store its being what it is; while the Son, in a lesser degree than the Father, extends only to rational beings

[for he is second to the Father]; and to a still lesser degree the Holy Spirit penetrates only to the saints" [i.e., to the consecrated members of the Christian community]. "So that according to this theory, the power of the Father is greater than that of the Son and the Holy Spirit, and again that of the Holy Spirit is superior to the other holy agencies."[3]

Jerome's only significant variant from this is his description of the Son as actually "less" (*minorem*) than the Father, and the Holy Spirit as "inferior" (*inferiorem*) to the Son,[4] which I take to be, a tendentious distortion of Origen's meaning. Justinian, with creditable attention to accuracy, speaks only of the Son as ἐλαττόνως . . . φθάνων, and the Holy Spirit ἔτι ἡττόνως, which does not, I would maintain, imply the sort of essential subordinationism of which Jerome is certainly accusing him.

Rufinus, of course, is concerned to soften the effect of this troublesome doctrine as far as he, in good conscience, can. If we were dependent on Rufinus alone, we would derive a very muted impression of Origen's theory. Here is his version (*De Princ.* I, 3, 5):

"I am of the opinion, then, that the activity of the Father and the Son is to be seen both in saints and in sinners, in rational men and in dumb animals, yes, and even in lifeless things and in absolutely everything that exists; but the activity of the Holy Spirit does not extend at all either to lifeless things, or to things that have life but yet are dumb, nor is it to be found in those who, though rational, still lie in wickedness and are not wholly converted to better things. Only in those who are already turning to better things and walking in the ways of Jesus Christ, that is, who are engaged in good deeds and who abide in God, is the work of the Holy Spirit, I think, to be found."[5] (Trans. Butterworth)

The distinction in extent of power between the Father and the Son, as we can see, has been here thoroughly obscured. They are both represented as being concerned with the whole of creation, as opposed to the Holy Spirit's exclusive concern with "the saints." With the help of our other evidence, however, we can, I think, discern what doctrine Rufinus was faced with. The Father alone extends his power "to lifeless things and to absolutely everything that exists," whereas the Son's power extends to all living things, both rational and irrational. The influence of the Holy Spirit, in turn, extends only to that class of rational beings which Origen's Gnostic predecessors classed as "pneumatics," those "saved" individuals endowed not only with soul but with *pneuma*. Origen is prepared to recognize such a class of person; his only objection to the Gnostic position, and it is a vehement one, is that he denies that this class is a closed one—any human being may acquire pneumatic status.

However, I am concerned in this paper not primarily with the significance of this doctrine in Origen's thought, but rather with its possible sources or analogues in contemporary Platonism.[6] To throw any light on this it is unfortunately necessary to move on approximately two centuries, down to the time of Proclus, and then to see if we can work our way back from there to the early decades of the third century.

In Proposition 57 of his *Elements of Theology,* Proclus advances a general principle concerning the range of activity of causal principles that, it seems to me, bears a remarkable resemblance to the doctrine of Origen. For our present purpose, I fear that it will be necessary to quote it in full:

> *Every cause both operates prior to its consequent and gives rise to a greater number of posterior terms.*
>
> For if it is a cause, it is more perfect and more powerful than its consequent. And if so, it must cause a greater number of effects: for greater power produces more effects, equal power, equal effects, and lesser power, fewer; and the power which can produce the greater effects upon a like subject can produce also the lesser, whereas a power capable of the lesser will not necessarily be capable of the greater. If, then, the cause is more powerful than its consequent, it is productive of a greater number of effects.
>
> But again, the powers which are in the consequent are present in a greater measure in the cause. For all that is produced by secondary beings is produced in a greater measure by prior and more determinative principles. The cause, then, is cooperative in the production of all that the consequent is capable of producing.
>
> And if it first produces the consequent itself, it is of course plain that it is operative before the latter in the activity which produces it. Thus every cause operates both prior to its consequent and in conjunction with it, and likewise gives rise to further effects posterior to it. [*Corollary:*] From this it is apparent that what Soul causes is caused also by Intelligence, but not all that Intelligence causes is caused by Soul: Intelligence operates prior to Soul; and what Soul bestows on secondary existences Intelligence bestows in a greater measure; and at a level where Soul is no longer operative Intelligence irradiates with its own gifts things on which Soul has not bestowed itself—for even the inanimate participates Intelligence, or the creative activity of Intelligence, in so far as it participates Form.
>
> Again, what Intelligence causes is also caused by the Good, but not conversely. For even privation of Form is from the Good, since it is the source of all things; but Intelligence, being Form, cannot give rise to privation.[7] (Trans. Dodds)

The theory presented here can be traced back, as Dodds points out in his excellent note *ad loc.,* as far as Syrianus, who enunciates it in his commentary on the *Metaphysics* (p. 59, 17 Kroll),[8] but no further. Iamblichus, as we shall see in a moment, has a rather different theory, and neither Porphyry nor Plotinus seems to make any use of it.

Proclus' theory is a consequence of certain other principles of his metaphysics. First, the principle that *every productive cause is superior to that which it produces* (Prop. 7); then, the immediately preceding proposition to the present one (56), that *all that is produced by secondary beings is in a greater measure produced from those prior and more determinative principles from which the secondary were themselves derived.* His doctrine is securely underpinned by a rigorous logical framework. The supreme principle, which he here terms the Good, rather than the One, in recognition, perhaps, of its causal role, extends its *energeia* to the lowest reaches of creation, even to what is unformed, negations (*stereseis*), and the chiefest of *stereseis,* matter itself (this is made clear by Syrianus, in the passage quoted in note 8). The second hypostasis, *Nous,* extends its influence not just to rational beings, as one might expect, but, precisely by virtue of the fact that it is a higher principle than Soul, which is the life principle, it extends also lower than Soul, to all entities that have Form, animate or inanimate, by reason of its role as bestower of Form. Soul itself, being the lowest of the hypostases, extends least far, taking in only what has life, be it rational or irrational.

It should be plain that, while there are striking similarities between the schemes of Origen and of Proclus (or should we say, of the Athenian school?), there are also considerable differences. The ranges of influence of the three hypostases are quite different in each case. What remains to be decided is, first, whether this theory can be traced in Platonism any further back than Syrianus, and on the other hand, whether Origen's doctrine sounds like something that he devised himself from the whole cloth, or is rather an adaptation of an already existing theory to his own particular requirements.

To take the second problem first, it is surely noticeable that, particularly in the case of the range of influence of the Holy Spirit, Origen's demarcation of influence does not seem to correspond to a natural division in the universe. Traditional divisions would be rather between rational and irrational animals, animate and inanimate objects, material and immaterial being; at the top of the scale pure Unity, at the bottom unformed, undifferentiated matter. Within this scale, and within the known metaphysical scheme of second-century Platonism, it is not difficult to fabricate a plausible triad of principles with concentric spheres of influence. Both Albinus, in the *Didaskalikos,* and Numenius, in his surviving fragments, present us with a triad of First God or Father, Second God or Demiurge (both of these, admittedly, being Intellects of a sort, but the First God being, according to Albinus, also "nobler than Intellect,"[9] according to Numenius Intellect "at rest"[10]), and finally World Soul. It would be easy to construct a Platonic theory of spheres of influence, according to which the Father extended his activity to all creation, even as far as matter—there is, after all, a school of thought in Platonism, traceable back to Eudorus of Alexandria,[11] and appearing in the *Chaldaean Oracles,*[12] according to which God is the creator even of matter, while the power of the Demiurge extends to all that which is endowed with Form, it being the Demiurge's particular task to create the material cosmos; the Soul would then extend to all that had soul. The only problem with such a construction is that there is absolutely no evidence for it. And yet Origen's scheme has a distinct look of being adapted to a special purpose. He was presented with a third principle which was precisely not Soul, but Spirit, and Soul and Spirit were sharply distinguished in the tradition from which Origen sprang, going back to St. Paul. The *hagion pneuma* could not be responsible for all that had soul; it could only be responsible for the *pneumatikoi*, the "saints." So Origen had to adapt, even at the cost of incurring the Platonist reproach of splitting up reality like a bad butcher, not at the joints.

Let us turn back to our first problem: what is the ancestry of this theory in the Platonic tradition? I have come upon only one clue, and it is not a very satisfactory one.

In the course of a comment on *Alcibiades* I, 115A, Olympiodorus reports, first, the theory of Proclus concerning the extension of influences of the hypostases, and then, in contrast to it, that of Iamblichus:[13]

> But the divine Iamblichus does not distinguish the higher principles from the lower by the greater extent of their influence (for all the principles, in his view, extend downwards as far as matter; for this is a dogma of his, that, irrespective of at what point a principle begins to operate, it does not cease its operation before extending to the lowest level; for even if it is stronger, nevertheless the fact of its greater separation can create a balancing factor, rendering it weaker), but he distinguishes them by the fact that the influence of the higher principles is more piercing (*drimutera*). For we strive for Being more basically than for Life, and for Life more basically than for Intelligence.

Iamblichus is actually talking here, not of the three basic hypostases, but rather of the three moments of the hypostasis of *Nous,* Being, Life, and Intelligence, but this does not affect the nature of his argument. The language of Olympiodorus does not admit of certainty, but it sounds to me rather as if Iamblichus is here presented as arguing against a previous view (he is actually presented as arguing against Proclus, which is impossible). If this were so, it would be evidence that the theory goes back at least to early Neoplatonism, and was only revived by Syrianus. Now, in his comments recorded elsewhere, Iamblichus is frequently to be found in opposition both to Amelius and to Porphyry, and with either of these we can find linked the name of Numenius.[14]

However, at this point the trail gives out. We cannot be sure that Iamblichus is in fact contradicting anyone. We are left with the reflection that there is much that we do not know about the doctrines of the three last-mentioned figures, and even less about the mysterious figure who provides a link between Numenius and Neoplatonism on the one hand, and Origen on the other, Ammonius Saccas. All one can say is that the doctrine would fit, not uncomfortably, into what we know of second-century Platonist speculation.

There is another aspect to this theory which, it must be noted, had no attraction for Origen, but did for the later Platonists, and this is the theurgic aspect. The theory speculates that, in a powerful sense, the lower down the scale of nature an entity is situated, the more closely it is linked with higher principles. This provides an excellent philosophical justification for making use of stones, plants, and animals in the performance of magical rituals; they are actually nearer to one god or another than we are, being direct products of the divine realm. Such a theory would accord well with the doctrines of the *Chaldaean Oracles,* another major influence on Neoplatonism from Porphyry onwards, and themselves a second-century production more or less contemporary with Numenius, but once again the available sources fail us. All we find attested, and that only in Psellus' summary of Chaldaean doctrine, is a doctrine of *sympatheia.*[15]

I remain convinced, however, that Origen's theory and Proclus' theory are applications of the same doctrine, and that this doctrine was not invented by Origen. Further than that, at the moment, I cannot go.

3

A Neoplatonic Commentary on the Christian Trinity: Marius Victorinus

MARY T. CLARK

Marius Victorinus Afer, a famous Roman rhetor, was born in Africa between 281 and 291. He had a fine classical education and an extensive knowledge of philosophy. From Africa he traveled to Rome where he became well known as a teacher of rhetoric. His statue was even erected in the Roman forum. Probably to assist his students, he wrote commentaries on Cicero's works, composed his own treatises on grammar and logic, and translated some key philosophical treatises from Greek into Latin.

Those of us who heard of Marius Victorinus from Saint Augustine's *Confessions*[1] met him there first as the translator of the "books of the Platonists" which Augustine borrowed from a very proud man whose identity has never been completely established. The reading of these books removed some of Augustine's intellectual obstacles to the acceptance of the truth of certain scriptural statements about God. Feeling himself unable to live according to these truths, however, Augustine applied for help to a Christian priest in Milan, Simplicianus (later a bishop), and discovered that he had known Marius Victorinus. Victorinus had discussed his conversion with Simplicianus, telling him how the reading of Scripture had convinced Victorinus that Christianity should be embraced. One cannot help wondering which scriptural texts influenced Victorinus to believe in Christ. Was it the Prologue to Saint John's Gospel as some have suggested? There he would read: "In the beginning was the Word, and the Word was with God; and the Word was God. All things were made through him, and without him was made nothing that has been made. In him was life, and the life was the light of men. And the light shines in the darkness; and the darkness grasped it not." Pierre Hadot[2] is one who points out that Victorinus could recognize in this Prologue all the Neoplatonic principles: God, Intelligence, Soul, matter, and even certain Porphyrian positions: the Intelligence, originally confused with the First Principle, then distinguished from him; the creation of the intelligible world; the double aspect of the Intelligence or Logos—life, and light; the creation of the sensible world; the role of the soul testifying to the divine presence in the world. Hadot even suggests[3] that the Platonist who was in the habit of saying, according to Simplicianus, that Saint John's Prologue "should be written in letters of gold and hung up in all the churches in the most conspicuous place," was Victorinus himself. On the other hand, H. Dörrie[4] considers that this advice to write large the Prologue in the churches was not given by someone friendly to Christianity but by an anti-Christian Platonist who thought that Christianity added nothing to Platonism. He thought that in John's words Christians would either recognize the heretical character of the Fourth Gospel, or there would be a general conversion to Platonism. But let us consider for the moment that Hadot is right and that Victorinus did recognize the correlation between the Christian and the pagan Divine Logos. This raises the question then as to why Victorinus would bother at all with baptism if he merely recognized the coincidence of Christian and Neoplatonic doctrines in John's Prologue. What Victorinus could know as a Neoplatonist could scarcely be the reason for his believing as a Christian.

I

I want to suggest that other texts of Scripture deeply moved Victorinus, texts in John and Paul that spoke of the Divine Condescension. His full reading of Scripture made Victorinus aware of the mystery of God's love for mankind and called forth his faith. His later writings show him to be humbled before this awareness of the mystery of God's salvific concern for the world. In his first book *Against Arius,* Victorinus wrote:

> For this is "a great mystery": that God "emptied himself, when he was in the form of God," then that he suffered, first by being in the flesh and sharing the lot of human birth and being raised upon the cross. These things, however, would not be marvelous, if he had come only from man, or from nothing, or from God by creation. For what would "he emptied himself" mean if he was-not before he was in the flesh? And what was he? He said: "equal to God." But if he had been created from nothing, how is he equal? That is why it is "a great mystery which was manifested in the flesh."[5]

Plotinus, we remember, had said: "It is not lawful for those who have become wicked to demand others to be their saviors and to sacrifice themselves in answer to their prayers."[6] While this was not an anti-Christian remark on Plotinus' part, but rather witnesses to his conviction that men have a duty to their world and to themselves to live on their highest level, one can find missing here any realization that a savior might volunteer to sacrifice himself even for the culpable man. And Porphyry's philosophy, as far as I know, makes no room for such Divine Condescension.

Despite Victorinus' embracing of the mystery of faith—God's love for man—he remained very Neoplatonic in seeing the Christian life to be the interior life of knowledge, a call to live on the spiritual level. Although the corporal works of mercy undoubtedly belong in the lives of those who wished to follow Christ by doing what he did for people—healing and helping—the importance of Christian spirituality through the ages, that is, the interior life, was definitely directed and influenced by Christian Neoplatonists like Victorinus, Augustine, and Dionysius the Areopagite. Victorinus taught that Christ was universal life, bringing a higher life and knowledge of the intelligible world into the sensible world to lead people to God.[7] Therefore, according to Victorinus, after Christ's death the hidden Christ continues to act in the Holy Spirit, principle of intelligible knowledge. Souls are then illuminated by this hidden Christ, the Spirit of understanding.[8]

Thus, for Victorinus, neither the creation of the world by God nor the incarnation of God's Son diminished the intelligible world. He asserts[9] against Candidus that the process of the sensible manifestation of divine power does not change the divine substance. This procession has reality only in the creatures that benefit from it. In the divine substance itself there is intense activity. All action is derived from the Logos with whom activity is identified: "the first two are one, yet differ insofar as the Father is actual existence, that is, substantiality, while the Son is existential act."[10] With the Logos in the Father, activity is power. This power is deployed through the Logos Father, the maker of the world, and is manifested in a sensible manner when souls (preexisting in the Logos) begin to descend into the sensible world. "For your Logos is the seed of the 'to be' of all things, but you are the interior power of this seed."[11] But there is another work of the Logos which Victorinus finds in Scripture expressing divine concern for the return of souls. This is the sensible manifestation of the Logos, his incarnation, death, resurrection, ascension, and the diffusion of the Spirit into souls. Victorinus expressed it this way:

> For the darkness and ignorance of the soul, violated by material powers, had need of the help of eternal light so that the Logos of the soul and the Logos of the flesh after the destruction of corruption by the mystery of that death leading to resurrection, could thus raise up souls and bodies under the guidance of the Holy Spirit to divine and lifegiving intelligences, uplifted by knowledge, faith, and love.[12]

For Victorinus, therefore, the mystery includes the descent of Divine Life through the Son into the world, and the ascent of thought through the Spirit to the Father. Such is the work of the twofold Logos:

For he is life, he is knowledge, in both directions having been efficacious for the salvation of souls, by the mystery of the Cross and thus by life, because we had to be freed from death, and by the mystery of knowledge also, by the Holy Spirit, because he was given as teacher, and "taught" all things and gave "testimony" to Christ.[13]

This is the economy of salvation attainable by faith in the mystery which is the Gospel, the truth of divine love that is good news. To know the mystery is to know the Logos dialoguing with the world; only the Spirit can give this knowledge of the Logos. "The Father speaks to the Son, the Son to the world."[14] And as to the Holy Spirit, Victorinus says that he has ". . . already set forth in many books that he [the Holy Spirit] is Jesus Christ himself but in another mode, Jesus Christ hidden, interior, dialoguing with souls. . . ."[15]

II

What then does the Logos give? It seems to have been important for Victorinus that the Son of God can provide a certain positive knowledge of God—a knowledge of his concern for the world he created and saved, and a knowledge of the inner structure of the divine life—which was a closed book to philosophical reason. It is right to recognize that when we try to reason about God, there is more about him that we do not know than we know. But is it possible to quench the desire to know as much as possible about God? Like everyone else, Victorinus had this desire. In his reading of Scripture he at last discovered the source of positive theology. "No one has ever seen God except the only Son who is in the bosom of the Father; he has explained him."[16]

Therefore, although he may have found the coincidence of Neoplatonic and Christian Trinitarian doctrines in Saint John's Prologue, Victorinus searched the whole New Testament to hear Christ explain the triadic nature of the God who "so loved the world."

He found what he was seeking, chiefly in John's Gospel and Paul's Epistles. From the many texts he cites, I shall choose only a few that proved formative of Victorinus' understanding of God as triune.

In John 5:26 he read: "For as the Father has life in himself, even so he has given to the Son also to have life in himself." From this Victorinus learned that the Son was aptly called life and, moreover, was as self-begetting as the Father.

And in 2 Philippians 2:5–7, he read of Christ Jesus "who though he was in the form of God, did not consider being equal to God a thing to be clung to, but emptied himself taking the form of a slave and being made like unto men. And appearing in the form of man, he humbled himself, becoming obedient to death, even to death on a cross. Therefore, God also has exalted him and has bestowed upon him the name that is above every name, so that at the name of Jesus every knee should bend, of those in heaven, on earth and under the earth, and every tongue should confess that the Lord Jesus Christ is in the glory of God the Father."

Again in John 14:26, he read: "These things I have spoken to you while yet dwelling with you. But the Advocate, the Holy Spirit, whom the Father will send in my name, he will teach you all things, and bring to your mind whatever I have said to you."

Thus life in the divine world is intelligible life. The Son is the principle of life, and the Holy Spirit is the principle of intellectual knowledge. Therefore, as John's Prologue says, the Logos is life and light which illuminates every man born into the world. The Logos is dyadic, the manifested one, Christ in the flesh, and the hidden one, the Holy Spirit. And the Father whose Be-ing is unknowable in itself, is manifested in Christ who said: "Philip, he who sees me sees also the Father. How canst thou say, 'Show us the Father?' Dost thou not believe that I am in the Father and the Father in me?"[17]

I have given rather fully these scriptural quotations most used by Victorinus, to show that he was able to draw from Scripture an understanding of the triune God as *esse-vivere-intelligere,* not in descending order but as mutually implicated in one another. The theory of implication and predominance dominates Victorinus' theological synthesis.

III

How then can one say that Victorinus' understanding of the Trinity was a Neo-platonic one?

One can say this perhaps in the sense that the Neoplatonic philosophy of the *Anonymous Commentary on the Parmenides* and of the *Commentary on the Chaldaean Oracles* enabled Victorinus to recognize that the processive reality of the Trinitarian God was not contradictory to reason. P. Hadot has documented[18] the Porphyrian materials which he thinks Victorinus used to defend the consubstantiality of Father, Son, and Spirit, but he includes the *Anonymous Commentary on the Parmenides* among the Porphyrian works. Whether Hadot has sufficient evidence from the extant writings of Porphyry to declare that Victorinus depends on him for his Neoplatonism is a weighty question. Are we certain that Porphyry authored the *Anonymous Commentary?* I believe that Dominic O'Meara seems justified in calling attention to the ". . . character of the available evidence [as to what Porphyry really taught] insofar as this implies interpretative limitations."[19] I believe that we should try to learn far more than we now know about Victorinus' knowledge of the Eastern theologians who discussed the *homoousios.* More attention might be paid to Marcellus of Ancyra who interpreted *homoousion* in the sense of identity and whose dynamic conception of God as the living, active, energetic biblical God is quite like Victorinus' notion of God. Marcellus speaks of God as never without his Word which was in him as *dynamis* and which emerged for God's work of creation and revelation as *energeia.* This monad God expands not in essence so that we can speak of three *ousias,* or three hypostases or three persons, but in activity alone. While it is true that Marcellus' theology is constructed in opposition to Origen's subordinationism, the suspicion of Marcellus' Sabellianism dominated the Eastern church's opposition to *homoousion.*[20]

Nevertheless, from Victorinus' own writings we do know that he believed that the Unitarians of the day (Neo-Arians) and the upholders of "similarity in substance" (followers of Basil of Ancyra), had made philosophical mistakes. Therefore, in addition to recourse to Scripture for understanding the Trinity, Victorinus felt obliged to argue philosophically. To do this, he had choices to make. Which philosophy available to the fourth-century theologians was best adapted to convey the possibility of a triune God, each of the three distinct from one another, but all three equally God? If one began with the data from Revelation, then the main teaching of Plotinus on the subordination of the two later hypostases could not be used. Yet Plotinus had discovered in the soul's structure an image of the structure of the intelligible world, and he had recognized the mutual implication of *esse, vivere, intelligere.*[21] Moreover, Plotinus had spoken of the soul and its activity as consubstantial. From his scriptural reading Victorinus thought he had to reject what Arius agreed with: that where there is emanation, there must be inferiority. The Nicene Creed had specified that neither inferiority nor posteriority was expressed by consubstantiality. At the dawn of Western theology it seems to have been Victorinus' task to show philosophically how this was possible. In Scripture he had learned that all that the Son has is received from the Father; he was also familiar with the texts that emphasized the infinite *esse* of God. By not accepting the Plotinian principle, "No one gives what he has," Victorinus kept the Son and the Spirit equal to the Father in being, while distinguished from him and from each other by the activity which predominated in each. In feeling free to call God *Esse,* a reality found in all things, he was able also to find in his system a place for positive philosophical theology. There was at hand, moreover, in the fourth century a philosophy which referred to the First Principle of all as Being. This was the philosophy present in the *Anonymous Commentary on the Parmenides* (attributed by Hadot to Porphyry) where we read:

> See then if Plato has not also the air of someone who allows us to seize a hidden teaching: for the One, who is beyond Substance and Being, is neither Being nor substance nor act but rather, it acts and is itself pure act, so that it is itself "To Be," that which is before Being. By participating in this "To Be" the second one receives from this "To Be" a derived being; such is "to participate in Being."[22]

The "commentator" goes on to speak of the derivatives from the One-Being. The prepositions used of the Son and the Spirit in Scripture also indicated that the second and third Persons were definable by reduction to the One. The *ek* or *ex* could refer to begetting; the Spirit being sent *ab* the Father and the Son refers to the Spirit's presence in the First or the One; and *in* the Holy Spirit one returns to Father and Son. This metaphysics of prepositions expresses the Western emphasis on the unity of God. The mutual implication of *esse, vivere, intelligere*[23] served Victorinus well in his effort to declare the absolute unity of the Trinity. This had been previously admitted by Plotinus[24] and was to be acknowledged by Augustine also.[25]

Thus Victorinus did not distort Christian teachings by importing Neoplatonic fragments into his exposition of the Trinity. He experienced a profound harmony between Neoplatonism and Christianity. He detected a structural relationship between Neoplatonic philosophy as he conceived it and the Trinitarian doctrine of the Church as derived from the scriptural use of common names for Father, Son, and Spirit as well as proper names. For in both fourth-century Neoplatonism and Christianity there is admitted the preexistence of the *Nous* or of the Logos in the bosom of the First Principle; Porphyrian Neoplatonism as rehabilitated by Hadot asserts a consubstantiality between God and the intelligible world which emanates from him.[26]

IV

One should not, of course, discuss Victorinus' use of Neoplatonism apart from the questions he faced. It is important to realize that he wrote his treatises in response to Arianism in general, to Neo-Arianism in particular, and to those who objected to the use of the word "consubstantial" in the Nicene Creed, namely, the followers of Basil of Ancyra.

In responding to the Arians who took the word "unbegotten" as the distinguishing feature of the Father, the word "begotten" as that of the Son, Victorinus used the Plotinian notion of God as *causa sui*,[27] self-begetting.

To the Neo-Arians who said that the Son was created and not generated inasmuch as generation would imply a mutation in God, Victorinus argued that the correct Neoplatonic understanding of the divine generation is such that it is understood to provide no modification in the generator.[28]

To the theologians united against consubstantiality, Victorinus speaks in Aristotelian language. Consubstantial as used in the Creed denotes that there is only one numerical individual substance of God, and this substance is simple. Therefore, Basil of Ancyra is philosophically in error in speaking of the Son as similar in substance to the Father. Similarity occurs by way of qualities; in God all is substantial.[29]

As is to be expected, Victorinus forsakes his Neoplatonism when he tries to prove to the Latin Homeans that the terms "*ousia*" and "*homoousion*" are conformed to scriptural and ecclesiastical language. But in *Adversus Arium* I, when he uses scriptural authority for the consubstantiality and distinctness of individuals within the Godhead by way of common and proper names, substantial and personal names (Spirit, Logos, *Nous*, Wisdom, Substance),[30] he does not hesitate to use the philosophical theory of predominance.

Moreover, the concept of *agere* which functioned both in the *Anonymous Commentary* and in Porphyry's *Commentary on the Chaldaean Oracles* was used centrally by Victorinus to safeguard the Christian revelation of the Son's equality with the Father. "For God is power and the Logos is action, but each is in the other."[31]

By recognizing activity as a transcendental and by admitting that God belongs to the realm of Being, Victorinus was able to speak of God as dynamic *Esse*. The activity of God is to live and to understand. This helped Victorinus to distinguish the essential attributes of God from the personal denominations of the three. He therefore taught that *esse* (*substantia*), *vivere* (*forma*), and *intelligere* (*notio*) are shared by all three. All three are transcendental, predicated of the First Principle.

Hence the Son and Spirit by sharing these essential attributes were in no way inferior to the Father, being also self-begetting.

In the movement of life there is the expression of God by his Son; in the movement of understanding there is conversion to the Father in the Spirit through knowledge and love. The Father's self-revelation is life and wisdom.

In the Trinity the Holy Spirit is the principle of the identity of the three after the Son's dynamic procession. In the world the Father wills the creation and creates through the Son, recreating in the Holy Spirit. Therefore, for us also the Holy Spirit is the principle of identity with God. It is evident throughout this work that Victorinus used the Platonic categories of identity, distinction, repose, and movement to express the procession from the Father and the return to the Father. These divine realities are mutually inclusive, each in all and all in each.

The external activity of God reflects his inner essence as Three Persons:

> You give "to be" to all,
> Thou, Son, givest form,
> Thou, Spirit, reform. O Blessed Trinity.[32]

Thus the structure of the act of creation expresses the structure of God.

Whereas Plotinus distributed being and intelligence and life among the two hypostases which follow the One, invoking the principle "No one gives what he has," Victorinus concentrated these in the one triune God. In doing so he allowed for an analogy of dynamic being. All things participate to a certain extent in the attributes of dynamic being. Life is everywhere. "For these three in their progress, as we shall show, have shared with all existents . . . existence, life, understanding, which they give to them according to the proper capacity of things. . . ."[33]

And so, although Victorinus uses abstract vocabulary, his philosophy is concrete and existentialist, a view of being as spontaneous and dynamic. He is impelled to use infinitives to express the dynamism of reality. Energy is the Father, form is the Son: *vivens* and *vita*.

V

And if it was proposed that he held the principal activity of the Christian life to be the intellectual one of detaching oneself from sensible knowledge to keep the soul united with the Divine Spirit, the Spirit of wisdom and revelation, yet we should not ignore the fact that he linked the interior movement of divine life with the rhythm of human history.[34] And he respects the value of time, especially as the time for faith. In his *Commentary on the Ephesians* he clearly teaches that salvation is from faith in Christ. And yet, it is undeniable that Victorinus understands faith to be the knowledge of Christ or of the Spirit, a uniting knowledge that leads the soul back to its original state of Spirit. But this faith-knowledge is not the soul's own achievement; it is the gift of God. Very dear to Victorinus is the theme of Christ as the true light. The soul is the light (this he learned from Neoplatonism), but not the "true light" (this he learned from Scripture).[35]

With this faith in Christ and in the mystery of his salvific concern for the world, there is no doubt of the essential Christianity of Victorinus the man. We can also add that as a theologian, his metaphysical reflection on the scriptural revelation of the triune God was expressed Neoplatonically largely because he found this appropriate to help those who in making philosophical errors had misinterpreted Scripture.

CONCLUSION

How important are these early and intricate speculations on the internal relations of the Trinity? Has Victorinus' Trinitarian theology any lasting significance?

First of all, his work, along with that of others, witnesses to the birth of dogmatic theology and to the role—the carefully limited role—of philosophy in that birth. His work needs to be more widely known and studied. No forward movement in theology is to be expected without a critical acceptance of what was adequate in the theological tradition and a critical rejection of what was inadequate. If historians of theology pass on the theological tradition, they will assist those who are trying to think theologically today. Theologians who confront the contemporary questions should be informed by the past, though not bound by it in the sense of being prevented from progressing, through reflection upon the experience of the Christian community.

In the early theology of the Trinity we see an effort to reflect upon the Christian texts of the Gospels and the Epistles by a Tertullian and an Origen whose Stoic and Plotinian frameworks prevented them from reaching any adequate formulation of the Trinity. At Nicaea, Athanasius used the word "consubstantial" to say that the three Persons are identical to each other, all three being numerically one God. This was a scriptural insight, not a Hellenic one, and no crusade for dehellenization should induce one to forsake Nicaea. Dogma had to develop as it did if the true interpretation of scriptural revelation was to be rescued from theological misinterpretations. Surely dogma is no substitute for Scripture which appeals to all those who wish to be saved and to experience the full worthwhileness of human existence, but dogma may be a necessity for the critical intelligence of those who wish to be assured of the truth of the Gospels. The dogmatic effort is a work of analysis and interpretation and synthesis, an approach to Scripture as true. The Church has provided dogma because it is the guardian of the truth of Scriptures so that they may do their saving work for individuals who come to them.

Thus Athanasius, after reading the Son's scriptural testimony to his Father and himself, used the word "consubstantial" to indicate that all that is said of the Father is also to be said of the Son, except that the Son is Son and not Father. Therefore, the Son is the same substance as the Father but not the same person.

Admittedly, it is a far better thing to live by the Gospels than merely to know what they are saying, but is the former possible without the latter? Dogmas are explicitations of Scripture; they are statements about what is going on there or being affirmed there; they are its truth dimension, significant for persons whose humanness includes a strong intellectual element.

Whereas Athanasius, in independence of any one philosphical tradition, was defining the dogma of the Trinity by using the word "consubstantial," Victorinus belonged to that second generation of post-Nicene theologians who had to consider whether the word "consubstantial" said too much or too little. He felt it necessary to evaluate the Nicene interpretation of the Trinity. And so he did this within the framework of his own convictions of the relation between the three principles of the intelligible world as he understood them through Neoplatonic philosophy in the fourth century. In evaluating the Nicene dogma, he not only formulated a philosophical defense of the possibility of consubstantiality, but he returned to the Christian texts that declared the identity and distinction of Father, Son, and Spirit.

Thus we perceive here two stages of dogma: its conciliar expression as an interpretation of Scripture, and the philosophical defense of its coherence as expressed in theology, in particular in the Trinitarian theology of Marius Victorinus who utilized the Platonic categories and Neoplatonic metaphysics.

The Nicene Creed, however, was only the first dogmatic statement on the Trinity. With the use of more adequate theological method and more adequate philosophical categories, man's desire to understand more deeply the life of the Trinity and its significance for our Christian lives may lead to dogmatic development. This will happen as theologians continue to appropriate past theology critically, that is, to make explicit any implicit incoherence. In any appropriation of the past which necessarily precedes true development of dogma, the Trinitarian treatises of Marius Victorinus the African should not be ignored. For any advance in Christology, a thorough knowledge of Trinitarian theology is fundamental.

In conclusion we may note that Victorinus' argument with the Neo-Arians of his day was an argument against those who resisted development. If he were alive today, what philosophical categories would he use to come to a better understanding of the Trinity? We do not know, but we can say that he would still argue against those who resist development, yet he would argue even more strongly against those for whom development means nothing less than the denial of dogma.

4

The Neoplatonism of Saint Augustine

JOHN J. O'MEARA

have written a good deal on this topic in books and articles, fairly evenly spread out over the last quarter of a century. They bear witness to the inevitable evolution of my ideas on this subject.

During the period there was sustained interest in this field, a great deal of it generated by H. I. Marrou, P. Courcelle, and P. Henry, who, with others, contributed an Augustinian dimension to the remarkable school of late Hellenistic religion and philosophy at Paris, deriving from F. Cumont and J. Bidez, and more recently associated with the names of, for example, A. J. P. Festugière and Ch. H. Puech. There were, of course, others, both in France and far from its confines, who regarded Paris as the center of their studies in this field. And, naturally, I must allude very discreetly indeed to the reigning generation—to such as J. Pépin and P. Hadot—not to say to the very promising group of younger scholars whose formation has been directly or indirectly affected by what I call the Neoplatonic and Augustinian school of Paris.

A great support in more recent times for this scholarly movement was the existence of the Études Augustiniennes maintained by Père G. Folliet and his community in the rue François 1ᵉʳ (now in rue de l'Abbaye). Not only have they

continued to publish their *Revue des Études Augustiniennes,* which contains also
an exhaustive bibliography of what is published on Augustine and, of course,
Augustine and Neoplatonism, but they arranged a famous Augustinian Congress in
Paris in 1954 that was dominated by the topic to which we are now addressing
ourselves. The intense interest and controversy that appeared in relation to this
subject on that occasion may be seen in the pages of the third volume of the proceedings, *Augustinus Magister* (Paris, 1954), which reports the more than lively
discussions. I shall never forget the interjection of F. Chatillon: "Quant à Plotin,
votre Plotin, eh bien! flûte pour Plotin!"

This vigorous remark was one of the last protestations on one side in an
embattled dispute with which you may not all be familiar. In 1888 A. Harnack
and G. Boissier had put forward a view, expounded in its heyday by P. Alfaric in
his *L'évolution intellectuelle de saint Augustin* (Paris 1918), which in effect said
that it was not until *long after* his "conversion" that Augustine accepted the
Christian faith in opposition to Neoplatonism. In the context of the time and in the
light, for example, of the career of Synesius, the professing Neoplatonist bishop
of Cyrene, such a view is not extravagant. From the time of C. Boyer's counter-
attack in 1920, however, this view became gradually untenable—hence F.
Chatillon's inelegant remark. Still the majority of scholars by 1954 would have
agreed that at the time of his conversion, Augustine's acceptance of Christianity
was sincere and that he was also deeply impressed by Neoplatonism. He, with
many others, thought (fondly as it proved later) that there could be a synthesis
between the Christian faith and Neoplatonic reason since indeed the one God had
to be the source for both authority and reason. It would, I think, be true to say
that since 1954 we are no longer interested in what is now called the "false"
problem of whether Augustine at any particular time was a Christian rather than
a Neoplatonist or vice versa. To us he now seems to have been a Christian of
his time who held certain views that were abhorrent to Neoplatonism but nevertheless had been much influenced by Neoplatonism in not unimportant ways.

A second problem had in the meantime emerged: which Neoplatonist,
Plotinus (204/5–269/70) or Porphyry (232/3–ca. 305) was responsible for this
Neoplatonist influence on Augustine? W. Theiler (whose death occurred early in
1977) was breast high for Porphyry; P. Henry for Plotinus. In my own introduction to the *Contra Academicos* I had already made it clear that in my view "both
Plotinus and Porphyry are well represented"[1] in that work. To that point, claims for
the dominating influence of Plotinus were standard. Since then and, I am happy to
say, since my own *Porphyry's Philosophy from the Oracles in Augustine* (Paris
1959), P. Hadot's very lon̄ ̄ review of it in the *Revue des Études Augustiniennes*
(VI. 3, 1960, pp. 205–244) and his own subsequent work, *Porphyre et Victorinus,*
and the Entretiens held on Porphyry at the Fondation Hardt in Geneva (1966),
Porphyry has gained enormously in his reputation as a philosopher and is allowed
an important role, alongside his master Plotinus, in influencing Augustine.

So much by way of a *status quaestionis.* But there are some other preliminary
remarks which it may be useful to make.

Recently Edward Booth has drawn attention to the eclectic character of Neoplatonism. It was in fact the most influential of the "eclectic contemplative philosophies, with their triple ultimate beings and their doctrines of salvation (which) were the background of Christian Trinitarianism."[2] The spirit of the Roman world, in which Plotinus and Porphyry lived, may have been responsible for some—though hardly all—of the eclectic character of Neoplatonism. The Roman spirit was profoundly sceptical, embracing only the probable, pragmatic and necessarily, therefore, eclectic. I recall vividly how startled I was when I read the opinion of the great Latinist Ernout that Lucretius was not concerned with how true the physical theory of Democritus was on which he based his system: it seemed to work; that was enough.[3] Now I am not saying that Plotinus' approach to truth is the same as that of Lucretius. But I am saying that the Neoplatonists were eclectic.

So was Augustine who was on this point strikingly Roman. Listen to this tidy example from chapter 28 of the twenty-second book of the *City of God*. The topic is the Christian doctrine of the resurrection of the body which the Neoplatonists refused absolutely to countenance:

> The Platonists agree with us that even blessed souls will return to bodies, as Plato says, but will nevertheless not return to any evils, as Porphyry says, and take this also from Varro, that they will return to the same bodies, in which they were formerly, then their whole difficulty about the resurrection of the flesh for eternity will be solved.

It is to be noticed that Augustine is not writing flippantly, although one suspects that if he were challenged on this piece of jig-sawing he would have disengaged himself quickly enough. But a remarkable feature of Augustine's writing is his tendency to use the *ballon d'essai*: "This theory," he writes in his first extant work, "about the Academics I have sometimes, as far as I could, thought probable. If it is false, I do not mind."[4] This inconsequential attitude to doctrine propounded by others or even himself is highlighted even more in his other well known tendency to believe that philosophers propounded one thing to the public but propounded very different and sometimes opposite views to their inner circle: it is the old business of exoteric and esoteric doctrines.

But if Augustine was Roman in his eclectic attitude to the truths of physics and logic, he was also Roman in his passionate attachment to ethics. I have often felt disappointed by his handling of philosophical themes in the earlier part of the *City of God*—though I hasten to add both that the controversial nature of that work offered him some excuse, and he does demonstrate a profound aptitude for philosophical speculation elsewhere—but I have always been impressed by his strong passion for social and moral issues. His praise of the high moral and social qualities of Brutus, Torquatus, Curtius, the Decii, Regulus, Cincinnatus, and others is emphatic and sincere.

Quidquid recipitur recipitur ad modum recipientis. The fact that Augustine borrowed from the Neoplatonists what he borrowed from them, and how he used his borrowings, all these reflect his own character and interests. I have written on this topic fairly comprehensively in, for example, *Recherches Augustiniennes* I (1958, pp. 91–111) and in my *Charter of Christendom* (1961, pp. 62–87) and elsewhere. Very briefly, Augustine accepted the Neoplatonic doctrine of an incorporeal Creator, the immortality of the soul, and the existence of Providence and mediatory salvation. Porphyry appeared to Augustine to espouse something like the Christian Trinity and a rudimentary notion of Grace. Augustine had much to criticize in the precise formulation by the Neoplatonists of their doctrines. His criticisms have been usefully set forth by Edward Booth in the article to which I have already referred.[5]

I should now like to look a little, but, necessarily, very quickly, at the particular points of contact which I judge to be of greatest significance between Augustine on the one hand and Plotinus and Porphyry on the other.

In an article in the *Revue Internationale de Philosophie*'s celebration of a Plotinian centenary in 1970,[6] I stressed what I called the conversion syndrome in Augustine's thought and its inspiration in Plotinus, principally in *Ennead* I. 6 "On Beauty." Here Plotinus truly passes on the mystical spell of Plato's *Symposium* to be taken up again by Augustine in a number of passages of the *Confessions* where, according to Courcelle,[7] Augustine describes his attempts to achieve Plotinian ecstasy. I am convinced that the impression that Augustine received from reading Plotinus I. 6, which made it possible for him to abandon materialism in any explanation of reality, abode with him forever. It was not so much Plotinus' articulation of immaterialist doctrine that affected him, as the profound insight that the emotional, almost mystical concentration on the hypostases afforded him:

> The reasoning faculty drew away my thoughts from the power of habit, withdrawing itself from those troops of contradictory phantasms; that so it might find what that light was, whereby it was bedewed, when, without all doubting, it cried out, "That the unchangeable was to be preferred to the changeable;" whence also it knew That Unchangeable, which, unless it had in some way known, it had had no sure ground to prefer it to the changeable. And thus with the flash of one trembling glance it arrived at That Which Is. But I could not fix my gaze thereon; and my infirmity being struck back, I was thrown again on my wonted habits, carrying along with me only a loving memory thereof, and a longing for what I had, as it were, perceived the odour of, but was not able to feed on. Yet dwelt there with me a remembrance of Thee.[8]

Again in the so-called vision of Ostia, he speaks about touching on eternal wisdom: "Could this (touching) be continued on, and other visions of kind far unlike be withdrawn, and this one ravish, and absorb and wrap up its beholder amid these inward joys, so that life might be for ever like that one moment of understanding which we now sighed after?"[9]

It will be observed that the elevation here described by Augustine uses the emotions if only to dismiss them. The *practical* aspect of the matter is in fact represented by the purification of the senses. This purification was fully propounded by both Plotinus and Porphyry and in due course by Augustine. The approach, then, changing somewhat from the metaphysical to the moral, becomes a theme congenial to Roman moralism, be it in Sallust, Seneca, or Saint Augustine.

The Latin language had (and has) an extraordinary power to seize upon the substance of a complicated consideration and express it pithily, memorably, and emotionally. Greek is more intellectual; but when it comes to expressing the whole of human experience and of the *lacrimae rerum*, Latin speaks grandly for the human heart. Over and over again Augustine sums up the necessity to turn to, to be converted to, the Father and to turn away from the things of this world. One can see this in the argument of a whole work such as the *City of God*: *fecerunt itaque ciuitates duas amores duo, terrenam scilicet amor sui usque ad contemptum Dei, caelestem uero amor Dei usque ad contemptum sui.*[10] Or one can see it in the phrases now hackneyed from too much casual use: *inquietum est cor nostrum, donec requiescat in te*: *noverim me noverim te, ut amem te et contemnam me.* These phrases are highly rhetorical, but their very jingle is part of their usefulness and appeal to the many. We should not be misled for all that; they enshrine the very core of Plotinus' explanation of the origin of things:

ὃν γὰρ τέλειον τῷ μηδὲν ζητεῖν μηδὲ ἔχειν μηδὲ δεῖσθαι οἷον ὑπερερρύη καὶ τὸ ὑπερπλῆρες αὐτοῦ πεποίηκεν ἄλλο. τὸ δὲ γενόμενον εἰς αὐτὸ ἐπεστράφη καὶ ἐπληρώθη καὶ ἐγένετο πρὸς αὐτὸ βλέπον καὶ νοῦς οὗτος. καὶ ἡ μὲν πρὸς ἐκεῖνο στάσις αὐτοῦ τὸ ὂν ἐποίησεν.[11]

Augustine did not quite follow Plotinus in the explanation of the creation of the *Nous*, the first being, by the One, but he did preserve the general structure and vocabulary. In particular the term *conversio*, "turning to," was for him an emotional touchstone of deep and lasting importance. The *Confessions* is the story of his own and of everyman's conversion to God. The *City of God* is the same theme writ large in terms of all angels and humanity that ever was or will be. The intellectual inspiration is in Plotinus.

I have been alluding to the salvational element that Augustine—and others—have discerned in Plotinus. But the other Neoplatonist who influenced Augustine (as we know from Augustine's own testimony), Porphyry, is much more explicit on the theme of salvation—which may well afford some explanation as to why we have until recently tended to rate Porphyry rather less than did Augustine, and why Augustine gives more prominence to him than to Plotinus.

Porphyry was for Augustine not only the greatest of recent philosophers but was one who, although he had abandoned or at least rejected and finally attacked Christianity most forcefully, had also examined its claims and, in his view, came very close to it. Porphyry, Augustine says in the *City of God*,[12] had accepted the God of the Hebrews and had extolled the virtues of Christ—as a man, only, however. Pride and the demons had prevented him not only from accepting the divinity of the Christ who had become incarnate and had died on a cross, but also from appreciating the virtues of Christians and the enduring mission of the Church. But Porphyry's salvationism and eclecticism seemed especially useful to Augustine. Augustine refers to him as follows:

> When Porphyry says that no one system of thought has yet embraced a doctrine that embodies a universal path to the liberation of the soul, no, neither the truest of

philosophies, nor the moral ideas and practices of the Indians, nor the initiation of the Chaldaeans, nor any other way of life, and adds that this same path has not yet been brought to his attention in the course of his research into history, he is undoubtedly acknowledging that some such path exists though it had not yet come to his attention. So dissatisfied was he with the results of his devoted study of the liberation of the soul and with what his reputation, higher in the eyes of others than in his own, credited him with discovering and maintaining.[13]

It was the nearness of Porphyry's approach—despite his ultimate fierce hostility—to Christianity that induced Augustine to give more extensive notice to Porphyry than to Plotinus and to praise him more. We must recognize this dominating fact in our assessment of Augustine's *own* admission of Neoplatonist influence on him.

The influences of Plotinus and Porphyry on Augustine as indicated so far could be described as important indeed but, especially, *dramatic*. At any rate Augustine's description of them is dramatic and, certainly in relation to the influence of Porphyry, also rather politic. There was a doctrinal influence involved, but it tends to attract our notice less. Nevertheless, the influence of both Plotinus and Porphyry at the doctrinal level, even if ultimately rejected, was wider and deeper than has so far been suggested here. Some of this may have been imbibed directly from a reading of these authors probably for the most part in translation. Some may have come to Augustine orally through his Christian–Neoplatonist friends and acquaintances in Milan. At any rate we now know, thanks to the fruitful labors of Berthold Altaner,[14] quite an amount on the influence of the Greek Neoplatonist Fathers—Basil, the Gregories, Irenaeus, Athanasius, and Origen—on Augustine, manifesting itself at all stages of his life.

I shall end with some comments on the work of Augustine perhaps best known under the title *Hexaemeron* in the earlier medieval period, and, under the title *de Genesi ad litteram,* very little known in more recent centuries. Only one translation of this work into a modern language, French, has been available and that only since 1972.[15] An English translation by John Taylor (of Seattle) should appear fairly soon. This work, Augustine's fourth attempt to comment (as literally as possible) on the first chapters of Genesis, was finished when its author was about sixty-one years of age. It is, therefore, a rather late and mature work and testifies to the permanent influence of Neoplatonism on his thoughts.

I am discussing elsewhere[16] the extent to which Augustine in the *de Genesi ad litteram* depends upon, for example, Plotinus' doctrine on the λόγος for his fundamental and very philosophical understanding of creation as described in Genesis. Likewise I hope to treat at some future time his use in the *de Genesi ad litteram* of Porphyry's idea of *spiritus* for his equally fundamental and equally philosophical understanding of the afterlife. There are other points of influence, such as that of Plotinus' ideas on Providence or Porphyry's angelology (and this was most significant). Here, however, let me mention briefly one instance only of the influence of Plotinus *and* Porphyry, taking them—as for the most part, perhaps they should be—together, as seen in the *de Genesi ad litteram.*

Fundamental to the Neoplatonist system and elaborated with great emphasis in Plotinus is the doctrine that the Father, the One, is beyond being and beyond not only all sensible but also all rational or even intellectual perception:

> (13) Thus the One is in truth beyond all statement: any affirmation is of a thing; but "all-transcending, resting above even the most august divine Mind"—this is the only true description, since it does not make it a thing among things, nor name it where no name could identify it: we can but try to indicate, in our own feeble way, something concerning it. . . . The Transcendent, thus, neither knows itself nor is known in itself. (14) . . . We have neither knowledge nor intellection of it (οὐδὲ γνῶσιν οὐδὲ νόησιν ἔχομεν αὐτοῦ), . . . we can and do state what it is not, while we are silent as to what it is (καὶ γὰρ λέγομεν, ὃ μὴ ἔστιν· ὃ δέ ἐστιν, οὐ λέγομεν).[17]

Porphyry and his translator, Victorinus, may well have been agents through whom the idea of the unknowability of the One was transmitted to Augustine. In his *Sententiae* he writes: θεωρεῖται δὲ ἀνοησίᾳ κρεῖττον νοήσεως.[18]

At any rate Augustine even in the early *de ordine* speaks of God as "known better in not being known": *qui scitur melius nesciendo*.[19] In the *de Genesi ad litteram* he has a remarkable passage stressing how God is not any *thing* but that he is nearer to us, nevertheless, than the many things he made:

> Although, I say, it is not possible to say anything of that substance (i.e., God) and there is no way whatever of one man saying anything about it to another except by commandeering some words related to times and places—whereas he is before all times and before all places—nevertheless he is nearer to us, he who made us, than the many things which were made. For in him we live and move and are. . . . It is a greater labor to find them than him, by whom they were made. To become aware of him with a faithful mind from anything, however insignificant, is better in its incomparable blessedness than to comprehend the whole universe of things.[20]

Augustine's use of the *theologia negativa* is, thus, influenced by the Plotinian "Father" or One, whether directly or through Porphyry, or through the Greek Fathers such as Gregory Nazianzen, orally or through writing. The extent to which Augustine's works are heavily marked by this negative theology has been much obscured by what one might call historical institutional theology in the West. This has tended to play down the influence of Platonism in, for example, Aquinas and even more in Augustine, where its presence is more obvious.

From the few instances of Neoplatonic influence on Augustine that I have given you, you will observe that the topic is by no means a simple one. Nor is there any reason why it should be. Neoplatonism, to begin with, was not one, unaltering doctrine, even in Plotinus. After Plotinus it evolved in various ways and, some would say, in curious directions. But above all, the recipient of the influence, Augustine, was a complicated character. Augustine for most of his life as a writer was a Christian bishop deeply committed in literally a sequence of critical controversies, the heat of which was undoubtedly raised significantly by his own ardent temperament. Over and over again, and notably in the *City of God*, he turns aside from a full discussion of some profound problem in order to maintain his general and well-directed polemic. Indeed one can say that the less polemical he is, the more philosophical. It could hardly have been otherwise.

Augustine at the same time was something of an artist and a religious genius. Some have spoken of the warring passions that rent his body. His mind, too, was racked by apparently conflicting loyalties, especially the drive to commend God's claim on us, which appeared to be *absolute,* and at the same time to sympathize with the erring needs of the human heart. In fact he was loyal to both—can be quoted to support both sides—and so can appear to contradict himself.

There is something of that enduring split within him in regard to Neoplatonism too. To the extent—which was in this case quite absolute—that he accepted the incarnation and the resurrection of Christ's and the human body, to that extent he rejected the immaterialism of the Neoplatonists—an absolutely fundamental point. In general, then, I regard Gilson's judgment that Augustine inhibited Neoplatonic influence in the West rather than transmitted it as true.

And yet the traditional practical asceticism of the West, which manifested itself in an actual hostility to the body, however that body is honored in the resurrection of the person, is deeply marked with Platonic dualism. Similarly Augustine sought the rational understanding of the problems and mysteries of Christian theology, perhaps progressively so as time went on, in Neoplatonic sources. Even in the last book of the *City of God,* while opting for the view that in the afterlife our corporeal eyes will see God, he does not omit to give a Neoplatonic view which centers on assimilation of mind with God rather than vision of any kind, however glorified, of corporeal eyes.[21] The matter was not made easier by the knowledge that even Neoplatonic immaterialism was by some understood in a sense involving some kind of matter, however attenuated.

There is no simple statement adequate to describe Augustine's use of the Neoplatonists. I hope, nevertheless, that I have succeeded in conveying to you in some plausible manner how manifold that use might have been.

II

Later Greek and Byzantine Thought

5

Some Later Neoplatonic Views on Divine Creation and the Eternity of the World

GÉRARD VERBEKE

The Aristotelian doctrine of the eternity of the world has been accepted not only by pagan philosophers, but also by Christian thinkers. Synesius of Cyrene, bishop of Ptolemais, one of the five cities of the Libyan Pentapolis, when he was converted to Christianity did not reject the eternity of the world.[1] That is no wonder: it is true that Christian theologians generally interpreted Plato's *Timaeus* in the sense of a creation in time, and yet the eternity of the world is not incompatible with the notion of a divine Creator and Providence.

In the Alexandrian school the eternity of the world was generally accepted. The teaching of Ammonius is transmitted to us through Philoponus' commentary on the *Physics*. Unfortunately, we only possess fragments of this commentary on Book VIII. Moreover, Philoponus does not merely echo the teaching of his master; he also introduces some personal views and remarks. Looking at the parts of the commentary which have been preserved, we notice in several passages objections to and criticisms of the doctrine of the eternity of the world. Presumably, these criticisms don't spring from Ammonius, a former pupil of Proclus in Athens, but are the views of Philoponus himself. Moreover, Philoponus refers to his commentary on *Physics* VIII where he presented a critical investigation of the Aristotelian doctrine. In the Alexandrian circle Philoponus seemingly was an exception. Olympiodorus, while he was not a Christian, did not oppose Christianity: apparently he thought of Christian religion as a faith for uneducated people. Themistius, when he was prefect of Byzantium, had already adopted a similar attitude: instead of fighting against the Christians, he endeavored rather to show the pagan way of life to be superior to Christianity. No wonder that Olympiodorus remains faithful to the Aristotelian teaching on the eternity of the world.[2] It is more amazing that a Christian teacher like Elias, and probably also David and Stephen of Alexandria, professed the same doctrine.[3] With respect to the Athenian school, Proclus undoubtedly maintained the eternity of the world: it is against him that Philoponus in 529 wrote his famous treatise *De aeternitate mundi contra Proclum*.[4] Presumably, the successors of Proclus, Isidorus, and Damascius, adopted the same position.[5] In any case, Simplicius showed the utmost opposition to the views of Philoponus. During the second half of the thirteenth century, at the time of the Averroistic controversy, the question of the eternity of the world was again violently discussed: the main issue at that time was whether from a philosophical viewpoint we should not adhere to the Aristotelian view, although contrary to Christian belief.

Thanks to the information supplied by Damascius in his *Vita Isidori,* we know that Ammonius had been compelled to make an agreement with the bishop of Alexandria, so that Christian pupils might attend his lectures and that he could get the necessary subventions for the working of the school. This agreement probably was contracted with the patriarch Athanasius II and dates back to 489–496.[6] Damascius violently reproves the attitude of his Alexandrian colleague.[7] Unfortunately, we lack precise information concerning the concessions made by Ammonius: did he recant some doctrines, for example, the eternity and the divinity of the world? Did he allow himself to be baptized? We do not know.[8] It is not impossible, for example, that Ammonius deliberately entrusted Philoponus with the edition of his lectures in order to appease the fears and suspicions of the Christian community. Regardless, we learn from Simplicius that Ammonius wrote a work in which many arguments are put forward showing that Aristotle considered God to be the creative cause of the universe, not only its final cause.[9] Surely that was an important step towards a rapprochement between Aristotelianism and Christianity.

The teaching of Olympiodorus diverges on many important topics from Christian doctrine; for example, he accepts that suicide may be justified in some circumstances and dismisses the Christian belief in an everlasting punishment. He admits only one single God, the first cause of the universe; the other divinities are intermediary beings between God and the world; they may even be considered to be attributes or functions of God. In this respect Olympiodorus comes rather close to Christian belief.[10]

Let us now examine the teaching of Philoponus and Simplicius on the two questions already mentioned, firstly that of the eternity of the world. According to H. D. Saffrey, Philoponus arrived at the school of Ammonius circa 510; he was already a Christian and about 20 years of age.[11] His commentary on the *Physics* dates back to 517. Although the text of Book VIII is only partly preserved, there are, in the course of his exposition, unequivocal indications of the author's opposition to the eternity of the world.[12] Philoponus wonders what we should think of the sentence saying that nothing could derive from nothing (*nihil ex nihilo*).[13] Quite obviously, being in the absolute sense could not spring from being, because it already would exist before coming to be. Could it proceed from nonbeing? Apparently not, for being, before coming to be, must be able to become; so it derives from something preexistent, a material principle; consequently, it does not proceed from nonbeing.[14] Philoponus replies that this argument is valid only if matter actually subsists before being is produced. He acknowledges however that whatever comes to be, originates from something existent in the sense of an efficient cause, for what comes to be need not necessarily proceed from something in the sense of a material principle. The Creator is able to cause not only the form, but also the matter; hence, it is possible that being stems from nonbeing and that matter is made jointly with the form by a creative cause.[15] Philoponus comes here to the heart of the problem: Aristotle states that every movement presupposes another one and we have to agree with him insofar as finite causality is concerned. The question however arises whether there is not another mode of causation, one that does not presuppose a preexistent matter, but causes the concrete being in whatever it involves. In this case, being in a way proceeds from nonbeing, because it does not presuppose a material principle out of which it has been effected; but on the other hand it springs from being, for it could only come to be by the activity of a creative cause.[16] Is this causation a real movement? By no means, for there is no material principle securing the continuity of the becoming.[17] In this context, Philoponus states that in Aristotle's view the forms of the beings do not derive from any merging of elements; the soul is not the mere result of a combination of elements. Consequently, the forms can proceed only from nonbeing, and the same holds with respect to matter: matter also must stem from nonbeing. In our author's view there is not only a coming-to-be that occurs through a process of generation from preexistent matter, but also the full and total causation of a being from nothing.[18]

In his commentary on Book III of the *Physics* Philoponus states that neither the world nor time exists from eternity and he expounds several arguments to support his viewpoint. If the world had always existed, it would include an infinite number of men having lived already: this is not in keeping with the teaching of Aristotle, who repudiates any infinite in act. Moreover, it would entail the possibility of traversing the infinite in act, for if it can be brought into being, it may be traversed. Besides, something would be greater than the infinite: children being born every day are added to the infinite multitude of men who already existed. Hence the infinite in act might increase indefinitely. Moreover, if every generation counts an infinite multitude of ancestors, the infinite will be produced an infinite number of times. In Philoponus' view all these consequences are absurd and could not be avoided, for it makes no sense to contend that in the case under consideration the infinite extends in one direction only because the present instant constitutes a borderline. The author replies that this specification is not applicable to numbers and not even to continuous quantity.[19] Could we say that in Aristotle's view the infinite could not be brought into being at once, but could be produced progressively? Philoponus answers that Aristotle purely and simply dismisses the infinite in act. It would even be more acceptable that there is an infinite multitude of men at the present instant, than to admit it with regard to the past; for if one accepts it regarding the past, one has to admit that this infinite number may be traversed, that it constantly increases and that the infinite is brought into being an infinite number of times.[20] It clearly follows from these passages and from the references to Book VIII of the commentary that Philoponus, when he edited the lectures of Ammonius on Aristotle's *Physics,* firmly repudiated the eternity of the world and attributed to God a creative activity capable of originating things without preexistent matter.[21]

In Book VI of the *Contra Aristotelem* which belongs to a later period, Philoponus deals with the same problems. Although the work is lost, it is possible to get some idea of its content thanks to the information provided by Simplicius in his commentary on the *Physics.*[22] One of the major objections of Philoponus to the eternity of the world is related to the Aristotelian definition of movement, which is declared to be incompatible with the doctrine in question. Movement is the act of what is movable in potency: the definition clearly implies that the movable in potency exists prior to the movement. Consequently, movement could not exist from eternity, if the movable in potency is always anterior to the movement. As a result, the definition of movement elaborated by Aristotle is not universal.[23] Philoponus however does not agree with Aristotle on that issue: he clearly understood that Aristotle proved the eternity of the world starting from the fact that any movement presupposes already the existence of what is movable in potency. In his view, however, this is not always true: some perishable beings move from the very beginning of their existence; there is the example of fire that, as soon as it exists, moves upwards.[24] Formulating this criticism, Philoponus attacks the very core of the Aristotelian argument: according to the Stagirite, a first movement has to be excluded because any movement implies the preexistence of a movable in potency.[25] Philoponus also contends that all present movements become unintelligible if the world already exists from eternity. For then every movement presupposes an infinite number of previous movements: if we want to explain a particular movement, we have to go back indefinitely in the series of antecedent factors; we could not avoid a *regressus in infinitum,* which means the denial of any explanation.[26] Moreover, all present movements are added to those of the past; that leads to the evidently absurd notion of an infinite constantly increasing.[27] What about the movements of the heavenly bodies? Philoponus points to the fact that the circular movements of some heavenly bodies are more frequent than those of others; the orbits of Jupiter, for example, are three times as frequent as those of Cronos, whereas those of the latter are as infinite as the former. So one infinite would be three times as large as another one.[28] Considering that the doctrine of the eternity of the world leads to absurd conclusions, Philoponus contends it ought to be dropped. Hence the world must have begun at some time in the past; it could not have existed from eternity. The question however remains concerning the future: will movement and time continue indefinitely in the future?[29] The answer must evidently be negative: no finite body could ever possess an infinite power; the argument is used by Aristotle in order to prove that the First Principle has no corporeal size. The power which is contained in the world could only be finite, which implies that the world could not continue to exist indefinitely.[30] Moreover, all beings in the world are compounded of matter and form and whatever is compounded in that way is perishable because matter is not always linked to the same form.[31] All those arguments of Philoponus belong to the field of philosophy; their inspiration is even Aristotelian. The criticism of the Greek master is undertaken from within his own system, without appealing to the authority of other philosophers or to arguments of a religious character. Philoponus endeavors to refute Aristotle through Aristotle himself.

Our author also examines the Aristotelian argument concerning the eternity of time and he comes to the same conviction—that the demonstration is inconclusive. In his view we could not assert that all instants are at the borderline of a past and a future: it would be a *petitio principii*. If time started, the first instant is not at the frontier of a past and a future.[32] Does time always refer to a previous time? If time began, we should ask the question, what was before time? Philoponus replies that in this case the term "before" has to be interpreted in a nontemporal sense because it does not refer to a temporal dimension.[33] Furthermore, the author contends that anterior and posterior do not always involve a temporal dimension. The mind without being in time grasps its objects the one after the other. God also wants things to take place in some successive order, and yet there is no temporal dimension in divine willing.[34] God knows the past and the future: does it follow that divine knowledge bears the stamp of temporality? By no means.[35] According to our author time as well as the world began. He quite disagrees with those who contend that time never started, but that the world had a beginning. In this respect he agrees with Plato whom he believes to be intrinsically coherent: time as well as the world does not exist from eternity, but had a beginning.[36]

Still, a further question has to be taken into consideration: how did the world, movement, and time ever begin to exist? The answer of Philoponus is quite unambiguous: the world began by an act of the divine will, which does not imply anything preexistent and does not involve any temporal dimension. It is not impossible for God to originate something from nothing: it is enough for him to will something to be and it exists, for he not only makes the form, but also the matter. It would be wrong to conceive of the generation of the world in the way of the ancient cosmogonies: the world has not been generated, it is not the result of a process of coming-to-be; it has been produced from nonbeing and in an atemporal way.[37] In order to support and illustrate his viewpoint, Philoponus refers to the works of nature and artistic activity. Prime matter has not been generated by nature and it does not pass away in the way of perishable beings; it has been made from nonbeing. Where do the forms in natural beings and works of art come from? Because they do not preexist in any way, they could only proceed from nonbeing.[38] Consequently, God created the world in an atemporal way by a sheer act of willing. Does this creation introduce any change in the divine perfection? By no means, because the creative act is atemporal; it is beyond any temporal succession. The divine willing by which the world begins to exist does not introduce into God any temporal extension nor any change because this willing is not inserted in the unsteadiness of temporal succession.[39]

Let us now proceed to the study of Simplicius' reaction to the interpretation of the Alexandrian scholar. One is immediately struck by the violence of tone adopted by the Athenian professor. Is there any personal spite involved? This is hard to believe because Simplicius contends never to have met Philoponus, which is perfectly acceptable if the one worked in Alexandria and the other in Athens. Is it rather a kind of grudge between two schools? That is more likely. Damascius also did not spare Ammonius, and the troubles of the school of Athens from 529 onwards certainly did not contribute to appease the atmosphere. Even if Justinian did not really close the school of Athens, as A. Cameron believes, but tried to prevent pagans from teaching in it, nevertheless this institution had to cope with conditions that were much more difficult than those of the Alexandrian school.[40] Simplicius repeatedly states that the objections of Philoponus are foolish but dangerous because they impress people who have not received a strong philosophical education. In Simplicius' view Philoponus is a traitor who abandons the precious legacy of Greek thought in order to cling to Egyptian mythology. The author makes fun of the narrative of Genesis, of the creation in six days, of a God who created the sun on the fourth day. He is indignant that a representative of the Alexandrian school surrenders to these poor mythological accounts.[41]

With respect to the eternity of movement, Simplicius declares the position of Aristotle to be perfectly coherent.[42] In his view the definition of movement as it is formulated by Aristotle is universal and not incompatible with the eternity of the world. For the movable must always exist prior to the movement, even in the case of eternal movement. Let us take circular movement: it is never given at once, so that each stage of the revolving refers to an anterior stage.[43] What Aristotle intends to show, on the basis of his definition, is the impossibility of a first movement: each movement is inserted in a process without beginning and without end.[44] It is useless also to contend that some beings already move from the very beginning of their existence. Simplicius introduces a distinction between perfect and imperfect potency. If fire moves upwards from its origin, it is because it has a perfect potency to do it; if it had an imperfect potency only, it would be unable to do that. Precisely in the case of an imperfect potency, Aristotle maintains that the movable must exist prior to the movement.[45] On the level of second causes, it is apparently impossible to refute the Aristotelian reasoning; from this viewpoint each movement is connected with a prior movement. The question arises however whether there is no opposition between the eternity of movement and the Aristotelian teaching concerning the infinite in act. According to Simplicius there is no contradiction involved, for in the case of movement or change the infinite in question does not totally exist at once. What in Aristotle's view could never be brought about is an infinite that exists totally at once. Besides, a movement without beginning is not yet infinite at present because it is marked by a boundary; in other words, it is not infinite in both directions. As a result a movement that occurs now does not simply have an infinite number of antecedents; the fire that burns now is not unintelligible because the event is located at the limit of a series which, though being without beginning, ends at this term.[46] Simplicius stresses the transformations of elements into each other: these changes are comparable to a circular movement without beginning. Things would be different if the number of forms happened to be infinite, but that is not the case. There is a limited number of forms and within this framework the transformations take place. The fact that this cycle is going on from eternity does not present any difficulty as to the explanation of a present event. As a matter of fact, if the number of forms were infinite, then our knowledge would be impossible and generation itself would be excluded.[47]

How then are we to conceive of the temporal dimension? Simplicius believes that on this subject there is a perfect agreement between Plato and Aristotle: the world has been shaped in the image of an eternal pattern, which means that it exists in a temporal dimension without beginning or end.[48] As to the Aristotelian argument saying that each element of time refers to a previous time, it is perfectly consistent: if there were a beginning of time, the question would arise as to what was "before" that beginning and in Simplicius' view the term "before" could only have a temporal meaning.[49] The author also states the Aristotelian conception of the instant to be correct. Is it a *petitio principii*? Not at all, because it is not the same to hold time to exist from eternity and to say that the instant is an intermediary (μέσον).[50]

One of the major criticisms Simplicius makes of the theory of Philoponus refers to divine immutability. The author dismisses any form of change in God. In his view it is inconsistent to believe that God was firstly inactive, then proceeded to the creation of the elements and further entrusted nature with the control of the transformations of the elements and the making of bodies from those elements.[51] Simplicius is convinced that this conception is incompatible with divine immutability. The author does not agree with Philoponus who declares that the anterior and posterior do not always refer to a temporal dimension: if the mind grasps its objects one after another, it could not be indivisible or unextended; the passage from one object to another is not possible without temporal extension.[52] According to Simplicius, the mind does not think the objects of its knowledge by passing from one object to another (μεταβατικῶς), but by distinguishing each one from each other.[53] In this respect the author is echoing a Plotinian distinction between the knowing of the mind and that of the soul: the former is a permanent intuition of all the intelligibles, whereas the latter is a discursive knowledge passing constantly from one intelligible object to another. In order to vindicate Aristotle's viewpoint concerning the eternity of the world, Simplicius emphasizes the difference between a process of generation and a creation out of nothing: what is generated proceeds from what already exists and passes away also into what exists;[54] moreover, any change occurs through the action of an external factor. The same holds with respect to decomposition: in Aristotle's view, it is a change occurring in time. By considering the final result only, one could say that decomposition takes place instantaneously.[55] If one draws attention only to the process of generation and passing away, one could not but accept that process to be without beginning or end. The creative activity of God is an integral causation that does not start from a preexistent matter: God makes things in an atemporal way (ἀχρόνως), hence he originates them always.[56] What is made by the Creator out of nothing does not come to be by generation; so the author concludes that it possesses an eternal substance.[57] According to him Aristotle asserts that what immediately springs from God (ἀμέσως) is eternal. If God made matter, he created it from eternity. The same holds with respect to the forms common to all corporeal things: stemming directly from God they must exist from eternity and will never pass away.[58] As to the objection that no finite body could possess an infinite power, the author makes a distinction between the power of moving and the power of being moved. The power of moving eternally could not simultaneously exist in a finite body, whereas it is not impossible that the power of being moved eternally exists in a limited body.[59]

It is noticeable that the disagreement between Philoponus and Simplicius does not concern the concept of creation as an integral causation: both authors accept that God makes beings out of nothing. Philoponus however declares that the world could not exist from eternity and that it came into existence by a creative act which is beyond movement and time; in his view this act is not incompatible with the divine immutability. Simplicius, on the contrary, teaches that the process of coming-to-be and passing away occurring in the world could never have started because it always refers to a previous movement. In his view it is not possible that God ever caused this becoming to start through a creative act: appealing to a Neoplatonic argument, the author asserts that whatever springs from God directly must be eternal. It is quite true that according to the Stagirite the first heaven is what is moved immediately by the Unmoved Mover; through the regularity and eternity of its movement it expresses the perfection of the moving principle. It would however be wrong to state that Aristotle's theory concerning the eternity of the world was based on the nature of creative causation. The concept of an integral causation was foreign to the mind of the Greek master.

The commentary of Simplicius on Aristotle's *Physics* is particularly interesting thanks to the rich information it provides concerning the doctrines of previous philosophers. His interpretation shows a great erudition, but it is not always faithful to the authentic thought of Aristotle. The first cause of Aristotle is not that of Simplicius and this is not the only case in which Simplicius gave to Aristotelian thought a turn that does not correspond to its original content. A similar distortion may be found in the interpretation of the intricate question of chance and fortune. It is more difficult to formulate a judgment about the commentary of Philoponus: to what extent does it reflect the teaching of Ammonius? In any case, the interpretation is very penetrating, especially in those passages where the author criticizes the doctrine of Aristotle and expresses manifestly his own ideas. Alfarabi takes Philoponus to task for settling a philosophical question with the help of religious doctrines:[60] nothing is less true, as W. Wieland has already noticed. Philoponus, rather, uses Aristotelian philosophy in order to refute Aristotle.[61] On the other hand he appeals to the concept of creation against the eternity of the world: he very sharply notices, perhaps also under the influence of Ammonius, that creation as an integral causation is not a movement and does not belong to the continuous process of coming-to-be and passing away. Thanks mainly to the concept of creation, the author escapes from the eternity of movement and time.

6

John Philoponus and Stephanus of Alexandria: Two Neoplatonic Christian Commentators on Aristotle?

HENRY BLUMENTHAL

"Two Neoplatonic Christian commentators on Aristotle?" The query is crucial, and could equally well come at three points in the title of this paper. It could come after the word "two" because it is not yet clear how much difference there, in fact, is between the commentaries of Philoponus and Stephanus on Book 3 of Aristotle's *de Anima*—it is these two commentaries with which I shall be primarily concerned. We now have Stephanus of Alexandria's exposition of this book in the transmitted text of Philoponus' commentary, while Philoponus' own survives only in a thirteenth-century Latin version by William of Moerbeke, and only for chapters 4–8 at that; it is also to some extent reflected in the paraphrase commentary by Sophonias,[1] which should probably be dated to the fourteenth century. So that is one question. One could also place the query after "Christian." Their philosophical background is manifestly Neoplatonic, but were they both, or was only Stephanus, Christian at the time when they wrote their commentaries—or gave the lectures on which the commentaries as we have them are based?[2] Yet again one could put it after "commentators." Were they Christians whose exposition of Aristotle *thereby* differed from what it would have been had they been pagans, or commentators on Aristotle who were no more than incidentally Christian? In other words, do the Christian convictions that both may have had bear in any way on their reading of Aristotle? And if they do, how can we detect the operation of this bias? Finally, we might ask how much these men were genuinely commentators on Aristotle at all.

Let us deal first with what should, at first sight, be the easiest of these questions: one commentator, or two? On a superficial level three sets of differences immediately present themselves. First, a crude measure, but informative nevertheless, is the scale of the commentaries. In the one Neoplatonic commentary which survives intact, that of Simplicius (?Priscian),[3] the commentary on Book 3 is twice as long as that on Book 1, and three-quarters as long again as that on Book 2, whereas in Stephanus' version (or whatever it is), the commentary on Book 3 is only four-fifths as long as Philoponus' on Book 1, and not much longer—some twenty pages—than Philoponus' on Book 2.[4] Now this might be a sign of different interests rather than anything else, but should at least be noted as a possible indication of difference. More significant is that within Book 3 itself, the relative length of discussion in different passages is not always the same. Sometimes Philoponus has more to say on one passage, at others Stephanus will give a long exposition of texts on which Philoponus has very little to say.

Second, we have a difference relating to the organization of the material. Philoponus' commentary continues with no marked breaks or divisions other than those arising from the text on which it is a commentary. Stephanus', on the other hand, falls into that series of divisions into *theōria* and *praxis* which seems to have been codified by Olympiodorus, though it can be traced back to Proclus.[5]

Third, we have a matter of scholarly practice. Stephanus' commentary, but not Philoponus', contains numerous named references to earlier commentators (or philosophers assumed to be commentators—especially Alexander and Plutarch, perhaps the only previous authors of full-scale commentaries on the *de Anima*, or at least Book 3 of it) and a continuous examination and dissection of the views of both these and others. That this apparent difference was not due to excisions by the Latin translator can be seen at once by a comparison with Philoponus on Books 1 and 2, as well as his other commentaries. Only Alexander constitutes an exception, both in the Latin *de Anima* commentary and elsewhere. But it must not be thought that the translator never made changes or additions: in the exposition of 3.4 we have a note on the fact that Greek *morion*, unlike Latin *pars*, was neuter, which cannot have been in the original. Thus we have here a *prima facie* case for distinguishing our two commentators as independent authorities—within the limits of independence at this point in the tradition. We have not yet excluded the possibility that they produced different presentations of a similar commentary; the formulation here is deliberately vague since, theoretically at least, straight dependence and common descent are equally possible. But a look at both the structure and the detailed contents of some of the comparable parts of each commentary will show that they are in fact independent.

By way of example let us take the opening discussion of 3.4, where Aristotle turns from imagination to thought, from the irrational to the rational soul. This latter distinction is one that is not present in Aristotle's treatise—it is mentioned only in passing in a later discussion, and attributed to persons unnamed[6]—but it is of course one of the major concerns of the Neoplatonist commentators, our two as well as Simplicius, who were much preoccupied with allocating the soul's faculties and activities to its higher or lower sections. Thus *phantasia*, working as it does with both, naturally presented peculiar difficulties, which are prominent in the exposition of *de Anima* 3.3.[7] Some of these are also conspicuous in the treatment of 3.4, where they are relevant insofar as it is necessary to establish how far reason and intellect involve imagination.

A brief look at the structure of the two expositions of 3.4 will show that the two commentaries cannot simply be identified. Philoponus, but not Stephanus, gives a short introduction to the discussions that are to follow. Both commentaries then tell us that Aristotle is setting out to answer three questions. Since Aristotle himself does not say this, it is probably part of the commentary tradition.[8] Aristotle himself says that whether or not the part of the soul by which it knows and thinks is separable—thus indicating that he does not himself intend to deal with that question in this place—we must ask how this part of soul differs from others, and how thinking takes place. Thus Aristotle asks *two* questions: the commentators, with their own special concerns clearly influencing their reading of Aristotle, have him ask three. According to Philoponus these are:

1. Is the rational soul separate or inseparable?
2. How does it differ from the sensible (*a sensu*)?
3. How does intellection happen in us?[9]

Stephanus' list is not, however, the same. The three questions he gives are:

1. Is the soul destructible or not?
2. How is the rational soul different from the sensible?
3. How does intellection take place?[10]

In these lists only the second and third questions more or less coincide. The first in Stephanus' list could be an implication of the one given by Philoponus, which is closer to what Aristotle actually says. The second and third, as we have said, do go back to Aristotle himself, but in the first the commentators have taken the words in which Aristotle puts aside the question of separability, as he repeatedly does, and turned them into a third question which not only reflects their own interests, but which is clearly more important to them than the other two. These however are Neoplatonic—or perhaps just simply Platonic—interests, and not Christian ones, though they do of course relate to Christian problems. The answers given are in any case firmly in the Platonic tradition.

A curious mixture of Neoplatonic aims and Aristotelian content emerges from Stephanus' *theōria*, the preliminary general discussion of matters under investigation in this section.[11] Stephanus announces that he will deal with the first two of the three questions, and start with the second because the second helps towards an answer to the first. Proceeding thus, he distinguishes rational soul from sensation—let us remember that the distinction of a rational soul from an irrational one does not figure in Aristotle's discussion—and argues that, though they have certain features in common, they differ in their reaction to intense stimuli. While this point is of course raised by Aristotle himself later in the treatise,[12] he does not draw the conclusion that is produced by Stephanus, namely that the very fact that *nous* thrives on intenser stimuli, and is helped by them to deal with the lesser ones, is a strong indication of its eternity. Neither this arrangement of the arguments nor the argument itself is to be found in Philoponus' discussion of this chapter. Nor is the second argument: that since *nous* can and does think all things, it must be incorporeal and eternal. The preoccupations that emerge from these discussions (preoccupations with discerning the differences between the levels of soul, and with the question of immortality) are of course highly relevant to our last question, how much these works are in fact commentaries on Aristotle. The answer suggested by this section is that they are rather meditations arising from the text of Aristotle, and that is an answer that can easily be reinforced by other evidence. The most conspicuous is the Neoplatonizing treatment of the next chapter, 3.5, which introduces into the exposition of Aristotle the whole Neoplatonic debate on the status of the individual *nous*.[13] Similarly we have the assumption that Aristotle must be talking in terms of a detachable soul on the Platonic model, patently wrong but consistently maintained by all the Neoplatonic commentators, in spite of some attempts by Philoponus to understand Aristotle in his own terms.[14] Thus the whole discussion of 3.4 is based on a consequence of the Platonic model, namely that the soul uses the body as a tool or instrument.

In the sequel the two discussions diverge further, and even when the same or similar points are made, the order in which they are introduced is not the same. Philoponus continues[15] by discussing how the intellect might be a part of the soul, and argues that Aristotle has used the term improperly. He maintains that in the soul the part must be coterminous with the whole, and this means that either the whole soul would be immortal, or not; whereas Aristotle has previously said that we are dealing with a different section of the soul. Further, the word "soul" is used equivocally, just as, for example, "sun" may mean the body or its light, and "Ajax" may refer either to the son of Telamon or a mysterious Trojan: neither of these examples is to be found in Stephanus. At the equivalent point in his discussion, Stephanus gives us the views of Plutarch and Alexander on the significance of the *lemma*,[16] but does not involve himself in the meaning of "part" until after he has dealt with the meanings of *nous,* which in the Philoponus commentary are discussed immediately after the section on "part."[17]

If we compare the two discussions of the senses of *nous* we find a similar account given by both commentators, though again the presentation differs. Philoponus goes straight on to consider three senses of *nous*,[18] while Stephanus gives us his view of what Aristotle means after telling us that Alexander and Plutarch take them differently. He discusses their treatments in some detail, and also explains Ammonius' differences with them before going on to his own position.[19]

Philoponus, on the other hand, states his own position first and then goes on to discuss certain views of Alexander, which Stephanus mentioned at a correspondingly earlier stage. Here, apart from the difference of presentation, we find that the two commentators have produced substantially different accounts of Alexander's position. Alexander, as is well known, held that the strictly human intellect was mortal, and that the active intellect was external to the individual. Now, according to Philoponus, Alexander was unable to deny that intellect was such as he has told us Aristotle's intellect was, citing the Aristotelian description of it as pure or unmixed and impassible. Therefore, says Philoponus, because he could not go against these pronouncements, Alexander said that Aristotle was talking about the universal intellect.[20] Stephanus, on the other hand, says that in order to maintain his position, Alexander did just what Philoponus said—rightly—he was unable to do, namely that he attacked the idea that *nous* was pure, impassible, and separate.[21] Here, on a point of considerable importance, they give manifestly conflicting accounts of Alexander, the only authority whom Philoponus cites by name in this part of his commentary.

Here, then, are a few examples, which could be multiplied without difficulty, of the difference in presentation and substance between the two commentators. They should suffice without multiplication to show that we have before us two separate commentaries, and not merely different versions of a typical and traditional Alexandrian lecture course on the *de Anima*. Yet certain similarities of approach are clearly present.

Now that we have established that we are dealing with two separate commentaries, we must turn to the question of their authors' religion. In Stephanus' case the mere fact of his Christianity (suggested by his name, his date, and his occupation of an official chair at Constantinople,[22] as well as the occasional pronouncement)[23] should be accepted[24]—its importance is another matter—but in that of Philoponus there is a problem. Here we must expand the point about being Christian at the time of composition of the *de Anima* commentary, or indeed of any of the Philoponus commentaries.[25]

Until recently, then, it has been commonly thought, lack of evidence from antiquity notwithstanding, that Philoponus had begun his philosophical activities as a pagan and subsequently become a convert to Christianity—to which his name John suggests, but does not prove, allegiance—after he had written his commentaries. This is the view of Gudeman in his generally unsatisfactory *Pauly* article, and has been maintained by others since.[26] In a book difficult of access—it was published in occupied France—R. Vancourt treated Philoponus as if he were a Christian when he wrote the *de Anima* commentary.[27] Subsequently E. Evrard, examining the chronological relationships of Philoponus' *oeuvre*, mainly on the basis of his views on the movement of the heavenly bodies and his understanding of Aristotle's fifth element, has argued that there is no chronological separation between the commentaries and the other works, and in particular that the *de Aeternitate Mundi contra Proclum* was written before the commentary on the *Meteorologica*.[28] That in itself, if correct, as I think it is, is sufficient to destroy the traditional position. It would mean that we cannot be sure that there was in fact any time when he was a pagan. Evrard proceeded to examine briefly the *de Anima* commentary, and to suggest that the apparently non-Christian views in it, on the preexistence of the soul and the immortality of the luminous body, are explicable in terms of an Origenism which, he thinks, survived at Alexandria. He further suggested, following Vancourt, that Philoponus' explanation of *de Anima* 3.5 was influenced by the wish to select from the field a view not incompatible with Christianity, namely that we have a single soul of which the intellect is part.

To take the second point first. Whether or not Philoponus was a Christian is probably irrelevant; the choice he makes is explicable in terms of the Neoplatonic tradition: three of the four views presented in the commentary are in fact Neoplatonic views, and are connected with Aristotle only insofar as the Neoplatonists thought they and Aristotle were expounding the same philosophy. I have examined this matter in some detail elsewhere, so shall not pursue the point now, but simply say that what Philoponus—and Stephanus—did was to adopt the standard and orthodox Neoplatonic view about the human intellect, namely that it is single and fully descended.[29] Insofar as that is what they did, we cannot attach great significance to their choice. It remains possible that Christian prejudice affected it, but it is unnecessary to introduce it into the discussion of their motives. Ironically, the problems presented by the Platonic view of the soul could be solved by reading Aristotle in the way we think he should be read, which is just what his interpreters in antiquity did not normally do. Thus a more straightforward reading of Aristotle might be a result of Christian bias, and one might consider in this context Aquinas' interpretation of 3.5.[30] As for luminous bodies, these, or pneumatic ones, were characteristic of Platonists and Platonizers alike.[31]

Similar explanations may be offered of Philoponus' view that the world was created in time. Like the dispute about the status of the intellect, this too reflects a long-standing and well-known controversy among Platonists after Plato. The point at issue was, of course, the interpretation of Plato's *Timaeus*. This is another controversy whose details need not concern us here. It need only be recalled that the view that the world was created in time was not a function of Christian readings of Plato, but can be traced back to Plato's immediate pupils—if not to Plato himself—and reappears at intervals thereafter.[32] In this matter too, Christian conceptions are compatible with the view offered and may have influenced its choice but, here again, the internal history of the Platonic tradition offers sufficient explanation of the facts.

Whatever one's assessment of Philoponus' Christianity and its influence on his views about these questions might be, it is clear that it was not otherwise sufficiently pervasive to prevent him from producing Neoplatonic material that is not strictly compatible with Christianity, at least in the course of background outline exposition. Thus, in speaking of the various levels of perfection and knowledge of different faculties of soul, he will say of *nous* that it is more obscure than reason in that its activities rarely penetrate to men, and then only to a few.[33] This seems at first sight to make intellect external. Insofar as it does, it is inconsistent with the understanding of 3.5 manifested by both Philoponus himself and Stephanus, who, as we have mentioned, chooses that Neoplatonic view of human intellect which holds it to be single and internal. Any doubts that might remain about the presence of material ill-suited to Christian ideas may be resolved by a reading of the preface to Philoponus' exegesis of Book 1.

The determination of Philoponus' position does, of course, present unusual difficulties because his views were by no means orthodox. Not only was he a monophysite (that is straightforward enough), but he struck at least one of his contemporaries as having deceived himself by holding views appropriate to the very pagans he ostensibly attacked. This was Cosmas Indicopleustes, the Traveler to India.[34] Cosmas may not have been a man of great philosophical culture or acumen, and he may not have known that Philoponus was a late convert—possibly because he was not—but this view of Philoponus should at least put us on our guard against saying that he was not a Christian at the time he wrote the *de Anima* commentary just because it manifests strange views about man and his nature.

And such views are present. If one were to set out some criteria for establishing whether or not a writer was Christian, one might think of the following: 1) a refusal to accept the soul's preexistence, though that is subject to the difficulty about Origenism already mentioned;[35] or more significantly, 2) disembodied existence after death of the normal Platonist type[36]—Porphyry had singled out reincarnation with a body for a scornful attack in his work *Against the Christians;*[37] and 3) the absence of the belief that the soul is capable of attaining salvation, or union with higher Being, by its own unaided efforts.[38] By these criteria Philoponus fails to qualify. All these views may be found right at the start of his commentary, in the preface. There we have the soul's preexistence[39] (which may not be crucial), survival after death without the body,[40] and several references to soul's assimilation to *nous* by habituation, or the practice of the cathartic virtues,[41] with no word of any help from above. We have already suggested that heresy rather than paganism may, at least in part, be the explanation of all this. If however one is trying to show that he held pagan views in the commentaries, and Christian views elsewhere, one has to show that there is a clear measure of inconsistency between the commentaries and those works which are indisputably part of Philoponus' writings *qua* Christian. Now when one looks at some of his views on the soul in this light, the opposite turns out to be the case. Thus what he has to say in his disquisition on the creation of the world, the *de Opificio Mundi,* about the ensoulment of the embryo turns out to be, shall we say, easily compatible with Neoplatonic views on the subject.[42] In particular, he divides the soul into two, a rational and an irrational part. Animals other than man have an irrational soul inseparably united to the body. Man in addition has a separate part (*chōriston*) which is the rational soul. He makes the distinction in connection with Aristotle's definition of the soul, and he treats that definition in a way that is not difficult to recognize as Neoplatonic, comparable not only with what Philoponus himself says in his commentary on the *de Anima,* but also with the explanation offered by Simplicius, who has never been suspected of Christianity.[43] What he does is to say that part of the soul is an entelechy of the body, as music is an activity of the lyre; while another part is separate like a sailor on a ship (or a charioteer)—an old image going back to the hesitation at *de Anima* 2.1,[44] a passage vigorously exploited by several Neoplatonists.[45] On this basis we should have to treat the *de Opificio Mundi* as a non-Christian work, which it patently is not. Therefore the appearance of the same view in works of uncertain status cannot be taken to show that they are pagan in doctrine, let alone in authorship.

As for vocabulary that might indicate Christian training or ways of thinking, there is virtually none in Philoponus. What there is, a reference to angels and the essence of angels,[46] may be a medieval insertion. That Moerbeke did not always, as is commonly thought, provide a straight literal translation is shown by the discussion, mentioned above, of the fact that the word Aristotle uses for "part" in 429 a 10 is, unlike its Latin equivalent, neuter.[47] If however we compare this situation with that in Stephanus, its significance is diminished. Given that Stephanus was a Christian writer, we might expect a higher incidence of Christian vocabulary. But apart from a very short section[48] to which Professor Westerink has already drawn attention,[49] and which, if it alone survived, would give a very different impression from the whole, there is virtually none in the part of the commentary that covers chapters 1–8, some 124 pages in all. The section that is an exception to this rule and has some Christian terminology actually embedded in the text, has *angeloi* in the Christian rather than the Neoplatonic sense, a reference to *eusebē dogmata* clearly meaning Christian (by now a standard sense,[50] as opposed to Platonic) doctrines, and also one to *theos,* again in the Christian rather than the normal Greek sense. In addition there is an apparently approving reference to Providence (*pronoia*) as a name for God.[51] Possibly one should add here a number of ambiguous references to faculties vouchsafed to us by the demiurge,[52] who could be either the ordinary Platonists' demiurge or the Almighty in Platonic disguise, and the tag "he said and it happened" (*eipe kai egeneto*) which seems to allude to the Genesis account of creation.[53]

With these we should perhaps put the terminology of the section-ending marks. The usual form of these in Stephanus is *en toutois hē theōria sun theōi plēroutai*: "here, with God's help, ends the general discussion" or, *en hois hē prāxis sun theōi plēroutai*: "here, with God's help, ends the lecture." For comparison, the pagan Olympiodorus uses slightly different formulae, such as *tauta ekhei hē theōria*: "this is the content of the general discussion," without any mention of divine aid. These appear uniformly in the commentaries on Aristotle's *Meteorologica,* Plato's *Gorgias* and *Phaedo,* and also the *First Alcibiades.* In the commentaries on Platonic and pseudo-Platonic works, however, there are separate section headings for the lectures, of the type *praxis sun theōi*: "lecture, with God's help," followed by a numeral. Now the Olympiodorus commentaries are probably editions by students,[54] and it could well be they—or even later copyists—who put in the non-integral chapter headings. If that is so, and if the chapter-end markings in Stephanus are not also later additions, more skillfully inserted so as to have the appearance of being integral to the text, then we do have at least a superficial mark of Stephanus' beliefs. "Superficial" must be stressed because there are, as we have seen, other explanations of his choices as a commentator. As for Philoponus, one would not expect to find comparable expressions in his text, given the absence of the organization of material to which they belong.

All this indicates, at least by way of sample, that Christianity was, at most, of little importance in the composition of these commentaries and the selection of the views they express. Further exemplification of this point would not be difficult, but space precludes it here.

Instead we must now come to our last question, how much were these men genuinely commentators on Aristotle. It is a question that is not as difficult as the others, though the obvious answer is misleading. Superficially, the answer must be yes, of course they were. They did after all write, or provide the material for, commentaries in the sense of exegetical works discussing the interpretation of texts. And when we consider primarily philological explanation of what unclear passages of Aristotle mean, then their opinion as interpreters of the text deserves to be respected in a perfectly straightforward way. The difficulty comes at the next level, that of philosophical exposition. And here things are a good deal less straightforward. Enough has probably been said in the earlier part of this paper to indicate the kind of answer that might be given, and there is no need to spend very long on it now. It should already be clear that we have to admit that we are not dealing with mere exposition of a difficult thinker. At this point it might be as well to state that what is being said does not imply that it is possible to explain a philosophical text without some involvement in philosophy, and perhaps some proneness to introduce one's own opinions. Nevertheless, the Neoplatonic commentators are a special case. Like some of the scholastics, the Neoplatonists' professed aim was to expound a given body of truth: for the Neoplatonists this was the philosophy of Plato, with which that of Aristotle was held, in the main, to coincide. It should not need to be said here that the words that are presented as an interpretation of Plato (whether with obvious labels like Proclus' *On Plato's Theology* or others less obvious like the *Enneads*[55]) are in fact presentations of views which Plato would not have recognized as his own without becoming the victim of an elaborate Socratic elicitation of truths that he never knew he knew. With Aristotle the situation is not all that different, for the reasons we have mentioned. To these we may add the local conditions in Alexandria in the time of Ammonius and Philoponus which made Aristotle preferable as the vehicle for Neoplatonic philosophy.[56] Some of the differences might be attributed to the nature of the Aristotelian treatises discussed, for these afford only the occasional opportunity for the higher flights of Neoplatonic speculation. If we had a set of commentaries on the *Metaphysics*, things might be different: that of Syrianus on a few of the less potentially explosive books of that work is sufficient indication of what can be done.

By way of summary let us review our initial questions. "Two?" Yes, that is clear. "Two Christian?" To this the answer is less clear. One, certainly, that is Stephanus; the other probably yes too, but not to an extent or on doctrinal lines that would be easily detectable on any page of his commentary, and this, on the whole, is true of Stephanus too. "Two Christian commentators?" then, in the sense we have defined, No: even Stephanus offered primarily Neoplatonic exposition. Philoponus, as we have suggested, wrote a commentary not deeply imbued with such Christian convictions as he may have held at the material time. If his course had included one, it would be particularly interesting to have Stephanus' equivalent of Philoponus' general introduction to Book 1, in which he sets out his own views, and which is full of the sort of Neoplatonism that would be likely to give doctrinal offense. Possibly in the interval the climate of opinion which Justinian was trying to promote by his measures, such as they were, against the public teaching of pagan philosophy[57]—and I would strongly stress public—may at last have had its effects. But that is speculation. Speculation should, of course, normally be discouraged, but I would like to close with some more. It has never been clear why, instead of Philoponus' commentary on Book 3 of the *de Anima*, we have that of Stephanus. Philoponus' was not lost. It was still available to Moerbeke in the thirteenth century and to Sophonias perhaps a century later still.[58] Yet our earliest manuscripts of Philoponus, which date back to the eleventh and twelfth centuries,[59] already contain the pseudepigraphic commentary for Book 3. Is the reason perhaps that at the time when these manuscripts, or their predecessors, were compiled, Philoponus' work was regarded as suspect—whether the cause was such apparent paganism as impressed itself on contemporaries like Cosmas and some modern scholars, or his notorious monophysitism—and the opportunity was taken to substitute the work of Stephanus on that part of the *de Anima* which was, more than any other, theologically delicate?[60]

7

New Objective Links Between the Pseudo-Dionysius and Proclus

HENRI-DOMINIQUE SAFFREY

I already drew attention, twelve years ago, to "a (first) objective link between the Pseudo-Dionysius and Proclus."[1] In fact, I had then proposed to explain the formation of the Dionysian *hapax legomenon*: *theandricos,* as a derivative of the name Theandrites of a Semitic divinity in whose honor we know that Proclus composed a hymn. Allow me to recall the result I arrived at: "The Semitic god Theandrios, honored in Arabia, was known to Proclus from his journey to Asia. He consecrated to him a hymn under the name of Theandrites. This hymn was familiar to the Neoplatonic school. Marinus and Damascius make allusion to it. John of Scythopolis (the first commentator of the Dionysian Corpus), without wanting to, likewise betrayed the knowledge he had of it in trying to justify in the Pseudo-Dionysius a facile and culpable concordism. In the same stroke, he established an objective link between the Dionysian Corpus and the milieu of the school of Proclus and of his immediate successors."[2] I had described this link as *objective,* since it depends neither on a hypothesis on the identity of the author of the Dionysian Corpus, nor on a doctrinal interpretation.

It is proper, indeed, to note that the Dionysian question has been most often raised with the sole purpose of identifying the anonymous author who hides behind the pseudonym of Saint Paul's convert, Dionysius the Areopagite. In my humble opinion, this undertaking is a priori hopeless. It consists, in effect, in constructing on the basis of some data contained in the Corpus, themselves more or less well interpreted, a sort of "identikit" picture of its author, and then in trying to put on this "identikit" picture a name drawn from the *Who's Who* of Christian society between, let us say, the third and the sixth centuries. I denounce this method as dangerous and illusory. It supposes, in effect, that one can on the one hand effectively construct a sufficiently exact "identikit" picture, and on the other that one has a quasi-complete knowledge of the prosopography of the Christian Empire—two conditions that are, on the evidence, beyond our reach. It is not surprising then that there have been proposed for the author of the Dionysian Corpus identifications as varied and fantastic as Ammonius Saccas, the master of Plotinus, or Damascius, the last diadochus of the Academy in Athens, or Peter the Iberian, or again, although this hypothesis is infinitely more reasonable, Peter the Fuller.[3] And many more! Ronald Hathaway has recorded twenty-two different identifications.

No less illusory, in my view, are the doctrinal interpretations and the vague parallelisms that led to seeing the Pseudo-Dionysius on the one hand as a disciple either of Plotinus, Iamblichus, Proclus, or Damascius, or on the other hand as either a father of the church connected with Origen or with the Cappadocians or with some heretical sect, or an obscure Oriental monk—in particular a Syrian. In this also, most often, they succeed only in explaining *obscurum per obscurius*.

I believe then that research must be pursued outside of these blind alleys, and it is a modest contribution in this direction that I want to present here. I propose then to expose some new links between the Pseudo-Dionysius and Proclus. These objective links, it seems to me, are of two kinds. First the links in vocabulary, that is, the words that are met with only in Proclus or the Pseudo-Dionysius or John of Scythopolis. These parallels in vocabulary seem to me particularly safe from any improper interpretation and can thus constitute a solid base for reasoning. Next, there are the structural links that disclose rigorous parallelisms in the structure of thinking. Thanks to the *Elements of Theology* and *Platonic Theology*, one is quite familiar now with the map of reality according to Proclus, and with how it differs, for example, from that of Iamblichus. One can thus investigate how the Pseudo-Dionysius took over these elements of structure and how he admitted them or did not admit them into his system. This particularly fruitful approach, which had been inaugurated in a very remarkable manner, in view of the state of the editions of the text available to him, by Hugo Koch in 1900 in his work *Pseudo-Dionysius Areopagita in seinen Beziehungen zum Neuplatonismus und Mysterienwesen,* has been brilliantly readopted in recent years on a much more solid basis by René Roques in *L'univers dionysien: Structure hiérarchique du monde selon le Pseudo-Denys* (Paris, 1954), and Jan Vanneste in *Le mystère de Dieu, essai sur la structure rationelle de la doctrine mystique du pseudo-Denys l'Aréopagite* (Paris, 1959), works which deal principally with the *Hierarchies* and with the *Mystical Theology*; Eugenio Corsini, *Il trattato "De divinis nomini-*

bus" dello Pseudo-Dionigi e i commenti neoplatonici al Parmenide (Torino, 1962) and Bernhard Brons, *Gott und die Seienden, Untersuchungen zum Verhältnis von neuplatonischer Metaphysik und christlicher Tradition bei Dionysius Areo pagita* (Göttingen, 1976), which have examined rather the *Divine Names*; and the latest in date, last but not least, Stephen Gersh, *From Iamblichus to Eriugena, an Investigation of the Prehistory and Evolution of the Pseudo-Dionysian Tradition* (Leiden, 1978). The results of these researches are impressive; they show a close structural connection between Dionysian thought and the Proclian stage of Neoplatonic doctrine.

Having said that, I shall follow now a third path, which I consider particularly fruitful for disclosing the objective links between the Pseudo-Dionysius and Proclus, that is the path I had already followed in my first study, that which consists in examining the scholia of John of Scythopolis. Indeed, if John of Scythopolis, as Hans Urs von Balthasar has shown,[4] is the first commentator on the Dionysian Corpus and probably an accomplice in what must be called the Dionysian fiction, it is without doubt no exaggeration to present him as the first to have systematically researched these objective links between the Pseudo-Dionysius and Proclus. What, in fact, does he set out to do? In reading the text of Dionysius, every time he encounters a term or an expression that might sound strange to the ear of a Christian who believed he was reading a contemporary of Saint Paul, he endeavors to answer in advance the objections that cannot fail to be raised. Naturally his intention is to justify the Dionysian fiction, but at the same time and without wanting to, he exposes it. We need only read him with attention in order to enter into his game and draw profit from it. Thus, as I demonstrated in my first article, in order to defend Dionysius for having constructed his neologism *theandricos* on the name of the Semitic god Theandrites, he shows us that he is quite familiar with the existence of this god and the devotion paid to him in the Neoplatonist school of Athens. We are at first surprised, but from that very fact we understand that he is showing the cloven hoof, and instead of justifying Dionysius, he is pointing out to us an objective link that exists between the Athenian Neoplatonic circle and himself, that is Dionysius also. That is why I should like to make an appeal here for the undertaking of a critical edition of these scholia and for the successful conclusion of the systematic study of them.[5] The following are other cases of the same type that will demonstrate to you the interest of this task.

As we know, one had not to wait until the sixteenth century to raise doubts about the authenticity of the Dionysian Corpus, since John of Scythopolis informs us that the citation by Dionysius of a phrase from Ignatius of Antioch, occurring in the *Divine Names,* had already aroused suspicions. Here is the note of John of Scythopolis on the Dionysian lemma: Ὁ θεῖος Ἰγνάτιος.[6] "These words," he says, "have led certain people to think they can reject the present treatise as not being by the divine Dionysius, since they say that Ignatius comes after him [they knew, in fact, through Eusebius of Caesarea, that Ignatius of Antioch had been martyred under Trajan, between A.D. 98 and 117, and according to the *Chronology* of Eusebius more probably in 107]; how then can someone who is later be cited?

But this is how they have thought it possible to arrange it. Saint Paul, who baptised Dionysius, was in time later than Saint Peter, whom Ignatius succeeded as bishop of Antioch at the time that Peter left for Rome; now, Saint Paul survived for a long time after the baptism of Dionysius, and Dionysius lived still later than Saint Paul. On the other hand," continues John of Scythopolis, "the evangelist John to whom Dionysius wrote a reply [this is Letter X of the Corpus] was deported to Patmos under Domitian. Thus Ignatius suffered martyrdom before Domitian, so that he is earlier than Dionysius." We can see that in order to defend Dionysius, John of Scythopolis does not jib at any improbability, even though it forces the chronology in an impossible manner. It is there that we discover, as I have said, his complicity in the Dionysian fiction, which makes him at the same time a privileged witness and a singularly suspect one.

But in the Pseudo-Dionysius there are not only fantastic chronologies; there are also expressions which, not being traditional in Christian literature, necessitated an explanation. Here is a good example of this. At the beginning of Chapter 9 of the *Divine Names,* Dionysius asserts that the following pairings of attributes are attributed to the Cause of all beings: "great and small," "identical and different," "similar and dissimilar," "rest and movement" [one may say in passing that one would recognize here the pairs of attributes of the One in the second hypothesis of the *Parmenides* according to the interpretation of Syrianus and of Proclus]. "Well," he says, "we must examine also all that is manifested to us from these statues that are the divine names, τούτων τῶν θεωνυμικῶν ἀγαλμάτων." I am obliged to translate literally this, at first sight, very strange expression: "those statues that are the divine names." At that point John of Scythopolis really felt it necessary to give an explanation and here is his gloss:[7] "It is with perfect wisdom that he speaks of *the statues that are the divine names,* for he extends this notion which he borrows from the Greeks by applying it to the truth. The Greeks, as a matter of fact, made up objects resembling statues without feet or hands which they called Hermes; they made them hollow with a door in the style of cupboards. Inside these statues they placed statues of the gods they adored, and from the outside they closed the Hermes. These Hermes thus appeared valueless, but inside they contained the beauties of their gods. It is in this way then that this passage too must be understood: those names from sacred Scripture, such as 'small' or 'to be seated,' etc., which are used concerning the God who alone exists and who alone is real, are not worthy to be spoken of God: but if these names are explained and if they are interpreted in a manner worthy of God, then they contain, within, the statues and the divine imprints of the glory of God."

Here is a very interesting passage and a very significant one. The comparison of the divine names with the statues of the gods is habitual in the Athenian Neoplatonists. It is met with in Proclus in the chapter devoted to *Divine Names* in the *Platonic Theology,* Book I, chapter 29:[8] "Just as," says Proclus, "the demiurgic intellect brings into existence in matter the appearances of the very first Forms it contains in itself, produces temporal images of eternal beings, divisible images of indivisible beings, and from beings which are really beings produces images which have the consistency of shadow, in the same way, I think, our scientific knowledge also, which takes as its model the productive activity of the Intellect, makes by means of discourse similitudes of all the other realities and particularly of the gods themselves: what in them is without complexity it represents by the complex, what is simple by the diverse, what is unified by multiplicity. Since then it produces the names in that way, our scientific knowledge presents them in this ultimate degree as images of divine beings; in fact, *it produces each name as a statue of the gods,* and just as theurgy invokes the generous goodness of the gods with a view to the illumination of statues artificially constructed, so also intellective knowledge related to divine beings, by composition and divisions of articulated sounds, reveals the hidden being of the gods." As theurges animate the statues of the gods and there demonstrate their presence, so language in composing the names of the gods expresses their nature and makes them present intellectually.

This doctrine is constant in Proclus and this passage is not an isolated one. Here for example is what he says again in his *Commentary on the Cratylus.*[9] He asks himself: "In what consists the art whereby names are made?" And he replies: ". . . It is that there exists in the soul a certain power which has the capacity to make copies . . . and by virtue of that power, the soul can assimilate itself to superior beings, gods, angels, demons; . . . that is why it makes statues of gods and of demons; and when it wants to bring into being likenesses, in a certain way immaterial and engendered by reason alone, of the First Beings, it produces out of itself, and with the help of verbal representation, the substance of the names; and just as the art of mysteries by means of certain ineffable symbols makes the statues here below like the gods and ready to receive the divine illuminations, in the same way the art of the regular formation of words, by that same power of assimilation, *brings into existence names like statues of the realities.* . . ." This passage is still clearer than the preceding one: through language, the soul makes verbal representations of the gods, as the sculptor carves their statues. To finish, in a quite general formula in the *Commentary on the Parmenides,*[10] Proclus states: "The names, since they are rational statues of the realities, are as a first consideration the names of immaterial forms, and as a secondary consideration the names of sensible forms." This doctrine of the divine names considered as verbal statues of the gods is thus well attested in Proclus.

Nevertheless, it must not be concluded from this that Proclus was its inventor. It is probable that he has taken over this comparison from his predecessor Syrianus, for we know of two texts in which we find an echo of the views of Syrianus on this subject. As is known, the *Commentary on the Phaedrus* of Hermias, the fellow-pupil of Proclus in the school of Syrianus, is no more than the report of the lectures of their common master.[11] The author wonders why Socrates accuses himself of having sinned against the divinity; it is, he says, because he used the name of the god Eros in the manner of the common man, "for," he adds,[12] "the names of the gods must be adored where they happen to be placed, as are their symbols, their statues and their images, which the soul holds as sacred." Here the divine names are objects of adoration like the statues. The other text comes to us from a contemporary of Syrianus, who had studied with him in Athens, Hierocles,[13] who says, in his *Commentary on the Golden Verses,*[14] that "the name of Zeus is a symbol and a sonorous expression of his demiurgic being, from the fact that the first people to have given names to realities, by these names as by means of images caused their powers to appear, in the same way that the best carvers of statues do so by a superabundance of technical ability." Here also, the name of Zeus is considered as a sonorous expression, whereas the statue is a visual image of it. One sees that in these two texts, which could have been written in the generation that precedes Proclus, his theory of the divine names, statues of the gods, was in the course of formation. Finally, it is Damascius, in what remains to us of his *Commentary on the Philebus*, who brings us a last testimony from the same period. When he is commenting on the famous remark of Socrates in the *Philebus*,[15] "I have always had for the names of the gods a more than human reverence, a fear which goes beyond all bounds," he informs us that a certain Democritus called the divine names ἀγάλματα φωνήεντα. "vocal statues" of the gods.[16] Naturally this Democritus is not the one from Abdera, and L. G. Westerink has identified him with a Platonist who must be placed in the generations after Iamblichus since he is again cited by the same Damascius, in his notes on the *Phaedo,* where his opinion is adduced after that of Theodore of Asine, the contemporary of Iamblichus, and in combination with that of Plutarch of Athens, the master of Syrianus and Proclus.[17]

Thus, all these testimonies agree in bringing us back to the beginning of the fifth century, to the time when Plutarch of Athens and Syrianus were teaching in the Neoplatonic school in Athens. All the same, a proof *a contrario* of the fact that it is impossible to take this doctrine of the divine names considered as divine statues back as far as Iamblichus can be drawn from two texts. The first embraces chapters 4 and 5 of Book VII of the *De mysteriis* of Iamblichus.[18] It is here that we find Iamblichus engaged in justifying the religious use of divine names without apparent significance or even of names that he calls "barbaric," that is, purely and simply transcribed from a language alien to the Greek. If these names have to be used, for Iamblichus as for the whole Greek tradition, it is evidently because they express in a mystical manner the divine essence itself. But never does he establish the parallelism between the divine names and the statues of the gods. Yet it is there that one would have expected this development if it had already been in fashion. But here is a still more precise example. In a letter from the emperor Julian, the disciple of Maximus of Ephesus, himself of the second generation after Iamblichus, there is a very clear allusion to three degrees in divine representations: there are the gods themselves beyond all representation; next there are the stars which are visible gods, images of the invisible gods; but as one cannot offer them corporeal worship, there are finally the statues of the gods. Here it is a question solely of material statues, and not at all of those "rational" or "vocal" statues that are the divine names.[19] For Julian also, what will become the theory of Proclus has not yet been developed.

One may moreover suspect the reason why the Platonists of Athens developed this theory of divine names as spiritual substitutes for the statues of the gods, is that through the effect of imperial decrees, the statues of the gods began at that time to disappear from their temples. We know that Proclus was an eyewitness to the removal of the statue of Athena from the Acropolis of Athens, and that at the time at which this was happening, he saw in a dream the goddess herself who said to him: "Lady Athenais intends to stay with you."[20] Dating from that day, she would have as temple the home of Proclus, and would be honored in his heart and that of his disciples. It is then only to the Platonists of the generations of Syrianus and of Proclus that one must attribute this devotion to the divine names as having taken the place of devotion to the statues of the gods. As John of Scythopolis saw perfectly, the expression of the Pseudo-Dionysius, "the statues that are the divine names," can only be understood in this context, and moreover that is what he explicitly states when he writes: "Dionysius transfers this notion which he borrows from the Greeks in applying it to truth."

But he still says something more. Indeed John of Scythopolis illustrates this doctrine by an argument that one could describe as drawn from folklore, the custom of the Greeks, according to him, of making statues containing inside them other statues for the worship of the gods, placed there as if in cupboards. To my knowledge, this supposed observation is not confirmed by any archaeological discovery. But it is evidently not an observation,[21] but a literary reminiscence, and from a famous text, that of the *Symposium* of Plato, in which Alcibiades compares Socrates to a Silenus. The passage is familiar:[22] "Socrates is just like those Silenus figures that are seen displayed in the sculpture studios and which the artists represent holding a pipe or a flute; if they are opened in the middle, it can be seen that inside they contain figurines of gods," a comparison taken up again and developed a few lines further on:[23] "Socrates is ignorant of all things, and he knows nothing, but he gives himself airs! Is this not the behavior of a Silenus? Yes, nothing could be more so! This ignorance, in fact, is the outer wrapping of the person, just as the carved Silenus is; but inside, once it is opened up, of what a great quantity of wisdom is it full, have you any idea, companions of this feast?" There should be no doubt that it is this comparison by Alcibiades between Socrates and a Silenus that John of Scythopolis has in mind, for no Hermes has ever been seen to be hollow and serve as a cupboard for relics, but if one considers that the word that has been translated as "sculpture studio" is in Greek τὸ ἑρμογλυφεῖον,[24] which means literally "a place where Hermes figures are carved" (a Hermes indicates in this case a statue in general), one will guess that it is from this that John of Scythopolis has taken his Hermes figures that have taken the place of the Silenus figures that were no longer made in his time, though there still existed in Athens "the street of the statue-makers" of which Plutarch speaks in his treatise *On the demon of Socrates*.[25] And if there is need, we would be confirmed in this conviction by another literary reference to this same passage of the *Symposium* that we find in a letter of Synesius of Cyrene who must have belonged to the same circle as Proclus and the Pseudo-Dionysius, where it is said that "in Athens the craftsmen made statues of Aphrodite and the Graces and divine beauties of this kind, enclosing them in statues of Silenus and of satyrs."[26] Now it is well known that this type of literature regurgitates literary reminiscences rather than concrete observations. However this may be, if we are to consider this little dissertation of John of

Scythopolis as a literary reference to the *Symposium,* this reference brings us back once again to Proclus, for there is no evidence, as John M. Dillon has noted, for a commentary by Iamblichus on this dialogue.[27] On the other hand, a valuable scholium to one of the dissertations of Proclus on the *Republic* provides us with an explicit reference to a *Commentary on the discourse of Diotima* by that author, which could have been a part of a complete commentary on the *Symposium.*[28] In any case, in the *Commentary on the Alcibiades,*[29] we can read from the pen of Proclus a precise reference to the passage in the *Symposium* with which we are concerned: "That the young man [Alcibiades] . . . has been made better, one can see," says Proclus, "in the *Symposium* of Plato, where even in a state of drunkeness, Alcibiades is represented as full of admiration for 'philosophic discourse'[30] . . . and swearing that he condemns not only himself but also his ignorance of himself each time he listens to Socrates speaking and remains in blissful admiration for 'the interior statues'[31] of his virtues which are so worthy of veneration and respect." This is a direct allusion to the comparison of Socrates with a Silenus in appearance ugly and filled with interior beauties.

All this analysis leads us, again in this case, to the following conclusion: we cannot understand this bizarre expression "the statues that are the divine names" used by the Pseudo-Dionysius, except with reference to a doctrine and a mode of speech in common use in the fifth-century Neoplatonic school of Athens, and the very suggestive explanations of John of Scythopolis bring us back directly to the master of that School, the Neoplatonist Proclus. Here also, I believe, one must speak of an objective link between the Pseudo-Dionysius and Proclus.

Here again is another example, less picturesque but not less significant. At the beginning of the treatise on the *Divine Names* (chap. 1, par. 4), Dionysius wishes to recall what he calls "the song of praise of the theologians," that is, the names of God which evoke his beneficent action towards us.[32] These names are Monad and Henad, which signify our unification, and Triad, which signifies the existence of all things, a cause which is described as wise, beautiful and friendly to men. It is to be noted that only the last name is really evangelical, since it is drawn from the "philanthropy of God" announced by Saint Paul in his Epistle to Titus.[33] After this list, Dionysius continues on: "And all the other theurgic lights" that he has received from Holy Scripture (τὰ Λογία) and from his divinely inspired masters (οἱ ἐνθέοι ἡμῶν καθηγέμονες).[34] One will agree with me that this language is not at all biblical nor even patristic; it can be clearly recognized as that of Proclus, when he speaks, as so often he does, of the *Chaldaean Oracles,* which are in fact his Holy Scripture, and of his master Syrianus, who is his true theologian. To mention it in passing, investigation has not yet been concluded on the borrowings of Dionysius from the language of the *Chaldaean Oracles* which were long since pointed out by Willy Theiler in his review of the *Indices Pseudo-Dionysiani* in the *Theologische Literaturzeitung* of 1944.[35] Having come to the word *theurgicos,* John of Scythopolis felt that, here again and rightly so, an explanation must be given, and here is his gloss:[36] "He calls *theurgic lights* the teachings of the saints, in so far as they produce a light of knowledge, and who make gods of those who believe." *Theourgos* was the proper term for the author of the *Chaldaean Oracles,* themselves always designated under the title of *Logia,* and "to make gods" was a formal definition of theurgy. These words and their derivatives recur forty-seven times in the Dionysian Corpus,[37] and one can scarcely estimate the strange impression they could have made on the ears of Christians to whom these words were entirely new. It is true that Dionysius had not hesitated to call the eucharistic rites themselves τὰ θεουργὰ μυστήρια, the mysteries by which one is made a god.[38] That may be all very well again for the sacraments; however, that the lights of theology may be called "theurgic" is hardly a Christian claim, but links up with that of Proclus for whom faith in the *Oracles* "places not only the universal souls but also ours in the ineffable and unknowable class of the gods."[39] It is by no means a question of the traditional doctrine of the deification of the Christian, for to make gods in naming the gods is to elevate the believer to the divine level itself, the ultimate goal of pagan theurgy. Once again, to forestall any wrong interpretation of the words of Dionysius, John of Scythopolis offers us an explanation altogether pagan and without any basis in the Christian tradition. He does not even seem to take account of this!

Up to now I have shown that the scholia of John of Scythopolis very often play the role of indicators of objective links between the Pseudo-Dionysius and Proclus. I should now like to draw attention to the fact that there exist direct links between the Pseudo-Dionysius and Proclus, for there are in the works of Dionysius quotations from Proclus. Hugo Koch and after him Willy Theiler have already recorded a first quotation in chapter 2, paragraph 7 of the *Divine Names.*[40] Dionysius says, concerning the divine persons, the following: "We have received from the tradition of the Holy Scriptures that the Father is the divinity that plays the role of source (πηγαία, a word once again from the *Chaldaean Oracles*), Jesus and the Spirit are, if one may speak in this way, divinely born buds from a divinity capable of engendering God and, so to speak, flowers and lights above being." As one can confirm, these names are not used in this form of the Father, of the Son or of the Spirit, in the Bible,[41] but the last element of the phrase, οἷον ἄνθη καὶ ὑπερούσια φῶτα, is found exactly in the *De malorum subsistentia* of Proclus, speaking precisely of the gods and of their providence. This last text is preserved only in a medieval Latin translation that we owe to William of Moerbeke, but his Latin is a perfect transfer of the Greek: *velut flores et supersubstantialia lumina.*[42] By reason of this striking parallelism, the last editor of the *De malorum subsistentia,* Helmut Boese, felt authorized to detect in it a quotation, independent in both cases, from the *Chaldaean Oracles,* for one can discover in it the end of a hexameter. All the same a doubt remains, because the word ὑπερούσιος has never been attested in the *Oracles.* For my part, I should be inclined rather to recognize a liberal Proclian combination of words coming from the *Oracles* (the words "flowers" and "lights") and to think that it is in Proclus, and in this treatise from which, moreover, he so abundantly drew inspiration, that Dionysius found this combination of words that fascinated him.

But here is another example which appears to me to be beyond doubt. This quotation is found also in the *Divine Names,* in chapter 5, paragraph 5. Let us recall that in the scholia of John of Scythopolis on the preceding paragraph which treats of the eternity of God, Werner Beierwaltes and his collaborator Richard Kannicht discovered extensive use of the treatise of Plotinus on the same subject.[43] In this paragraph, Dionysius wishes to move from beings and eternities to their cause, and this is what he writes:[44] "For all beings and for all eternities, existence comes from Him who preexists. All eternity and all time came forth from him, and He who preexists is the principle and cause of all eternity and of all time, briefly of all that exists in any way whatsoever, that is that everything participates in him and he is never separated from anything. He is before all things and everything subsists in him." In that last phrase: "He is before all things and everything subsists in him," one will have recognized a word-for-word quotation from Saint Paul (Colossians 1:17), which will not be surprising from the pen of Dionysius. But in the preceding phrase, which defines in some way the manner in which He who preexists all (that is, the First Cause) is principle and cause, when Dionysius says: "Everything participates in him and he is never separated from anything," I recognize a quotation no less literal from Proclus, for it is in these terms that he also defines the First Cause in at least two passages of the *Platonic Theology*. Here is the first:[45] "It must be," says Proclus, "that the first principle of all beings is participated in by all, since it can never be separated from anything, being the cause of all that is said to exist in whatever manner." And the second:[46] "It must be that the cause of everything that exists is that in which everything that exists participates . . . and which is never separated from anything of that which is said to exist in any way." One may note the perfect identity of expression in Proclus and in Dionysius, and moreover the second part of the formula, "which is never separated from anything," comes directly from the *Parmenides* of Plato.[47] In quoting Proclus in this way, Dionysius lets it be seen in which school he was trained, and naturally he has sought to mask this dependence by the quotation from Saint Paul which he coupled with that from Proclus. This is a process with which he is quite familiar. Some lines further on,[48] Dionysius replaces the word designating the Platonic ideas, τὰ παραδείγματα, by the word, οἱ προορισμοί, introduced as a word derived from theology, ἡ θεολογία. One would be quite at pains to find this word in the Bible. It is met with in Origen in the sense of a "decree of the divine will," but it is the gloss of John of Scythopolis that shows the way, for he reveals that this word is drawn by Dionysius from the very προορίζειν used by Paul in Romans 8:30, "those he has predestined."[49] Those determinations in God whereby he predestines the elect, these are the Ideas—a purely nominal Christianization of a Platonic notion, and an interpretation quite peculiar to the Pseudo-Dionysius, without real support in the patristic tradition; and once again, a subtle trace of the connivance of John of Scythopolis with Dionysius, since it is only through his gloss that we understand the origin of a term which the editors had never been able to discover.

Before finishing, I should like to recall the very fine study by the late Sheldon-Williams, *Henads and Angels: Proclus and pseudo-Dionysius.*[50] One will be able to reread it in the light of what we have established in the introduction to volume III of the *Platonic Theology* of Proclus on the origin and the significance of the doctrine of the divine henads.[51] The inquiry into the use of the word "henad" in philosophical and theological literature between the fourth and the sixth centuries has revealed that this word is very rare before Proclus and that in particular it is completely unknown to Iamblichus and his disciples.[52] And now we know that it is Syrianus who, in his interpretation of the first and second hypotheses of the *Parmenides,* invented the doctrine of the divine henads as the first degree in the hierarchy of the gods below the One, True God. Proclus, through his *Commentary on the Parmenides* and his *Platonic Theology,* was the great diffuser of that doctrine. That is why the simple fact that we find the word *"henas"* employed seven times in the work of the Pseudo-Dionysius, classes it automatically in the line of Syrianus and Proclus.[53] And the fact that he speaks in the plural of "the angelic henads," thus identifying the angels with the henads,[54] and calls God: "the unifying Henad of all henads,"[55] recalling the term of Proclus "Henad of the henads" used for the One,[56] shows that he was familiar with the doctrine of the divine henads. Of course he could not accept it as it was, and it was not to appear in his work except by implication. Nevertheless, the trace of it that we find once again constitutes an objective link between the Pseudo-Dionysius and Proclus.

At the conclusion of these reflections I must guard against falling myself into the temptation of making identifications that I criticized at the beginning. All I have wanted to do was to produce evidence of new objective links between the Pseudo-Dionysius and Proclus. I remark only that they increase and multiply accordingly as the research proceeds, and I am sure that still many more of them will be discovered. I shall only say in conclusion that by this means are confirmed two statements in relation to the Pseudo-Dionysius, the first by one of the earliest and the other by the most recent of the historians of Neoplatonism. The first is that of Thomas Whittaker who presented Dionysius as "some Christian Platonist trained in the Athenian School;"[57] the other is that of Carlos Steel who has recently characterized the Dionysian Corpus as the final stage in that sort of rivalry between pagan Platonism and Christianity "which finally absorbed it and neutralized it as a pagan ideology."[58] It was merely to establish a dialogue which has been prolonged through the Middle Ages right down to our time.

8

The Problem of General Concepts in Neoplatonism and Byzantine Thought

LINOS BENAKIS

Within the framework of a conference having as its theme the relationship between Neoplatonism and Christian thought, the object of my paper is to point out the relationship between the two traditions on a specific problem. This is the problem of "universals," *universalia,* with which the philosophy of the later Greek and medieval periods, both in the West and in the East, was very much concerned.

I shall not therefore deal with the general problem of the relationship between Neoplatonism and Byzantine philosophy. In my article "The Study of Byzantine Philosophy: Critical Survey 1949–1971" (Athens, 1971),[1] I have reviewed critically some earlier approaches to the presumed total dependence of the Byzantines on Neoplatonism, and have drawn attention to other, more correct, views presented in more recent publications, which defend the position that external similarities (basically in terminology) and partial relationships do not imply substantial internal general dependence. However, this basic issue is not directly affected by whatever conclusions may be established through the analysis of the special theme under consideration here.

Thus I can enter directly upon my subject, taking as my starting point a passage from a representative treatise by the Byzantine philosopher of the thirteenth and fourteenth centuries Nicephoros Choumnos (d. 1327), which has the characteristic title "Discourse against Plato regarding Matter and Forms, that neither is matter prior to bodies nor are species separate, but these are together."

The philosopher categorically rejects both the existence of separate (Platonic) Forms prior to the Creator and the creation of the world out of preexistent and uncreated matter, in order to defend the thesis of "continuous procreation," that is, the uninterrupted successive presence of the Forms in the perceptible world and hence its "incorruptibility." Nicephoros Choumnos' thesis is found in the following paragraph (lines 261–276 in my translation):[2]

> Nor is it correct for us to conceive Forms that have a permanent separate existence and are prior to those things whose Forms they are. The contrary is true. Because, since the first man was created by the Creator in the manner we have said—namely as a reasoning mortal animal made to give birth to his own kind and not to one different from him, indeed having this capacity as something which belongs to his substance—every other man who has come into being from him has exactly the same shape, kind, and substance as the first man was made to have.
>
> Therefore, by proceeding inductively from all individual instances of man and by looking at the first man, and also at those after him, and so on continuously, we find that which is common to all and has not changed in the slightest. This we recognize as the species of man; in defining this, we say that man is a reasoning mortal animal, and this definition is valid for every man and for his kind.
>
> In this manner, therefore, the Form and the kind are not prior to the particulars (as Plato says), but rather they are *what we conceive afterwards with the mind and thus define accordingly.*

Choumnos' view of the Forms is an inevitable consequence of his rejection of the self-existence of Form and its ontological presence prior to sensible particulars. Since the Forms acquire existence only in formed creations, they are perceived only *a posteriori* at the time when the knowing subject discerns them on the basis of the common characteristics which are to be found in all individuals of the same species and thus constitute the basis for their definition. (Our philosopher's position becomes clearer with the application of this principle, as we have seen above, to the example of man.)

It is clear that this fourteenth-century philosopher has understood the transition in meaning from "Forms" to "general concepts"; and in a way that enabled him to take a stand in relation to the so-called "*universalia* problem."

Now that our knowledge of the historical perspective and of related texts has been improved,[3] I believe that this Byzantine philosopher's formulation—which holds for other earlier Byzantine philosophers as well—also indicates his dependence, in his questions, terminology and solutions, on the systematic discussion of certain issues in the Greek philosophy of later antiquity. These issues involved questions as to what the Forms (the universal substances) represent as general definitions of beings (1) in themselves, (2) in relation to sensible individual things ("the many"), and (3) in relation to the knowing subject.

The answers to these questions were elaborated for the first time and *with a clear metaphysical reorientation, as we shall see, in the Neoplatonic school of Alexandria in the fifth and sixth centuries* both by its leader, Ammonius of Hermias, and his disciples and successors, Asclepius, Olympiodorus, Philoponus, Stephanus, Elias, David, and others, all commentators on the logical writings of Aristotle.[4]

This particular branch of Neoplatonism, in its interpretation of Aristotle, shows, comparatively speaking, the smallest influence of Neoplatonic doctrine. For this reason, the commentaries of Ammonius' disciples on Aristotle served as the most conducive bridge for the teaching of Greek philosophy in the Christian world. With regard to the mode of existence of an ultimate reality, the Alexandrian school did not espouse extreme positions and, hence, it adopted a moderate solution to the problem of general concepts.

The formulation of the problem by the Alexandrian scholiasts, its influence on the later Greek–Byzantine tradition, on Arabic philosophy and on the thought of many well-known Western philosophers, forms one of the new chapters in the history of the problems of ontology and of knowledge in their later phases. It is a chapter that still awaits its final form, hopefully to replace what we read in the accounts still presented in various histories of philosophy and in monographs on the *universalia* problem.

This is not the occasion to present a more systematic exposition of the *universalia* problem from its beginning up to the period which interests us. I would like only to draw attention to the fact that we must place within the historical period I have mentioned the emergence of a new solution that diverges basically from "Platonism" (by which of course I mean every type that meets the prerequisites of realism but is not restricted to the historical Plato[5]), namely the solution of "conceptual realism" (or "conceptualism" where the term is not taken in the psychological sense[6]). This is the interpretation of the universal as a concept of the knowing subject (ἐν τῇ διανοίᾳ, *conceptus mentis*), a concept no longer regarded as prior to sensible things (*ante res*), nor simply in things (*in rebus*), but derived from individual sensible things through the conceptual apprehension of their common characteristics.

It is this position which emerges with the elaboration of the problem by the Alexandrian Neoplatonists on the basis of a Neoplatonic transformation of the Aristotelian teaching on substance, and in association with the preservation of the Platonic Forms conceived now as *the thoughts of the demiurge,* the God-Creator.

In our opinion, this solution represents more fully the Greek medieval tradition, and must be considered a *variation* of Platonic and Aristotelian realism and not of nominalism, as it is usually called and which prevails in Western philosophy where this variation is also present as a compromise between realism (Scotus) and nominalism (Roscelinus), making its appearance with the influence of the Arabic philosopher Avicenna (who borrows from the school of Ammonius) on Anselm (d. 1109) and particularly on Abelard (d. 1142).

Aristotle's criticisms of Plato (to a certain degree well-founded, in other ways not) also obviously belong to the history of the problem of the nature of general concepts. Since the arguments are complex, I will point out only those elements which have influenced the formation of the *universalia* problem in postclassical and medieval thought.

The Aristotelian criticism was valid in the case of the so-called "third man" argument, and so as long as it was directed against the doctrine of the Form as "exemplar" and of natural things as its "images." Specifically, the Aristotelian criticism focuses on the objectivization of ideal beings (and more precisely on their transformation into things of the same ontological type as concrete objects), but it does not at all deal with the principally Platonic doctrine of the existence of ideal beings.

From the criticism of Aristotle it does not follow that Forms do not exist, but only that, if they exist, they cannot be something of the same type as that of individual sensible things.

From this perspective, it becomes clear why we must not bring Aristotle into the realism (Platonism)–nominalism dispute. The Aristotelian position must be classified, not under nominalism, but rather under realism. Aristotle is in fact in substantial agreement with Plato on the position that it is not possible for scientific knowledge to exist if we deny some sense of objective reality to the universal. The difference between Plato and Aristotle is that the latter believes that it is not necessary to attribute a *separate* existence to the universal. The universal (the Aristotelian kind, εἶδος) exists, but only together with the particulars and within them.

This means that both philosophers agree on exactly the same point, once we locate the weakness of the Platonic system (that is, that in order to explain the possibility of general [scientific] knowledge, it is not necessary to accept, as Plato does, abstract ideal objects). But of course the position of Aristotle was too far from a semantical interpretation of language to be able to solve the problem of knowledge of the universal without its direct association with the existence of ideal substances.

The opposition to which later metaphysicians attached such significance was formulated, as we know, as follows: Plato accepted "universals prior to the sensible objects" (*universalia ante res*); Aristotle held that "universals are in the objects" (*universalia in rebus*).

From the metaphysical viewpoint of each philosopher, the contrast becomes profound: Plato deifies the form (ἰδέα) and undervalues the world of sensible objects; Aristotle bases his realism on the role of "first substance" (πρώτη οὐσία, substance in the primary sense). But if we strip the problem logically of its metaphysical appendages, that is, if we eliminate the issue of whether the universals are prior to the objects or are in the objects, we may come to regard it today as being basically a pseudo-problem arising from the tendency to objectify or concretize universality, a tendency which was cultivated persistently in postclassical and medieval philosophy.

We insist, therefore, on the assumption that the only problem, which there is any sense in putting forward, is the simple question of whether ideal abstract objects *exist or not*, whether they have an objective reality or not.

Nevertheless, in the historical course of questioning, the contrast prevails between the two teachings on the "place" (location) of universals, a contrast which is sustained, as we have said, by the spirit of an era in which the objectivization of conceivable Being leads to the *universalia* problem. This tendency becomes even more pronounced when the nominalistic solution is added: *universalia post res* (the universal is merely a subjective concept subsequent to the object; the universals are neither abstract beings nor attributes common to their particulars, but general words, simple names, creations of the mind, *flatus vocis*).

In this paper I am concerned basically with the starting point of the dispute, which I believe also explains its course within the Eastern branch of medieval philosophy, that of Greek Byzantium. This starting point is to be found in the era of the Neoplatonic commentators on Aristotle. During this period one further transformation of the Platonic Forms was brought about. Nurtured in the New Academy or in the Middle Stoa (Posidonius), and intensively cultivated by Philo of Alexandria, it passed as a generally accepted interpretation in Middle Platonism, Neoplatonism, and in Christian writers. It is *the identification of Forms with the thoughts of God,* and furthermore with the creative intellect, the *Nous* of the demiurge.

Without intending to disregard the fact that we find the first seeds of the problem regarding general concepts much earlier in the Cynics (Antisthenes), in the successors of Plato and Aristotle (Xenocrates and Xenarchos, first century B.C.), as well as in the Stoa and Plotinus, it is indisputable that Porphyry (in the third century) was the first clearly to formulate the problem in the very first paragraph of his famous *Isagoge*.[7] Porphyry here posed three questions:

1. Are the kinds and Forms (general classes and characterizations of identical forms) existing substances or do they exist only in the mind (are a subjective concept)?
2. Do they have bodily substance or not?
3. Do they have an existence separate from sensible objects or do they exist only in them?

The first question is the only acceptable one from a scientific point of view, as we have already explained.

The second question derives from the tendency to objectify ideal substances, as we have also seen.

The third question constitutes historically the first formulation of the problem *universalia ante res* (universals prior to the objects)–*universalia in rebus* (universals in the objects).

It is characteristic that Porphyry explicitly avoided taking a position on the questions which he himself formulated: "I shall refrain from speaking about these things, because the treatment of such a subject is extremely deep and needs another, more profound, examination." He never made this investigation in any of his works. This attitude of his certainly constituted a great stimulation for later discussions, which became ever more sharp since the questions were particularly difficult to answer.

Porphyry's problematic soon passed into the West, thanks to the Latin translation of his *Isagoge* by Boethius (d. 525). Boethius, in the commentary which he wrote on the *Categories,* prescribed the solution which was later named "pure" (psychological) conceptualism: our mind has the capacity to separate (by abstraction) whatever appears inseparable in the sensible world.

In the East, the school of Ammonius (at about the same time as Boethius, who was also Ammonius' student, and about two centuries after Porphyry) formulated the same questions as follows, according to our free rendering:

1. Is there any knowledge of beings transcending our sense experience but having no less real existence and not being mere figments of the mind? In other words: Do the Forms or ideal beings, that is, the universals (genera and species), have existence in themselves, having thus, apart from their mental reality, also a suprasubjective reality?

2. (And since the answer to question 1 is affirmative), what exactly is this "reality" of the ideal beings?

As we see, the questions of the Alexandrian philosophers are correctly centered on the first and philosophically more legitimate question in Porphyry's *Isagoge.* In association with this first question, of course, the others can also be solved.

The problem of the real existence of mental (ideal) beings appears to be an acute one to the commentators of the school of Ammonius, *insofar as it has to do with the determination of the relationship between "first" and "second" substances* in Aristotle.

Why, Ammonius asks, does Aristotle name the concrete (individual) *ousia* "first substance," and the universal "second substance"—the latter being surely more primary, more important, superior (τιμιωτέρα)? Because, he answers, that which is prior in nature (the universal) is for us (as knowing subjects) secondary (posterior). From the particulars we are led to the general, to universals. For this reason, he comments, Aristotle was careful not to speak of first substance (particulars) as if "it primarily and in the highest degree *exists*" but says that "it primarily and most certainly is *said*" (not καὶ πρώτως καὶ μάλιστα ἔστιν, but καὶ πρώτως καὶ μάλιστα λεγομένη).

Philoponus also explains the superiority of the universal (second substance) by the principle that "the cause has a higher degree of existence than the effect," and justifies Aristotle's terminology by saying that in the *Categories* the philosopher is speaking to novices, and that it is for this reason that he names "first" the substance, appears later, "after a long time, when reason has shone within us" from the particulars to the universal, because second substance, which is the main substance, appears late, "after a long time, when reason has shone within us" (ὀψέ, τοῦ λόγου ἐν ἡμῖν ἐλλάμψαντος).

Simplicius gives the same explanation (after he has pointed out the superiority of the universals "under which particulars are classed and from which they derive"). That is, in the *Categories* the investigation of substance starts out "from a semantic relationship" (ἀπὸ σημαντικῆς σχέσεως), and for this reason its examination is undertaken from the standpoint of first substances (those prior in relation to us, that is individual, sensible beings). Similar views are found in the other commentators of the same school.

Summarizing the position of the Alexandrians, we see that they accept a double order of beings: the order of the being of things and the order of the cognitive subject. The first order is manifested "in nature," independently of thought and human knowledge. It is the order and hierarchy of the first causes of beings which is reflected also in particulars but without being identical with these. The second order starts where the first ends, and, following an inverse course, tries to reach the beginning of being. While the first order is ontological and creative (Asclepius: οὐσία τῶν τῇδε προακτικὴ καὶ δημιουργική), the second is cognitive or, rather, "recognitive." With regard to their courses, the two orders are not parallel but run in opposite directions.

In this analysis, the Neoplatonic scholiasts do not place simple general concepts in the first order, the order of universals (those prior in nature), but they see there a supersubjective reality. Even more, it is a reality prior to the mind of man, a reality given to him. Thus the universal, the ideal substance (genera and species), has priority in being and value in relation to concrete substance.

Thus, the universal-ideal substances not only have a reality independent of the knowing subject, but they also have an existence truer than that of sensible beings. The terms "more valuable," "to a higher degree," and "senior" (τιμιώτερον, κρεῖττον, πρεσβύτερον) for intelligible substance are not only symbolic but must be evaluated in the context of ontological definitions. The universal is the truly "first" substance (even if called the "second"), above the particular substance in the ontological order; and this primacy would not occur if the intelligible were purely a conceptual reality. (If that were the case, the intelligible would not determine the sensible, but the sensible would prescribe its rules to the rational.)

This evaluation of the degree of existence of the universal in relation to the particular has one more consequence: for the Alexandrian scholiasts, the particular has an even truer existence *within* the universal than it has by itself. Certainly this would be impossible if the universal had the mode of existence of a simple general concept of the mind.

Here a second group of problems appears, which leads to further discussion of the character of the reality of the universal. I can only state here the conclusion of this discussion.

The Neoplatonists accept a gradation of being and indeed within intelligible being. It is a gradation with reference not only to first (sensible) subtance, but more importantly to second (intelligible) substance. The higher level is always the ontological basis (the presupposition) for the lower. The higher the ascent (ὑπερβεβηκέναι, ὑπέρβασις, ὑπερβατόν, terms used by the Alexandrians), the stronger and more comprehensive being, as supportive of other beings, becomes. In Ammonius' own formulation: κάτωθεν μὲν ἀπὸ τῶν ἀτόμων . . . πλήθει μὲν στενοῦται . . . δυνάμει δὲ αὔξεται.[8]

We now come to the second question posed by the Alexandrian commentators: What actually is the real character of the existence of *universalia*? We have first a negative definition (consistent with the above): The reality—the state of existence—of the ideal is not identical with the way in which sensible particulars exist.

One of the arguments for this is the following: species and genera (man, animal) "seem" (φαίνεται) to designate a concrete individual in each case, but in truth they designate plurality and quality, because they indicate the "community" and the "collection" (κοινωνίαν καὶ συναγωγήν) of particular substances. (For this reason, Ammonius says, Aristotle does not say that the form is "the what as quality" but "the what with regard to substance": περὶ οὐσίαν τὸ ποῖον.)

Thus "universal" substance (1) is something distinct from concrete particular substance (without this implying its individualization—I simply mention the problem, since it figures in one of Aristotle's arguments for the rejection of the Forms: the argument "of the doubling of the world"); (2) it also defines substantial quality and is not simply a qualitative predicate of particular substances (for this reason it does not need the qualitatively defined particular in order to exist, as the latter needs it).

Next follows a positive definition from which a really surprising thesis emerges: The universal needs the particular substance, not in order for it to exist but in order to be expressed in it (Ammonius: οὐ γὰρ δέεται τὸ καθόλου τῶν πρώτων οὐσιῶν, τοῦτ' ἔστιν τῶν μερικῶν, ἵνα συστῇ (πρὸς σύστασιν), ἀλλ' ἵνα κατ' ἐκείνων ῥηθῇ).

But I must now turn to certain final positions that are of direct interest for the later history of the problem of ideal beings or general concepts. For the Alexandrian Neoplatonic commentators:

1. The "separate" existence of universals does not have the same form as that of the sensible particulars. (Thus Aristotle's criticism of Plato for introducing a "separation" of reality into two worlds through the theory of Forms is refuted.)

2. In the texts under consideration we do not have any hint that the commentators postulate a domain of Forms existing somewhere, close to, or outside, the natural world-order.

3. What is more, it is maintained that the Forms exist within particular concrete objects, or rather that the particular objects express the Form itself which appears in them.

However, the appearance of the Form does not mean that what appears (the phenomenon) is identified with the Form; the phenomenon does not cease to be the representation of the Form, its copy, a way for the Form to appear. And that is why the phenomena (the ways in which the Forms appear) are always inferior to their Form. (Compare the concept of the transcendence of the Form in relation to its representation in the sensible: transcendence has meaning precisely on the presupposition of a presence of the Form within the objects).

On the other hand (as has been shown above), the existence of the universal as universal does not cease with its presence in particulars. In the natural reality of time and space we also have gradations of being. The intelligible which is embodied in the sensible is the strongest, the fullest region of being. Besides, this difference in the value of the intelligible region even in its bodily shape—given that the intelligible never coincides absolutely with its bodily shape—expresses a kind of "separation" of the intelligible from the natural. (We may note here the Platonic–Aristotelian opposition on the separation of the two world-orders and the reconciliatory efforts of the Neoplatonists.)

It is true that the terminology used by the commentators to express the above relationship gives at first sight the impression that they mean an existence of the universal which is independent from the particulars. But a careful study leaves no doubt that they accept different modes of existence in being as a whole; there are different degrees of ontological fullness in the gradations of being with regard to both the intelligible and the natural world.

Thus we learn that (as Philoponus says):

1. Particular concrete objects (first substances) constitute for being the subject or substratum (ὑπόκεινται) in either of the following ways:
   a) for the qualities/events of the sensible world, so as to exist in the sensible world (ὑπόκεινται πρὸς ὕπαρξιν);
   b) for the universals, so as to be predicated (ὑπόκεινται πρὸς κατηγορίαν).
2. The intelligibles and the phenomena are mutually dependent.

We cannot think of the intelligible as intelligible without contrasting it to the sensible. And we cannot speak of sensible phenomena without using simultaneously the concept of the intelligible. For this reason the mutual interdependence of the universal and the particular occurs not only in the region of the intelligible, but also in that of concrete individual existence.

We can now understand the final position, which has great significance: universals are necessarily subordinated to the function of our mind in apprehending and expressing them (νοεῖν καὶ λέγειν αὐτά). From this standpoint, their characterization as *a posteriori* (as subsequent to the particulars) becomes understandable. (I will return to this topic.)

At this point I shall simply refer to one interesting dispute of the Alexandrians with the most reliable commentator on Aristotle, Alexander of Aphrodisias. Olympiodorus and Elias defend the priority of the universal *in nature as well as in logic*. As we know, for Alexander, only the particulars are prior in nature. This simple reference is necessary in order to draw attention to a critical point which throws light on the final definition of the mode of existence of universals: the Alexandrians maintain that the universal is prior in nature even when they admit that the universal appears only in the particular sensibles and ceases to be in their absence.

But what ceases to be? That is the crucial point, ensuing from the discussion on the priority of what is prior in nature, and which has a bearing on the final solution. The universal which ceases to be in the absence of particulars is not that which is "prior to the particulars," τὸ πρὸ τῶν πολλῶν (= the kind, the Form in the mind of the God-Creator, as we shall see), but *that which "applies to the particulars*," τὸ ἐπὶ τοῖς πολλοῖς, namely *the conceptual apprehension of the universal*.

Thus we come to the final designation of the universal, according to the school of Ammonius. It must be understood as an attempt (1) to preserve the Platonic doctrine of the Forms as the ideal substances (models) of creation, residing in the mind of the Creator (as his thoughts). This last idea—that the Forms, which in the human soul are discrete and separate, are found collectively in the Divine Mind, being identical with it—is the result of the Neoplatonic transformation of Platonic and Aristotelian elements in the postclassical tradition (at least after Philo) of the doctrine of the Forms. It is *a transformation which facilitated considerably the new solution*.

It is also an attempt (2) to validate the thesis of the ontological priority and permanence of the universal against the sensible particular, since if the sensible (first substance) is abolished, it is not the universal (second substance) *itself* which ceases to exist, but *only its apprehension by the mind*.[9]

In conclusion, the solution involves *a triple mode of existence of the universal*.[10] Universals (genera and species) are, therefore, for the Alexandrian Neoplatonists:

1. *prior to particulars* (πρὸ τῶν πολλῶν), in the mind of the Creator. This doctrine is attributed explicitly to Plato and represents—as they believe!—his teaching on the Forms.[11]

2. *within the particulars* (ἐν τοῖς πολλοῖς), inseparable from the sensible concrete objects of the natural world. This is the Aristotelian "material form" (ἔνυλον εἶδος) or "first substance" (πρώτη οὐσία).

3. *applied to the particulars and conceptual* (ἐπὶ τοῖς πολλοῖς καὶ ἐννοηματικά). According to the precise formulation in Philoponus: "Those which are in our mind are seen to apply to the many particulars and are subsequent to them." (It is significant that Philoponus refutes here the opinion of a certain Eustathius, unknown to us, and that of Porphyry, and calls on "those who speak more correctly, of whom one is Iamblichus, who says that the aim of the Aristotelian *Categories* for the philosopher is to speak about the φωναί [meaning the five most general categories] signifying objects through their meaning.") From this passage it appears that the Alexandrian scholiasts consider also the third mode of existence of the universal ἐπὶ τοῖς πολλοῖς to be consistent with Aristotelian teaching, the most correct interpretation of which they find in the Neoplatonic branch headed by Iamblichus. Philoponus says explicitly: "Aristotle always calls genera those applying to the many (τὰ ἐπὶ τοῖς πολλοῖς) and being objects of our thought (ἐννοηματικά)." But it is clear that we have here Stoic influence, at least indirectly. Furthermore, there are other Stoic elements in the example of "the seal and its waxen copies" which the Alexandrians used.

Let us now reread the definition given by the Byzantine philosopher Nicephoros Choumnos: "Therefore, taking into consideration all men by induction and looking at precisely that first man, who is the origin, and at those after him and so on continuously, that which we find *common to all* (ἐπὶ πάντων ταὐτόν) . . . this we recognize as the species (the general concept) of man," etc.

We can easily see the common line of thought which, it may be noticed, used a similar terminology.

We find this line of interpretation throughout the Byzantine period, specifically in the texts of Ioannes Italos (1023–ca. 1085), Eustratios of Nicaea (1050–1120), who is also a commentator on the *Posterior Analytics,* Nicephoros Blemmydis (1197–1272), and even later in Georgios Scholarios and Bessarion, but not in Plethon.

Unfortunately a treatise devoted to the subject by Photius (820–893), which he himself mentions, has not survived. But in his brief essay, "Various questions for discussion on genera and species," he shows clearly and vividly a knowledge of the history of the problem of general concepts. Photius gives us an original elaboration of only one specific aspect of this problem, Porphyry's second question as to whether the Forms are incorporeal or corporeal. Photius characterizes his own solution as "no less elegant than that of the Greek philosophers." His answer is as follows: "Universals are corporeal (not bodies) and indicative of subjects (not indicating themselves), developing the existence of these (not causing them to subsist) and reporting the substantification of the parts within them (not providing it) and are names signifying substances through appropriate meaning (names not possessed by the beings themselves)."[12]

In the same text we find a rejection of the Platonic Forms. He also clearly states that "the philosophers of better taste applied genera and species to the many and within the many" (τὰ μὲν ἐπὶ τοῖς πολλοῖς, τὰ δὲ ἐν τοῖς πολλοῖς). This means that Photius, too, is close to Aristotelian realism as the Neoplatonic scholiasts elaborated it. An important indication is the presence of the phrase ἐπὶ τοῖς πολλοῖς in his definition.

My thesis, therefore, is that in Byzantine philosophy the discussion of the problem of general concepts does not resemble the dispute as we know it in the West. In the Greek East, there is an almost universal acceptance of the solution of the Alexandrian Neoplatonic commentators of Aristotle, which we can characterize as (moderate) "conceptual realism." We do not find a nominalistic solution, because, as has been indicated, general concepts for them were not simple concepts or mere names, stripped of every reality and "existing" only in the human mind.

In fact, the new phrase which the Alexandrians introduce and the Byzantines adopt (ἐπὶ τοῖς πολλοῖς καὶ ὑστερογενῆ τὰ καθόλου: universals applying to the many and subsequent to the particulars) is not equivalent to the *post res* of the *universalia* dispute, that is, the position of the nominalists, as one might believe, and has in fact been maintained by some.

On the basis of the texts of Philoponus and also of those of the Byzantine Eustratios of Nicaea, who in his comments on Aristotle shows an admirable knowledge of the sources (this same Eustratios uttered the bold statement that "throughout all his divine sayings Jesus reasons in the Aristotelian way"![13]), we see that the *a posteriori* status of general concepts does not alter their "substantial status," their mode of existence. Their existence is always within sensible particulars and together with these; the universals that are conceived by the mind by abstraction of the common characteristics of the particular sensibles are the Aristotelian "second" substances (ὕστερα equals ἡμῖν δεύτερα).

There is one more reason why universals, as objects of thought, come after sensible substances. They are posterior to their creative and determinating causes, namely the ideal substances in the mind of the demiurge. This last thesis is accepted particularly by Christian thinkers, who consider the Forms, as we have seen, to be the thoughts of the demiurge and the creative causes of all beings.

For a more analytical presentation of the Byzantine writers one would have to consult the texts, which unfortunately remain to a great extent unedited.[14] I wish only to refer to two recent publications of mine, which offer an interpretation of Byzantine philosophical texts, together with a new critical edition and with the necessary identification of the sources used: Nicephoros Choumnos, "On Matter and Forms"; Michael Psellos, "On the Forms of which Plato speaks," *Philosophia* (Athens), vol. 3 (1973) and vols. 5–6 (1975–1976).

One final remark: in the West the Alexandrian solution has rather the character, as I have said, of a compromise solution between the contrasting positions of realism and nominalism. It is represented in the twelfth century and thereafter by Abelard, Albertus Magnus, Thomas Aquinas, and others. The link is generally considered to be the Arab Avicenna (980–1037), who certainly borrows from the last scholiasts of the school of Ammonius, Elias and David. However, it would be interesting to investigate the Greek—Latin connection from as early as the time of Photius and after.

III

Medieval Latin Thought

9

The Primacy of Existence in the Thought of Eriugena

G. H. ALLARD

One can scarcely be mistaken in asserting that Neoplatonism—whether it be Christian or not—is fundamentally an "essentialist" philosophy; by that I mean that it is a system of thought at the core of which a universe of essences and intelligible beings is organized according to relationships of causality which are universal, timeless and necessary, a system in the face of which phenomenal realities possess little or no ontological density. In this respect the thought of Eriugena marks an important date in the history of Neoplatonism since it bears witness to a profound change in its customary perspectives. Indeed, the acute awareness that Eriugena has of the idea of existence, perceived as the ontological pole complementary to essence, leads him, so to speak, to shift the observation post of reality and to look in the other direction: the approach to being, to intelligible beings, is now mediated by existence, by "existents." Polarized in this way, thought succeeds in integrating quite naturally the spatiotemporal realities and in conferring on them not only a decisive gnosiological function, but also a new ontological status. This increased sensitivity towards the idea of existence, need we emphasize, does not of course entirely destroy the quite Neoplatonic structure of Eriugena's thought, but it does already suffice to shake the edifice to the extent to which Eriugenian thought sets out to distinguish, in the heart of being, between what is (*quod est*) and the crude radical fact of existing (*esse*). I shall certainly not be able within the framework of this paper to examine the various influences which affected the thinking of Eriugena on this question;[1] but it does remain that the mental equipment which he inherited and which he transformed in such an original manner enabled him to make a completely new reading of the dogma of creation. It is precisely on this theme of *creatio ex nihilo* and on its philosophical consequences that I want first to spend a little time.

I

My attention was drawn to this little explored dimension of Eriugenian thought on the occasion of the computerization of the text of his *Expositiones in Ierarchiam coelestem* which Mlle. Barbet has edited in the *Corpus christianorum* series (1975); together with my colleague S. Lusignan I had to consolidate the *index verborum latinorum* for both the commentary of Eriugena and the text commented on (Dionysius) and translated into Latin by Eriugena. When considering the range of frequency that the same word may undergo according to where it appears in Dionysuis' commented text or in the commentary, I was struck by the frequency of the words relating to creation (*creator, creare, creaturae, ex nihilo*) which recur in fact 135 times in the commentary as against once in the commented text. To my first source of astonishment was added a second: in fact, I established that this single representative of the family of words relating to creation,[2] which occurs only once, could itself also have been completely absent from the *Celestial Hierarchy* if our translator had chosen, just as Hilduin did, to render the Dionysian *demiourgos* by the term "*opifex.*" This "slight alteration" makes of Eriugena a very bad translator but perhaps a better philosopher than Hilduin; what is in any case certain is that this intervention reveals in him an obvious concern to adjust the Dionysian text to his personal problematics.[3] For Dionysius, as we know, the action of the demiurge is "an action organizing" things and relations between beings.[4] There is no doubt that the Dionysian demiurge is unique, transcendent, and is Providence; in this respect, we are here far from the hypostatic universe of Iamblichus or of Proclus.[5] But the question presents itself: is the god of Dionysius a creator in the biblical sense of the term, that is, the principle and cause of the radical appearing of things and beings *ex nihilo* in time and in space? The idea of *ex nihilo* is absent from the vocabulary and from the thought of Dionysius. This absence is significant; it indicates that Dionysius does not so much consider the question of the "radical *origin* of being," which is that of *existence,* as that of the intelligibility of "what is", that is, the necessary and intelligible order that governs beings and essences.[6] Thus it is being and the cause of being that holds his attention—his thought is polarized by the "what is," the essence, the substance, and he is consequently insensitive to the first springing forth of beings into intelligible or spatiotemporal existence. In this context, the demiurge is the cause and principle of *being* but not of *existence;* according to Dionysius' own terms, it is ἀρχή

. . . καὶ οὐσία . . . οὐσίας . . . πρὸς τὸ εἶναι παραγαγών[7] or again αἰτίαν οὐσιοποιὸν εἶναι:[8] it is a manufacturer (*opifex*) of order among the essences (the beings), or better still it establishes and gives the rank of essence (being) to all that is as intelligible.[9]

Eriugena is not unaware of the precise meaning of the action of the demiurge of Dionysius, for on occasion he translates very fairly the πρὸς τὸ εἶναι οὐσίας πρώτας παραγαγών or the οὐσιοποιὸν εἶναι as "causa substantifica."[10] But it has not been sufficiently noted that each time he renders the Dionysian δημιουργός by "*creator*," Eriugena modifies its implication by adding a dimension alien to Dionysius because it is unknown to him. In Book III of the *De divisione naturae (DDN)*,[11] the divinity is defined as a "causa existentium omnium"; still in the same book,[12] he takes up on his own account the celebrated eulogy that Dionysius addresses to Being (ON) in the *Divine Names*; but this time the divinity (the demiurge) is "creator existentis subsistentiae," "existentis substitutor," "causa existentium." It is for this reason that in the *Expositiones in Ierarchiam coelestem*,[13] where Eriugena intentionally attributes to Dionysius the concept and the word "*creator*," one must, to my mind, translate the passage "primasque essentias ad esse adducens" by "he brings the first essences (beings, substances) to existence." For the action of the Eriugenian god proceeds *ex nihilo*, and from this fact, it raises the idea of *origin* (i.e., that of *existence*). The Eriugenian god can no longer be, as was the case for Dionysius, a simple supervisor of the essences since, if one takes into account the narrative of Genesis, it must be recognized as the principle and cause of the radical and total emergence of all beings (intelligible and spatio-corporeal). Thus from the the conceptual and operational point of view, the idea of the demiurge becomes inadequate, and parallel with this, essence itself, which in itself is eternal, universal, infinite, and simple, has become powerless to signify the temporal emergence of beings, outside of their cause, into created finitude. It is for this reason that Eriugena summons up the idea of a creator and the concept of existence. "Divina providentia" he writes, "universitatem conditae creaturae ex non existentibus in existentia produxit,"[14] or again: "Deus creat igitur omnia quae de nihilo adduxit ut sint ex non esse in esse . . . ita omne quod dicitur existere non in seipso existit sed participatione vere existentis naturae existit."[15] It is in this "*existential*" sense that one must understand the famous passage of Dionysius for which Eriugena seems to have a marked preference: "esse omnium est superesse divinitas."[16] Generally this passage of Dionysius is translated in the following way: "The superessential divinity (i.e., beyond being) is the being of everything."[17] This translation appears to me to give a faithful rendering of the thought of Dionysius; in fact, we know that the demiurge operates at the level of the essences that it establishes. Thus it is in some way anterior and superior to them as principle and as cause, that is, beyond being and eminently unknowable. On the other hand when the same ideas are ascribed to the authorship of Eriugena, it seems to me that there is a danger of misinterpreting his thought. It has not been sufficiently remarked that Eriugena is once again altering the Dionysian text, precisely in the words that immediately precede the passage we are discussing, and it seems thus to be given a new context and a new meaning. We read in the *Expositiones*:

"existentia omnia esse ejus participant."[18] The expression "existentia omnia" leaves no doubt, in my opinion, as to the way in which the "esse omnium" of the preceding phrase is to be understood: it is a question of the very existence of beings, of all the *existents* of whom it must be postulated that they participate in the *esse* of that which is *causa existentis,* since they are not themselves the principle of their own existence. This is my reading of line 132: "Thus all the existents participate in its existence." We are already a long way away from Dionysius. Is it possible then to render the line that follows without taking account of this context? Henceforth the proposition "esse omnium est superesse divinitas" can be understood in this way: "superexisting divinity is the very existence of all existents." Such a translation does more justice, it seems to me, to the constant efforts that Eriugenian thought makes to remain resolutely, in what refers to relations between God and the world, on the level of existents and of existence and not of beings and being (as is the case with Dionysius). This change of perspective once recognized, there could be no meaning, indeed there would even be a contradiction, in translating the "esse omnium est superesse divinitas" by "the superessential divinity is the being of everything," in the eyes of Eriugena. It is a trap that he managed to avoid. For our author, as we know, no essence (divine or created) can know itself or be known; the term "superessentialis" signifies exactly that conviction: "qui dicit superessentialis est, non quid est dicit, sed quid non est."[19] Now to state that superessential divinity (i.e., that of which one knows nothing essential) is the being of everything, is the equivalent, in good logic, of attributing a predicate, thus a determination, to a subject of which one does not know the essence. Here, consequently, is a proposition that, in addition to being contradictory, is far from being enlightening. On the other hand if one says: the superexisting divinity is the existence of everything, one is conveying that there is in God the Creator such an abundance and such a fullness of existence that they overflow onto all the existents of which he is the principle. From this viewpoint, not only does the proposition recover its coherence, but again it makes sense, for it appeals both in its subject (*superesse divinitas*) and in its predicate (*esse omnium*) to significations upon which thought has seized since only the *quia est* of the creatures and of the creator are accessible to it. Existence (*quia est*) is even the immediate datum of the Eriugenian *cogito,*[20] and it is from this first fundamental angle that human thought approaches the knowledge of God: "causa omnium . . . solummodo cognoscitur esse."[21]

Thus one can better understand how, by means of this reversal of viewpoint, Eriugena thought fit in the *De praedestinatione*[22] to invert even the order of the words that belong almost as of right to God, enumerating the verbs before the nouns: "quaedam sunt quasi propria quorum exempla sunt in verbis, quidem sum, es, erat, esse; in nominibus vero essentia, veritas, virtus, sapientia, scientia. . . ." Not only does Eriugena distinguish between the *esse* and the *quod est* in God, but he equally differentiates in him the *quod est* from the *qui est.*[23] These grammatical infrastructures to which Eriugenian thought has reference and from which it takes support, are of such a kind as to dissipate all ambiguity concerning his conception of divinity: being is not an anonymous principle, but is personal, and in relation to the affirmative discourse which the human mind can conduct on the question, being is pure activity, absolute existence, the cause of existence, indeed even the establisher of the existents. Here is how he defines "creation": "creatio est omnium existentium substitutio;"[24] one can better imagine now the reasons which urged him to prefer the word *creator* to that of *"demiourgos"* and to call upon the concept of *existence* and of *existents* rather than that of the too essentialist *being* and *beings*. It is not without interest to note that each time that Eriugena encounters the expression *ta onta* in the Greek authors, he generally renders it by *existentia* in preference to *entia*. This last term is in fact totally absent from the *Expositiones* and appears only twice in the *DDN* and that within a quotation from Dionysius;[25] on the other hand the word *"existentia"* (the existents) occurs 158 times in the *DDN* and 18 times in the *Expositiones*. These constant alterations express a clear intention on the part of Eriugena which is that of bending the meaning of the word in the direction of his system, and they manifest from this fact that a change is in the course of being produced at the very core of Eriugenian Neoplatonism, of which the keystone has become the *creator,* the supreme existent, the principle and cause of all existence. Consequently, one need not be surprised to see Eriugena modify, for example, the fourfold division of things of Dionysius;[26] while the latter classifies beings into nonliving, living, rational, and intellectual, Eriugena corrects the first category and writes in *existentia*[27]—an interesting correction! It informs us that in his eyes existence is the first step of the universal scale of beings.

II

We have seen up to now the lexicographical precedence which Eriugena accords to the constellation of the words *"esse," "existere," "existentia."* It is time to ask oneself what are the metaphysical consequences of this choice—what function and what meaning does he intend to give to the concept of existence? While Eriugenian man understands himself as an existent or knows himself as existing, he gives to existence the role of a fundamental gnosiological principle; to express it in a word—which, though bizarre, you will forgive—I believe that existence has, in the system of Eriugena, the function of an "ousiophany." It is striking to establish the extreme consistency and the close correspondence that exist between the different levels of discourse in the Eriugenian text, so much so that the theologian is in perfect harmony with the metaphysician, the logician, the poet, and the dialectician. Just as the spring that flows[28] appears to the eyes of the poet as an epiphany of what is taking place "in secretis sinibus Naturae", just as creation in its entirety is from the theological viewpoint a theophany, so existence for the metaphysician makes manifest the essence, in the manner in which the accidents (περιοχαί) reveal the substance for the logician, or as the individual, in the dialectical order of genus and species, is in a way found to be the ultimate limit of their revelation.[29] In the *Expositiones*[30] Eriugena tells us that the proper activity of the creator consists in leading the essences to existence, "adduxit eas, videlicet essentias, ad esse," and he adds immediately "ad essentiam plane," that is, that their accession to existence enables what was latent to be made manifest, what was invisible to be made visible, and what was unknowable to be knowable. In the *De divisione naturae* it is still more explicit: "invenies," says the master to the disciple, "*ousian* omnino in omnibus quae sunt, per se ipsam incomprehensibilem non solum sensui sed etiam intellectui esse. Atque ideo ex his veluti circumstantiis suis intelligitur existere, loco dico, quantitate, situ; additur etiam his tempus. Intra haec siquidem, veluti intra quosdam fines circumpositos, essentia cognoscitur circumcludi."[31] To exist, consequently, in the mind of our author, is for essence to possess the accidents whose principal mission is to allow the sense or the intellect to grasp not what it is (the *quid*), but at least that it exists (the *quia*). That is to say that the demarcations confirmed through the fact of existence enable essence to be better circumscribed, in some sense to be accounted for, just as the predicates explain the substantive of the proposition—in a word, to allow it to be made visible: "Deus ad visibilem essentiam adduxit."[32]

This "ousiophany" corresponds very exactly to the third mode according to which things are said *esse* and *non esse*. "Quicquid enim ipsarum causarum in materia formata, in temporibus et locis per generationem cognoscitur, quadam humana consuetudine dicitur esse. Quicquid vero adhuc in ipsis naturae sinibus continetur, neque in materia formata, vel loco vel tempore, ceterisque accidentibus apparet, eadem praedicta consuetudine dicitur non esse."[33] In this context of the spatiotemporal generation of things outside of their causes and of their principle (which is called etymologically *ex-sistere*), it is suitable to speak rather of *phusis* than of *ousia*: "nam graeci *phusin* pro *ousia* et *ousian* pro *phusei* saepissime commutant. Horum siquidem nominum proprietas est, *ousian,* i.e., essentiam, de eo quod nec corrumpi, nec minui in omni creatura sive visibili sive intelligibili potest predicari; *phusin* vero, hoc est naturam de generatione essentiae per loca et tempora in aliqua materia, quae et corrumpi et augeri et minui potest, diversisque accidentibus affici. . . . Omnis itaque creatura quantum in suis rationibus subsistit, *ousia* est; in quantum vero in aliqua materia procreatur, *phusis*."[34] Now the fundamental characteristic of every created existing nature is to be generated in time and space: "omnium itaque existentium essentia localis et temporalis est";[35] furthermore, these categories are the two first accidents to be comprehended: "videsne igitur locum tempusque ante omnia quae sunt intelligi?," the master asks the disciple who assents to the idea that time and space constitute in fact the very containers which delimit the essence.[36] As containers, they exercise a necessary gnosiological priority: "Necessario enim ea quae continent prius intelliguntur quam ea quae continentur."[37] As time and space first and then all the other categories contain and delimit the *ens creatum,* so they serve as a necessary mediation to the understanding of the content, that is, of essence, and thus they come to fix as the point of departure in the epistemological path existence itself, preeminent principle of "ousiophany."

III

This view of things entails grave consequences, of which a first important one consists for Eriugena in conferring (thanks to that "ousiophany" which has just been mentioned) on existence, on the spatiotemporal and phenomenal realities a preferential gnosiological status. But a second consequence, which is even more spectacular than the first, of which it is moreover the corollary, concerns the metaphysical theory of Eriugena. Postulating as the keystone of totality (the *to pan*) a creating divinity, no longer solely demiurgic but the cause of existence, generator of natures *in loco et tempore,* Eriugena saw himself gradually being constrained to integrate existence into the ontological order as the pole complementary to essence. He expresses his explanation of the subject in connection with his division of the five modes of *esse/non esse* in the opening passages of the *De divisione naturae.* According to the fourth mode, our author reports, "ea solummodo quae solo comprehenduntur intellectu, dicitur vere esse; quae vero per generationem, materiae distensionibus, locorum quoque spatiis temporumque motibus variantur, colliguntur, solvuntur, vere dicuntur non esse, ut sunt omnia corpora quae nasci et corrumpi possunt."[38] One can recognize here the opinion of the philosophers for whom being is identified exclusively with the intelligible. And Eriugena adds: this sense of the word "*esse*" is plausible (*non improbabiliter*). It is a judgment filled with deference towards his masters in philosophy, and it is doubtless in order to do justice to them and to make his enumeration more complete that he inserts this fourth mode. But one feels that he does not adhere to this opinion; how could he, without leaving himself open to contradicting the instructions that *reason* itself and the customary manner of speech of human beings have laid down for him on the way in which *esse/non esse* are to be understood—instructions that he passes on to us when speaking of the first and third modes. Of the first he tells us: "ratio suadet omnia quae corporeo sensui vel intelligentiae perceptioni succumbunt, posse rationabiliter dici esse; ea vero quae per excellentiam suae naturae, non solum *uleon* id est omnem sensum sed etiam intellectum rationemque fugiunt, jure videri non esse."[39] *Esse* then signifies to devote oneself to the "prehension," or rather to the comprehension, of the senses or of the intellect, which, it must be emphasized, can happen only at the moment when essence, by definition incomprehensible, is revealed through accidents: "quicquid autem in omni creatura, vel sensu corporeo percipitur, seu intellectu consideratur, nihil aliud est nisi quoddam accidens incomprehensibile per se, ut dictum est, uniuscujusque essentiae."[40] In this context, thought can no longer discount the accidental in order to attain to substance, nor discount existence in order to gain access to essence; the *quid est* presents itself for our recognition under the form of the *quia est.* Essence then is bound up with existence, in a definitive way.

We discover the same concept expressed in the third mode, applied this time to the study of the entire visible universe. Eriugena informs us here that the fact, for the world, of existing in the flesh of the visible, that is, of having been projected outside of its causes (divine or primordial) and of being extended in time and in space, constitutes a supplementary perfection, a completeness: "Tertius modus non incongrue inspicitur in his quibus hujus mundi visibilis plenitudo perficitur."[41] Here then is *ousiophany*; the fact that an essence is placed in spatio-temporal existence and clothed in its accidents confers on it a fullness, a completeness that it did not possess as essence pure and unadorned, withdrawn as it was from every human perception or intellection. We know that, for Eriugena, that which cannot be understood is in a certain way imperfect in the face of the connatural need of visibility which thought experiences, or, to put the matter differently, that which escapes all epiphany or manifestation does not exist. That is why he will say of God, who is pure infinite essence, outside of time and space, simple, without any accident, that he is *tenebrositas,* positive pure nothingness.[42] In spite of everything he will have lacked in these infinite perfections the complementary and ultimate perfection of revealing himself in his theophanies as supreme Existent and cause of existence, for, deprived of knowing the *quia est,* the human mind could not even guess at the superessential perfections of the *quid est.*

IV

I hope I may be allowed, in coming to the end of this paper, not to draw conclusions nor to sum what has been said, but rather to express very briefly two general considerations that come to my mind following upon this commentary on the Eriugenian text. First, I want to say that Neoplatonism did not emerge intact or unscathed from its encounter with the Christianity of Eriugena, and neither did his Christianity, but that is another story. Second, the original synthesis that Eriugena succeeded in elaborating with the aid of his precursors represents a decisive turning point in the history of Western ontology. Indeed, if my understanding of Eriugenian thought is correct, it must be recognized henceforth that Eriugena, through the triple primacy that he attributes to existence (lexicographical, gnosiological, and ontological), reversed the order of Neoplatonic values without all the same abandoning them, and was well in advance of Thomas Aquinas and his Arab and Latin predecessors in introducing the concept of existence into the field of Western consciousness.

10

The Overcoming of the Neoplatonic Triad of Being, Life, and Intellect by Saint Thomas Aquinas

CORNELIO FABRO

Just as the twelfth century is characterized by the diffusion of Platonism, so the thirteenth century bears the dominant mark of Aristotle, but an Aristotle who remains, even in Saint Thomas Aquinas, present and operative along with Platonic elements put into circulation by Neoplatonism. The commentary on the *De causis* can be considered to be the final step in the process of Saint Thomas' absorption of Neoplatonism. This commentary, which was occasioned by the appearance in the West of Proclus' *Elements of Theology,* constitutes his discharge of a grave intellectual obligation to strike a theoretical balance in regard to all his earlier speculation.[1] Today no further doubt remains that Dionysius the Areopagite also drew heavily on the works of Proclus, if not in fact on the early *Elements of Theology*. Although Saint Thomas himself was unaware of this dependency, he explicates the *De causis* by constant appeal to Proclus, integrates the two, that is, Proclus and the *De causis,* and even corrects them both by using Dionysius.

What we might call "absolute realism," characteristic of the great speculative tradition which begins with Parmenides, achieves its perfect systematic expression in Proclus. We can best realize that this is no accident if we recall that Proclus has also left important mathematical works. The informing principle of his *Elements of Theology* is the total and direct transformation of relations of formal universality into relations of reality and of causality, and this according to a fabric of relations which intersect one another as infinite lines and centers. What is involved here is a most complete and bold metaphysics of being, one in which "the real cause" is nothing other than the reflection of the logical "Because" and in which the Aristotelian apparatus of genus, species, and difference has been transformed into an objective hierarchy of being and powers.[2] There is thereby developed in the most extravagant form the systematic affirmation of that which we have elsewhere called "coexistence." As Thomas observes:

> According to Platonic theory, whatever is found present in many things should be reduced to a first which, by its very essence, is such as that which others are said to be through participation in it. Hence, in this theory, infinite powers are reduced to a first which is by essence Infinity of power—not that it is a participated power found in some subsisting thing, but that it is something which subsists of itself.[3]

Consequently, the classification of the first causes corresponds to grades of universality of the formalities themselves. However, the situation is not very clear in Thomas' exposition, which remains closely bound to the text of the *De causis*. The most obvious scheme is that there is, first of all, the One and the Good, which is followed by *ens* or *esse ipsum* and then by intelligence, life, and finally the world of bodies. On the contrary, between the Good and *esse* there are in fact at least two intermediaries, namely, *aeternitas,* which measures duration, and *infinitas,* which measures *esse*. There is thus an *esse superius aeternitate et ante aeternitatem,* namely, the first cause which is the cause of eternity, just as there is an *esse cum aeternitate,* which is the *intelligentia,* and also an *esse post aeternitatem,* which is the *esse* of the soul and of the corporeal world.[4] Even more, *infinitas* seems to accomplish this function, at least according to Saint Thomas' exposition, that is, an infinity that is situated above *esse* itself. But it is also clear that this first infinity, in turn, participates in the One and the Good that is above it. Ideal infinity is thus the mediator (μεταξύ) between the Good and the entire sphere of being.[5]

Following *infinitas idealis* there is then *ens ideale* or *esse separatum*. The Good is the very first cause, since it extends itself even to "nonbeing," which is matter for the Platonists. *Aeternitas* and *infinitas* are the ideal forms of all the separate forms, but the "separated" *esse* embraces all existing things. Proclus himself wrote with respect to that *esse*: "Omnium participantium divina proprietate et deificatorum primum est et supremum ens."[6] The commentary of Saint Thomas faithfully follows the line of Proclus by setting in relief the intensive emergence of being (*ens*), which is said, from this point of view, to follow immediately after the Good (*Bonum*).[7] Saint Thomas, as has already been noted, gives to the *De causis* an intermediate position between the *esse separatum,* which is the first created ideal form of Proclus, and the *esse participatum communiter in omnibus existentibus* set forth by Dionysius. He thus has the *De causis* assert an *esse participatum in primo gradu entis creati quod est esse superius,* which is therefore the highest form of created participations and is to be found in the highest sphere of reality.[8] This formal emergence of *esse* involves the most intimate immanence, which is the effect of its closeness to pure *esse* itself.[9] While Saint Thomas interprets this *esse purum* as the first cause itself,[10] the text cited is too vague to authorize so important an identification, one that would break the rhythm characteristic of the Neoplatonic deductions. The difficulty of the question is to determine whether the dialectic of participation has to function with the binary rhythm of Christian creationism, namely, that of *esse per essentiam* and *esse per participationem*, or rather with the ternary rhythm of Proclus, namely, that of the participated, the participations and the things that do the participating. The text of the *De causis* does not provide sufficient support to allow Thomas to detach himself from his source on so decisive a point.[11]

It is not easy to orient oneself in the obscure forest of the Neoplatonic doctrine of "processions" (πρόοδοι), especially that of the first intelligible triad, so as to be able to determine the relations that the first three hypostases have both with the One and also among themselves. For Plotinus the order is as follows: there first comes the One, from which proceeds Intelligence, and from the latter proceeds the Soul, which serves as the intermediary between the Intelligence and matter.[12] The One is also called the First (τὸ πρῶτον) and the Good (τἀγαθόν) because everything depends on it and everything aspires to it in being, life, and thought. It is also called the Simple (τὸ ἁπλοῦν), the Absolute (τὸ αὐταρχές), and the Infinite (τὸ ἄπειρον). The Intelligence contains the ideas (εἴδη) or pure forms, which are essences (οὐσίαι) and real beings (τὰ ὄντως ὄντα). They are also the intelligibles which compose the intelligible world (κόσμος νοητός) itself. The universal Soul (ἡ ψυχὴ ὅλη), or *Anima mundi* (ψυχὴ τοῦ κόσμου), causes and contains in itself all the particular souls.

The most important point for us is to determine whether the One and the Good is placed at the beginning of the series as the first of three hypostases, or whether it remains in itself separated from every relation with that which proceeds forth. In Porphyry, who declared his fidelity to Plotinus, it seems that the triad does exclude from itself the One, which remains outside it as its very principle. In Proclus, who here interests us more, the procession of the triads is complicated by tortured derivations of a metaphysical arithmetic, one that confronts us with an exasperating formal dreariness. The One and the Good thus seems to be left in its total isolation, while the first triad is arranged according to a structure that repeats itself, at diverse levels, with the same dialectical urgency. In *Platonic Theology*, the fundamental "diremption" seems to be the following: τὸ ὄν, ἡ ζωή, ὁ νοῦς that is, being, life, and intelligence, a triad that is said to be found everywhere (πανταχοῦ) according to the principle of πάντα ἐν πᾶσιν. The sphere of being is οὐσία, which comprehends the totality of the intelligibles; νοῦς embraces the sphere of the intelligent principles; and ζωή, the sphere of souls as principles of motion in the material world. Corresponding triads are those of πέρας, ἄπειρον, μικτόν, and μονή, πρόοδος, ἐπιστροφή.[13] This ternary rhythm, which unfolds below the One in endless complications, forms the key to the system of Proclus, which in turn inspired the *De causis*.

The context of the fourth proposition of the *De causis,* which sees the reason for the multiplicity of the intelligences in the composition of the finite and infinite, involves the thesis of an *esse separatum* which is not God but which can be called the *esse purum subsistens* because it is the first formality or the "head of the series" in the order of *esse.*[14]

Platonic *causality,* understood as ideal subsistence, descends from the abstract to the concrete. It falls in straight lines and is divided in parallel cascadings. Metaphysical causality and noetic causality always exist here on the same plane and according to a perfect coincidence of relations. Although the principle of separation (χωρισμός) first divides and spreads reality apart into a fabric of scaled participations, it then unifies and constrains it with an iron structure of relations of necessary inclusion. Saint Thomas finds in Proclus' metaphysics of identity a logical and continuous development of the principles of Plato. In a word, the order of causality is symmetrical to that of universality:

> Among these forms, however, he introduced this order: that to the degree that a certain form is more universal, to this degree it is more simple and prior as a cause, for it is participated in by posterior forms. It is just as if we were to say that animal is participated in by man, and life by animal, and so on for the other forms. The ultimate, in which all else participates and which does not itself participate in anything else, is the One itself, the separate Good which he said was the supreme God and the first cause of all things. Hence the following proposition, proposition 116, is introduced in Proclus' book: "Every god is capable of participating, . . . except the One."[15]

Since the intellects know only through participation in the intelligibles, the intellects follow the intelligibles in both the real and causal orders. But in his commentary—why I don't know—Thomas makes the intelligent beings to be the separate forms or pure formal unities (ἑνάδες) of Proclus.[16] In any case, the causal derivation is divided according to Saint Thomas in two intentional currents, so to speak, one that is metaphysical and another that is noetic. For the soul, too, there is a participation of divinity, not through the direct communication of the ideal intellect but by means of the divine intellects. Bodies themselves, in their turn, participate in the divine by way of the divine souls.[17] The latter are the first divine hypostases (or "heads of the series") that constitute the source of causal derivation in their own genus and in subalternated genera.[18] Accordingly, the noble soul (*anima nobilis*), which presides over the whole corporeal world, has a double operation: (1) a divine operation insofar as it is a principle of movement for the whole of nature, and (2) the operation of understanding things. There is also a double participation, and therefore a double causality and a double dependence.[19]

Saint Thomas recognizes that in this doctrine of a descending, scaled causality there may lie hidden a grave danger for Christian creationism. However, he not only absolves the author of the *De causis* of all error, but he even appeals to the Platonists themselves, who conceived derived causalities according to the mode of participation and not of creation. The causality of the formalities following upon *esse* would therefore be of a complementary nature and not of a creative or constitutive nature. The key to the turn which Thomas' commentary has taken here is the presupposition already mentioned, that is, that for the *De causis*—and here Saint Thomas extends this presupposition to the Platonists—*esse separatum* is God, the creator of the being of all things.[20] The mitigation which the *De causis* would introduce into the rigid Neoplatonic doctrines of vertical causality is formulated by Saint Thomas in proposition XVIII (XVII), which truly represents the nucleus of the Thomistic metaphysics of causality. It is that God, the First Being, gives being to all other things by means of creation (*ens primum . . . dat esse omnibus . . . per modum creationis*), while the other hypostases, namely, life (*vita*) and intelligence (*intelligentia*), give that which they give not through the mode of creation (*per modum creationis*) but through the mode of a form (*per modum formae*).[21] In his commentary on this proposition, Saint Thomas leaves the defense of this graduated or scaled creative causality to the Platonists, but he absolves of all blame the *De causis*, which here becomes allied with Dionysius— he had set up a like alliance for its position regarding the separate forms in God. It thus remains—and this is the important result for this dialectic—that there are two modes of causality, one by way of creating (which relates to *esse*), and the other by way of an informing (which relates to the other formalities).[22]

We already know the decisive application that Saint Thomas makes here of the notion of intensive *esse*:

> Because therefore thinking (*intelligere*) presupposes living and living presupposes being (*esse*) and being does not presuppose anything else prior to it, so it is that the first being (*ens*) "gives being (*esse*) to all things by means of creation." But "first life," whatever this may be, gives life not by means of creation but after the manner of a form, that is, by forming. And a similar account is to be given of intelligence.[23]

Indeed, Saint Thomas is persuaded that the *De causis* corrects itself at this point:

> From which it is clear that when he said above that intelligence was the cause of soul, he did not understand this to mean that it was a creative cause, but merely that it was a cause by way of informing.[24]

The meaning of the formulae of the *De causis* now seems beyond discussion: the superior intelligences cause the inferior, and the inferior intelligences in turn cause the souls.[25] Saint Thomas' open recognition of this is very significant with respect to what can be called the theoretical tension internal to Thomism. Nevertheless, the only causality that can be attributed to separate substances, that is, the intelligences and angels, in regard to inferior substances is one of a dispositive nature. However, it is not possible to state that causality any more precisely. The *De causis* remains, then, faithful on this fundamental point to its Neoplatonic source.[26]

The incomplete treatise *De substantiis separatis* seems to represent Thomas' final stance towards Platonism, that is, Neoplatonism. Since the exposition is free and not tied to a text, it proceeds (as it seems) with a greater synthetic and critical power. It also constitutes the last word of the Angelic Doctor on these, the most difficult problems of metaphysics. We shall therefore briefly analyze its basic structure and salient doctrines.

A. The first chapter, which concerns the ancient philosophers (*De opinionibus antiquorum philosophorum*),[27] is mostly of a historical introductory nature. Four principal stages are indicated in the demonstration of the existence of spiritual substances: (1) the first philosophers, who were still ignorant of the nature of spirit; (2) Anaxagoras, who introduces the intellect only as a distinguishing principle of the cosmos; (3) Plato and the "Platonists"; and (4) Aristotle. If, for the first two stages, Saint Thomas still relies on the exposition of Aristotle, he enlarges his perspective in regard to Platonism and follows the new sources that he has now come to know. For the first time, the Platonic method of separation to attain the *veritas fixa* of the separate universals is directly related to the method of intellectual abstraction. This method is itself divided into two branches, namely, mathematical abstraction and physical abstraction.[28] According to Saint Thomas, Plato had envisaged two spheres of formal, separate beings, namely, that of mathematics and that of abstract universals, which he called *species* or *ideas*. However, an important difference is to be noted between the two spheres. While in the sphere of mathematical abstraction one can think of many individuals of the same species (for example, two equal lines or two equilateral triangles), in the sphere of abstraction of universals this is not possible. For example, man taken in his universality is only one in species. For this reason, Thomas explains, Plato placed the sphere of mathematical relations as intermediate between the species or separate ideas and the singular sensibles. Insofar as there can be many individuals of the same species in the mathematical sphere, that sphere bears a likeness to sensible singulars; insofar as the relations are abstract, it bears a likeness to the universals.

B. There then follows an analytical description of a metaphysical structure of the world that is still attributed to Plato, but which in reality gathers together the development of Neoplatonism as it can be found, for example, in Proclus. That structure consists of the triad of the *unparticipated,* the *things which are participated in* or *participations,* and those *things which participate*.

1. The general principle and doctrine of the subsistent One. The direct correspondence between the logical and the real orders fixes the primacy of the One and the Good:

> Further, among forms themselves, he posited a certain order, on the ground that according as something was simpler in the intellect, so far was it prior within the order of things. Now that which is first in the intellect is the One and the Good; for he understands nothing who does not understand something one and good, and the one and the good follow upon one another. Hence Plato held that the first Idea of the One, which he called the One-in-itself and the Good-in-itself, was the first principle of things and this Idea he said was the highest God.[29]

Up to this point there is nothing new in comparison with the commentary on the *De causis*. However, what follows regarding the classification of the secondary unities, of the separate intellects, and of the souls reveals a greater penetration and adherence to the text of Proclus than that found in Thomas' commentary on the *De causis*. The fidelity to Proclus, even if not complete, is more visible.

2. The separate derived unities and the second gods:

> Under this One, he established among the substances separate from matter, diverse orders of participating and participated beings, all of which orders he called secondary gods, as being certain secondary unities below the first simple unity.

There is a descending nexus of causality:

> Again, inasmuch as all forms participate in the One, the intellect likewise must participate in the forms of things in order to have understanding. Therefore, just as under the highest God, who is the prime unity, simple and unparticipated, other forms of things exist as secondary unities and gods,[30] so, under the order of these forms or unities, he posited an order of separate intellects, which participate in the above-mentioned forms in order to have actual understanding. Among these intellects, an intellect is higher according as it is nearer to the first intellect[31] which has full participation in the forms; just as among the gods or unities, that one is higher which shares more perfectly in the first unity.

A higher mode of cognition is attributed to the second gods (or "participations"):

> Although Plato distinguished between the gods and the intellects, he did not mean to imply that the gods could not have understanding. It was his desire, rather, that they should understand in a supra-intellectual manner; that is, instead of understanding by participating in certain forms, they should have understanding through themselves, with the proviso that every one of them was good and one only through participating in the first One and Good.[32]

Why does Saint Thomas not also apply this extension to the first One and to the Good? For the reason that he had already noticed, namely, that knowing for Platonism is inferior to the incommunicable reality of the First. Analogously, if the second unities or gods or separate forms understood, they would also participate in the intelligibles, and the intelligibles would no longer be the foundation of the participation in understanding on the part of the intellects.

3. The hierarchy of souls:

> Again, because we see that certain souls possess understanding which, however, does not befit a soul by the fact that it is a soul, otherwise it would follow that every soul is an intellect and that it would be intelligent in its whole nature, he further posited that under the order of the separate intellects, there was an order of souls, the nobler of which participate in intellectual power, while the lowest of them are lacking in it.

The dignity of souls in the cosmic function is assigned to them with respect to bodies:

> Again, because bodies do not seem to be capable of moving themselves, . . . , Plato held that self-motion belongs to bodies insofar as they participate in soul, since those bodies lacking in this participation, are not moved, unless they are moved by an-

other. Whence he considered it to be an essential property of souls that they move themselves.[33]

4. The hierarchy of bodies. A novelty of this classification is the aerial bodies or ethereal bodies of demons of which Apuleius speaks. It is a question of a body internal to the soul, invisible and perpetual as the soul itself.[34] And just as among men there are the good and the bad, so too are demons divided into the good and the bad. There are thus four orders of intermediate beings between us men and the supreme God. Below the One there are the second gods, the separate intellects, the celestial souls, and the good and bad demons.

5. The derivation of beings. The immediate creation of *esse* by God and the mediate production of the sphere of the real:

> Influenced by these reasons, the Platonists held that in the case of all immaterial substances and, in general, all existing things, God is immediately the cause of being according to the aforementioned mode of production which is without change or motion. But they posited a certain order of causality in the aforementioned substances according to other participations in the divine goodness.[35]

The participations of the concrete are directly related to the subsistent universals of the respective formalities as, for example, man will participate in bipedness and animality.[36] Turning a bit further on to explain the division of spiritual substances, Saint Thomas, again citing the Platonists, mentions by name Plotinus (from Book IX of Saint Augustine's *City of God*), and he closes his exposition with a citation from the *Elements of Theology* of Proclus himself.[37]

Platonic causality is actuated as a participation that is the "presence" of the cause in the thing caused. Causality shows itself to be a defense and a recovery of the *unity* of the real insofar as the multiplicity of the effects is gathered into the unity of the cause. In turn, that cause has value—as cause—precisely insofar as it is a unifying principle in its own undivided immobile reality. In this way, causality becomes the verification and systematic foundation of the Parmenidean unity of the real. The complex causal hierarchies, which were devised by Neoplatonism and systematized by Proclus, actuate this program of unification which in Plato had remained suspended and dispersed in formal multiplicities. These latter multiplicities were set next to the One and each of them was placed one next to the other but without any clear and effective relation of dependence among them. Moreover, the relation between the ideal Platonic form and the sensible participants was a relation of "similitude," and this relation was equally affirmed for all the various relations that ran between the world of Ideas and that of reality. As a result, the abyss of separation between the intelligible world and the sensible world was left intact, and the world of ideal reality was contained in itself as an autocratic collection of pure Ideas, uncontaminated by sensible reality, which is itself subject to the vicissitudes of time according to the rhythm of generation and corruption.

Neoplatonism steadfastly maintains itself in this perspective of an "absolute realism" which makes the Good and the One to precede *esse* and places it outside

God. However, having been made more self-conscious by Aristotle's critique of *chorismos,* Neoplatonism thought to fill up the abyss of separation by the theory of the hypostases or higher unities. Consequently, while the *transcendence* of the ideal forms represents the first moment of the truth of being, the *immanence* of the same forms is the equally necessary second moment. Indeed, Platonic causality is resolved in this second moment of immanence. It is not so much a matter of explaining the "becoming" of reality—since the world itself stands before us and we ourselves are continually subject to its changes—it is, rather, a matter of individuating that which everywhere in the respective natures is always that which it is, and of discovering it in the form of an immutable presence. In this way, the reality of our experience does not properly exist in virtue of that which it is, but it exists, rather, thanks to that which it is *not.* That is to say, the real that we experience exists by means of that higher formality that maintains and penetrates everything with its power.

Saint Thomas brilliantly grasped the Neoplatonic innovation and his commentary on the *De causis* is the continuous explicit confirmation of it. The difficult point for all of this speculation lies in the divergence that remains between the formal unification of the real in itself and the concrete unity of the real of our experience. While Platonism opted for formal unity and lost real unity, Aristotelianism, on the other hand, opted for real unity but lost formal unity, or at least it reduced that formal unity to a universal in the human mind. In neither of the two do we reach the unification of the real in a supreme unity coeternal with God.[38] In this regard, the diversity of formulations that immediately leaps to the eye (both at the beginning and also in the very structure of the work of Proclus and of the *De causis*) is symptomatic.[39] With a perfect Platonic orthodoxy, the *Elements* opens with a prologue that treats of the One and of the Many (propositions 1–6), which is of course the central problem of Plato's *Parmenides.*[40] Such a prologue is missing in the *De causis,* and it would seem that nowhere in his commentary does Saint Thomas expressly follow any of these first propositions of the *Elements.* On the other hand, the *De causis* immediately begins in proposition I with the universal theory of causality which sums up the whole doctrine of the treatise and constitutes the motto that made it so famous in the Middle Ages: "Every primary cause has more influence over what it causes than does the secondary universal cause" (*Omnis causa primaria plus est influens super causatum suum quam causa universalis secunda*).[41] The universal theorem of dependence is later completed with propositions IX (VIII), XVI (XV), XVIII (XVII), XIX (XVIII), and XXII (XXI), and it is Saint Thomas himself who relates these aphorisms to one another. As to the commentary connected to the text, which seems to be by another author, possible Arab and also unknown, while it is on a noteworthy speculative level, it often leaves Thomas perplexed, and he prefers to concentrate on the text of Proclus himself.

The commentary of Saint Thomas on the *De causis* has a well-defined character. It aims to demonstrate the absolute dominion of God, the First Cause, and his unity insofar as he is the *ipsum esse subsistens,* and to do so according to the reduction of intensive *esse* proposed by Dionysius.[42] The fundamental agreement of the doctrines of the *De causis* with those of Proclus is beyond discussion, and the Dionysian turn effected by Saint Thomas in his commentary concerns his own synthesis and transcends his interpretation of the text. This comes to light right from the first proposition. Where the *De causis* says: "Omnis causa primaria plus est influens . . . quam causa universalis secunda," Saint Thomas begins his own commentary by writing simply, that is, without adding anything else: "Cause prima plus influit in effectum quam causa secunda." The subject of the *De causis,* "omnis causa primaria," evidently stands for the plural because there are many primary causes in Neoplatonism, that is, all the primary forms or unities (ἐνάδες): every head of a series in the formal order, as we have seen, can be called "causa universalis primaria."[43] However, let us now turn to Thomas' commentary on the doctrinal content of this prologue, which he divides into a corollary and a conclusion: both of these points are taken from propositions 56 and 57 of Proclus' *Elements of Theology.*

The example adduced as the first argument (*esse, vivum, homo . . .*) proceeds by reference to the formal causes, and in this consists the Neoplatonic method of establishing a direct relation between real principles and formal reasons: ". . . in quibus quanto forma est universalior, tanto prior esse videtur." However, in Thomas' interpretation of the example, the transcendental Platonic causality suddenly undergoes an explicit Aristotelian twist by means of the theory of substantial change. The principle that in formal causes: "quanto forma est universalior, tanto prior esse videtur . . ." holds for the three indicated formalities: *homo* indicates the specific form, *vivum vel animal* refers to the *forma generis,* and *esse* signifies *id quod est omnibus commune.* In the processes of generation and corruption, the more universal formality reveals itself as the more fundamental and primitive: in generation, *esse* is delineated first, then *animal,* and then *homo,* while in corruption, *homo* is lost first (that is, the use of reason!), then "vita . . . et remanet ipsum ens quod non corrumpitur."[44]

In the exposition that follows, Saint Thomas prefers Proclus to the *De causis.* For Proclus, the First Cause has greater influence because it is the cause of the very operation with which the second cause causes the effect and it is therefore of help to the second cause. For the *De causis,* however, reason, which is the second cause, is the effect of the First Cause. Indeed, the First Cause is cause of the very substance of the second cause, because the operative power itself of the second cause originates from the First Cause. Such being the case, it is not simply a matter of helping the second cause, but of establishing the very causality to be found in that cause:

> Therefore, that the second cause is the cause of an effect is something it has from the First Cause. Therefore, to be the cause of an effect belongs primarily to the First Cause, secondarily to the second cause. But what is prior among all things is more greatly [to a greater degree], since the more perfect are prior in nature. Therefore the First Cause is the cause of an effect to a greater degree than is the second cause.[45]

Since the influence of the First Cause is, first of all, the most intense, it is therefore the most profound in its efficacy and the most universal in its extension.

In the second place, the First Cause is the last to abandon the object, "tardius recedit": here the felicitous expression of the *De causis*, which speaks of a "greater vehemence"[46] of the influence of the First Cause on the effect of the second cause, holds for a while the attention of Saint Thomas.

However, the demonstration of the third point, ". . . quia prius advenit," turns immediately to the two propositions cited from Proclus and extends in an Aristotelian manner the verification of the principle to the other kinds of causality, namely, material and efficient causality. Neither Proclus nor the *De causis* had of course thought of doing this. Thomas argues this for efficient causes in the following fashion:

> For it is evident that the more an efficient cause is prior, the more does its power extend to many things. Hence its proper effect should be more common. Indeed the proper effect of the second cause is found in fewer things and hence is more particular. For the First Cause itself produces or moves the second efficient cause, and hence is a cause of its acting.[47]

In these resolute remarks is condensed the entire doctrine of transcendental causality which, in Platonism, issues from and absorbs into itself the whole cycle of causality.

Finally, the First Cause—the term itself indicates this—precedes in activity the second cause: "prius advenit . . ." No one could state more explicitly the triumph over Aristotelian immanence, which attributes to form, itself tied to matter, priority in being and activity. But in his entire commentary Saint Thomas always avoids this direct confrontation, which is still premature. He gets around the obstacle in a very skillful fashion in that the primacy which had been attributed to formal causes is now conceded to efficient causes. To justify turning things upside down Thomas does not invoke Aristotle, as we might have expected, but he again cites Proclus:

> Therefore the three above-mentioned aspects which have been touched upon [the first cause "has greater influence . . ., leaves later, arrives earlier"] are found primordially in efficient causes and from this it is clear that the derivation goes out toward formal causes. Hence the word "to influence" ["to flow into"] is used here and Proclus uses the word "production"[48] which expresses the causality of an efficient cause.[49]

This change of front is of great importance for Saint Thomas in that, if we can take our departure from efficient causes as the prime analogate (*princeps analogatum*) of causes, we can also arrive at demonstrating the creation of prime matter. This demonstration is in fact one of the principal objectives of Thomas' commentary. No one can fail to notice that the direct creation of matter by God signifies creation itself and the total dependence of all being on God. The doctrine is here introduced by the analogy of the artisan who takes hold of the matter of nature. And so God, the first and supreme artisan, must be the creator of nature itself and therefore also of matter:

> The First Cause of all things is compared to the whole of nature, just as nature is compared to art. Hence that which first subsists in all of nature is from the First Cause of all things and is particularized in each individual by the work of second causes.[50]

The final application of the proposition in its three moments holds good for the order of final causes: this too is an extension of obvious Aristotelian inspiration, but it presents us with the unexpected reduction of the final cause to the efficient cause:

> For it is for the sake of the ultimate end, which is universal, that other ends are sought, the desire for which comes after the desire of the ultimate end and which ceases before it. But the essence (*ratio*) of this order [of cause] is reduced to the genus of efficient cause, for the end is cause insofar as it moves an efficient cause to act, and thus, insofar as it has the nature of that which moves, it belongs in some way to the genus of efficient cause.[51]

It is clear that this process of reducing the second causes to the First Cause is applied within the sphere of direct *per se* subordination and it is not effected through that *per accidens* subordination that lacks all rule or restraint. And so through his radical reflection on principle taken as act, Aquinas has overcome the static and circular dialectic of the Platonic triads (ὄν, ζωή, νοῦς) in such fashion as to make *esse ipsum* emerge as the constitutive metaphysics of God and also to make participated *esse* (*actus essendi*) emerge as the act of all acts and the perfection of all perfections.

11

The Problem of the Reality and Multiplicity of Divine Ideas in Christian Neoplatonism

W. NORRIS CLARKE

My purpose in this paper is to trace a chapter in the history of ideas within the broad stream of Neoplatonism as it passes into Christian thought. The theme is one that caused special difficulties to Christian thinkers as they tried to adapt the old wine of Neoplatonic metaphysics to the new wineskins of Christian theism. My intention is not to focus in detail on just what each thinker involved held, as a matter primarily of historical scholarship. My interest will rather be focused primarily on the basic philosophical problem itself, and on tracing out the general *types* of solutions tried out by various key thinkers along the line from Plato to Saint Thomas. The problem is this: For Plato and all pre-Christian Platonists the world of ideas was "the really real"; hence, the multiplicity of the ideas and their mutual distinctions were also real, though in the mutual togetherness proper to all spiritual reality. Such multiplicity, however, was not admitted into the highest Principle, the supreme One, who by nature had to be absolutely simple to be absolutely one. But the Christian God, as personally knowing and loving all creatures and exercising providence over every individual, had to contain this world of archetypal ideas within his own mind, in the Logos. Yet the real being of God was also held to be infinite and simple; the only real multiplicity allowed within it was that of the relational distinction of the three Persons: Father, Son, and Holy Spirit. How would it be possible to put all these doctrines together without internal contradiction in a consistent doctrine of God? The story of the various efforts to meet the problem is a fascinating and illuminating study in the history of ideas. Let us retrace the principle moments in it.

PLATO

For Plato himself it is clear that the world of ideas possesses a strong dose of reality. The breakthrough to discover the abiding presence of this transcendent dimension of reality, for the first time in the history of Western thought, must have been a powerful, almost intoxicating, experience for him, as though a veil had been pulled aside to reveal at last the splendor of the truly real, in comparison with which our changing world of sensible objects was only a shadowlike imperfect image. No modern neo-Kantian or analytic philosophy reinterpretation of the theory of ideas as merely conceptual or linguistic categories should be allowed to vitiate the strength of Plato's ontological commitment to the objective reality of ideas, however this be finally interpreted.[1] But when we come to the relation between the world of ideas and the mind as knowing them, clouds of ambiguity begin to thicken. *Where* are the ideas? What is their ontological "location" or ground? Do they constitute an independent dimension of reality on their own, whose autonomous light is then passively received by any mind knowing them? Or do they reside in some ultimate mind that supports them by always thinking about them?

With respect to the human mind it is clear that the world of ideas constitutes a realm that is ontologically quite independent of our minds. We do not just make them up; our knowledge is true because they are there. The matter is more obscure when we come to the demiurge of the *Timaeus*. No direct statement is made; but the images used suggest that the demiurge, in order to create an ordered cosmos, contemplates and copies an objective world of ideas that is already given even for him; it is the natural object of his contemplation, as it is for all the gods and unfallen souls who drive their chariots across the eternal heaven of ideas, but it is not something they think up or produce out of their own substance but which they gaze on as already given. Contemplation, the highest act of any Platonic mind, is a motionless reception, not a productive act.[2]

This leaves the ultimate status and ground of the world of ideas veiled in obscurity for Plato. The sparsely adumbrated doctrine of the One and the Good as the ultimate source for both ideas and minds does significantly complete the picture. But it is never made clear whether the Good is a mind or something above it, whatever that might mean. There are indeed highly significant hints in the *Timaeus* and the *Sophist* that the whole world of ideas is part of a single great living unity. But the generation of the world of ideas by the Good, even if conceived as ultimate mind, which Plato never calls it, is quite compatible with the objective reality and the multiplicity of this world as the really real. In any case, the ultimate relation between the world of ideas and mind remains unfinished business in Plato, a legacy for his successors to unravel.

PLOTINUS

When we come to Plotinus—I will pass over the intermediate preparatory stages of Middle Platonism—a major resolution of the problem has been achieved, but with serious internal tensions still remaining. On the one hand, the ideas are now firmly located ontologically within the divine *Nous*; they no longer float in ambiguous ontological independence, but are eternally thought by this eternal mind as its connatural object. As a result the ideas themselves, though immutable, immaterial, and eternal, are alive with the very life of the divine Mind itself, each one a unique, self-thinking, spiritual perspective on the whole of reality.

On the other hand, there still remains a strong dose of the old Platonic realism of ideas, and this creates a tension between two somewhat conflicting perspectives on the status of the ideas in Plotinus—a tension that it does not seem to me that he completely resolves. This tension concerns the relation of priority between the *Nous* and the ideas: Is the *Nous* absolutely prior in nature (not, of course, in time) to the ideas, the realm of authentic being, as generative act to its product? Or do the ideas have a certain priority over the *Nous* as the true existence over the act that contemplates it? Or is there simultaneous reciprocal dependence, inherence, or even identity without any priority at all?

We would be tempted at first, viewing the problem from within the central dynamic perspective of the descending flow of emanation from the One, to assert that obviously the *Nous* (or Intellectual Principle) has priority over the realm of being or ideas, as their generating source. As the *Nous,* emanating from the One, turns back toward the One in its first ontological "moment," as an empty and formless ocean of potentiality, it is fecundated, so to speak, by its contemplation of the splendor of the One and bursts forth into producing the whole multiple world of ideas in atemporal ordered sequence (corresponding to the inner order of the intelligible numbers, one, two, . . .).[3] This dynamic perspective is certainly present in Plotinus, but surfaces only occasionally and briefly. I might add, speaking in my own name as philosopher, that in this direction lies, it seems to me, the only satisfactory metaphysical explanation of the relation between mind and ideas: the absolute priority of mind, as ultimate spiritual agent, over all ideas; existential act must always precede idea. This perspective gradually became dominant in Neoplatonism, both Christian and Islamic, after Plotinus, and in most modern thought. But it is still a minor chord in Plotinus himself.

There is another and more prominent perspective in Plotinus, however, which runs through the whole gamut of his works, both early and late; here the old Platonic priority of being over intelligence still stubbornly holds on and is never explicitly negated by Plotinus. This can be found especially in *Ennead* V, 9, "The Intellectual Principle, the Ideas, and the Authentic Existent," a very early treatise (no. 5) in chronological order. The first point developed here is that the ideas cannot be outside the Intellectual Principle, otherwise its truth would be insecure and its knowledge imperfect. The ideas must thus be part of the very self of the *Nous,* identical with its being as a single unitary life flowing through all the distinct parts. But Plotinus goes on to say more, giving a certain priority to the ideas over the *Nous* as thinking principle, so that they seem to constitute the very life of the *Nous* itself.

> Being true knowledge, it actually is everything of which it takes cognizance; it carries as its own content the intellectual act and the intellectual object since it carries the Intellectual Principle which actually is the Primals and is always self-present and is in its nature an Act . . . but always self-gathered, the very Being of the collective total, not an extern creating things by the act of knowing them. Not by its thinking God does God come to be; not by its thinking Movement does movement arise. Hence it is an error to call the Ideas intellections in the sense that, upon an intellectual act in this Principle, one such idea or another is made to exist or exists. No: the object of this intellection must exist before the intellective act (must be the very content not the creation of the Intellectual Principle). How else could this Principle come to know it. . . .
>
> If the Intellectual Principle were envisaged as preceding Being, it would at once become a Principle whose expression, its intellectual Act, achieves and engenders the Beings; but, since we are compelled to think of existence as preceding that which knows it, we can but think that the Beings are the actual content of the knowing principle and that the very act, the intellection, is inherent to the Beings, as fire stands equipped from the beginning with fire-act; in this conception the Beings contain the Intellectual Principle as one and the same with themselves, as their own activity. But Being is itself an activity; there is one activity, then, in both or, rather, both are one thing.[4]

The above presents a significantly different perspective: here the inner being and act of the ideas seems to constitute the very act of the *Nous* itself, rather than the *Nous* giving them its own being by actively thinking them up. The older Platonic conception of mind, here faithfully reproduced, seems to be that mind as such, even the divine Mind, is by nature contemplative, not constitutive, of its object. This position, however, leaves open the difficulty we saw earlier in Plato, that is, what is the ultimate ground for the unified multiplicity of the world of ideas? It seems to be an exigency for intelligibility that only the active power of a unitary mind can ground both the multiple reality of the ideas and their mutual correlation into a single unified system. That is why the later more dynamic perspective in Plotinus, that of the *Nous* as generative of the world of ideas, is more metaphysically satisfying, and is the one that actually dominated in the subsequent history of Neoplatonism.

Even though priority is occasionally given to *Nous* over the ideas, the strong realism of the ideas still remains undimmed in Plotinus. And it is this that forbids allowing the world of ideas to be in the One. Since the ideas are really real, true being, and really multiple or distinct, and the One as pure unity cannot tolerate the slightest shadow of multiplicity within itself, even that between mind and idea, the entire world of ideas or true being must be relegated to a lower level of divinity, the second hypostasis or *Nous*.[5]

THE EARLY CHRISTIAN FATHERS

When the first philosophically minded and trained Christian thinkers took over the Neoplatonic philosophical framework to use in the intellectual explication of their faith, during the third and fourth centuries, they had to make two drastic changes in the matter which concerns us. First, the subordinationist hierarchy of divine hypostases in Plotinus had to be condensed into a single supreme divine principle, in which the three Persons within the divine nature were perfectly coequal in perfection of being, distinguished only by internal relations of origin, not by differing levels of perfection. Thus the Word or Logos, the Second Person, corresponding analogously to Plotinus' *Nous,* was declared perfectly coequal with the Father (corresponding analogously to Plotinus' One) sharing the identical divine nature and perfection. Secondly, the single supreme God of the Christians was identically creator of the universe through knowledge and free act of love, and exercised personal providence over each and every individual creature. This required that the one divine Mind, the same for all three Persons but attributed by special aptness to the Word or Logos, contain the distinct knowledge of every creature as well as the universal archetypal ideal patterns guiding the creation of the world according to reason. The old Platonic and Neoplatonic world of ideas, enriched with the distinct knowledge of individuals, is now incorporated directly into the one supreme divine nature itself. Christian thinkers simply had to do this to do justice to their own revelation, and they had no hesitation, but rather took pride, in doing so.

The metaphysical repercussions, however, of making the above changes in Neoplatonic tradition were of seismic proportions, and did not seem to be recognized very clearly for some time in their full philosophical implications. Two basic Neoplatonic axioms have now been violated. First, knowing a distinct multiplicity of objects, even only as ideas, is no longer considered an inferior mode of being, weakening and compromising the radical purity of unqualified unity and simplicity in the One. To know multiplicity is no longer a weakness, but a positive perfection, part of the glory, of a One that is *personal.* To *know* multiplicity is not to *become* multiple oneself. Secondly, purely relational multiplicity even within the real being or nature of the One is no longer a compromise or destruction of its unity, but an enrichment. The highest form of unity is now not aloneness but communion of Persons with one mind and will. We are not concerned here with this second principle, relational multiplicity within the nature of the One. Our concern is limited to the status of the world of ideas within the divine Mind.

It was one thing for Christian thinkers to *assert* that the world of ideas must be within the divine Mind as Logos, in order that God may personally know and love his creatures. But it is another thing to come to grips successfully with the metaphysical problems involved in thus adapting the Neoplatonic doctrine of the world of ideas. In particular, what about the strong realism of ideas as true being, the really real, which was so deeply ingrained in the whole Platonic tradition, no less, in fact even more, in Plotinus than in Plato himself? If the ideas remain, as always in this tradition, true and real being, they must also be really multiple. Does this not introduce an immense multiplicity of real beings, an immense real pluralism, within the very being of God himself, thus negating his infinite simplicity? In orthodox Christian doctrine, as it was gradually worked out, the only distinct realities allowed in God were relations, and the only real relations allowed were relations of origin resulting in the three Persons. But if all the divine ideas are also authentic, hence, real being, and at the same time distinct from each other in the intelligible (real) order, then there is not only a multiplicity of distinct real beings within God himself but a still greater multiplicity of real relations between them. For the relations between ideas are clearly distinctly intelligible, and for every traditional Platonist whatever is intelligible is also real.[6]

It is not clear to me that the Greek Fathers ever came to grips explicitly with this metaphysical problem of the reality of the divine ideas in God, aside from asserting that God knew them all with a single act of knowledge, which Plotinus would also admit. (I would be very happy to receive any information from my colleagues on this point, since patristics is not my field and I have not had the time in preparing this paper to do extensive study on this point.) My general impression is that we will have to wait till a later period to find explicit metaphysical discussion on this point.

Let us turn briefly to Saint Augustine in the West, as a prime example, it seems to me, of avoiding the issue. He holds simultaneously two metaphysical doctrines that I do not see that he has brought together in a consistent whole. On the one hand, one of his central doctrines, learned, as he tells us, from the Platonists, is that of divine exemplarism, namely, that the divine Mind contains the ideal exemplars, the *rationes aeternae,* of all created things, according to which he creates them by willing them to be, to be *expressed,* outside of himself as real creatures, as real *essentiae.*[7] It should be noted along the way that Augustine is careful not to call the divine ideas *essentiae aeternae,* the eternal essences of things, but only *rationes aeternae*—eternal "reasons" or exemplary ideas, models. Since the concrete term *ens, entia* did not yet exist in Latin in Augustine's time—it was introduced deliberately by Boethius centuries later—*essentia* was the standard noun derivative from the verb *esse* used in Augustine's time for referring to existential being.[8] Hence, on the one hand, one might be led to believe that these *rationes aeternae* were not considered by Augustine to be a realm of true being, in God, since the entire universe of real being was created in time freely, not from all eternity, as these *rationes* necessarily existed in the mind of God.

On the other hand, when Augustine comes to an explicit discussion and definition of what it means to be—to be a being—his criterion of true being is quite unambiguously the old Platonic one of immutability; to *be* is to be *immutable,* to be identically and immutably *what* one is. His texts could hardly be more forceful:

There is only one immutable substance or essence, which is God, to which being itself (*ipsum esse*), from which essence draws its name, belongs supremely and in all truth. For that which changes does not keep its very being, and that which is capable of changing, even if it does not change, is capable of not being what it was. There only remains, therefore, that which not only does not change but is even absolutely incapable of changing which we can truthfully and honestly speak of as a being.[9]

Being (*esse*) is the name for immutability (*incommutabilitatis*). For all that changes ceases to be what it was and begins to be what it was not. True being, authentic being, genuine being is not possessed save by that which does not change.[10]

Being (*esse*) refers to that which abides. Hence that which is said to be in the supreme and maximal way is so called because of its perdurance in itself.[11]

All change makes not to be what once was; therefore he truly is who is without change.[12]

The difficulty here for a Christian thinker is that this criterion for true being is verified perfectly by the divine ideas, as well as by God himself in his own being. The ideas in God are indeed eternal and immutable, as the ideal patterns for all creatures and the ground for all truth, which by its nature must be immutable. Since they perfectly verify the criterion, they should indeed be true being, real being for Augustine, just as they were for Plato and Plotinus, from whom the doctrine of divine ideas was directly inherited. Yet strangely enough, Augustine never quite seems to draw this conclusion and speak explicitly of the divine ideas as real being in themselves. He just seems to drop the point, to pull back into discreet silence just before he gets into metaphysical trouble. It is, however, common Augustinian doctrine that things are present more truly and nobly in the divine ideas of them than in their mutable, imperfect, created existence. Perhaps he did not see clearly the difficulty of the ideas as real multiplicity in God, as did Plotinus; or perhaps he did see it, but did not know quite what to do with it, and just quietly let it drop. At any rate, he gives us no clear philosophical principles by which to solve it.[13]

JOHN SCOTTUS ERIUGENA

Let us now skip to a later Christian Neoplatonist, the early medieval thinker John Scottus Eriugena, whose thought has the advantage for our purposes of bringing together both the Augustinian and the Dionysian traditions. Its special interest lies in that the problems that remained latent and untreated by Saint Augustine now come out into the open with striking sharpness in this daring but by no means always consistent thinker.

The point that concerns us is the ontological status of the second division of nature in the vast cosmic schema of John Scottus' *De Divisione Naturae,* namely, *natura creata et creans.* This comprises the divine exemplary ideas or, as he calls them, the "primordial causes," which are the "first creation" of God, coeternal with the divine Word, but always dependent on the Word, in whom they subsist.

They are created but also creating in their turn, charged with the power to unfold and produce the whole material cosmos spread out in space and time.[14]

The first point to notice is the strong Platonic realism of this realm of creative ideas. This is the realm of true being below God (who, for John Scottus, is the superessential Source above being itself).[15] It is in this ideal realm that all creatures, especially the sensible world of creation, have their true being, perfect and immutable; they are more real, they more truly exist, in these eternal idea-causes than in themselves as the explicated effects or emanations of these causes, for the latter are not merely abstract ideas or static models but causal forces charged with creative power of their own, though deriving, of course, from their higher Principle. Thus each one of us exists more truly in the eternal idea of man than in our own temporally spread out existence in this lower material world. We have here one of the strongest statements of what is to be a favorite theme of Christian Neoplatonists all through the Middle Ages, at least in the pre-Scholastic period.[16]

The realism of these primordial causes is also borne out by the assertion that they have been "made," "formed," "created" by God as the first level of creation—a stronger term than any previous Christian thinker had used to refer to the divine ideas, though, to do him justice, he sometimes warns that "created" here is not used in as strong and proper a meaning as its ordinary sense as applied to the second creation, that of the present contingent world. These primordial causes are produced *by* the Father *in* the Word from all eternity, in whom they subsist; yet as made (produced) they deserve to be called created. But what is created by God and which, itself, has causal power must certainly be real, and because immutable, also eternal, and spiritual, that is, authentic being, of which the changing world of bodies is but a shadowy image or participation. No statements of Augustine about the being of this realm of divine ideas are nearly as strong and clear as those found in John Scottus. It looks as though the Neoplatonic world of true being in the *Nous* has reappeared with new vigor and splendor.

It is a little surprising, therefore, to discover that, when Eriugena comes to speak of the mode of being of these primordial causes in the Word, with respect to their real multiplicity and distinction, he asserts in the strongest possible terms that in the divine Word they are absolutely "simple, one, unseparated," perfectly identical with the Word's own being, and "indistinguishable, without differentiae," until they unfold in their actual effects in the space-time sensible world.[17] To illustrate how they subsist in simply unity in the Word, he uses the example of how all numbers are present in the monad before division and how all lines are present in the point that is the center of a circle, with no distinction until they begin to unfold from the center.

Here I have the impression that Eriugena is being a better Christian than a Neoplatonist. I do not see how he can consistently hold both the real being and plurality of the primordial causes and also their perfect simplicity, unity, and identity with the Word as subsisting in it. Plotinus in fact holds the exact opposite, and would object as follows: The way that all numbers are in the number one and all lines in the point at the center of the circle is indeed the way that all things are precontained in the highest principle, the One, who is "the potentiality of all things" (*dynamis pantōn*) without being any of them. But this is not the way the ideas, the realm of true being, are in the second hypostasis, the *Nous*. There they are indeed held together in the unity of a single undivided spiritual life of intelligence; but this unity is a complex unity, not a simple one; it includes all the distinct intelligibilities of each Idea-Being as intelligibly distinct (though not separated or divided), as well as the distinction between the *Nous* as subject and the realm of being as intelligible object. It is precisely because of this multiplicity that the world of ideas can have no place in the perfect, simple unity of the One, but only in a lower, less unified hypostasis.[18]

But there seems to be no trace in Eriugena of these reservations about the perfect unity and simplicity of the primordial causes in the Word. It is not clear how he can have it both ways, though if he is to remain both a good Christian and a good Neoplatonist he must try. Here we have the latent tension between the conflicting demands of the two traditions coming sharply to a head, since Eriugena pushes each one all the way to the limit. It is a remarkable case of the coincidence of opposites. If one looks at this apparent impasse as a speculative philosopher, there seems to be only one possible way in which one could hold onto both sides of the opposition without contradiction, although this "solution" brings its own new train of problems with it. Suppose that one were to hold that true being, the very being of the primordial causes, is *nothing else but* their being thought by God. Their truth is identical with their being. In this case since the *act* of knowing or thinking them is one single simple act, and they have *no other being* save their being thought, it could be said that their being, as identical with the act of thinking in the Word and never really emanating out from it to possess their own distinct being—until, of course, they are unfolded in the material cosmos—is really one single simple being identical with the Word.

In fact, it seems that this is precisely what Eriugena himself has followed, at least in certain of his strong formulations, such as:

> For the understanding of all things in God is the essence of all things . . . all things are precisely because they are foreknown. For the essence of all things is nothing but the knowledge of all things in the Divine Wisdom. For in Him we live and move and have our being. For, as St. Dionysius says, the knowledge of the things that are is the things that are.[19]

> For the understanding of things is what things really are, in the words of St. Dionysius: "The knowledge of things that are is the things that are."[20]

It is true that Eriugena does qualify this identity here and elsewhere by calling the divine knowledge the cause of the things that are, so that cause and effect would seem to be distinguished. But if this distinction is pushed too far, hardened into the strong Aristotelian real distinction between cause and effect—and I think this is also true in its own mitigated way in Neoplatonism—then his position on the unity, simplicity, and identity of the primordial causes in the Word will collapse. Only in the relation between thought and its self-generated ideas can there be a real identity of being between cause and effect, *granted* that the ideas have no being of their own.

I have two remarks to make about this doctrine of the identity of thought and being in Eriugena. First, if this is the case, it is now easy to understand how all creatures can be more truly in God, that is, in his knowledge, than in themselves, since it is this knowledge that in fact constitutes their true and perfect being. Another daring doctrine of Eriugena also becomes clear: in a sense, man himself is the creator of the material world, because he holds it together in unity in his own mind, as participating in the divine wisdom, and the material world exists more truly and perfectly even in man's mind than in itself. Again true being is identical with being known. We are here on the edge, if not over the edge, of something like the Hegelian mode of idealism, as has often been pointed out. We will consider the philosophical difficulties of this position later.

Secondly, it seems to me that here Eriugena has gone farther than Plotinus and classic Neoplatonism itself, and in a sense dramatically reversed the old Platonic realism, which on the other hand he seems to be strongly asserting and certainly wishes to assert. For in the Plotinian *Nous,* or world of true being, as we have seen, even though the ideas are held together in the unity of a single unified spiritual life, the act of divine intelligence, still this life, this unity of the world of being and knowing, is a multiplex unity, an intelligible (hence, real) diversity in unity and unity in diversity. The ideas truly emanate from the *Nous,* while remaining within it, to the extent that they are distinguished as subject and object; also the ideas truly have being within them, so much so that it is almost equally legitimate to say that the *Nous* itself is constituted in being by its union with the ideas as to say that the ideas are constituted in being by the *Nous*—there is a kind of reciprocal priority between them; a strong dosage of the old Platonic realism of ideas as in themselves true being still remains. Nothing like this can be found in Eriugena. In no way can it be said that the Word for him is constituted by the ideas it eternally thinks. The relation of dependence is strictly one-way, asymmetrical. His solution is Christian; can it still be called authentically Neoplatonic? I doubt it.

Let us now turn briefly to some of the purely metaphysical difficulties inherent in the Neoplatonic side of Eriugena's doctrine of the divine ideas as true being, with the result that we, like all creatures, exist more truly in our primordial idea-causes in God than in our own "explicated" temporal existence in ourselves—the third division of nature, that which is created but does not create. If this position is taken literally and in full seriousness, then the problem arises, What is the point of this unfolding of our true being, already present from all eternity in God, into our present lesser mode of existence? What is the point of our existential struggle for salvation in human history in a lesser mode of being when we are already perfect in our truest being in God? The whole value of human history, including that of the Incarnation and temporal life of Christ himself, seems to become so secondary and "accidental," as he puts it, that it becomes disturbingly ambiguous, if not tinged with unreality. His only answer seems to be the classic Neoplatonic one, a purely impersonal kind of metaphysical law of emanation—that the emanation must go on to its furthest multiplicity, that the Craftsman of the universe would not have shown forth the fullness of his power unless he had made all that could be made and unfolded all the oppositions between creatures and not just their harmonies. It should be remembered that in the second division of nature, the primordial causes, there are no oppositions or *differentiae* between the various genera and species; all is perfect togetherness.

This is a typical Neoplatonic theme or axiom of emanation, that the great chain of being must unfold all the way to the limit of its possibilities, by an inherent necessity of the self-diffusiveness of the Good. But such a view of the value and meaning of the contingent world as only an inferior ontological state of the *same* world at a higher level is hardly compatible with the inspiration of Christian personalism, where the supreme locus of value is the existential dimension of freely given personal love, moral nobility, and so on. The subject of the salvific redemption of Christ and the final beatific vision in the heavenly Jerusalem is not the eternally perfect, immutable idea of man, but the unique contingent individual John Smith who has worked out his salvation freely with the help of God on the stage of human history. In a word, there is a profound metaphysical, epistemological, and religious ambiguity in the Neoplatonic conception of the relation of the ideas to true being, not indeed in the presence of exemplary ideas of all things in God, but in their ontological evaluation, namely, that the true being of anything is found more fully, as true being, in its idea state in the mind of God than in itself. The classic Neoplatonic worldview of reality is not ultimately a personalism. The tension, if not contradiction, between this metaphysical view of reality and that implicit in any authentic Christian personalism seems to me to be profound and irreconcilable; it remains one of the central unsolved problems haunting Christian Neoplatonists—also, I might add, Islamic and Sufi Neoplatonists—throughout the pre-Scholastic Middle Ages. To sum it up, as this problem surfaces in John Scottus Eriugena, I do not think he can hold, if he is to be a consistent and authentically Christian thinker, *both* that the primordial causes are absolutely simple and one in the Word, which a Christian must hold, *and* that the true being of all creatures resides in these divine ideas, rather than in their own contingent being in history, which a traditional Neoplatonist should hold. One of these two positions will have to give way if a consistent Christian metaphysics is to develop. But for this we have to look beyond the daring and seminal, but not always consistent, brilliance of John Scottus Eriugena.

In thus casting doubts on the metaphysical consistency and Christian assimilability of the cherished Neoplatonic theme that our true being is found in, consists in, the eternal idea of ourselves in the mind of God, I do not wish to deny the power and fruitfulness of the theme as it functioned—understood somewhat loosely, without pressing its metaphysical implications too rigorously—as a guide for spiritual development in the rich flowering of Christian spirituality during the Middle Ages. The operative concept here is that we understand our true self and come to realize it by turning toward and striving to fulfill the ideal model or exemplar of our fulfilled selves that God holds eternally to his mind and draws us toward by the magnetism of his goodness. Our true selves are indeed *seen* in God's ideas of us, and this vision is pregnant with the magnetic drawing power of the Good. But this does not require the further metaphysical commitment that our true being, our true selves, literally *is,* consists in, the divine idea of us. But it took a long time for these underlying metaphysical issues to be worked out explicitly in medieval Christian thought.

THE SCHOOL OF CHARTRES

Let us now move several centuries down the line and take a brief look at another Christian Neoplatonist treatment of the same problem. This is the famous School of Chartres, known for its exaggerated Platonic realism of ideas.[21] Its main themes are really a revival of John Scottus Eriugena with some original variations. The themes we are interested in are the realism of the divine ideas and their ontological status in the mind of God. Again we find almost the identical position of Eriugena. The true being of creatures is found in the divine ideas, which Thierry of Chartres, perhaps the most daring of the school, calls *formae nativae.* These are found in their pure state in the mind of God, and become imprisoned and diminished by union with matter. As Clarembald of Arras tells us, the true being of anything comes from its form: *omne esse ex forma est . . . quoniam forma perfectio rei et integritas est.*[22] But all these forms as in God become a single simple form; God is the *forma essendi* of all forms and through them of all things.[23] But as they exist in God these exemplary forms are not yet explicated or unfolded as they are in the created world. Just as all numbers are already precontained in the simple unity of the monad or number one, so all forms are *complicatae* (enfolded as the opposite of unfolded) in the unity of one form in God. As Thierry puts it in a striking image, in God all forms fall back into the one: "The forms of all things, considered in the divine mind, are in a certain way one form, collapsed in some inexplicable way into the simplicity of the divine form."[24] And thus "every form without matter is God himself."[25]

Clarembald of Arras explains further how the many forms are enfolded without real plurality in the one:

> Every multitude lies hidden in the simplicity of unity, and when in the serial process of numeration a second is numbered after the one and a third after the second, then finally a certain form of plurality flowing from unity is recognized, and so without otherness there can be no plurality.[26]

Here again, it seems to me, we run into the same unresolved tension as we found in Eriugena. It is indeed an authentically Christian metaphysical doctrine that all ideas are identical in being with the one perfectly simple being of the divine Mind. But I submit that this is not an authentically Neoplatonic doctrine; the ideas in the divine *Nous* for all classic Neoplatonists are already unfolded in their distinct intelligible multiplicity and hence in their plurality of being, thus forming the system of true being as integrated plurality—a plurality, however, without spatial or temporal separation, held together in the unity-multiplicity whole of a single spiritual life. (It is indeed true—this was objected to me in the discussion of the paper—that the ideas, like all things, are in a sense in the One, as the "power of all things" [*dynamis pantōn*]. But this is in a mode of supereminent simplicity, as in the power of the cause from which all else emanates, not in the mode of distinct intelligibility or of true being as in the *Nous*. The realm of being is below the pure unity of the One.) And if the thinkers of the school of Chartres insist that these divine ideas or native forms, though simple and one in God, are nonetheless the true being of all things, then we have a metaphysical impasse. *Either* this is a metaphysical contradiction or incoherence, *or* true being is nothing but its being thought, has no being of its own but only that of the act that thinks it. This seems to me the conversion of the Neoplatonic realism into a latent idealism that is quite foreign to the original inspiration of the doctrine, and, I believe, to the explicit intentions of the Christian Neoplatonist thinkers themselves. Which side of the dilemma did they actually opt for? I have the impression that they were just not that clearly aware of the metaphysical implications of their thought and made no clear option, but remained oscillating ambiguously somewhere in the middle, unwilling to give up either end of the opposition.

But to be fair to them, the blame is not entirely theirs. They are trying to cope with the rich but enigmatic heritage of the Pseudo-Dionysius, who in his turn has tried to impose a new dialectic of the unmanifest-manifest divinity on the old Neoplatonic doctrine of the emanation of the world of ideas and the *Nous* from the One, but without making it that clear that some significantly new metaphysical laws have been introduced. Although something similar to the unmanifest-manifest dialectic can certainly be found in classical Neoplatonism, still the particular way in which Pseudo-Dionysius interprets it to hold onto the ontological simplicity of God—in terms of the divine "energies" which are both divine, God as *manifested,* and yet somehow multiple—seems to me to have a strong dose of oriental as well as Neoplatonic roots, unless one considers it an original creative Christian adaptation of Neoplatonism. I cannot go into this complicated but intriguing problem here. The Dionysian doctrine has remarkable affinities with the Hindu notion of the *shakti,* or divine power, of the "manifest" Brahman at work in the world. It was given central prominence later in the Eastern Orthodox theology of Gregory Palamas, but was rejected by Western Scholastic theologians. Like the doctrine of multiple divine ideas, it is filled with metaphysical tensions of its own.

THIRTEENTH-CENTURY SCHOLASTICISM

We now come to a decisive new chapter in the history of our problem, one that finally provides a coherent metaphysical resolution to the almost 1000 years of tension within Christian Neoplatonism. This solution emerges gradually during the twelfth century, due to the struggle over the reality of universals, and finally comes to a head in thirteenth-century Scholasticism. Here the technical precision demanded of professors trained in Aristotelian logic and functioning in a professional academic community could no longer be satisfied with inspiring but metaphysically fuzzy pantheistic-*sounding* formulas that at the same time repudiated pantheism, or with the simple assertion of unexplicated paradoxes held together by metaphors such as "all forms fall back into the simplicity of the one divine form." The crucial decision is finally made: the Platonic realism of ideas must once and for all be given up.

There seems to have been a fairly wide consensus on this point, though, as we shall see, not universal. It was not only the Aristotelian current of Albert and Thomas Aquinas that sponsored it: leading Augustinians such as Saint Bonaventure also agreed. In fact the latter provides us with an admirably succinct summary of the basic position:

> God knows things through their eternal "reasons" (*rationes aeternae*). . . . But these eternal intelligibilities are not the true essences and quiddities of things, since they are not other than the Creator, whereas creature and Creator necessarily have different essences. And therefore it is necessary that they be exemplary forms and hence *similitudines representativae* of things themselves. Consequently these are intelligibilities whereby things that are are made known (*rationes cognoscendi*), because knowledge, precisely as knowledge, signifies assimilation and expression between knower and known. And therefore we must assert, as the holy doctors say and reason shows, that God knows things through their similitudes.[27]

The die is cast. The divine ideas are no longer the very forms, the true being, of creatures, but their intentional similitudes, whose only being is that of the one divine act of knowing. (It is quite true—as was objected in the discussion—that the divine ideas in Bonaventure seem to have a greater ontological density and dynamism than in Saint Thomas. But this remains the *creative* dynamism of the Word itself and is not the true being of creatures as for John Scottus. The very next question after the above quotation, whether there is any real multiplicity in the divine ideas, makes this clear beyond the shadow of a doubt. Hence, the suggestion made that he qualifies his position in the next paragraph is entirely without textual foundation.) But the firmest and clearest grounding for this common position is provided by Thomas Aquinas, with his new metaphysics of the composition of essence and act of existence (*esse*) in creatures and the location of the real perfection of beings no longer on the side of form but on the act of existence of which form is limiting principle.[28] Thus creatures have no true being until God as creative cause gives them their own intrinsic act of existence, which is not their intelligible essence but a distinct act by which form itself comes to be as a determinant structure of a real being. As creatures are precontained in the divine ideas, they simply do not yet have this act of their own intrinsic *esse*, hence are not yet properly beings at all, let alone the really real. Their "subjective" being is identified entirely with the being of the simple act of divine intelligence which "thinks them up" (*adinvenire* is the word Saint Thomas carefully picks out, which means to invent or think up, not discover, which would be *invenire*) as possible limited modes of participation in his own infinite act of *esse subsistens*.[29] Thus their entire being *is* their *being-thought-about* by God, in a single simple act without any plurality of real being, though there is a clear plurality and distinction on the level of the objective intelligible content thought about by this one act. In a word, in the new technical terminology, the divine ideas are now only the "signifying signs of things" (*intentiones rerum*), not things themselves; their being is *esse intentionale* not *esse naturale* or *reale.*[30] This crucial distinction between *esse intentionale* and *esse naturale,* in terms of which alone the doctrine makes sense, is the one piece that has been conspicuously missing from the entire Platonic tradition, and for good reasons. To have admitted it would have blown up classical Platonism from within, or at least forced such a profound adaptation as to involve almost a change of essence. The term itself is an inheritance neither of the Platonic nor even the Aristotelian tradition, but from Arabic sources.

This single stroke of distinguishing the subjective being of ideas, which is nothing but the act of the mind that thinks them, from their objective content, their intentional meaning and reference which can be multiple and distinct, opened the way at last to a metaphysically coherent assimilation of the whole Eriugenian doctrine of the presence of the divine ideas in the Word in a single, simple act prior to any plurality. The latter was indeed a brilliant insight of Christian Neoplatonism, but one that could not make sense unless the doctrine that accompanied it in Eriugena—that of the ideas as true being in themselves—was jettisoned. The divorce was painful, but inevitable. But this move also entailed the dropping of another cherished theme of classical Neoplatonism, namely, that the passage from the divine ideas, or realm of true being, to their unfolded exemplifications in the contingent world of matter is a passage to a lower mode of being, a degradation or diminution in being. Creation now becomes, on the contrary, a positive expansion from the merely mental being of the world of divine ideas to a new dimension of true being "outside" the divine Mind (*extra causas*), as an enrichment of the universe through a gracious free sharing of its own real perfection; for this real perfection is always in the line of actual *esse,* and this was not yet accomplished in the realm of the divine ideas by themselves.

The same move also forced, if not the total giving up, at least the drastic toning down and reinterpretation of another closely linked theme long cherished by Christian Neoplatonists in the pre-Scholastic period following the lead of Augustine himself.[31] This is the notion that all creatures exist in a higher, more perfect state in the exemplary idea of each of them in the mind of God than in their own created being—especially so, but not exclusively, in the case of material beings. This theme still keeps recurring in the spiritual writings of Christian Neoplatonists, used as a potent motivation and intellectual model for spiritual growth.[32] But its literal metaphysical force is now toned down.

Clearly Thomas Aquinas cannot hold this as a metaphysical doctrine—and not even Bonaventure, if he is to remain consistent with his text quoted above. For if, as I am present in the mind of God, I do not yet possess any slightest trace of my own intrinsic act of *esse,* in proportion to which alone is measured all my real participation in the perfection of God, then it cannot be literally asserted that I *exist,* have my true being, in a higher and more perfect state in God's idea of me than in my own contingent created existence in myself. It is true that my *intelligibility,* the *intelligible content* of the divine idea of me, exists in a higher, more perfect way in God than in me; but this is still not my true being, my *esse.*

Thomas is quite aware that he is laying aside a long and venerable Augustinian tradition. But as is his wont in so doing, he never directly contradicts it, but reinterprets it to draw the most he can out of it without compromising his own metaphysical integrity.[33] Thus in the present case he is quite willing to admit that there is a certain fulfillment for a material being to exist, as known, in a spiritual intelligence, *a fortiori* in God's, since in being thus known the material mode of existence is transposed into a spiritual one, that of intentional existence, which is identical with the spiritual act of the mind knowing it. But this fulfillment can exist only if the material being already exists in its own material being and is *also* known in a spiritual mode. The real being of the material thing does not *consist* in its being known and the latter state cannot be substituted for the former with the full value retained. It does remain true, however, that the perfection of our real being is *represented*, held before us by the divine idea as an ideal goal, a final cause, drawing towards its actual *real*ization through the drawing power of the Good reflected in it. It functions thus as a powerful *motivation* for spiritual growth toward the fulfillment of our true being to-be-realized; but it is not this true being already existing in the mind of God. For if the latter were literally the case, why bother with working out on an inferior level the same perfection already given on a higher level? This was the enigma haunting, as we saw, Eriugena's emanation from the second to the third division of nature—a problem to which he gave no recognizably Christian solution.

All did not agree, however, with this deontologizing of the divine ideas. Henry of Ghent, teaching in Paris at the end of the thirteenth century, and drawing his inspiration both from Avicenna and Neoplatonism, complains that the more "current theological opinion" has gone too far in rejecting the doctrine of Eriugena and reducing the divine ideas to nothing but understood "modes of imitability of the divine essence (*rationes imitabilitatis*)." To this he opposes "the position excellently expressed by Avicenna in his *Metaphysics,* according to which the ideas signify the very essences of things."[34] Expounding this position elsewhere he distinguished between two aspects of the ideas: (1) "the essences of things in the divine knowledge as objects known . . . which are really other (*secundum rem aliae*) than the divine nature"; and (2) "the *rationes* by which these are known, which are really identical with the divine nature."[35] To explain this he introduces his own technical terms of a distinction between an idea and its *ideatum* or object, and a distinction between the being of essence and the being of existence (*esse essentiae* and *esse existentiale*):

> Since therefore the ideas in God exercise causality in every way over the things of which they are the forms, by constituting them in both their *esse essentiae* and their *esse existentiae,* and this according to the mode of the exemplary formal cause, therefore the relation of the divine idea to its *ideata* . . . is according to the first genus of relation, which is that between the producer and its product . . . so that it follows from the divine perfection that from the ideal *ratio* in God, the first essence of the creature flows forth in its *esse essentiae,* and secondly, through the mediation of the divine will, this same essence flows forth in its *esse existentiae.*[36]

But the introduction into Christian thought of this Avicennian attempt to salvage Neoplatonism in a creationist universe, by means of a world of possible essences which, as someone put it, "stands up stiff with reality" (the reality proper to essence in itself, distinct both from the idea that thinks it up and its later mode of created actual existence), did not find hospitable acceptance among the thirteenth-century and especially later Christian theologians. The ghost of John Scottus Eriugena was no longer welcome at the banquet of Christian theology, although the overtones of the doctrine do linger on in Duns Scotus and down through Descartes, Spinoza, and the early rationalism of modern philosophy.

FOURTEENTH-CENTURY NOMINALISM

We cannot conclude our story, however, without a brief word on the final denouement in medieval times. The thirteenth century gave birth to a careful balance between a firm maintaining of the presence and role of the divine ideas in God and a firm rejection of their identification with the true real being of creatures. The pendulum now swings all the way to the opposite extreme. The deontologizing of the divine ideas is pursued so relentlessly that the divine ideas themselves, even in their *esse intentionale,* finally disappear entirely. This is the work of William of Ockham and his nominalist followers. His sledgehammer metaphysics, pairing the principle of contradiction with the divine omnipotence, will allow no medium between full reality—evidenced by full real distinction and separability—and nothing at all. One of the first casualties is the *esse intentionale* of the great thirteenth-century metaphysical systems. Either the so-called divine ideas are real being, and thus real multiplicity, in God—which a Christian thinker cannot accept—or they are nothing at all. The divine ideas, venerable tradition though they be, must be resolutely jettisoned in the name of Christian thought purified of all pagan Platonism. Nothing in the divine nature is immutable or eternal except the being of God himself. But God is not an idea:

> The divine essence is not an idea, because I ask: the ideas are in the divine mind either subjectively or objectively. Not subjectively, because then there would be subjective plurality in the divine essence, which is manifestly false. Therefore they are there only objectively: but the divine essence does not exist only objectively (i.e., as the object of idea). Therefore it is not an idea.[37]

As Gabriel Biel, a later Ockhamist disciple, puts it succinctly:

> These two, namely, immutability or eternity, and multiplicity or plurality, do not seem compatible (for the divine essence, which is immutable and eternal, does not allow that plurality which is posited among the ideas—for each creatable thing has its own proper and distinct idea—and although this plurality is proper to the creature, immutability and eternity are not, but are proper to God alone).[38]

The so-called divine ideas must therefore be banished from God and identified simply with creatures themselves as the direct objects, without intermediary of any kind, of the divine act of knowing. The danger of this position, of course, as became all too clear with the unfolding of nominalism, was that, in the name of saving the divine simplicity, all intelligible structures of creatures as causally prior to creation also seem to have vanished from the divine mind, and we are threatened with an unfathomable abyss in God of pure unillumined will power which seems at the root of intelligence itself, leading to the substitution of divine will rather than intelligence as the ground of morality. As Biel does not hesitate to put it: "It is not because something is right or just that God wills it, but because God wills it therefore it is right and just."[39] With the banishment of the divine ideas, we have now come full circle in the spectrum of positions within Christian thought. The divine simplicity has been preserved, but at the expense of that other pillar of traditional Christian metaphysics, which Saint Thomas and other thirteenth-century Christian thinkers worked so hard to bring into equilibrium with the divine simplicity, the theory of divine exemplary ideas. The total negation of the Neo-platonic world of ideas is as unacceptable in Christian philosophical thought as its ultrarealism. A Christian metaphysics of God can survive only at a point of balance in the middle. Professor Anton Pegis has made the suggestion, in a brilliant article on "The Dilemma of Being and Unity,"[40] that in thus moving to such an extreme anti-Platonic position, Ockham and the nominalists are still the unconscious prisoners of Platonic thought, accepting uncritically one of its basic presuppositions; namely, that the world of intelligibility is necessarily and un-avoidably a world of real multiplicity. The Neoplatonists drew the conclusion that, since being and intelligibility were necessarily correlative partners, then the su-preme source of reality, the One, must be beyond both being and intelligibility. The nominalists drew the conclusion that, since the supreme principle must be being, Ultimate Being itself must be raised above intelligibility. But both conclu-sions proceed from the same premise. The only solution is to do away with the premise itself—that an intelligible order is necessarily linked to real multiplicity. It was this decisive move, rendering Christian Neoplatonism finally viable, that we owe to Saint Thomas and other Aristotelian-influenced thinkers of the thir-teenth century.

CONCLUSION

To sum up briefly, the key point I have tried to make, as a metaphysician reflecting on the history of a problem, is that, although large areas of Neoplato-nism can be assimilated for the profound enrichment of Christian thought, there is one doctrine that stubbornly resists coherent assimilation: this is the doctrine of the realism of ideas, that the true being of things consists in the pure ideas of them as found in the mind of God (or elsewhere). This is inconsistent first and foremost with the Christian notion of the existential identity of all the divine ideas, however distinct in their intelligibility or *esse intentionale,* with the one simple act of the divine mind thinking them, so that there is no real plurality in God outside that of the three divine Persons. It is also inconsistent, though this point remained more latent in actual medieval discussion, with the value given to created existence as the gift of God's love and the decisive value given to human salvation freely worked out in contingent history through the Incarnation of the Son of God and the free moral response of historical man. The chapter we have just studied illustrates once again that the encounter between Neoplatonism and Christian thought was a deeply challenging one, where genuine assimilation and viable synthesis could be brought about only by profound creative adaptation, in some cases even the final rejection, of some aspects of Neoplatonism.

12

Meister Eckhart on God as Absolute Unity

BERNARD McGINN

The history of the relation between Neoplatonism and Latin Christian theology is long and complicated, the names of its protagonists many. Ambrose and Augustine, Boethius, John the Scot, Bonaventure, Meister Eckhart, and Nicholas of Cusa are only some of the figures that would appear on any list of the major attempts to make use of Neoplatonic thought as a vehicle for the speculative appropriation of Christian belief. But brief reflection on the fates of these seven sages gives us pause. The views of two of them, John the Scot and Meister Eckhart, were subject to posthumous ecclesiastical condemnation, and Boethius, if safe from criticism in the medieval period, has been subject to accusations of being a "closet pagan" by modern scholars over the past century. Such condemnations and suspicions seem to confirm the feeling that Neoplatonic thought is at best a problematic (and frequently an unhelpful) language for the expression of Christian theology. Such general feelings, however, are rarely very useful for the historical theologian, except when tested and confirmed in particular cases. They are especially dangerous when the contrasted poles of the comparisons and contrasts (e.g., Neoplatonism and Christianity) are treated as clear and distinct systems miraculously exempt from historical development and change. The following essay attempts to study one example of the interaction between an important aspect of Neoplatonic thought, in this case the dialectical understanding of the One or Absolute Unity, and the Christian doctrine of God as found in one of the most controversial of the Christian Neoplatonists, Meister Eckhart.

This test case is a significant one. Along with John the Scot and Nicholas of Cusa, Eckhart is arguably the most systematic of the Latin Neoplatonic dialecticians, and he is the one who suffered the most for it. The majority of the twenty-eight propositions from his works condemned by Pope John XXII in the Bull "In agro dominico" of March 27, 1329, involve or imply aspects of his appropriation of Neoplatonism. Three of them (articles 23, 24, and 26) relate directly to his doctrine of God, the subject of this paper.

Nearly everyone agrees that there are problems in Meister Eckhart's doctrine of God. Less consensus is found about what the main problems are, and agreement about the best way to resolve them is rarer still. By its very mode of presentation Eckhart's thought invites, even encourages, disagreement and polemics among its interpreters. Not only the problem of the relative weight to be accorded the Latin and the German works, but also the occasional character of many surviving texts has bedeviled subsequent students. In a brief paper definitive solutions are not to be expected, but it may be possible to set out on the road that leads to a more adequate understanding of what the German Dominican taught concerning God as a way of illustrating the encounter between Neoplatonism and Christianity. This investigation will be in three unequal stages. First, a brief note of three major problems in Eckhart's teaching on God; second, an analysis of the Meister's interlocking theories of predication, analogy, and dialectic as a way of beginning to resolve the first of these problems; and third, a reflection on the nature of Christian Neoplatonism suggested by Eckhart's dialectic of the One.

As is well known, in the first of the *Parisian Questions,* dated 1302 or 1303, Eckhart denies the Thomistic thesis that existence (*esse*) and understanding (*intelligere*) are the same in God and affirms the priority of understanding to existence in the divine nature:[1] "I say that if there is anything in God that you want to call existence, it belongs to him through his understanding."[2] In the prologue to the *Opus Tripartitum,* which is probably late but cannot be dated with security, the first of the theological axioms analyzed is that "Existence (*esse*) is God." Here the Meister affirms that the four transcendental predicates of existence, unity, truth, and goodness can be applied to God alone in the proper sense, while the title and order of treatment suggests that he accords clear priority to *esse.* The many attempts to deal with this first problem in the German Dominican's doctrine of God may be broadly broken down into those which admit contradiction, surmising that Eckhart changed his mind,[3] and those that try to show the inner unity of the two texts either by appealing to diverse perspectives or by locating the presentations within a broader and more systematic treatment of Eckhartian theology.[4]

A second disputed area arises from the study of passages in some of the German works that seem to affirm a distinction between God and the Godhead.[5] Traditional Latin theology, enhanced by the condemnation of the supposed Trinitarian errors of Gilbert of Poitiers at the Council of Rheims in 1148, resisted any separation of the Trinity from a prior unmanifested divine essence. How seriously are we to take Eckhart's language then? The answer to this question depends on many prior issues concerning the relation of the German to the Latin works and the author's teaching on the Trinity. Many would agree with those who suspect that the distinction between God and the Godhead indicates that Eckhart viewed union with the divine nature in a way that was not distinctively Christian in the last analysis.[6] Others would contend that there is at least a definite priority of the divine unity over the Trinity in the Eckhartian view.[7]

A third problem follows hard apace. Perhaps no part of Eckhart's teaching was more controversial, in his own day as in ours, than his statements regarding the birth of the Word in the soul. The papal bull of condemnation refers to this teaching in six of its twenty-eight articles, and debate about the meaning of such claims as ". . . the Father generates me his Son and the same Son. Whatever God does is one, and for this reason He generates me his Son without any distinction"[8] has continued to our own day. Eckhart defended his pronouncements with vigor in his response to his accusers, the *Rechtfertigungsschrift* or *Defense*. He even said that he had never taught that a part of the soul was uncreated, a position that may seem contradictory to assertions in his surviving works.[9] But the Meister was a true Scholastic, well able to invoke a distinction where others would see only a contradiction. Where does the truth lie? The massive problems surrounding Eckhart's teaching on the birth of the Word in the soul, while more directly related to his theological anthropology than to his doctrine of God, necessarily have profound ramifications for the latter. One can take Eckhart's *Defense* at face value and see nothing more in his teaching than traditional theology expressed in novel language,[10] or one can discern seemingly inevitable pantheistic implications of the birth of the Word in the soul.

These three problems are too complex to be open to any brief and facile solution. Within the limits of a paper, however, it may be possible to suggest an avenue of approach to the language contrasting God as *esse* and God as *intelligere* that will show that there is no contradiction in this area of the Meister's thought.

Like most well-trained Schoolmen, Eckhart was a logician as well as a metaphysician and theologian. Perhaps beginning at the humble level of his theory of predication may both help avoid errors in loftier domains and also hint at the systematic coherence of this thought. Most notably in the prologues to the *Opus Tripartitum*,[11] though not absent elsewhere,[12] we find in Eckhart a doctrine regarding two modes of predicating terms that, while it is based upon the teaching of Aristotle and Aquinas, has quite different implications. Thomas had used the distinction between two-term and three-term propositions to reflect on the nature of the language we use about created reality. A two-term proposition (*secundum adiacens*), one in which the verb stands as the second term, intends to affirm that the action predicated is really taking place. Thus *Socrates currit* or *Socrates est* affirm that Socrates really is running or really exists. A three-term proposition (*tertium adiacens*), on the other hand, one in which the verb "is" serves as the copula uniting the subject with a predicate and thus forms the third element in the sentence, does not make any assertion about the actual relation of subject and predicate, but only about their logical relation. Thus, *Socrates est albus* affirms that whiteness is logically compatible with Socrates without direct consideration of whether or not Socrates really exists.[13]

Eckhart, on the other hand, used the distinction between *secundum adiacens* propositions like "X exists," and *tertium adiacens* propositions like "X is this," to reflect on the difference between the language we use about God and the way we speak of created reality. While he nowhere denies the Thomistic application of both kinds of propositions to created being, his analyses concentrate upon the preeminent case of the transcendental terms of existence, unity, truth, and goodness.

> For when I say that something exists, or I predicate one, true, or good, these four terms feature in the predicate as the second term (*secundum adiacens*) and are used formally and substantively. But when I say that something is this, for instance a stone, and that it is one stone, a true stone, or a good this, namely a stone, these four terms are used as the third term (*tertium adiacens*) of the proposition. They are not predicates but the copula, or they are placed near the predicate.[14]

Eckhart's use of the distinction here rests upon the difference between unlimited and limited predication. Two-term propositions imply the unlimited possession of the predicate, its absolute fullness, the negation of its negation.[15] Hence in the case of the transcendentals, they can properly apply to God alone. "God alone properly speaking exists and is called being, one, true, and good."[16] In three-term propositions the key is the particularity of the predicate, the "this" or "that." The transcendental term is here reduced to a "kind of copula"[17] that connects predicate and subject according to a manner of classification, that is, "X is in the class of those things that are particular according to existence or unity, and so on." This logic of propositions coheres exactly with the well-known distinction between *esse simpliciter* and *esse hoc et hoc* which Eckhart uses throughout the prologues and elsewhere to express the separation between God and creation.[18]

This overriding sense of the difference between God and creation expressed in the two types of predication is helpful for understanding some of the peculiarities of Eckhart's doctrine of analogy.[19] Here again, while the terminology has its starting place in Thomas Aquinas, the development takes a very different direction. The *Parisian Questions* note that nothing is formally in both the cause and the effect if the cause is a true cause,[20] and since only analogous causes are true causes for Eckhart,[21] we should not be surprised that the Meister's understanding of analogy is centered on formal opposition rather than on proportionality, intrinsic attribution, or participation. In a classic text like that in the *Sermons and Lectures on Ecclesiasticus* (nn. 52–54),[22] we are told that

> . . . analogates have nothing of the form according to which they are analogically ordered (*analogantur*) rooted in positive fashion in themselves, but every created being is analogically ordered to God in being, truth, and goodness. Therefore, every created being radically and positively possesses existence, life, and wisdom from and in God and not in itself.[23]

This analogy of "extrinsic attribution" is found throughout the Latin and German works.[24] It is at the root of the denial of *esse* of God in the *Parisian Questions*,[25] and is also found in the vernacular *Book of Divine Consolation*.[26] It seems less important to debate whether this doctrine of analogy results in a mere quasi-Lutheran imputation of being to creatures as E. Gilson argued,[27] or a fleeting sense of loaned being as J. Koch held,[28] than to recognize that what is most distinctive about Eckhart's analogy is its ability to reverse itself.[29] If *esse* and the other transcendentals are understood as referring to the existence of creatures, the terms cannot be used of God; rather, he must be seen as something above such existence. If *esse* is taken *simpliciter*, it is properly predicated of God in *secundum adiacens* propositions and improperly predicated of created reality in *tertium adiacens* ones. The observation that Eckhart's notion of analogy is a two-edged sword is not meant to deny that he usually strikes with one side, that is, that explicit treatments of analogy are usually designed to affirm something of God and deny it of creatures,[30] or to affirm something from the point of view of principial knowing, as C. F. Kelley would have it.[31] One of the propositions for which the Meister was condemned was that "All creatures are pure nothing. I do not say that they are a little something or anything, but that they are pure nothing."[32]

Predication and analogy call out for dialectic to complete the picture. These are not three different approaches or methods; they are more correctly seen as three levels of increasing depth in Eckhart's presentation of God and his relation to creation.[33] What the dialectical level shows is that the inner meaning of *secundum adiacens* predication and of the reversible analogy of *esse* and *intelligere* as God-language is best expressed in the *unum* (the One, or Absolute Unity) that simultaneously manifests both the utter transcendence and the perfect immanence of the divine nature.

In his exegesis of Wisdom 7:27, "And since Wisdom is one, it can do all things," Eckhart gives the most sustained treatment of the dialectic of divine transcendence and immanence found in his corpus. He begins from the specification of the first of the related poles of the meaning of *unum*: ". . . the term 'the One' is the same as 'indistinct,' for all distinct things are two or more, but all indistinct things are one."[34] Right from the outset, he associates *esse* with the indistinction of the *unum,* thus hinting at the important relation between this text and his prologues.[35] "Saying that God is one," as he puts it, "is to say that God is indistinct from all things, which is the property of the first and highest *esse* and its overflowing goodness."[36] On the basis of this pole of indistinction three proofs are advanced that God is one.[37] Then the first part of the text closes with a brief remark that preludes the investigation of the other pole of the dialectical understanding of *unum*: "Therefore, it must be recognized now that the term 'the One' sounds negative but is in reality affirmative. It is the negation of negation which is the purest affirmation and the fullness of the term affirmed."[38]

In the second part of his treatment Eckhart further analyzes *unum* and its relation to multiplicity in order to advance a single argument for the unity of divine wisdom. The argument centers on an extended consideration of the meaning of "negation of negation," perhaps the most detailed of all the Meister's treatments of this key notion. Because *unum* adds nothing to *esse* except negation, that is, the affirmation that it is nothing else than itself, ". . . it is immediately related to *esse* and signifies the purity and core and peak of *esse* itself, something which even the term *esse* does not."[39] Hence Absolute Unity or the One belongs most properly to God, even more than such other transcendental terms as Truth and Goodness. The conclusion reached through the investigation of the notion of Absolute Unity is then buttressed at the end of the second part by an appeal to Macrobius, Boethius, and Proclus on the relation between the opposition/distinction and participation/indistinction of the One and of number.[40]

This sets the stage for the third and most interesting part of the exposition. Drawing together what has already been implied, Eckhart shows how the two poles of *unum*, both involving negative and positive moments, cannot be separated, but are indissolubly linked in a dialectical coincidence of opposites. "Nothing is as distinct from number and what is numbered or numerable, that is, what is created, as God, and yet nothing is as indistinct."[41] Three proofs are advanced to demonstrate distinction or transcendence and three proofs of indistinction or immanence. The first two arguments for the complete transcendence of the One over creation can be seen as parallels to the separation between God and creation implied in the Meister's doctrines of predication and of analogy. The third proof is new and it is a dialectical one:

> Everything which is distinguished by indistinction is the more distinct insofar as it is indistinct, because it is distinguished by its own indistinction. Conversely, it is the more indistinct insofar as it is distinct, because it is distinguished from indistinction by its own distinction. Therefore, it will be the more indistinct insofar as it is distinct and vice versa.[42]

In order to grasp the import of this crucial but dense passage, it may be helpful to paraphrase the key sentences in terms of transcendence and immanence and their relation to the language of *esse*. "Everything which is distinguished by indistinction is the more distinct insofar as it is indistinct, because it is distinguished by its own indistinction" can be read as: "Everything which is transcendent by reason of immanence is the more transcendent insofar as it is immanent, because it is made transcendent by its own immanence." In brief, God transcends creation because he is immanent to all creatures, or, in the language of existence, God alone is true *esse*. The following sentence, ". . . it is the more indistinct insofar as it is distinct, because it is distinguished from indistinction by its own distinction," means that: "It is more immanent insofar as it is transcendent because it differs (transcendently) from immanence by a difference that is no difference at all." Briefly put, God is the more immanent to creatures the more he transcends them because the distinguishing characteristic of the One is its indistinction from all things. In the language of *esse*, God is immanent to all creatures as their transcendental existence.[43] Thus while this text initially may sound like a mere verbal game or wordplay (and no one would want to deny that Eckhart loved verbal games), the play is meant to reveal, insofar as human language ever can reveal, the dynamics of the relation between God and creation.

The same structure of argument is repeated in the three proofs of the indistinction or immanence of the One in all things. The first is perfunctory, the second a summary of an earlier argument, the third is dialectical and crucial. "Nothing is as indistinct from anything as from that from which it is indistinguished by its own distinction. But everything that is numbered or created is indistinguished from God by its own distinction, as said above. Therefore, nothing is so indistinct and consequently one. The Indistinct and the One are the same; hence God and any creature whatever are indistinct."[44] The exposition concludes by a return to the exegesis of the Scripture verse. Having demonstrated that wisdom is One, Eckhart gives three arguments that it can do all things by applying the seventeenth axiom of the *Liber de causis*, ". . . insofar as a thing is simpler and more unified, it is stronger and more powerful, able to do many things."[45]

Space precludes a detailed consideration of other passages, but it is easy to show that the fundamental lines of this text from the *Commentary on Wisdom* appear throughout Eckhart's treatments of the divine nature. The first pole of the dialectic, the understanding of *unum* as *indistinctum*, that is, the "not-to-be-distinguished,"[46] and therefore as properly predicated of God alone, is constant throughout the Meister's works.[47] The other pole—namely, that *unum* signifies complete self-identity, the negation of negation that is the purest and highest form of affirmation—according to J. Quint's enumeration appears fifteen times in the Latin works and in some detail in the twenty-first of the German Sermons.[48] Although Thomas Aquinas had twice spoken of unity as the negation of negation,[49] it seems difficult to deny some influence to William of Moerbeke's translation of Proclus' *Commentary on the Parmenides* on the important place of negation of negation in Eckhart's thought, however different the uses of the Athenian and the Thuringian may have been.[50]

What is most characteristic of Eckhart's understanding of God as Absolute Unity is the dialectical way in which it demonstrates the coincidence of opposites of divine transcendence and immanence. Even the passages in which the Meister explains the dialectical relation of God and creatures in slightly different language, such as the *Commentary on Exodus* (20:3–4), where a polarity of *similitudo/dissimilitudo* is joined to that of *distinctio/indistinctio*,[51] do not fundamentally depart from the message of the *Commentary on Wisdom*. Among the many texts that treat of the dialectic in explicit or implicit fashion,[52] it may be worthwhile to single out two in order to reveal how the Meister communicated his teaching to the broader audience of the Sermons. In the Latin Sermon IV, on the text from Romans 11:36, "Ex ipso, per ipsum et in ipso sunt omnia," Eckhart gives a concise summary of four anthropological implications of the dialectic of distinction and indistinction. The third is the most significant:

> Because, just as God is completely indistinct in himself according to his nature, in that He is truly and most properly one and most distinct from other things, so too man in God is indistinct from all things in God (for "everything is in Him") and at the same time completely distinct from all things.[53]

A similar anthropological application is present in the well-known German Sermon, "Blessed are the Poor," where it is more daringly formulated as a technique to invite the soul to break through beyond the realm of opposition implied in the terms "Creator" and "creature" to the region where the opposites dialectically coincide.

> Where man still preserves something in himself, he preserves distinction. This is why I pray God to rid me of God, for my essential being is above God insofar as we comprehend God as the principle of creatures. Indeed, in God's own being, where God is raised above all being and all distinctions, I was myself, I willed myself, and I knew myself to create this man that I am.[54]

It is now time to ask how the inherently dialectical character of Eckhart's doctrine of God as Absolute Unity helps to solve the problem presented at the outset. Specifically, how does God as *unum* relate to the teaching of the prologues on God as *esse* and to the claim of the *Parisian Questions* that *intelligere* and not *esse* is more adequate in speaking of the divine nature?

The relation between *esse* and *unum* as the *puritas essendi* should be evident from the texts analyzed. No theme in Eckhart is more constant than his identification of God with *esse simpliciter*.[55] But the texts from the *Parisian Questions* and elsewhere that suggest the limitations of the language of *esse* must be taken seriously. These strictures spring not only from the reverse analogy of which Eckhart was so fond (i.e., if *esse* is properly predicated of creatures, it cannot apply to God), but also from the implications of the transcendental uses of "*esse.*" While it is never incorrect to say that God as *esse simpliciter* is also the *esse omnium,* or existence of all things, the term "*esse*" seems semantically less capable of revealing the dialectical coincidence of transcendence and immanence in the same way that *unum* understood as the *negatio negationis* and *puritas essendi* does.

The similarities and differences in the dialectical availability of *esse* and of *unum* are well illustrated by a series of passages in the *Commentary on John.* In exegeting John 3:34 Eckhart appropriates the One (*li unum*) to the divine substance, the unity underlying the three Persons of the Trinity, while *ens, verum,* and *bonum* are ascribed to the Father, Son, and Holy Spirit.[56] But in his treatment of John 10:30 ("The Father and I are one"), the Meister reverses this and identifies *esse* as what is absolute and undetermined in God, that is, the Godhead or essence, so that *unum* (". . . that which among the four transcendentals is most immediately related to *esse*") is ascribed to the Father, and *verum* and *bonum* to the Son and Holy Spirit.[57] But the *unum* of which Eckhart speaks in this and similar passages is not identical with the full range of the dialectical understanding of *unum* of the Wisdom commentary. It represents only an aspect of it, that of the distinction that first sets *esse* off from all multiplicity and makes the Father the first productive principle within God and in creation.[58] In this passage, however, the Meister does seem to suggest that *esse,* when properly understood, can also reveal the dialectical relations within the Godhead and between God and all things, for it is described as *absolutum* (or distinct) and *indeterminatum* (or indistinct). This dialectic in the key of *esse* comes out more strongly in a passage from the extended *Commentary on John* (14:8):

> The idea of being is that it is something common and indistinct and distinguished from other things by its own indistinction. In the same way, God is distinguished by his indistinction from any other distinct thing, and this is why in the Godhead the essence or existence is unbegotten and does not beget. The One points to distinction by its particular property; it is indistinct in itself, but distinct from other things and therefore it is personal and belongs to a supposit capable of acting. Hence the saints attribute the One or unity in the Godhead to the first supposit or person, namely, the Father.[59]

Such passages demonstrate that both forms of language can be used to explore the same territory, though it is significant to note that in Eckhart's surviving works no treatment of the dialectical character of *esse* is as richly developed as the passage on *unum* of the *Wisdom* commentary.

Finally, the broad lines of the relation of *esse/unum* and *intelligere* are clear enough, even though all the implications and ramifications are quite complex. To understand is to become *one,* or better, to *be one,* with what is understood—if we keep this fundamental insight in mind, the seeming contradictions of Eckhart's earlier and later formulations of the relation of *esse* and *intelligere* begin to recede.[60] The solution is obvious in Latin Sermon XXIX where the German Dominican advances eleven reasons for the priority of *unum* in the creature's striving toward God as a basis for reflecting on the intimate unity of *unum* and *intelligere.* Eckhart claims that Absolute Unity or the One is proper to the intellect alone, because all material beings are composed of matter and form, and immaterial beings are also composed, at least of *essentia* and *esse,* and more radically of *esse* and *intelligere.*[61] God alone lacks these compositions because he is *one,* he is pure *esse* and totally *intellectus.*[62] Eckhart affirms: "Intellect is proper to God, and God is one. Therefore, to the extent that each thing has intellect or that which pertains to intellect, it also has God, the One, and unity with God. For the one God is intellect and intellect is the one God."[63] The *puritas essendi* and the *puritas intelligendi* are fundamentally identical in the indetermination of Absolute Unity which is also the *plenitudo* of all things.

The dialectical character of Eckhart's notion of God is not a new discovery. In his classic study *Théologie négative et connaissance de Dieu chez Maître Eckhart,* Vladimir Lossky put great stress upon it,[64] and M. de Gandillac later devoted a valuable paper to the Meister's dialectic.[65] But the term "dialectic" itself has meant different things to different interpreters, an ambiguity that may be at the root of the puzzling denial of some that there is any dialectic in Eckhart's thought at all.[66] So it may be worthwhile at this point to reflect on the sense in which dialectic is being used here.

In his essay on "Hegel and the Dialectic of the Ancient Philosophers," H. G. Gadamer notes that Hegel maintained that all three of the essential elements of dialectical thinking—thinking of determinations by themselves, simultaneously thinking of contradictory determinations, and the positive content of the higher unity of contradictory determinations—were present in ancient philosophy by the time of Plato.[67] Whether Hegel's interpretation of Plato was a simple misreading or a creative "refusal to listen" does not concern us here;[68] what does is Gadamer's observation that Hegel's reading of Plato had been largely shaped by Neoplatonism's theological-ontological interpretation of the *Parmenides.* Along with V. Lossky and M. de Gandillac, we should all probably want to distinguish between the dialectic of Hegel and that of the Meister Eckhart in many ways, but it does seem that Gadamer's three broad notes can provide us with the contours of a genus within which we may begin to distinguish species, and that the influence of the *Parmenides,* especially in its Neoplatonic readings, whether directly or indirectly available, affords important historical continuity to the history of dialectic in Western thought.

The real issue concerning the significance of dialectical thinking revolves around how the third element, the positive content of the higher unity of contradictory determinations, is conceived. Perhaps the beginning of wisdom here is a reflection upon the purposes for which dialectic was invoked, the kinds of problems the method was called upon to help resolve. I have suggested that for Meister Eckhart dialectical thinking functioned as a way to bring to speech in speculative fashion Christian belief in a God that was both utterly transcendent and yet perfectly immanent, more present to the creature than the creature was to itself. The use of Neoplatonic dialectic for this purpose has a long pedigree. As S. Gersh has pointed out, Christian Neoplatonists, beginning at least with the Pseudo-Dionysius, diverged from their pagan predecessors and contemporaries by shifting attention away from consideration of the emanationist structure of reality toward an attempt to investigate God considered as transcendent cause, immanent cause, and both transcendent and immanent cause at the same time.[69] Despite the preparation for this type of dialectic found in places in Plotinus,[70] it seems fair to say that in the light of the writings of the Pseudo-Dionysius, Maximus the Confessor, John the Scot, Eckhart, and Nicholas of Cusa (to name but the most outstanding), the full development of this particular application of dialectical method to the problem of God is distinctive of Christian Neoplatonism.[71]

We may, of course, wish to question the viability of such an approach. Many have felt uncomfortable with the theology of those listed above, as the condemnations of John the Scot and Eckhart demonstrate. That eminent twelfth-century Platonist, William of Conches, once felt constrained to declare indignantly: "Christianus sum, non academicus,"[72] but he may have been just another deluded intellectual. Another eminent Plato scholar, Friedrich Schleiermacher, was also accused of the reverse miracle of changing gospel wine into the water of human philosophy, though not that of Plato or Plotinus. Schleiermacher's answer, as put forth in his *Brief Outline of Theology,*[73] may be more helpful to us than William's. The Berlin theologian recognized both the necessity and the risks in using philosophical systems to help give systematic expression to Christian belief. For him philosophy was a real, if subordinate, "codeterminant" in the ever-unfolding task of the intellectual presentation of that Christian consciousness whose own internal development remained the primary reason for the continuing necessity of new dogmatic formulation.[74] Whether or not we are totally at one with Schleiermacher's formulation, once we admit the full entry of the historical dimension ("development of doctrine" for the optimists) into Christian belief, it seems hard to avoid some analogous explanation. Codetermination need not mean domination, nor does it imply the absence of criteria to discriminate useful appropriations of philosophy from less helpful ones. The history of the Christian adaptation of Neoplatonic understandings of the dialectic of the *Parmenides* suggests that one of the criteria of success is the degree to which the exigence for the transposition and reinterpretation of the language of the philosophical source in order to deal with issues more central to the consciousness of the Christian community is realized. Much of the debate over the propriety of a dialectic like Eckhart's as a language for Christian theology has not paid sufficient attention to this note of reinterpretation, but has tended to judge success on the grounds of conformity to more easily assimilated forms of language.

Discussion of the relation between varieties of dialectical thought and Christian theology has been so intense over the past generation that it would be impossible to try to summarize the state of the question here. On the basis of our study of Eckhart's doctrine of God, however, some of the misunderstandings of the early stages of the debate are evident. A good example of one misunderstanding can be found in E. Coreth's 1951 essay on the usefulness of dialectic in theology.[75] Coreth's negative response to the invocation of dialectic as a codeterminant in the task of Christian theology (admittedly addressed primarily to Hegel) helps us to understand the insufficiency at the roots of the discomfort that many have felt with the dialectical implications of Eckhart's thought. Coreth did see that both analogy and dialectic have similar functions—the mediation of the one and the many, identity and difference,[76] or, in our theological formulation, transcendence and immanence. But he was still dissatisfied with dialectic's ability to provide an answer consonant with Christian belief. His position was that dialectic formulates its positive and negative moments as opposition and identity rather than as unlikeness and likeness, and thus remains trapped in the categories of human logic that allow no openness to true transcendence.[77] But analogy is still a form of human speech and logic, and there is no getting around the fact that if we are to speak of God it must be done in a language that is our own. On the purely logical level, it remains to be proven that opposition and identity are less inadequate than unlikeness and likeness as a way of speaking about God. Historical doubt is not the equivalent of speculative certainty, especially when the minority view may not have been given a totally fair hearing.

Despite the a priori elements of his evaluation, Coreth's essay is a useful starting point for a consideration of the relation between Christian thought and dialectic, not least of all because of its direct influence upon V. Lossky's attempt to vindicate for Meister Eckhart a mediating position between Scholastic analogy and modern dialectical thought.[78] Lossky's response seems in many ways correct, though in need of expansion from at least two sides. From the historical viewpoint, his failure to integrate predication, analogy, and dialectic as increasingly more profound ways of dealing with the same set of problems at times led to confusion of the analogical and dialectical levels, though he was eminently correct in noting that the lack of synthesis in the crude sense sometimes attributed to Hegel in Eckhart did not mean the absence of what Gadamer would call a positive content of the higher unity of contradictory determinations.[79] From a theological viewpoint, Lossky wrote at a time when the acceptance of a plurality of theological languages, at least within the Roman Catholic tradition, was still highly suspect. If that monolithic view of theology has been overcome, we may hope that a more fruitful encounter between Eckhart's dialectic and contemporary views of God is both possible and desirable.

In concluding, we must remember that Eckhart's dialectical view of God was never meant to be mere abstract speculation. The positive content of the higher unity of contradictory determinations is as much a message about man as it is about God. Eckhart the preacher and Eckhart the teacher labored to the same end—to help each believer to a full union with the God who remains ever distinct and indistinct. The Dominican preacher's message that we are in God precisely because he is transcendent to us is strangely simple and at the same time baffling in its paradoxicality. The insoluble elements of his solution are not the least part of the attraction the great Meister continues to exert.

IV

RENAISSANCE THOUGHT

13

Neoplatonism and Christian Thought in the Fifteenth Century (Nicholas of Cusa and Marsilio Ficino)

MAURICE DE GANDILLAC

For Neoplatonism in the period between the end of the Middle Ages and the beginning of the modern period we shall consider here two significant witnesses who, taken together, occupy the entire fifteenth century, since Nicholas Krebs, who died in Todi in 1464, was born sixty years before on the right bank of the Moselle, in the little town of Kues (now merged with Bernkastel) and Marsilio Ficino, born in 1455 at Figline in the valley of the Arno, was to finish his life in Florence barely three months before the end of the quattrocento.

Apart from the differences in age (a whole generation) and country of origin, the contrasts between these two clerics are manifest. A canonist by formation, admitted to the Council of Basel to plead the cause of a great ecclesiastical lord who had supported him at the start of his career, soon taking the lead in the assembly through his learning and ability, joining the papal party as soon as the opponents of the pope had displayed their incompetence, a militant bishop and then a cardinal of the Curia, a mathematician but with a curiosity also for experimentation and observation, Nicholas is a man of action as well as a historian and philosopher. The son of a doctor and himself a doctor (though a theoretician rather than a practitioner), Marsilio lived far from the labors of public life; this humanist who was not ordained priest until 1474—after having completed his Latin translation of Plato—long enjoyed the leisure for scholarship that the patronage of the Medici secured for him.

In 1440 when presenting to Cardinal Cesarini the three books of the *De docta ignorantia,* the Cusan (in Latin, *Cusanus,* from the name of his home town) asked the indulgence of the Italians for his style, heavy and rich in neologisms. In fact, the language that the author uses says well, essentially, what it wants to say and, in his Paris edition of 1514, Lefèvre d'Etaples was not always well-inspired in "correcting," in his fashion, the text which appeared in Strasbourg in 1488. But in spite of a persistent legend—of which Cassirer still took advantage—Nicholas had only a superficial smattering of Greek. As Martin Honecker[1] has shown, he knew the alphabet and recognized some words, not at times without misconstructions; lacking a Latin translation, even with the aid of a lexicon, he could not draw much on the manuscripts brought from Byzantium. We know well that Ficino, on the contrary, an excellent Hellenist, was a good writer and at the same time a very sure translator.

Much rather than any influence—a problematic question—of the Mosellan on the Florentine, what authorizes us to compare these two Christian Platonists is first of all that apart from its Eleatic and Pythagorean sources, both of them willingly root the doctrine they venerate—this to a great extent under the influence of Proclus—in a mythical Orient; but it is especially the fact that if they discern more than one doctrinal nuance within the school and if they happen to share the same views on essential points, neither of the two is, however, fully conscious of the difference in the spiritual and philosophic climate between the time of Plato and that in which his later disciples lived and taught. One is not very surprised that the Cusan thought that he often heard the voice of the old master in the mouth of Dionysius or of Proclus. One is a little more surprised that Ficino, better armed philologically when he presents his Latin version of the *Enneads,* familiar though he is for decades with the real Plato, still invites his readers to listen to *Platonem ipsum sub Plotini persona loquentem.*

*   *   *

Vergerius de Buxis (or Giovanni Andreas dei Bussi) had been for six years the secretary of the Cusan; he appears as a "Platonic" interlocutor in the *Possest* of 1460 and in the *Directio speculantis* of 1462. In 1469 he published, under the patronage of Cardinal Bessarion—thanks to the industry of some German printers, in the studio founded in Rome in 1463 by Cardinal Barbo (the future Paul II)—an *incunabulum* that combined some works of Apuleius with the *Disciplinarum Platonis Epitome* then attributed to Alcinous, a work which had recently been translated by Balbo who had dedicated his work to Nicholas. It was a fine occasion for Bussi, now librarian to the Vatican, to address to the pope a dedicatory epistle and to unite in the same eulogy these two admirers of Plato, namely the two cardinals and friends, the Greek and the German.

This text is believed to be the oldest in which explicit mention is made of an 'intermediate age" (or Middle Age). Nicholas, dead for five years, appears in it as the indefatigable reader who had "held in his memory" *historias omnes, non priscas modo, sed mediae tempestatis, tum veteres, tum recentiores, usque ad nostra tempora,* but what is more important for us is that the author of this panegyric appears to place on the same level two *doctorum principes* who speaking truly—as he knew better than anyone—did not possess Greek culture in equal measure. After having presented the Cardinal of Nicaea, Bessarion, as *Platoni magna ratione affectissimus*—an affection, he thinks, that every judge "serious and of good sense" must approve—he does not hesitate to apply the same formula to the titular of Saint Peter in Chains: *id ipsum et de Nicolaeo Cusensi cardinale, dum viveret, Sancti Petri declaravi.*[2]

Among the Greeks in Italy there was frequent controversy between the devotees of Aristotle and the partisans of the Academy. In this regard Bessarion generally held conciliatory positions. However, in the same year in which the *Apuleius* of Bussi came out, he published (through the same printers) a defensive booklet entitled *In calomniatorem Platonis* against his compatriot George of Trebizond, guilty in his eyes of having accused all Platonists en bloc of "paganism." An even more sensitive point for this high ecclesiastical dignitary was that he had himself been the pupil of Gemistos Plethon, a mysterious personage whose pseudonym, as formerly that of Plotinus, already indicated a deep-seated attachment to Plato, but who pushed this cult far enough for the community of Mistra to become suspect to the orthodox, which provoked the material destruction of almost all his works. However, at the death of Plethon in 1452, Bessarion celebrated in emphatic terms this "Plato reincarnate."[3] Many questions have been asked about the secret sentiments of the Byzantine who passed over to the Romans. Above all, let us seize on this fidelity to Mistra as the guarantee of a very intimate relationship with Plato—a guarantee strong enough for Ficino in 1484 in the preface to the *Plato latinus* to connect mythically the foundation of the Academy in Florence and all his own labor with the discussion that could have taken place, more than a half century earlier, at the time of the Council of Union, between Cosimo de' Medici and Gemistos Plethon. What is more surprising is to find the Cusan, thanks to his secretary, in such erudite company.

In support of his statement Bussi invokes the care that Nicholas had taken to acquire the best translations of Proclus, watching over them as over very precious treasures. In fact, at least after 1444, he had in his possession Proclus' *In Parmenidem* and *Elementatio* in the faithful medieval translation of William of Moerbeke. MS Cus. 186 and MS Cus. 195, in which these works appear (the second containing also the *Liber de causis*), carry in the margin a number of annotations in the hand of the Cusan himself, who often read and reread them and drew excerpts from them that are to be found in certain of his own treatises, notably the *De principio* of 1459 (taken to be a sermon by Lefèvre d'Etaples and, under the title of "Tu quis es?," partially published as such among the *Excitationes*). Already in 1438, as a member of the delegation sent by the papal party to win over the emperor, the patriarch and the Eastern prelates (with a view to a rapid negotiation which resulted, under the Turkish menace, in a fragile concordate considered by the majority of the orthodox as a theological capitulation), he had brought back from Constantinople a Greek copy of the *Platonic Theology,* anticipating that Traversari would very quickly provide him with a translation. But he had to wait for twenty years to obtain from Balbo a Latin version, which also was from then on read often, reread and annotated, as MS Cus. 185 reveals.

In the previous century, confronted with a Greek manuscript of Plato, Petrarch had undergone a truly tantalizing torture. Better provided for, the Cusan possessed at an early stage, apart from the medieval translations by Aristippus of Plato (*Phaedo* and *Meno*), more recent translations done by Leonardo Bruni (*Phaedo, Apology, Crito,* and *Phaedrus*). MS Cus. 177, in which the two collections are combined, bears the sure signs of use, but less constant use than was made of the Latin texts of Proclus. In the last years of his life, when scarcely having the time to study them, the cardinal likewise had to hand the translations of the *Republic* and the *Laws* by Decembro and by George of Trebizond (MS Cus. 178 and MS Harl. 3261, which came from the library at Kues). It is probable, furthermore, that he had available late in life—although they have not been found—a version of the *Parmenides* by the same George of Trebizond (who, as one can see, was not such a fierce enemy of Plato) and of the *Letters* translated by Bruni. On the presence of the *Parmenides* among the books of the Cusan, a phrase of Bessarion in the *In calomniatorem* confirms the slightly ambiguous reference in the Letter to Paul II. Concerning the collection of Plato's *Letters,* a series of citations in the *Directio speculantis* of 1462 (chaps. 21–22) corroborates a note in MS Cus. 41, as has been pointed out by Raymond Klibansky.[4] Without ever ceasing to hear Plato through Proclus, it seems that in the last years of his life the cardinal read more of Plato's own works; he refers to them more often and with less imprecision.

And it is with him that he now very explicitly connects the *corpus dionysiacum.* Having available since 1443 the new translation of Traversari (in the copy that the future Nicholas V procured for him, MS Cus. 43), he confronts it, if not with the Greek text as he lets it be understood, at least with the old translations. In his *De concordantia catholica* of 1433, he was not afraid to call into question the authenticity of several decretals and, before Valla, that of the famous donation of Constantine; however, he does not seem to doubt that, despite the silence of the early Fathers, one must attribute to Paul's Athenian convert the texts belatedly made known under the name of Areopagite. But even while pointing out in passing this dependence of Dionysius in relation to the Apostle of the Gentiles (*Paulus apostolus ejusdem Dionysii magister* . . .),[5] he scarcely seems to refer to secrets that would have invested the author of the *Mystical Theology* with a quasi-apostolic authority. And indeed it should be noted that, if he suggests, again incidentally, a possible "sequence" from Dionysius to Proclus in the use of "apophatic" vocabulary (*Proclus* . . ., *Dionysium sequendo, unum et bonum, licet Plato ita primum nominaverit, de primo negat, quod penitus est ineffabile*),[6] in a not much earlier work—the *Tetralogus de non aliud, seu Directio speculantis* written in 1462 in which the cardinal, presented as a specialist on Dionysius, is in discussion with a Portuguese Aristotelian and those two ardent Platonists, namely Bussi and Balbo—he held it as "uncertain" that the author of the *In Parmenidem*, "certainly" later than the Areopagite, had known his works: *Proclum . . ., Dionysio Areopagita tempore posteriorem fuisse certum est. An autem Dionysii scripta viderit est incertum.*[7] And, in spite of a brief remark on the "laboring in vain" that Proclus imposed on himself in his *Platonic Theology* (in order to define, *ex conjecturis incertis*, the different kinds of "gods" and their relation to the sole eternal God),[8] rather than supposing, as Lefèvre again will, a distortion of the Dionysian tradition by pagan Neoplatonism, he explains evident doctrinal concurrences by a common fidelity to Plato: *Sicut Dionysius inquit unum quod est posterius uno simpliciter, ita et Proclus, Platonem referens, asserit.*[9]

The reference to the actual author of the *Parmenides*—not merely to his commentators—was very explicit as early as 1449 in the *Apologia doctae ignorantiae* in which the Cusan brings on the scene a "disciple" who is outraged by the accusations of ignorance made against his master by a professor from Heidelberg. After having evoked the precedent of Socrates, an excellent judge of his own *agnosia*, the spokesman for Nicholas cites several theorists on apophacy, notably that Avicenna who suspected, he thinks, the "coincidence" in God of the singular and the universal; but, it is to the "divine Plato" that he gives credit for the glory of having "beforehand" and "in a more perspicacious manner," "attempted to open up the way," followed by the "divine Dionysius" who "ofttimes" reproduced his words literally: *Acutius ante ipsum [Avicennam] divinus Plato in Parmenide conatus est viam pandere, quem adeo divinus Dionysius imitatus est ut saepius Platonis verba seriatim posuisse reperiatur.*[10]

We have here, certainly, only a "straining" towards the inaccessible, but in the eyes of a researcher who always held to what he calls "conjecture" or "approximation," the attempts of Plato are sufficient example for the Areopagite—supposed, however, to be familiar with other models—to be presented straight out as his "imitator." It was not at all as a simple mode of expression that Proclus used the adverb ἐνθέως to define the manner in which his master discovered the "most primary principle" (*Plat. Theol.* I, 3) and to evoke, according to *Phaedrus* 238d, his "divinely inspired mouth" (I, 4). The *divinus* that Nicholas applies simultaneously to the author of the *Parmenides* and that of the *Divine Names* has not for him the full value of the θεῖος of Proclus (reserved for Plato and his authentic disciples, the "very perspicacious" Aristotle meriting only the adjective δαιμόνιος), and finally[11] it will give place to a less emphatic *magnus*.

Having in his possession from the time of his early philosophic studies two Latin versions of the *Phaedo,* the Cusan doubtless had no need to await the translation of the *Platonic Theology* in order to find in it, from the first lines, the Platonic image of the "chase" (for the ὄντος θήρα of 66c he will only substitute a "quest for wisdom," a notion at once quite biblical and quite Pythagorean); but, it is certainly from the work of Proclus that he will borrow[12] the quotation from *I. Alcib.* 133b–c, on the "soul" (he adds "intellective") which, "returning into itself, can see all things and God." And the previous year, despite the restriction implied in the word *conari,* the reference to Proclus was very explicit when the cardinal, pushing far the display of his Platonic religion, was not afraid to write, in chapter 20 of the *Directio*:

> Plato autem, quem tantopere Proclus extollit tanquam deus fuerit humanatus, ad anterius semper respiciens, conatus est rerum videre substantiam ante omne nominabile. . . . Ex quo Platonem reor rerum substantiam seu principium in mente sua revelationis via percepisse.

But in ending the quotation here for greater effect, one might be misled. In fact, reechoing Romans 1:19—where Saint Paul, on the subject of divine anger, seems to be thinking of a theophany in some sense natural—what follows evokes the diffusive movement of light, which, if it did not offer itself to view, would remain invisible:

> Modo quo apostolus ad Romanos dicit se illis revelasse, quam equidem revelationem in lucis similitudine capio, quae sese per semetipsam visui inheerit. Et aliter non videtur neque cognoscitur quam ipsa se revelat, cum sit invisibilis.

Thus, for the Cusan, was not the pupil of Socrates, rather than a prophet or a wise man, the one of all the philosophers best able to grasp the fundamental need for a truly divine gift without which human intelligence would remain blind? In such a way only can it be explained that—hunting on the *campus lucis,* the fourth ground for a fruitful quest—the "great Plato" was able to rise *de Sole ad sapientiam per similitudinem,* opening the way for the "great Dionysius" who *de igne ad Deum et de Sole ad creatorem per proprietatum similitudines quas ennarat ascendit.*[13]

And it is without doubt that we must interpret, in a parallel fashion, the reference (*Directio,* chap. 20) to the last lines of Plato *Letter VI* (323d)—a text of extremely doubtful authenticity ("We shall all, on condition that we truly philosophize [ἂν ὄντως φιλοσοφῶμεν], come to know the god insofar as happy men can"), quite enigmatic all the same, and for which the cardinal substitutes an equivalent that better puts into relief the theme of the gift, accompanying it with a commentary directly inspired by Proclus:

> Haec Plato in epistolis sic se habere perbreviter exprimit, Deum ipsum dicens vigilantissime et constanter quaerenti se demum manifestare, quae Proclus quoque in Parmenidis commentariis resumit. Cum haec igitur vera supponant, animam inquit, quae quidem omnia posteriora, seipsam contemplans, in se animaliter complicat, ut vivo in speculo inspicere quae ejus participant vitam, et per ipsam vivunt vitaliterque subsistunt. Et quia illa in ipsa sunt, ipsa in sui similitudine sursum ascendit ad priora, quemadmodum haec Proclus in ejus recitat Theologia.

(For this last reference, compare in particular IV, 16).

But from the gracious effusion that allowed Plato such valuable insights, the last lines of the *De docta ignorantia* (III, 12)— addressed, like the Prologue, to Cardinal Cesarini—left it to be understood that Nicholas himself could have benefited. Thirteen years later, to introduce the Utopia of religious peace, he will make use of a classical procedure very dear to the Middle Ages, that of the *somnium.*

Was it simply a question of a rhetorical figure when he seemed to attribute to a celestial munificence (with the qualification, it is true, of an "I believe") the discovery of his own method, after a series of vain efforts? Here already the diffusion of light was at the center of every work; and the citation from James 1:17 on "the Father of Lights from whom comes every excellent gift" had evidently the value of a Dionysian reference:

> Accipe nunc, metuende pater, quae jamdudum attingere variis doctrinarum viis concupivi, sed prius non potui quousque in mari, me ex Graecia redeunte, credo superno dono a Patre luminum, a quo omne datum optimum, ad hoc ductus sum ut incompraehensibilia incompraehensibiliter amplecterer in docta ignorantia.

This gift received at full flood could not indeed dispense the Cusan from intensive recourse to *auctoritates*. From Anaxagoras to Cicero, from Trismegistes to Maïmonides, they are numerous in the *Learned Ignorance,* and more than once distorted or modified, as can be seen notably in the way in which the author makes use of the *corpus dionysiacum*. Thus, in I, 6—where the Areopagite is celebrated as *maximus divinorum scrutator* (but have we really here an "absolute" superlative?)—the Cusan, not content to refer back, quite naturally, to *Div. Nom.* V, 8, 824a ("God cannot be this without being that, here without being there"), to *Myst. Theol.* V, 1048b (which suggests a simultaneous surpassing of the *positio* and of the *ablatio*), and to the *Ep.* I, 1065a (knowledge of the divine "transcends thought and intellection"), justifies the coincidence of the *maximum absolutum* and the *minimum absolutum* which is affirmed throughout Book I, by referring curiously to the phrase in *Myst. Theol.* I, 3, 1000b where theology is called (according to Saint Bartholomew) that which is "at once the longest and the shortest." Citing then two phrases borrowed from *Guide for the Perplexed* (doubtless through the mediation of Eckhart who referred to it in his commentary on Exodus), he interprets a simple celebration of divine glory, in the face of which, according to Maïmonides, "wisdom is only ignorance," as if the question here was properly that of the *docta ignorantia,* "without which God cannot be found, as Dionysius, I believe, endeavored [*nisus est*] to show in many ways."

In the following chapter Dionysius seems to be cited through Thierry of Chartres, a source not mentioned by the author but from which he certainly borrows (in I, 8) the hypothetical link between the pseudo-Greek *ontas* and the Latin *unitas*. Thinking to read in the Areopagite that our intellection of God leads *magis ad nihil quam ad aliquid,*[14] Nicholas transcribes the statement in his own language, according to the "rule" of what he calls here a "sacred ignorance": *Sacra autem ignorantia me instruit hoc quod intellectui nihil videtur esse maximum incompraehensibile* (I, 17). In truth, that Cusan "Platonism" is presented in terms more Dionysian or more Proclian, that it is inspired by the school of Chartres or by Eckhart, indeed more simply by Augustine, it is so much less exclusive in that the author, from beginning to end of his work, ceaselessly affirmed a "concordance" (at least virtual) between "all the doctrines of the learned," provided that one understands them according to the true wish of those who (more or less clumsily) were only able to enunciate them in their own way.

In the very passage of the *Directio* (chap. 20) which evokes for the benefit of Plato a *revelationis via*, while the translator of the *Platonic Theology* underlines the accord between Dionysius, Proclus, and their common master, the cardinal hastens to universalize this agreement: *Forte sapientes idem dicere voluerunt de primo rerum principio, sed varie idipsum varie expresserunt.*

In this respect the author of the *De venatione* does not appear to differentiate at all between the revealed texts and the works of the philosophers: *Sacrae litterae et philosophi idem varie nominaverunt* (chap. 9). And this applies not only to the deuterocanonicals (chapters 1 and 13 refer to Ecclesiasticus as well as to Philo, supposed compiler of another "Wisdom"), but equally applies to the Pentateuch: in 1447, in the dialogue entitled *De genesi*, while his interlocutor underlines the divergences between the Mosaic recital of origins and the opinion of the *alii plerique*, Nicholas replies (without the restriction of any "perhaps"): *Qui de genesi locuti sunt idem dixerunt in variis modis.*[15] It remains to discover this *idem* in its various *modi*, and this quest does not proceed without serious misunderstandings. Thus, on reading Aristotle, some confuse the true *nunc aeternitatis* with that *immensurabilis duratio mundi* which raises no more doubt for the Cusan than for Eckhart. But on their side the "subtle" Platonists, if they recognize the transcendence of the *primum imparticibiliter superexaltatum*, not seeing that in him coincide *essentia et actus, actus et potentia*, indeed in a certain way *esse et non esse*, did not realize the immanence of the infinite and the theophanic value of that *innumerabilis multitudo particularium* which participates in the *idem absolutum* as much as of those particular beings *quodlibet est idem suiipsi*, in such a way that the unattainable shines forth "more clearly" in the universe.[16] The difficulty is not less when it is a question of sacred texts. There again for want of referring to the *intentio scribentis* (the great exegetic rule already so dear to Abelard), one is prevented from discovering the truth—beneath the "human mode" of the biblical narrative, with the contradictions and even the "absurdities" that literal readings of it imply—discerned, up to a certain point, only by the *prudentiores philosophi* and those whom Nicholas, preferring almost always the comparative to the superlative, designates rather vaguely as *in theologicis peritiores*. The apparent paradox here is that—according to the symbolic teaching on the fall that the Bible narrative contains—to aspire *sua vi in scientia Deo coaequari*, man falls into that form of ignorance which is only the death of the intellect.[17]

That is why, proudly modest, the Cusan pretends many times that his sole project would be to bring to light (as through spectacles, declares the *De beryllo* of 1458) the "arcane" which Plato hinted at when he dared to explore the *campus* of the *non aliud* (the third hunting ground of the *De venatione*, after the *docta ignorantia* and the *possest*), producing from his discovery a "brief" and "timid" survey, in order above all to "stimulate the very subtle minds with much."[18] It was a matter then for his successors, not indeed to achieve the unachievable, but to participate in a great collective work, without excluding the contribution of discredited thinkers like Protagoras, who were not wrong in recognizing in man a *mensura rerum*,[19] or like Epicurus, to whom Nicholas (misled by a fault in his manuscript of the Latin translation of Diogenes Laertius, and holding especially to the critique in the *Letter to Herodotus* concerning the pagan gods considered as subordinate guides) attributes the merit of having doubted that so many stars that populate the vast world should have been at the service of our little terrestrial region (*ad finem hujus terreni mundi*).[20]

But, astonishing above all is the apparent vanity of so many, sometimes unusual, *auctoritates*, if it is true (as the Cusan also states), that the most simple artisan—a maker of spoons on the Roman forum, he who called himself *idiota* (simply a private individual, in contrast to the *orator* and the *philosophus*)—can by his own powers decipher the "book of the world" and listen to the voice of wisdom which "cries out in the public places";[21] moreover, he does this not by drawing on some traditional treasure of accumulated experiences but by a precise analysis of the operations familiar to the merchants. This statement is illustrated, with different degrees of complexity, by the four dialogues of 1450: *De sapientia* I and II, *De mente,* and *De staticis experimentis.* In this last text—contemporary with *Transmutationes geometricae* and an early version of *Quadratura circuli*—the author boldly lends to the would-be "profane" the anticipation of very ingenious "mental experiments" founded on a universalized use of scales that would enable all bodies to be "weighed," including those that one supposes to be "light" (such as inhaled air and exhaled air), in order to establish a complete repertory of their properties by a quantification of all scientific knowledge.

With this wonderful confidence in the virtues of what Descartes would call good sense, the cardinal evokes the Socratic-Platonic origins of chapter 13 of the *De venatione,* with reference to the tenth hunting ground—that of *ordo*—when he states that the *puer Menon* [*sic*], questioned "according to order," replied correctly *ad cuncta geometrica* [*sic*]. But it must be seen what ambitious project should finally be served by a method so facile and at the same time so difficult: the establishment of a human community founded on conciliation between beliefs. Of this hope the canonist of Basel outlined as early as 1433, in the *De concordantia catholica,* some useful preliminaries, recalling that, following the most ancient traditions, the pope is nothing more, on three levels (the diocese of Rome, the patriarchate of the West, the universal Church), than the *primus inter pares.* Rallying to the sovereign pontiff, but without renouncing his ideal of "universal concordance," Nicholas, in 1452, at the time of his negotiations with the Hussites, specifies the conditions of every compromise: a possible and, indeed, even desirable variety of rites and customs, but a fundamental requirement of unity. However, the following year—while the fall of Constantinople indicated the failure of the precarious accord between Greeks and Latins proclaimed at Florence in 1439—the Cusan, in the *De pace fidei,* "dreams" of an extension of the religious "peace" through an agreement in dogma (the blending of many liturgical, sacramental, and linguistic concessions) with the Arabs and the Turks, the Tartars and the Indians. This project was returned to in 1461 (at a more limited and less utopian level) when the cardinal was writing his *Cribratio Alchorani* at the very moment when the Ottoman army was advancing along the Danube and when the humanist Pius II—after having offered the sultan as wages for a hypothetical conversion the derisory crown of the fallen Byzantine Basileus—prepared (quietly) for a very anachronistic crusade.

For the Cusan, it is not on the force of arms that the *pax fidei* can depend, but rather on a common reflection concerning the real content of differing creeds. While Ficino will assign himself as his first task the demonstration—by "reasons" borrowed above all from the Platonists—of the divine origin and the immortality of the soul (preambles without which Christian dogmas would remain, he thinks, inaccessible not only to readers of Lucretius—he, himself, in his youth was for some time an admirer of the *De natura rerum*—but to all those who interpret the Aristotelian noetic in the deceptive light of Alexander or of Averroës), the Cusan project is of another kind: it aims at discerning in all the doctrines of all times and of all countries, provided one knows how to extract their most profound intention, the presence, at least virtual, of the two Christian doctrines of the Trinity and the Incarnation; the one understood as based on relations between unity, equality, and connection (a theme very dear to the school of Chartres), the other referred to the requirement of an effective link between the divine infinite and the cosmic indefinite (called, in the *De docta ignorantia* II, 4, *infinitum contractum seu concretum*), a *nexus* which finds its "major possibility" in "human nature" taken in *summo gradu et omni plenitudine* (III, 3 and 4), that is to say in Jesus, "the perfect man," compared to a maximum polygon that forms one whole with the infinite circle in which it is inscribed, or again, according to a less mathematical vocabulary, *altissimum principiatum immediatissime principio unitum,* which, being at once active principle and passive material, could only be born *a matre sine virili semine* (III, 5).

Neither at Padua nor at Cologne had the Cusan obtained a master's degree in the arts nor had he donned the hat of a doctor of theology. It is somewhat through his chance reading, highly eclectic, that he instructed himself in the philosophical systems. From a Neo-Kantian perspective Cassirer has emphasized the role played for Nicholas by the "constructive" work of the intellect capable of forming some sorts of working concepts. But the most characteristic trait of Cusanism is the systematic recourse to a "dialectic" of opposites (remotely derived from the *Sophist* and the *Philebus,* reactivated by the Proclian reading of the *Parmenides,* but also by certain aspects of the style of Eckhart which abounds in the paradoxes of the "yes and no" sort). As for the influence of Ockham, of which one finds many traces in his way of considering, in counterpoint to the traditional realism of the intelligible, the mental formation of "notions," it partly determines the critical attitude of the cardinal faced with a *figura mundi* which—at least on essential points—was common to the disciples of Plato and those of Aristotle.

But there again, it is the principle of the "coincidences" (between maximum and minimum, hot and cold, rest and motion, circular and rectilinear, etc.) that allows the author of the *De docta ignorantia,* greatly exceeding the audaciousness of Parisian nominalism, to imagine a universe without assignable limits and deprived of a center; where the earth has ceased to be an immobile mass, dark and "base"; where the sun cannot be pure light and must contain, as all things do, dark patches (not having faultless lenses, the Cusan rather supposed than affirmed the existence of "black spots"); a universe above all without a fixed point, where each observer (Nicholas hypothetically describes the ascent of an astronaut), wherever he might be, would believe himself to be at the center of the world, in such a way that one could apply to the entire cosmos—with reference to the relativity of movement—the "theological" formula of the *Liber XXIV philosophorum,* taken up again by Alain de Lille, Saint Bonaventure, and many others, on the infinite sphere whose center is everywhere and its circumference nowhere:

> Machinam mundanam habere aut istam terram sensibilem aut aerem aut ignem vel aliud quodcunque pro centro fixo et immobili, variis motibus orbium consideratis, est impossibile. . . . Jam nobis manifestum est terram istam in veritate moveri, licet nobis hoc non appareat cum non apprehendimus motum nisi per quamdam comparationem ad fixum. . . . Propter hoc, cum semper cuilibet videatur quod, sive fuerit in terra sive sole aut alia stella, quod ipse sit in centro quasi immobili, et quod alia moveantur, ille certe semper alios et alios polos sibi constitueret. . . . Unde erit machina mundi quasi habens undique centrum et nullibi circumferentiam (II, 11 and 12).

However, the cosmological revolution is less complete here than it will be in Pascal, since the author explicitly adds that the true center and the true circumference of the undefined universe is God himself, *qui est undique et nullibi.* This immanence of the infinite the Platonists suspected only of being the *anima mundi,* without quite seeing that *natura* (or *spiritus universorum*) is *tota in toto et in qualibet parte.* But the Cusan often seems to distort the idea of the "number which moves itself," "made of the same and of the other," in the sense of what he calls (making use of an expression that comes from Boethius) the "natural complication of all the temporal order of things." If the Peripatetics criticize Platonism in this regard it is because they refuse the *medullaris intelligentia,* holding (perhaps without reason, *forte irrationabiliter*) to the *cortex verborum,* to a mode of expression that reifies the idea and separates it from its living source. More prudently, "a number of Christians"[22] have "acquiesced" to the Platonist view, understanding that in spite of some ambiguous expressions which appear to suppose "distinct reasons, posterior to God and anterior to things," placing them sometimes in a "guiding intelligence of the spheres," it is really a question, more or less confused, of the Word, that is, of the Son equal to the Father (II, 9).

Certain audacious consequences which the author of the *De docta ignorantia* draws from these views—the undefined character of a world which *terminus caret intra quos claudatur* (II, 11), the homogeneity between the sublunar and supralunar (the earth is a star like the others; there are probably inhabitants on the sun, II, 12)—announce a new reading of Neoplatonism (that of Giordano Bruno) that will remain, in its essentials, unknown to Ficino (for it is incidentally, and in order to praise circular movement, that he writes [*Plat. Theol.* IV, 1]: *Terra, si, ut voluit Aegesias, moveretur, in circulum moveretur,* adding immediately that this earth, *ut volunt plurimi, manet per superficiem,* all that is heavy being heaped up around it as in the center of the world). But it must be especially emphasized that, even where the Cusan makes use of concentric circles, in order to show the double envelopment of the sensible by the rational and of the rational by the intellectual, he corrects this schema by a figure of a quite different type, destined to show in what manner all creatures are simultaneously subject, in various degrees and fashions, to two clusters of influence, symbolized by two intersecting pyramids, corresponding to identity and difference, unity and multiplicity, light and darkness, but also, in a certain sense to God and nothingness: *Adverte quoniam Deus, qui est unitas, est basis lucis, basis vero tenebrae est nihil.*[23] Already, in the *De docta ignorantia* (II, 8–11), the theory of the *spiritus*— with explicit reference to ancient Stoicism—limited the hierarchical theme in suggesting an immense dynamic whole that has often been compared to the world of Leibnitz to the extent to which everything in it depends on everything and corresponds to everything (*quodlibet in quolibet*).

While preserving the terms "macrocosm" and "microcosm" (but in a universe which scarcely merits any longer the name of cosmos), Nicholas describes an undefined complex of interactions which leaves little room for astrology such as Ficino so willingly practiced. Without doubt, in the sermon *Ubi est,* delivered in 1456 on the feast of the Epiphany,[24] the preacher evokes with one word the sayings of Abumasar linking Judaism with Saturn, Islam with Venus, and Christianity with Mercury, but he does not attempt to define exactly the "signs" that announced the Nativity to the Magi. He prefers to take his inspiration from Eckhart's commentary on John 1:38 (*Rabbi, ubi habitas?*) in order to expatiate upon the divine "where," that "place of time" called eternity, "the never-ending motion" which is also "rest." And, without evoking any astral influence, he then outlines—in the line of the myth of Protagoras taken up and adapted by Gregory of Nyssa in the *Creation of Man*—a history of humanity at first deprived, then raised up, through culture and technology, to the true religion:

> Multi suo ingenio aut divina illuminatione varias artes invenerunt melius vivendi, ut qui artes mechanicas et seminandi et plantandi et negotiandi invenerunt, et alii qui politizandi et oeconomisandi regulas conscripserunt atque qui ethicam invenerunt. . . . Est deinde hiis artibus religio addita, in divina auctoritate et revelatione fundata (p. 96).

This progression has not the simplicity of a straight line. Although later than Jesus, Mohammed preached a truth that was partial and deformed. His historical mission was, however, to rescue untutored desert peoples from their superstitions and, although "deceived by the devil," to open to them an "easy way" towards the truth.[25] Throughout the Koranic formulae which explicitly reject them, the cardinal thinks he finds—implicit—Christian dogmas which, in their secret hearts, the best educated Muslims probably profess. Much more than the majority of his contemporaries, Nicholas foresees the spread of the inhabited earth and the variety of civilizations. (In the last book of *De concordantia* he already emphasizes them in relation to the Roman Empire which, contrary to the view supported by Dante, cannot lay claim to universality.) In spite of all the misfortunes of an age that does not encourage optimism (he, himself, struggles for years against the Duke of Tyrol and clashes, in his diocese of Brixen, with a section of his clergy), he seems to believe in progress. Not only can one better observe phenomena, spectacles are manufactured, printing is invented, but the cult of idols is regressing and the dream of a *pax fidei* corresponds certainly to what Ernst Bloch—inspired by the words of the Cusan—will call a *docta spes*.

It has been seen that among the thinkers who participated in the collective work, if Dionysius is at times presented as *cunctis acutior*,[26] Plato remains to the end the one who could see *aliquid plus aliis philosophis* (chap. 12), but in the same late text in which Nicholas confirms this advantage, showing himself all the more eirenic in that his recent reading of the *Vitae philosophorum* has notably enriched his information, he makes a very honorable place for Thales and for Anaxagoras, as well as for the Stoics, but still more for the *acutissimus Aristoteles* who is praised for having defined logic as the "most exact instrument" for the "pursuit as much for the true as for the conceivably true" (chap. 1), for having established a ternary theory of the syllogism analogically applicable to the *divinum opificium* (chap. 5), for being the one who, while limiting (in an erroneous manner) the action of the universal intellect to the *administratio coelestium*, was able to rise from sensible effects to the "first cause of all the causes" (chap. 8).

At the beginning of the *Learned Ignorance* (I, 1), he was already describing the Stagirite as *profundissimus* for having recognized that the radiance of daylight blinds the people of the night (following *Met.* α, I, 993b). A little later, irritated by the attacks of Wenck, he was sharply reproaching the "Aristotelian sect" for making use of the first principle which would prohibit every *ascensus ad mysticam theologiam*.[27] Nevertheless, in the *De mente* (chap. 13) the *idiota* learnedly expounds a theory of knowledge that holds the balance almost equally between Plato and Aristotle, moreover attributing more than one divergence to the use, in the two schools, of different vocabularies, one calling *anima mundi* what the other designates as *natura* and which is, in truth, *Deus omnia in omnibus operans* (called also *spiritus universorum*). Elsewhere[28] the cardinal will point out that the same first cause (unitrine as far as being efficient, formal, and final; another figure of the three divine Persons) is designated by the master of the Academy as *unum et bonum*, whereas the founder of the Lyceum presents it as *ens entium*—a formula so much more acceptable in that, according to the *Directio* (chap. 18), one of the major merits of Aristotle is to have stated that being is that which is "always sought and always in question" (*Met.* Z, 1, 1028b). The Cusan here anticipates, in a certain fashion, the exegesis of Aristotelian ontology that Pierre Aubenque will defend.[29]

Assuredly, the *De Beryllo* (chap. 25) underlines the error of the Stagirite when he is unwilling to admit in substance, side by side with form and matter, any more than a weak *privatio*, being unaware of the presence of a *nexus*. But in this respect it seems indeed that other thinkers went astray; the Cusan says so without mincing words: it is *omnes philosophos concordando* that Aristotle, extending in an unwarranted manner the range of application of the principle (a quite valid one) according to which contradictory judgments cannot be true at the same time, wrongly excludes from *substantia* this *tertium principium* in which coincided— according to Nicholas, in their infinitesimal degree and, so to speak, at the source of their differentiation—"contraries" such as the *minimum calor* and the *minimum frigus* (the tendency of which to be merged can be seen in the case of burning cold), the *minima tarditas* and the *minima velocitas* (the union of which can be imagined by observing a "sleeping" teetotum). These are physical analogues, Nicholas believes, of what are, for the geometrician, at the limit where they form a unity, the *minimus arcus* and the *minima chorda*. To have failed completely to grasp this was the common deficiency of searchers after wisdom, and for them it results, in Trinitarian theology, in semi-blindness. Less imprudent in this area than was Abelard, the Cusan professes in fact that even to the philosophers who spoke "with elegance" of the Father and the Word (not incarnate), this "principle of connection anterior to every duality" remained unknown, the *spiritus,* of which, the cardinal notes, no mention is made in the Gospel of John, the one to which most of the *Platonici* came closest.

In chapter 25 of the *De venatione,* making use of less radical formulae, the author notes only that "few philosophers" were aware of the *nexus unitatis et entitatis* (which *procedit ex unitate et aequalitate*), an invisible bond of love that makes all parts of the world hold together, a fire that nourishes the intelligence and alone procures for it complete happiness. Indeed it is possible that Aristotle had a presentiment of it when he defined that *intellectus penitus in actu* which turns back upon itself and *seipsum intelligit,* so producing the *delectatio summa.*[30] But Plato had a better inkling of it when he stated—if we are to believe Diogenes Laertius—that the "idea" is "at the same time one and multiple, stable and mobile."[31] It remains that properly speaking no *venator* explored through and through the ten hunting grounds listed by the Cusan. What restrained them particularly was their finitist prejudice. Most paradoxically, at least in the *Directio*—where he intends to take unto himself the Peripateticism of one of his interlocutors—it is again in the Stagirite that the author seems to recognize (apart from the merit, often emphasized, of judging *ratio* incapable of grasping *ipsam simplicissimam rerum quidditatem*; chap. 19) the implicit attribution of a *virtus infinita* to the Prime Mover, here assimilated, it is true, with the *non aliud, ante quantitatem et in omnibus omnia,* a true *forma formarum* and authentic *termini terminus* (chap. 10). On the other hand, even in the *De principio* of 1459, very closely inspired by the *In Parmenidem* of Proclus, the cardinal emphasizes the limits of a view according to which, in order to give form to the cosmos, the demiurge would have available only a finite number of notions. Not knowing the *Enneads* (in particular passages such as in V, 3, 15 or VI, 5, 9 which describe the One as a "total power" containing "infinite being and the multiple") he remains convinced that no Platonist grasped with "precision" the dyad of the two *infinitates*: the *finibilis* (called also, in other texts, *posse fieri*) and the *finiens* (or *posse facere*), the one situated *post,* the other *ante omne ens.*[32]

Also, even though Plato "saw better" than Aristotle the "generated" character of the world and the true role of time as an "image of eternity" (*De venatione,* chaps. 8 and 9), understanding even that man should try to become continually *Deo similior* (chap. 20), Nicholas is not at all sure that Plato grasped in its full significance (in spite of the *aliquid plus* that Nicholas accords to him some lines later on) the *naturale desiderium* under the impulsion of which our intellect endeavors (*conatur*) ceaselessly to explore an "infinite treasure" that it rightly "rejoices" (*gaudet*) in recovering, not at all "numerable" or "comprehensible," but "inexhaustible" inasmuch as "incomprehensible" (chap. 12). As background to the homily of Pope Leo invoked here and cited (*Nemo ad cognitionem veritatis magis propinquat quam qui intelligit in rebus divinis, etiam si multum proficiat, semper sibi superesse quod quaerat*),[33] the Cusan brings in the tradition of *epectasis* according to the spirit of Gregory of Nyssa.[34] But at the same time—through his concern for human toil during this life on earth, oriented towards a better knowledge of the created and towards a lasting understanding between peoples—it seems indeed that, in language that is partly inherited from Neoplatonism, he anticipates in a certain way the "modern" option of Lessing (which will also be that of Kant, at least in its moral): the call for an "infinite endeavor" in preference to an immediate gift of complete knowledge, which belongs only to God, not to his creature.

*   *   *

On the funeral monument erected in the sixteenth century in the cathedral in Florence, one could read of canon Marsilio that he, "the Father of Wisdom," had "restored to the light" the "Platonic dogma, through the fault of time hidden in the dust." And it is indeed like the awakening of some sleeping beauty that the Italian humanists experienced the *rinascimento*. But for Ficino it was like a sort of excavation at several levels corresponding to the historical vicissitudes of that same "dogma," each time forgotten and subsequently rediscovered.

When presenting in 1492 his translation of the *Enneads,* Ficino asserts—in a style that is dear to him—that at the beginning of 1484, when his Latin Plato was already in the press, it was the "heroic spirit" of Cosimo de' Medici (dead for twenty years) that sent him another "heroic spirit," that of the young Count de la Mirandola, inviting him to continue with his work by translating and commenting Plotinus, an intercession all the more charged with meaning in the eyes of Marsilio because Pico had first seen the light (under the same astral signs as he) in 1463 when there began at Careggi, at the urging of the Medici, the "rebirth of Plato."[35] In truth, being nourished above all on Aristotle, Pico came to Platonism rather as an "explorer" than as a "deserter,"[36] convinced moreover that between the two schools the difference must have been verbal in the majority of cases. A fortiori, he did not see any doctrinal opposition, but a development and an illustration, from the old Academy up to the final school of Athens. This was also the view of Ficino who, after having very rapidly completed his translation of Plotinus, addressed himself to the works of Porphyry and Iamblichus.

He did not believe, for all that, that the history of ancient Platonism presented a picture of a continual and harmonious flowering. As far back as 1469— the year, as we know, in which Andrea dei Bussi associated in a common eulogy the "Platonists" Bessarion and Nicholas of Cusa—the controversy between the cardinal of Nicaea and his compatriot George gave Marsilio an opportunity to retrace in broad outline the eclipses and revivals of the doctrine that must again, with courage, be defended and promoted. Thanking Bessarion for his vigorous pamphlet, he recalls that wisdom, after having shone with a sharp brilliance in the author of the *Phaedrus* (by some "gift divine"), grew dark in his very school through the fault of too-feeble successors. In order to explain this blacking out, Saint Augustine records a tradition that Arcesilaus had deliberately concealed the Platonic truth for fear that Zeno would alter it (*Contra Acad.* III, 17–19). Proclus describes the movement by which philosophy would, so to speak, have "withdrawn into itself" (*Plat. Theol.* I, 1).[37] Marsilio avoids the language of the ancient mysteries, and notably the Proclian metaphor[38] of a "reason" that surpasses itself and then achieves, thanks to the writings of Plato, a "Bacchic ecstasy." Preferring metaphors borrowed from the practice of alchemy, he shows the manner in which the "Platonic gold," at one time tarnished, recovered its brightness, thanks to an "intense fire," at first "in the dispensary of Plotinus, then in those of Porphyry, of Iamblichus, and afterwards of Proclus."[39]

We are concerned then with a kind of precious treasure, constantly under threat and at times lost, but whose origin dates from the night of time. In his *proemium* to his translation of the *Poimandres* (1463), the young Marsilio goes back to Atlas, whom he imagines as a contemporary of Moses and brother of Prometheus, himself a distant ancestor of Hermes Trismegistus, held to be the founder of "theology"—a variable list which, following a tradition coming doubtless from Syrianus, will include also Orpheus, Pythagoras, and Aglaophemus. Ficino soon adds to it Zoroaster who is for him the author of the *Chaldaean Oracles* and whom Gemistos Plethon placed on the same level as the founder of the Academy.[40] Indeed, at the time of the *De religione christiana* (1476), the author, a priest for two years and anxious to root Platonism in the Hebraic tradition, suggests that the Iranian prophet, perhaps earlier than Hermes, could have received teachings from Cham after the Deluge, or at least have associated with Abraham. But in the introduction to his Plotinus he presents a genealogy that does not introduce any biblical authority:

> Non absque providentia . . . factum est ut pia quaedam philosophia quondam et apud Persas sub Zoroastre, et apud Aegyptios sub Mercurio nasceretur, utrobique sibimet consona; nutriretur deinde apud Thraces sub Orpheo atque Aglaophema; adolesceret quoque mox sub Pythagora apud Graecos et Italos; tandem vero a divo Platone consummaretur Athenis.

But before taking a place, in his turn, among the successors or the restorers of this *pia philosophia,* Marsilio Ficino (introduced to the Medici by his father, a physician who had gained their confidence) was first at Pisa the pupil of the Peripatetic Tignosi. A little later, too captivated a reader of Lucretius, he disturbed Saint Antoninus, archbishop of Florence, who thought it prudent to advise him emphatically to study the *Summa contra Gentes.* From reading this our humanist drew sufficient profit to make use, in his *Platonica Theologia,* of many Thomistic arguments, not only in what concerns the divine attributes such as infinity, unity, and intellection (II, 2–9), but even in the matter of what constitutes the very heart of the work, the *immortalitas animarum,* for it is indeed to the

Angelic Doctor that Ficino owes the reasons he invokes for refusing to the "pure forms" all other composition than that of *esse* and *essentia* (V, 7–9). Only, while he very willingly names Saint Augustine and quotes him at length (for example in XII, 5–7 where there occur extended extracts from the *De vera religione,* from the *De musica,* and from the *De trinitate,* with introductory formulae such as *Sed juvat hic cum Augustino, ut saepe solemus, paulo latius pervagari*), his borrowings from Aquinas—qualified though he was as *christianae splendor theologiae* (XVIII, 8)—often remain anonymous, and more or less masked by stylistic transpositions.[41] Let us add that, in all his work, Marsilio will juxtapose with the Platonic formulae elements of Aristotelian and Stoic vocabulary (and theory), a customary mixture in Neoplatonism.

That being said, it is indeed Plato that from a very early stage he declares for, even at a time when he is only reading the *Timaeus* through Chalcidius and the *Phaedrus* in the translation of Bruni, during that period of apprenticeship when, in order to work out some scholarly dissertations ambitiously entitled *De Deo* and *De anima,* he takes inspiration from Proclus in the translations of Moerbeke, collecting from Apuleius and from Boethius the fragile information in his *Platonic Institutions* presented in 1456 to Landino and to Cosimo. This text, which was not well received, was never published. From then on, while studying medicine (probably in Bologna between 1457 and 1462), Ficino set himself very seriously (and, it seems, especially through his own means) to the study of Greek, a language whose difficulties he overcame sufficiently to translate, by way of an exercise, some poems of Hesiod, the Pseudo-Orpheus, Proclus, and parts of the *Chaldaean Oracles,* highly successful attempts that he made use of for numerous quotations in his *Platonica Theologia.*

In 1463, judging him well trained for the task of which he had been dreaming for a long time, Cosimo installed him in the villa of Careggi. Having gotten his hand in with the *Poimandres,* Marsilio began to translate—and to comment on— the Plato manuscript his protector entrusted to him, the Plut. gr. 59, 1 of the Laurentian library, without trying to distinguish, among the *Dialogues* and the *Letters,* between the doubtful and the apocryphal. By the following year, Cosimo, an invalid close to death, was able to read Ficino's versions of the *Parmenides* and of the *Philebus.* Of the latter dialogue the guest at Careggi soon gave a public reading, matched with his comments, in a monastery that was very probably that of Santa Maria degli Angeli. To those who were astonished at this, he declared that Platonic philosophy, *tanquam sacra, legenda est in sacris*; he even added, which corresponds well with his taste for intermediary spirits, *in conspectu angelorum.*[42]

During the brief years of his administration of public affairs, the "gouty" Piero de' Medici took little interest in Careggi. Lorenzo, on the contrary, gave a vital stimulus to the Academy, where reigned a fervor that made it almost a sanctuary (although it still remains highly doubtful that a lamp continually burnt there in front of a bust of Plato). On the seventh of November, 1468, he who would become known as the Magnificent (he would not succeed his father until the following month, but was already enjoying great prestige) organized a solemn repast, renewing, says Ficino (*De amore* I, 1) the tradition interrupted at the death of Porphyry. Around Bandini assembled, in addition to Marsilio and his father, the bishop of Fiesole and some companions, among them Landino and Cavalcanti. Each guest had the duty of commenting on the successive speeches that Plato has given his interlocutors in his *Symposium*. As they were recorded in the treatise *On love*, drafted by Marsilio shortly after the event, these exegetic propositions—in the style of Ficino, more homogeneous than those of the participants in the Platonic dialogue—constituted a sort of erotic philosophic mysticism, at times disparate and confused, but whose general meaning was quite indicative of Neoplatonic thought in the Florence of the Medici.

Let us say for the sake of simplicity that, according to this perspective, Eros, a very ancient god, born with Chaos and destined to fight it (I, 3), symbolizes the tendency, innate in us, towards the Beautiful, the son and splendor of the Good. To the heavenly Aphrodite, continually turned towards her father Ouranos (not Kronos as Plotinus suggested, thus substituting Intelligence for the One; III, 5, 2), corresponds the angelic intellect, identified with the second Plotinian hypostasis. The earthly Aphrodite is the Soul of the world, the power of a childbirth born at the same time of Zeus and of the *materia mundi* signified by Dione (II, 7). It is she who gives form to bodies and makes them beautiful enough to inspire lovers with such reciprocal attachments that each lives only for the other, or, to put it better, in the other (*Quotiens duo aliqui mutua se benevolentia complectuntur, iste in illo, ille in isto vivit*; II, 8). Thus Eros, son of this Aphrodite, holds together the things of heaven and those of earth, and it is from him that are born the arts, whose common principle is harmony (III, 2–3).

As for the burlesque recital of Aristophanes on the original androgyne, it must be understood of souls, not of men, and the duality that it describes concerns less the sexes than the two "lights" with which all were endowed at their creation: the one "innate," by which they can consider what is "equal and inferior" to them, the other "infused" (at the same time reminiscence and grace), so that they may contemplate what is "superior" to them (IV, 2). Having chosen to immerse themselves in bodies, there remains in them a trace of the *splendor infusus*, in such a way that by means of the four cardinal virtues—prudence leading to strength (masculine and solar), moderation (feminine and terrestrial), justice (androgynous and lunar)—they can purify themselves, reject the arrogance of him who trusts in his own powers and thus recover, under the stimulation of beautiful forms, their *pristina integritas* (IV, 5), attaining to a beatitude that (and he also goes back to the theme of *epectasis*) Ficino conceives as an appetite that feeds tirelessly on a "spectacle always new":

> Aeternus igitur amor, quo semper in Deum afficitur animus, efficit ut Deo semper tanquam novo spectaculo gaudeat. . . . Omni expulso fastidio, suo quodam ardore oblectamentum quasi novum jugiter accendit in animo redditque illum blanda et dulci fruitione beatum (IV, 6).

One is not greatly surprised that the guests at the banquet of the Medici acknowledge an essential role for the ambiguous beings that Plato called gods, souls of the stars, or demons, whereas Dionysius speaks rather of "angel ministers of God," but in this connection, thinks Benci, commenting on the speech of Socrates, *inter Platonem et Dionysium verborum potius est quam sententiae discrepatio* (VI, 3). By whatever name we call them, these messengers had originally, according to the qualities proper to the seven planets, transmitted to the souls "enveloped in a heavenly and luminous body" and descending towards the earth through the Milky Way and the constellation of Cancer, seven gifts which (as they are listed in the *De amore* VI, 4—*contemplationis acumen, gubernandi potestas, animositas, claritas sensuum, amoris ardor, interpretandi subtilitas,* and *foecunditas generandi*) scarcely correspond to the seven munificences of the Holy Spirit, and which moreover, especially the last three, quite "honorable" though they be because of their divine origin, creatures too often misuse. Let us add that the "demons" act in general according to the humors and temperaments of the bodies in which the souls are bogged down. Improving upon the Platonic distinctions, Benci enumerates, for example, three *venerei demones,* of which the first (the progeny of the heavenly Aphrodite) reserves its weapons for the choleric, the second (sent by the common Aphrodite) attacks rather the sanguine, and the third (coming from the planet Venus) prefers to aim its arrows at the phlegmatic (VI, 5).

These mediating powers taken together constitute the third level of a hierarchy on four levels, rising from the body to God: the major difference between the two intermediate degrees is that the *angeli mens,* which is called stable, total, and continuous, grasps things in an instant and in a global fashion (*uno aeternitatis puncto simul intelligit omnia*), whereas the *anima* is bound, by nature, to discursiveness and temporality, which is why Plato accords it an "ipsomotricity" that Aristotle misjudged, believing that it meant that the soul confers its movement on itself (VI, 15). In other passages Ficino and his spokesmen hold to a ternary order, that of *Letter II* (312e), evoking the beings of "second" and "third" rank which "gravitate around the King of the universe," but the *theologus Antonius* (none less than the bishop of Fiesole), who comments on the speech attributed to Pausanias, curiously assimilates this ternary order to a supposedly Zoroastrian triad (Ormuzd, Mithra, Ahriman), deprived of all dualist inner depth and merged in fact with the Plotinian hierarchy (*Deus-Mens-Anima* II, 4—compare the almost identical formulae of *Plat. Theol.* IV, 1). When Benci, on the subject of Eros the "magician" (*Symposium,* 203d), evokes in his turn the Iranian prophet, declaring (VI, 10) that for the same reason as Socrates he was "by nature" the "friend of demons" (as distinct from Apollonius of Tyana and Porphyry who owed to their sole "veneration" for these intermediary beings the privilege of magic powers), it is evident that only angels or favorable geniuses are in question.

Throughout the work, neither Plotinus nor Proclus is mentioned by name; they remain merged into the community of the *Platonici,* although Ficino notes certain divergences between them, notably concerning the existence of *mali demones,* evoked in a quite incidental fashion (VI, 4), but on which, he says, "certain Platonists" and the "Christian theologians" are in agreement. Several times he cites Ovid, Virgil, and even Lucretius (true, it is to describe certain aberrations of love, VII, 5 and 7). He happens in passing to invoke the authority of Aristotle, but as a *physicus,* on the subject of the "black bile" of those who, like Socrates or Sappho, seem *ad amandi artem propensissimi* (VI, 9), or of the supposed "spiritual vapor" that would escape through the eyes and, with women during the menstrual period, would be laden with droplets of blood capable of tarnishing their mirror (VIII, 4). In the *De amore,* conceived first and foremost as a *Commentarium in Convivium Platonis,* Christianity is placed, in a sort of a way, between parentheses, but the Trinitarian allusion (confirmed in the margin by a note by Marsilio and by the very title of the chapter, *Quomodo agendae sunt gratiae Spiritus Sancti qui nos ad hanc disputationem illuminavit atque accendit*) is not without significance right at the end of the book, when Cavalcanti, having expounded and explained, in the manner of Ficino, the speech of Alcibiades, in order in some way to make Him propitious, invokes "God whole and entire"— Power, Wisdom, and Love—that is Father, Son, and Holy Spirit (and not, as Marcel inexactly translates it, the power and the wisdom of Love):

> Nos autem amorem hunc adeo nobis propitium ea mente colemus et veneremus sapientiam et potentiam admiremur, ut, amore duce, totum, ut ita loquar, Deum habeamus propitium, ac totum amoris flagrantia diligentes, toto etiam amore perpetuo perfruamur (VII, 17).

Dated July 1469—some months before the *Letter* to Bessarion on the vicissitudes of Platonism—this commentary, in a tone at times peculiar and which was the basis of several malicious interpretations, was not to be published until 1484, two years after the *Platonica Theologia de immortalitate animarum* (completed, it seems, by 1474). In the meantime appeared two short works with the significant titles, *Concordantia Mosis et Platonis* and *Confirmatio christianorum per socratica.* Braccio Martello, to whom these texts are addressed, is disturbed by the position that "demons" hold in them. Ficino replies by invoking the double testimony of Plotinus and of Porphyry confirming that of Origen, in such a way that *non Plato solum, verum etiam Platonici cum nostra religione consentiant.*[43] Already in 1474 it was prompted by such a certitude that, under the guarantee of Lorenzo, he had decided to receive the sacrament of Holy Orders, thus attaining to a status which indeed, through the game of ecclesiastical benefices, assured him leisure for work, but which above all was to enable him (as he declares in the foreword of *De christiana religione*) to combine *philosophandi studium* with *pietatis officium.*

In pursuing his Platonist work, he thus considers that he was fulfilling his priestly vocation. His *Plotinus* completed, he translates several Neoplatonic texts, notably of Iamblichus, Porphyry, and Proclus, and then, as if in the same burst of enthusiasm, the *Divine Names* and the *Mystical Theology.* After which the Areopagite—qualified as *Platonicorum procul dubio summus*[44]—brings him back so to speak to the legendary sources of the *corpus dionysiacum.* From 1497 onward, grown old and disillusioned by the drama of Savonarola, which for him was not a very brilliant episode, he undertakes a commentary of the Pauline epistles which will not go beyond the first five chapters of Romans. For this work he is closely inspired by Aquinas, but—as has been seen with reference to several pages of the *Platonica theologia*—to make his own certain Thomistic arguments was not to break with a fundamental attachment to the "Platonic dogma." The epitaph drawn up by his colleagues by no means indicates that he had ever renounced the *Atticum decus* of which they congratulate him on having made a gift to his fatherland.

It seems that he remained faithful to the positions that he defended, for example, in 1492, against his friend Pico who deplored the attachment of Marsilio to astrology, preferring for his part to find support for his Christianity in the Cabbala, more easily reconcilable, he thought, with free will and the "dignity" of man (but this was not at all the view of his Roman censors). Ficino, at the beginning of his commentary on the *Parmenides,* counters with a general criticism of anyone who, neglecting the opinion of Proclus, wishes to reduce the divine dialogue to an exercise in logic. Disregarding the primacy of the Good and the One over Being, the author of the *De ente et uno* makes a concession to the Parisian (i.e., scholastic) style that Marsilio deems unacceptable. The following year, replying to the *Adversus astrologiam divinatricem* by the same Pico, he agreed that one must understand the astral signs in a "poetic" and "symbolic" sense, but would not concede anything on the essential points of his convictions.[45]

The role that "Platonic theology" properly plays in an apologetic quite different from that of Proclus remains to be determined. Dedicating his great work to *Lorenzo*—he who knew how to unite, as the author of the *Republic* wished, *philosophia* with *summa in rebus publicis auctoritas*—Ficino recognizes in Plato the merit that the Cusan pointed out in analogous terms of having understood that, just as the sun is visible only by its own diffusion, we know God only through the light that he confers on us:

> Plato, philosophorum pater, magnanime Laurenti, cum intelligeret quemadmodum se habet visus ad Solis lumen, ita se habere mentes omnes ad Deum, ideoque eas nihil unquam sine Dei lumine posse cognoscere. . . .

Thus all his philosophy—moral and dialectic, physical and mathematical—constitutes a "theology" and, since the consciousness of self, as Saint Augustine well saw, is the first condition of our accession to illumination, it is first proper to establish the divine character of the *mens creata.*

This undertaking is all the more necessary in that, in ever greater numbers, *perversa ingenia* challenge the authority of the faith. To those who had complained of his supposed "rationalism," Abelard objected that without arguments from reason, one can have scarcely any effect on subtle opponents. That is also the opinion of Ficino, convinced that Providence has very precisely entrusted him with the task of reviving the "Platonic reasons," most capable in his eyes of affecting the ungodly. His friend Pannonius, a humanist bishop but one who scarcely appreciates familiarity with geniuses and belief in celestial signs, suggests in a letter that the *renovatio antiquorum,* attributed by Marsilio to a happy planetary conjuncture, could be more "fortuitous" than "providential" and could depend less on "religion" than on "curiosity." He answers him by a defense of those superior spirits, true "ministers of God," of which the astral figures signify only (without determining them) the benevolent actions toward the *mentes humanae*, in such a way that even *fatum* is always at the service of *Providentia*.[46]

Already, in the foreword to the *De christiana religione*, Marsilio evoked eternal Wisdom which, since the beginning of time, has established a privileged liaison between the *divina mysteria* and the *verae sapientiae amatores*. Also, for the Persians as for the Jews, for the Indians and for the Gauls, as much in Egypt as in Ethiopia, the philosophical function was not separated from the sacerdotal dignity, so that no propagator of the *rectus cultus* could neglect the *ratio colendi*.[47] Ficino reproaches the Christians of his time with a double ignorance, that of the clerics whose religion is often pure superstition, and that of the philosophers who fail to recognize the only way capable of leading them to religion: hence this appeal addressed to the one and to the other: *Hortor igitur omnes atque precor philosophos quidem ut religionem vel capessant penitus vel attingant, sacerdotes autem legitime sapientiae studiis diligenter incumbant*. The *Letter* to Pannonius specifies it; these stubborn philosophers, for whom religion is an old wives' tale, are none other than the disciples of Alexander of Aphrodisias and Averroes, those who betraying Aristotle (*adversus Averroem graeca Aristotelis verba reclamant*; *Plat. Theol.* XV, 1) proclaim the human intellect either mortal like the body or common to all individuals.

Thus Ficino rediscovers the same enemies as Petrarch and one can see better the direction of his Platonism. Indeed he exonerates the Stagirite from the blasphemies that are erroneously shielded by his authority; he even attributes arguments to him on occasion (referring, for example, to his *Metaphysics* as to the existence of a multiplicity of angelic directors charged with moving the heavenly spheres; *Plat. Theol.* I, 5), but he judges his philosophy, even essentially, as much less "religious" than that of Plato, less apt therefore to serve as a propaedeutic *ad perfectam religionem*, that is, as the best of all those that constitute the genus of the *religio communis*. The *acuta ingenia* are nourished voluntarily on philosophic food, but if they receive the *esca philosophica* of a *philosophus religiosus* such as Plato, while they believe themselves to be philosophizing, they are already impregnating themselves with religion, which leads them more easily *ad meliorem religionis speciem sub genere compraehensam*. While awaiting the miracles that Providence, as it did in the time of the apostles, will doubtless not be slow to instigate in order that the specific character of the true faith may be made manifest, Ficino accomplishes a work of piety, since to make better known "the divine Plato and the great Plotinus" is to confirm *ratione philosophica ipsum religionis genus*.[48]

It might be thought that, in a certain way, by a "transsumption" of Cusan-type, Platonism as Ficino understands it, transcends itself to be merged at the upper limit into the truth common to all religions, that of Christianity, of course. This idea is not perhaps totally unknown to Marsilio who—to use the formulae in which Raymond Klibansky sees a possible echo of the *De pace fidei*—acclaims the variety of rites as a *mirabilis decor*, the sign of a providential will (*De christiana religione*, chap. 4). But the *religio communis* that he envisages, at one of the decisive stages of his argument, resembles rather a natural religion (although more poetical and magical than rationalistic). His essential aim is to throw the fullest light on the divinity and on the immortality of the soul. If it is true that the divine attributes demonstrable by means of *ratio philosophica* extend to the providential care of all creatures (*Plat. Theol.* II, 13), which does not at all exclude, as we know, the essential place left for the angels and demons (without forgetting heroes and geniuses), the "common religion" under its Platonic form— that of the wise man who "treats divinely of heavenly things" while Aristotle "speaks naturally of divine things"[49]—only indirectly (or in a premonitory fashion) makes way for the great Christian dogmas of the Trinity, Incarnation, and Redemption. Indeed Socrates, in his acceptance of unjust death, in the manner in which he came out of himself to converse with his *daimôn*, can pass, not for an *aemulus*, but for a *defensor* of Christ (that is, a pagan precursor parallel to the just men of the Old Testament[50]). And, in the *Concordia*, where Marsilio takes up again the same terms as Numenius, Plato appears quite like "another Moses," who has a presentiment of the creation, the fault of men expelled from a sort of earthly paradise (the Atlantis of the *Critias*!), the punishment of the wicked in another world, and even the veiled announcement of a *sacratior aliquis quam homo* coming to earth in order "to open up the sources of truth, finally followed by all." [51] It remains that nothing of all that can take the place of faith in Christ as it is revealed only by the *perfecta religio.*[52] In this regard the later texts that multiply the formulae of prudence do not lack continuity with the earlier works, to which moreover they willingly refer. In the same letter to a Dominican in which he suggests that Platonists such as Plotinus (pupil of the Christian Ammonius Saccas) or Proclus were able to read with profit the Gospel of John and the Dionysian writings, Ficino, in 1495, refers explicitly to what he wrote to Braccio Martello, that is, to his *Concordia* itself.[53] He could have evoked much earlier declarations, for example those in the *De religione christiana* (chaps. 8, 13, 23, etc.), as to the superiority of the apostle over the most subtle philosophers.

Let us add that, in this reading of Platonism, despite certain allusions to falls and punishments, the accent is scarcely placed on the resistance that the demiurgic work comes up against, nor on the indomitable aspect of certain forms of malice. Marsilio is the resolute opponent of all forms of gnosis of a Gnostic tendency (cf. notably *Plat. Theol.* II, 2). On the other hand he emphasizes the teeming life "everywhere present," which makes him indulgent towards the idea of a World Soul.[54]

If he invokes in passing the unlucky influx of Venus, particularly fearful when Saturn is opposed to the sun (for example, *De amore* IV, 4 and VII, 10–11), it pleases him to put confidence in Jupiter to counteract the misdeeds of Saturn (VI, 4–17). Despite his morose temperament (and a melancholy against which the *De triplici vita* of 1489 presents many remedies—dietary, astrological, and even "ecological"), in general he treats with much understanding the "sympathies" between planets (for the angels who move the spheres are all children of God, ministers of the same Father, *De amore* I, 8). In any case, never could the tyranny of Necessity prevail against the dominion—more ancient—of that Eros who, as

Orpheus said, "engenders all" and, in this way, "commands the three Parcae" (*De amore* V, 10–12). Below the transcendent God, "source of unity" (*Plat. Theol.* III, 1) within the scale leading from matter to the angels, Ficino emphasizes the continuities. With what he calls the "inert mass" of bodies (only recognized by Atomists) is linked, in fact, as of itself, the "efficacious quality" (brought to light by the Stoics) that in its turn leads to the "rational soul" (which Heraclitus described), then to the "angelic intelligence," the stage at which Anaxagoras stopped, leaving to Plato the concern to designate the "divine sun" toward which must turn the *purgata acies mentis* (I, 1).

As thunderbolt and mortars can prove, bodies have more power to the extent that they are less dense, nearer to air and fire, and the most humble forms, those that need a material substratum, act only through the immanence in them of an idea coming from the *primus mundani operis architectus* (I, 2 and 3). At the same time intelligent and intelligible, the angel remains motionless, a direct reflection of the operative principle. In an intermediary position, exactly in the center of the scale, the soul, like the moon, receives its light from on high; motionless by its substance, it is mobile through its works. Between the pure corporeal multiplicity and the divine unity (with the two intermediaries of quality or united multiplicity and of the angel or multiple unity), it alone forms the link between two infinities, that of the Good and that of primary matter, which, inasmuch as it aspires to Being, already participates in goodness (I, 4–6 to III, 1–2).

With its triple function (reason, anger, and concupiscence corresponding to brain, heart, and liver), the human soul is distinguished however from the *anima mundi,* indivisible and omnipresent, populated by demons, geniuses, and heroes, *vita mundo infusa* which the Stoics erroneously confused with the *summus Deus.* Although Saint Augustine and Saint Thomas judged the question of secondary importance, Marsilio wished that a council would explicitly confirm the thesis of the *Epinomis* (983b–c) on the souls of the spheres, intermediaries between ours and the *anima mundi,* but he scarcely seemed to doubt there would be a positive response that would harmonize with his astrological views (IV, 1). On the other hand, despite the opinion of Plotinus, he did not believe that the seminal reasons were finite in number, which would impose the image of an eternal return. And if it is true that the statement of Plato on the manufacture of souls by the acolytes of the demiurge seems to accord with Ficino's taste for mediations, Ficino here—not being afraid to invoke equally the authority of Aristotle as to the intellect coming from without (*Gen. Anim.* II, 3, 736a)—prefers the opinion of other "excellent Platonists" (Dionysius, Origen, Augustine) and asserts that, having been created *ex nihilo,* our souls owe their incorruptibility to a *virtus infinita* operating *sine medio* (V, 13 to X, 7–8). From this one can infer—Marsilio here comes close to Nicholas—that the *mens* also possesses, *quodammodo,* an "infinite virtue" thanks to which *non modo reperit infinitum actum qui Deus est, verum etiam potentiam infinitam quae est materia subdita Deo atque ad innumerabiles formas inde cap- iendas idonea* (VIII, 16).

Calling attention to certain disagreements between non-Christian Platonists (for example between Plotinus, on the one hand, and Porphyry and Proclus on the other) on the immortality of irrational souls, he passes quickly on, making use of a formula (*sed haec ipsi viderint*) that means: it is their business (V, 4). Most often he believes he discerns between all the *Platonici*—Greek, Arab, and Christian— a fundamental agreement, notably on the existence of the "ethereal body" which will belong to souls inasmuch as they are incorruptible (IX, 6), but still more on the motion by which the *mens,* as *imago Dei,* turns back on itself, reflecting in some way the divine radiance, and can thus rise towards God (XII, 3–4 to XIII, 4).

In the fall of souls, Ficino—who pretends to rely at the same time on Moses and on Zoroaster, on Hermes and on Plato—see less a revolt than a sickness. In spite of the disorder that it produces in the cosmos, he emphasizes particularly what remains of harmony, notably those marvels of instinct that he presents as the signs of a divine presence, recognized by Saint John and Saint Paul and which the ancients symbolized by their *Jovis omnia plena* (X, 3 to XII, 1). And he extols above all that *mens humana,* constantly illuminated by the *mens divina* and which possesses an *intuitus naturalis veri* (XII, 4). Through the enthusiasm which captivates it, it can have command over beasts and things in such a way that man becomes a sort of "emulator of God in his arts and governments" (XII, 3). Describing him as the most religious of beings, Ficino seems to attribute to him the final ambition to "become all," to "do all," to "surpass all," to be "everywhere and always," to know "the supreme riches and the highest pleasure" (XIV, 2).

These are certainly rhetorical formulae rather than a statement of some Promethean wish, but the magical background remains disquieting to the extent that Ficino affirms a parallelism between three systems of determination— Providence which governs intellects, Destiny which rules over souls, Nature who is mistress of bodies—so that not only miracles, but all the spells and incantations (to use the expressions that Marsilio knew well and which soon imposed themselves on Pomponazzi) come to be written in a certain way into the *lex aeterna.* The author of the *Platonica Theologia* does not appear to doubt that this doctrine is at the same time that of Iamblichus, of Proclus, of Avicenna, and of the "Christian theologians" (XIII, 2–5). But is it enough, to assure this harmonization, to take up again arguments against materialism and against Averroism (notably in Book XV) that are partly borrowed from the Thomistic arsenal, or, finally, confronted with the eschatological problem, to invite the reader to pass beyond the philosophical circumlocutions to follow the shorter way that he is offered by the *theologici christiani* (XVIII, 8)?

Without casting doubt on the good faith of the canon of Florence, one will simply recall, among so many other signs of a mode of expression through which are revealed singular modes of feeling and of thought, the very terms of which Marsilio makes use—spontaneously and not without naïveté—when he expresses his gratitude to the archbishop of Florence, Rinaldo Orsini, the brother-in-law of Lorenzo. This prelate, in fact, made the journey to Rome to see the pope personally and to prevent an imminent condemnation of the *Apologia* published in December 1489 by the author of the *De triplici vita* who was accused of allowing too much scope to astrology in the third part of the medical work. In truth it seems that his defense, on the contrary, aggravated his case. Saved by the representations of Orsini, he was not afraid to evoke Saturn, master of ravening wolves, and to compare the archbishop to the beneficent planet that neutralizes inauspicious influxes:

> Salve diu, salve semper, pastor bone, salus ovium. Pastor bonus animam suam ponit pro ovibus suis, ut ea et pascat et tueatur a lupis. Ita ut nuper agnum tuum Ficinum pie admodum ex voracibus luporum faucibus eruisti et Saturno jam nos graviter invadenti, tu quasi Jupiter es oppositus.[55]

14

Neoplatonism, the Greek Commentators, and Renaissance Aristotelianism

EDWARD P. MAHONEY

In this paper I should like to share with my fellow students of Neoplatonism the results of researches in medieval and Renaissance Aristotelianism that have brought to light interesting ways in which Neoplatonism came to have a special impact on the development of Renaissance Aristotelianism. It is certainly not my aim to exclude other possible ways in which Neoplatonism had its effect, but I do believe that historians of ancient Neoplatonism will themselves be surprised to learn of the pervasiveness of certain themes among supposed proponents of Aristotle during the fifteenth and sixteenth centuries. The two topics on which I wish to concentrate are (1) the influence on late fifteenth- and early sixteenth-century Aristotelianism of two late ancient commentators on Aristotle, namely, Themistius (317–388) and Simplicius (*fl.* 530),[1] and (2) a conceptual scheme of metaphysical hierarchy whose origins are clearly Neoplatonic and which was constantly debated during the same period.

THE GREEK COMMENTATORS
THEMISTIUS AND SIMPLICIUS—AND THEIR INFLUENCE
ON RENAISSANCE ARISTOTELIANISM

If we turn to the writings of two of the most famous philosophers at Padua during the fifteenth century, namely, Paul of Venice (d. 1429)[2] and Cajetan of Thiene (1387–1465),[3] we find no direct use of the writings of these Commentators in their own psychological writings. The situation is different with Nicoletto Vernia (d. 1499)[4] and his student, Agostino Nifo (ca. 1470–1538),[5] both of whom make extensive use of Themistius' paraphrases on the *De anima* in the translation of Ermolao Barbaro;[6] Simplicius' *Physics* and *De coelo* and the *De anima* traditionally attributed to him;[7] and Girolamo Donato's translation of the *De anima* of Alexander of Aphrodisias.[8] The work of Themistius had of course been known in the Middle Ages through the translation of William of Moerbeke, and it had played a role in the philosophical psychologies of Thomas Aquinas, Siger of Brabant, Henry Bate of Malines, and James of Viterbo, among others.[9]

In an early question on whether the intellective soul is united to the human body as its true substantial form, Nicoletto Vernia makes no use of the Commentators but presents a straightforward Averroist position.[10] However, in his *Contra perversam Averrois opinionem de unitate intellectus de animae felicitate questiones divinae*, finished perhaps in 1492 but only published in 1504 after Vernia's death, he makes constant use of the Greek Commentators on Aristotle, namely, Alexander, Themistius, and Simplicius, along with Albert the Great.[11] Although he cites both Ficino's translation of Plato and also that of Plotinus, Vernia culls his presentation of Plato's psychology from Albert, and he attributes essential elements of it to Aristotle as well as to Themistius and Simplicius. The intellective souls, which God has created from eternity, possess in themselves the forms of all intelligible things, but they no longer remember these forms after they have entered human bodies. Nonetheless, once the body is purged through study, the soul is excited to reminiscence since learning is for Plato a recollection, as Boethius also points out.[12] Vernia lists Themistius and Simplicius among those who hold that both Plato and Aristotle thought that intellective souls are many, have been created by God from eternity, are infused in the human body, and return to their respective stars at death, and he adds as a comment from the *De anima* attributed to Simplicius that any disagreement between the two is merely verbal.[13] He also quotes from Themistius' paraphrases on the *De anima* in Ermolao's translation to show that while the ancient Commentator presents a possible argument for the unity of the intellect based on the need of a teacher and student to know the same thing, he did not himself assent to such a view but rather argued against it.[14] Later in the treatise, Vernia reaffirms that Themistius was only presenting an argument in the text in question, and he adds that Themistius determined the problem in his comparison of the intellect to light.[15] What Vernia is referring to, of course, is the celebrated passage regarding illuminating and illuminated intellects, whose meaning had already been debated by philosophers in the late thirteenth century on the basis of Moerbeke's translation.[16] Paraphrasing Ermolao's translation, Vernia interprets Themistius to mean that there is one illuminating intellect for all men but many illuminated intellects, just as there is one sun although light itself is divided.[17] He also argues on the basis of other passages from Themistius' *De anima* that the individual human intellect survives death, and he denies that Themistius intended to have Aristotle disagree with Plato regarding preexistence and recollection.[18]

Vernia uses both Simplicius' *Physics* and also the *De anima* attributed to him in presenting his position on the soul and the intellect.[19] It must be admitted that Vernia is not wholly successful in welding together the ideas that he derives from the two works.[20] Among the things that Vernia takes from the *Physics* are that Plato and Aristotle both believe that the presence of the agent intellect to the sense image excites the soul to the knowledge that it previously possessed,[21] and also that the separation of the soul from the body does not involve a motion but simply the soul ceasing to illumine (*illustrare*) and to inform (*informare*) the human body by reason of some indisposition on the part of the latter.[22] From the *De anima* ascribed to Simplicius, Vernia appears to derive his own interpretation of Aristotle's doctrine of the agent and potential intellects, a doctrine which he also attributes to Plato. As we have already noted, Vernia assumes that both Plato and Aristotle held to the preexistence of the individual soul, which forgets all the intelligible species it possesses as soon as it is united to the body. The three stages of the soul's cognition can be considered in either an a priori or an a posteriori ordering. According to the a priori ordering, the soul first knows itself and things above it, then it somehow descends from itself to know the intelligible species that are innate to it, and lastly it flows wholly to the outside and thereby comes to know accidents and individual things. On the other hand, according to the a posteriori ordering, the soul first knows sensible things through the imagination, and it is then aroused by other sensible things to return to the innate intelligible species that it had forgotten and is thereby made to know material things perfectly, that is, through their causes, and finally it returns to itself and there contemplates both itself and higher beings. The possible or potential intellect is the soul before it flows outside; the speculative or habitual intellect is the soul as it has gone outside and then returned to grasp its innate intelligible species; and the agent intellect is the soul as it has returned from outside and contemplates both itself and higher things.[23] Vernia claims to find this same threefold mode of the soul's operating in the *Liber de causis,* which he attributes to Proclus.[24] What is lacking in Vernia's treatise is any discussion of the two intellects that stand above the individual human intellect.[25] It is most important to emphasize, however, that Vernia has read Simplicius to have held that the human intellect is multiplied, that is to say, individual in each human being, since his student, Agostino Nifo, and many other philosophers during the sixteenth century will interpret Simplicius in an opposed fashion.

In his commentary on Averroes' *Destructio destructionum,* published in 1497, Nifo quotes Ficino's translation of the *Enneads,* but only late in the commentary and not to decide any major doctrinal issue.[26] Simplicius' *De coelo* and *Physics* are mentioned, but not the *De anima* traditionally attributed to him.[27] On the other hand, in the early *De anima,* which was published in 1503, Nifo cites Alexander, Themistius, and Simplicius constantly, often showing parallels between Themistius and Simplicius, on the one side, and Plotinus, on the other side. He reads both Themistius and also Plotinus (*Enneads* I, 1, chaps. 7, 10, 12) to hold that the rational soul extends a "life" or "animation" from itself into the body, though in doing this he is being misled by the imprecision of Ermolao Barbaro's translation of Themistius. The latter often contains explanatory remarks as part of the translation itself.[28] In any case, Nifo's exegesis of Plotinus is clearly inspired in great part by Ficino's own commentary on the *Enneads* (I, 1, chaps. 1, 7, 8).[29] Nonetheless, it should be noted that Nifo himself does not present Aristotle as upholding this sort of "animation" theory, although both Ficino, who bases himself on Themistius, and Ermolao's translation of Themistius do so. Indeed, Nifo seems to have been heavily influenced by Ficino's commentary on the *Enneads* in his own analysis of Themistius' views on the relation of soul and body.

Throughout his early commentary on the *De anima,* Nifo makes constant use of the *De anima* ascribed to Simplicius. He underlines Simplicius' distinction of the soul perfecting the body as opposed to its using the body, but he appears neither to understand too well nor to emphasize sufficiently Simplicius' doctrine of the various "lives" of the soul.[30] Without doubt, one of the most fundamental doctrines of Simplicius is that of the three levels of intellect, which Nifo interprets as involving: (1) the unparticipated intellect—Nifo identifies this intellect with God, the first agent intellect; (2) the participated intellect, which while abiding in itself in unwavering fashion attaches the soul to itself; and, (3) lastly, the human soul and its intellect which, when it abides in itself in the unity and permanence within itself, is the actual intellect, just as it is the potential intellect as it proceeds forth to the outside.[31] Nifo takes the third intellect to be one for all men. While Nifo does not always interpret Simplicius' doctrine correctly, the important thing to notice is that he helped to initiate a tradition of interest in that Commentator's psychology that lasted throughout the sixteenth century among Aristotelian philosophers.[32] And as with Themistius, so Nifo again turns to Ficino's commentary on the *Enneads* to explicate both Simplicius and also what Simplicius attributes to Iamblichus.[33]

Once again in his *De intellectu,* also published in 1503, Nifo uses both Themistius and Simplicius, as well as Ficino's translation of and commentary on the *Enneads.* He claims to find in agreement Themistius, Iamblichus, and Plotinus in saying that there is one World Soul that subsists in itself but vivifies by other souls (called "lives," "animations," or "traces") all living things.[34] He thus believes that Thomas could not use Themistius effectively against the Averroist doctrine of the unity of the intellect, though he admits that Thomas' *De unitate intellectus contra Averroistas* contains other arguments from which the Averroists cannot escape.[35] It should be noted that Nifo, in clear opposition to Vernia, takes Themistius and Simplicius to hold, in agreement with Averroes, that the intellect is one in number for all men.[36] On the other hand, he believes that no matter what Themistius may espouse, various "Platonists" maintain the plurality of human souls—

Ammonius, Origen, Plotinus, Porphyry, Proclus, and Iamblichus—all mentioned by Ficino. From at least this point of view, the Neoplatonists support Christian belief. Nifo has here simply borrowed from Ficino yet another time.[37] We should also note that while Nifo realized the similarities between the Commentators, that is, Themistius and Simplicius, and Plotinus as presented by Ficino, neither he nor his fellow Aristotelians seem to have fully appreciated the Neoplatonic doctrine of the simultaneous one-and-many which provides the key to some of the ideas of these two Commentators.[38] We might add that Nifo's interest in the Commentators continued in his later *De immortalitate animae,* where he again interprets Themistius and Simplicius as maintaining one intellect for all men and again rejects Thomas' use of Themistius against Averroes in his *De unitate intellectus contra Averroistas.*[39]

The works of Themistius and Simplicius on the *De anima* continued to be cited and studied throughout the sixteenth century by such philosophers as Giulio Castellani, Marcantonio Passeri (Genua), Giovanni Faseolo, Francesco Vimercato, Federico Pendasio, Giacomo Zabarella, Antonio Montecatino, and Francesco Piccolomini.[40] The writings of Themistius and Simplicius brought with them a variety of Neoplatonic doctrines that were absorbed into the mainstream of sixteenth-century Aristotelianism. The origins of this use of the Commentators must of course be traced back to the use made of Themistius' *De anima* in the Moerbeke translation during the late Middle Ages, but the new translation of the work by Ermolao Barbaro and the latter's claim that Averroes had stolen his ideas from Alexander, Themistius, and Simplicius doubtless had much to do with renewed interest in Themistius' work.[41] Key points of contention that these ancient Commentators engendered among Renaissance Aristotelians concerned the unity of the intellect and the personal immortality of the soul. It is surely noteworthy that on occasion both topics much exercised religious authorities during the Middle Ages and the Renaissance.[42]

A CONCEPTUAL SCHEME TO ACCOUNT FOR METAPHYSICAL HIERARCHY—ITS NEOPLATONIC ORIGINS AND ITS INFLUENCE ON RENAISSANCE ARISTOTELIANS

Throughout Proclus' *Elements of Theology* there are scattered remarks setting forth a conceptual scheme that was to have great impact on Western Christian philosophy during the Middle Ages and the Renaissance. The scheme was also introduced into the West through the writings of Proclus[43] and the Pseudo-Dionysius,[44] the *Liber de causis,*[45] and some passages in Augustine.[46] Elsewhere I have traced the history of this scheme in the writings of over twenty philosophers, ranging from Albert the Great to John Locke.[47] I shall sketch out here only salient aspects of the scheme and the debates that it engendered. I shall take care to show what I take to be its potential for conflict with orthodox Christian thought.

The scheme involves taking God and matter (or non-being) as two poles or termini measuring all things and thereby determining their grade or rank in the hierarchy of reality. Spatial terms like "nearness" and "distance" play crucial roles in this scheme. The closer something is to God, the higher its grade, whereas the more it recedes from God and approaches matter (or non-being), the lower is its grade. The scheme is found in Albert the Great's commentary on the Pseudo-Dionysius' *De divinis nominibus* as well as in other of his works. The greater the falling away from the simplicity of the First Being, the greater a thing's diversity and composition. In like fashion, participation and approaching God are inter-related.[48] Aquinas too adopts the scheme in various of his writings, pointing out that God can be called a "measure" only by transferring the word from the category of quantity.[49] But what is important to emphasize is that Thomas is careful to point out that there always remains an infinite distance between God and his creatures.[50] That is to say, Thomas seems wary of certain aspects of the conceptual scheme. He explains in the *Summa,* for example, that things are called "distant" from God through an unlikeness of nature and grace, not through any physical distance, since God is in fact omnipresent.[51] The scheme is also to be found in the writings of Siger of Brabant,[52] Henry of Ghent,[53] Giles of Rome,[54] and Godfrey of Fontaines.[55] The sources used by these various medievals include the Pseudo-Dionysius' *De divinis nominibus,* the *Liber de causis,* and Proclus' own *Elements of Theology.*[56]

The fourteenth-century discussions regarding the "intension" and "remission" of forms had their effect on the fifteenth- and sixteenth-century developments.[57] Richard Swineshead's *De intensione et remissione qualitatis* played a central role in these later discussions.[58] Paul of Venice (d. 1429) will admit that the grade of things in the scale of being (*latitudo entis*) can be measured from the zero grade of being (*non gradus entis*), but he denies that measurement is possible in regard to the infinite grade (*ad gradum infinitum*), that is, God. He argues for this position on the grounds that the perfection of a man is no closer to the highest goodness than that of a horse, since in each case there will be an infinite distance from the finite grade of goodness to the infinite grade.[59] Not surprisingly, Marsilio Ficino (1433–1499) accepts the conceptual scheme and God as the primary measure of the grades of things in the hierarchy of being. One would expect this of a philosopher who translated and studied with care Plotinus, Proclus, and the Pseudo-Dionysius, and whose favorite medieval Christian philosopher was Thomas Aquinas.[60] He was also acquainted with Swineshead (Suiseth) and the so-called *calculatores* tradition.[61] Ficino shows special concern with the problem of how God can be infinite and yet measure the gradation of his creatures.[62] Indeed, Ficino at times speaks as though God were the highest (*summum*) or the first grade (*gradus primus*) within the genus of all things—so too had Thomas Aquinas—but further analysis of his fascinating but tortured attempts to solve this dilemma lies outside the scope of this paper.[63] What surely must be added is Ficino's denunciation of "certain barbarians" (*barbari quidem*)—Paul of Venice is doubtless the prime target—who deny that things can be measured by their approach (*accessus*) to God inasmuch as he is infinite and who assert instead that things are measured solely by their receding (*recessus*) from privation.[64] There was also a sharp interchange between George of Trebizond and Cardinal Bessarion on the same issue.[65]

The debate over whether or not the measuring should be taken only from the zero grade of being (*non gradus entis*) and not from God continued in such thinkers as Gabriele Zerbo (ca. 1435–1505),[66] Cardinal Domenico Grimani (1461–1523), and Pietro Pomponazzi (1462–1525), of whom only Grimani defends Swineshead's view as applied to the metaphysical hierarchy.[67] Pomponazzi denounces Swineshead and cites Aristotle, Averroes, Plato's *Philebus,* Ficino's *Platonic Theology,* the Pseudo-Dionysius' *De coelesti hierarchia,* and Augustine's *Confessions* (XII, 7) as authorities for the view that intension and remission are measured by approach to and receding from the highest grade of a latitude, a view that he himself accepts.[68] The Franciscan, Antonio Trombetta (1436–1517), accepts God alone as measuring things by their approach to or receding from him, but by omitting non-being he is simply being loyal to his intellectual master, John Duns Scotus.[69] In contrast, the contemporary Thomists, Thomas de Vio (1469–1534) and Jacobus Brutus, accept both God and prime matter as the measure of things, thus reasserting Thomas' view on the subject.[70]

The conceptual scheme of God and non-being or matter measuring the hierarchy of being, which is clearly Neoplatonic in origin, was adopted by various Renaissance philosophers who are usually identified with the Averroist tradition. In his commentary on the *Destructio destructionum* (1497), the medieval Latin translation of Averroes' *Incoherence of the Incoherence,* Agostino Nifo (ca. 1470–1538) frequently invokes the scheme in order to explicate Algazel and Averroes.[71] The *Liber de causis* is cited on several occasions, and Albert's and Thomas' works probably influenced him to adopt a participation metaphysics and to attribute it to Averroes.[72] In this and other of his works, Nifo takes Averroes to have adopted the scheme in order to explain the composition both of the Intelligences and of all other things.[73] Nifo's work had an impact on another so-called "Averroist," Marcantonio Zimara (1460–1532), who also attributes to Aristotle and Averroes a participation metaphysics and the conceptual scheme. However, Zimara goes beyond Nifo to seek other authorities for the scheme, not simply Augustine, but also the *De coelesti hierarchia,* the *Letters,* and the *De divinis nominibus* of Pseudo-Dionysius.[74] Both Zimara and Alessandro Achillini (1463–1512),[75] another Averroist who adopted the scheme, show special concern with the problem of how an infinite God can be said to measure things approaching to him, granted that he is always infinitely distant from them. Zimara tries to solve the dilemma by arguing that while God's perfection is formally infinite when taken in itself, it is not infinite when taken as imitable or participable by creatures.[76] Achillini, on the other hand, would say that only if God is finite, as Aristotle maintains, can he serve as a measure, but he also adds that he holds as the truth that the Intelligences are in fact infinitely distant from God. His solution would be, it appears, to fall back on the zero grade of being (*non gradus perfectionis entis*) as measuring the hierarchy of being.[77] Zimara attacks the *sophistae* and *calculatores* for just this position.[78]

The scheme is debated and either adopted or rejected by a variety of other sixteenth-century philosophers. For example, the Dominican Giovanni Crisostomo Javelli (ca. 1470–ca. 1538) appears to accept the scheme,[79] whereas Gaspare Contarini (1483–1542), one of Pomponazzi's students, makes God alone the measure and rejects the zero grade. By means of a tortured line of reasoning, Contarini argues that God can be considered as finite as well as infinite, at least insofar as he is free of the infinity of matter and multitude—he resembles the finiteness of the number one in comparison to other numbers.[80] The problem of reconciling the concept of an infinite God with taking him as the measure of all things as they approach or recede from him also vexed a group of thinkers of the late sixteenth century. In his *De motu libri decem,* Francesco Buonamici clearly takes God to be such a measure or standard. He interrelates the concepts of participation, "nearness," intension and remission, and the latitude of being.[81] Buonamici's solution as to how something that is of infinite perfection, and therefore unknown to us, could enable us to understand how much each thing approaches to it appears to be that God is known by us as finite.[82] Galileo Galilei (1564–1642) presents arguments against measuring things by their distance or receding from God in his *Juvenilia,* and in so doing he is rejecting the view of his own teacher, Buonamici.[83] On the other hand, one of Galileo's acquaintances at Pisa, Jacopo Mazzoni (1548–1598), does accept God as the measure of all other things. However, he is very concerned to answer the objection that an infinite God cannot serve as a measure. His reply, in short, is that the "closeness" and "distance" at stake mean nothing but a greater or lesser participation in infinite perfection.[84] Finally, Cesare Cremonini (1550–1631), Galileo's acquaintance at Padua, rejects the scheme as presented by Nifo and Zimara, and he makes pointed criticisms against using the word "to lack" (*deficere*) of the Intelligences in comparison with God.[85]

In this brief survey of the fate of the conceptual scheme during the Renaissance, one constant concern has become evident, namely, how to reconcile the concept of an infinite God of orthodox Christian theology with the notion of a God who measures all grades or levels in the hierarchy of being as things approach or draw near to him according to a set "distance." It is not surprising that some thinkers rejected that scheme as unreconcilable with the concept of an infinite God. On the other hand, it should be noted that Plotinus himself did consider God to be infinite and saw him as outside and beyond all measure, though he measured everything else.[86] Moreover, in contrast to Proclus, Plotinus seems eager to present God as outside any genus or even hierarchy.[87] Consequently, we should perhaps view the debate about the conceptual scheme as revealing not so much a conflict between Neoplatonism as such and Christian orthodoxy but rather as difficulties inherent in the hierarchical conceptions of such Neoplatonists as Proclus.[88] It is instructive to note that Philo and the early Church Fathers used the terminology of "enclosing, not enclosed" to bring out God's transcendence rather than that of "infinite distance."[89] In like fashion, a Church Father such as Gregory of Nyssa who knew both Plato and Neoplatonism appears to make no use of the scheme to explain metaphysical hierarchy.[90]

The present paper has examined two different areas in which Neoplatonism had an important influence on the course of Renaissance Aristotelianism, namely, in psychological analyses, through the writings of Themistius and Simplicius, and in the long history of discussions regarding a conceptual scheme of metaphysical hierarchy. This scheme had its roots in Proclus, with perhaps some anticipations in Plotinus, and was known to the Christian West through the Pseudo-Dionysius, the *Liber de causis,* and Augustine, as well as through Proclus' own *Elements of Theology.* It even had some history, though in a watered-down form, in early modern thought, but that is another story.[91]

15

Andreas Camutius on the Concord of Plato and Aristotle with Scripture

CHARLES B. SCHMITT

The more deeply one studies the philosophical thought of Western Europe during the fifteenth, sixteenth, and early seventeenth centuries, the more it becomes apparent that there are two dominating factors at work. I say this basing myself on the very imperfect state of our knowledge of the vast philosophical literature from the period that has not yet been assimilated into the general interpretative structure found in most syntheses of the thought of the Renaissance and early modern world. I am convinced that we are still very far from plumbing the depths of Renaissance thought, and even in those very few instances (e.g., Ficino, Pico, Pomponazzi, or Bruno) where we have a substantial interpretative literature, we are still not very close to having a complete understanding of these men's thought and their definitive place in the complex of Renaissance philosophy. Indeed, in the present paper, I hope to be able to add a footnote to the *fortuna* of Pico della Mirandola and Ficino in the sixteenth century.

The two principal factors of the Renaissance that I referred to above are that: (1) the continued importance of Aristotle as *the* dominant philosophical influence during the Renaissance is far greater than has been realized by interpreters up to now; and (2) the deep penetration of Neoplatonic thought in the Renaissance fabric, although generally emphasized by most interpreters at the expense of Aristotelianism, is both deeper and more widespread than generally thought. These two statements, of course, seem at first hearing to be mutually contradictory; and, so they are. They require explanation, qualification, and clarification.

Let us look at Aristotelianism first. The general interpretation of Aristotelianism found in most writers of history of philosophy and of intellectual history is that, after having had its day in the high Middle Ages, it declined rapidly in the fifteenth century to be replaced by humanism and Platonism. Recent work shows this to be patently false. In fact the real high point of Aristotelianism—quantitatively speaking—can be located in the fifteenth and sixteenth centuries. Leonardo Bruni's translations of the moral writings had few peers in terms of popularity in the fifteenth century.[1] Flodr's *Incunabula classicorum* shows clearly the degree to which Aristotelian editions dominated the classical revival in fifteenth-century printing:[2] there were 552 Aristotle editions in the fifteenth century compared to 389 of Cicero, 181 of Ovid, and 18 of Plato, to give a few illustrative examples. A similar pattern is to be found for the sixteenth century, though we are still far from having a reliable and fairly complete list of Aristotelian editions for the century.[3] I estimate there to be between 2000 and 3000 Aristotelian editions, commentaries, and expositions printed during the century, perhaps ten times as many as there were Platonic works. For most of the individual Aristotelian works more new Latin translations were made during the fifteenth and sixteenth centuries than during all earlier centuries combined.[4] There can be no doubt whatever that Aristotelian philosophy still dominated the West during the fifteenth and sixteenth centuries as much as it had done during the Middle Ages.

How then can I say that Neoplatonism also was even more influential during the Renaissance than normally supposed? Many years ago it was shown by Professor Fabro in his pioneering work that there was a far deeper penetration of Neoplatonic themes and doctrine in the thought of Thomas Aquinas than had previously been thought.[5] More recent research has substantiated and broadened his findings, so it is now generally accepted by all, save a few, that *Doctor Angelicus* is not necessarily equivalent to *Doctor Aristotelicus*. That is to say a very large amount of Neoplatonism went into the medieval Aristotelianism of the thirteenth and fourteenth centuries as well as of the twelfth century. What is not so well recognized yet, however, is that the same is true for the Renaissance. While many Aristotelians of the Renaissance wished to go back to the "true" Greek Aristotle— Zabarella is a good example—the interpretative framework of most Aristotelians still owed much to the Neoplatonism already present in the Middle Ages. Many aspects of medievalism were consciously removed from Renaissance Aristotelianism, ranging from linguistic formulation (e.g., *De generatione et corruptione* becomes the more classical *De ortu et interitu*)[6] to a rejection of fourteenth-century logic in the name of something closer to Aristotle.[7] Though there are many exceptions, and generalization on the matter is difficult, it is my view that the penetration of Neoplatonic themes and doctrines—in the broad syncretistic sense formulated by Ficino—became more widespread among Renaissance Aristotelians than it had been during the Middle Ages. Not only do some of the Neoplatonic themes favored by the Greek commentators on Aristotle (who were largely of Neoplatonic persuasion) become more central,[8] but much Hermetic and Neopythagorean doctrine finds its way into Aristotelian writers often under the guise of *prisca theologia,* a formulation of Ficino's much favored by Renaissance Neoplatonists, but by no means spurned by self-styled Aristotelians of the period. It has taken us some time to realize the degree to which *prisca* themes are to be found in Aristotelian writers and now, even nearly thirty years after Walker formulated *prisca theologia* as a functional descriptive term,[9] it is usually considered to be a doctrine of Renaissance Platonists and not Aristotelians.[10]

The result of all this is that when one looks closely at Aristotelian writers of the Renaissance, especially if one studies particular doctrines in detail, patently Neoplatonic doctrine is very often fused with Aristotelian, Platonic philosophy frequently being put into Aristotelian language so effectively as to conceal its true paternity. The insinuation of this Neoplatonic material into the Aristotelians comes about in various ways, several of which are worth briefly mentioning. First, there is frequently a conciliatory and syncretic motive on the part of Aristotelians to assimilate Platonic materials into a synthesis. Second, a particular Aristotelian will sometimes find some Peripatetic doctrine outmoded or questionable on philosophical or other grounds and will substitute a convenient and more suitable Platonic doctrine in its place. Third, certain pseudo-Aristotelian works of decidedly Neoplatonic inspiration were accepted as genuine and gave Aristotelianism a more Neoplatonic cast than it otherwise would have had. There are various other reasons for the absorption of Neoplatonism into Aristotelianism, but further discussion would take us too far off the track.

In conclusion to these introductory comments, let me emphasize once again my view that even if Aristotelianism (or as I would prefer it, "Aristotelianisms")[11] dominated Renaissance philosophy to a degree hitherto seldom recognized, Neoplatonism was also lurking everywhere, even in places where one would hardly expect it. Renaissance philosophy in general can be viewed as a wide variety of different eclecticisms, consisting of a nearly endless number of blends of a relatively limited number of constituents. "Eclecticism" in this sense is one of the most important contributions of the Renaissance Neoplatonic tradition stemming from Ficino. In that sense—a structural one—almost all of Renaissance philosophy can be seen as Neoplatonic.

Having made these preliminary comments, I would like to illustrate some of these ideas by a consideration of a Renaissance thinker, who, as far as I have been able to discover, has completely escaped the nets of modern students of the subject. Andrea Camuzio (Camutius) was of a distinguished family of medical men native to Italian Switzerland.[12] He fits into the general picture I have sketched in several different ways. In addition to writing medical works, he published various philosophical treatises that make use of Neoplatonic themes and sources, as well as Aristotelian ones; the names of Plato, Plotinus, and Pico occur frequently throughout his works. His general position, which owes much to Pico, emphasized the general philosophical agreement between Plato and Aristotle and interpreted both to be in harmony with Scripture, as the title of his first published works brings out so clearly. This work, directed towards Cristoforo Madruzzo, the Bishop of Trent, who was to play such a key role in the forthcoming Council, consists in a preface to a disputation held in Milan in December 1541 and bears the title *In Sacrarum literarum cum Aristotele et Platone concordia praefatio.*[13] Not only the title, but the content of the work as well hark back to Pico's endeavor of a *pax philosophica.* Before turning to a consideration of this brief work, however, let us examine Camuzio's life and activities insofar as they can be learned from the current state of our knowledge. The necessary archival and manuscript work has not yet been done to establish the details of his life. We must, therefore, make use of the information we have, realizing that not all of it is reliable.[14]

Camuzio (Andreas Camutius) was the son of Francesco, himself an eminent physician,[15] and of a family noted in medicine from the fifteenth to the seventeenth century. He was apparently born in Lugano, though in 1557, by a special dispensation, was granted Milanese citizenship and appears later as *mediolanensis.*[16] Secondary literature is silent or imprecise about the date of his birth, but it must have been about 1512, since he tells us in 1541 that he was then twenty-nine years old.[17] His life seems to break down into three periods: one in Pavia-Milan, a second one in Vienna, and finally one in Pisa, though we also know of his presence in Rome.[18] His studies were at the University of Pavia,[19] where he began teaching prognostics in 1536 and then logic and philosophy during the next few years.[20] After a period of medical practice in Milan (and perhaps elsewhere), he then taught theoretical medicine again at Pavia between 1559 and 1568.[21] During those years he published several works and was involved in a public disputation on medical topics in 1563 with Girolamo Cardano, whose account leads us to believe that Camuzio did not come off very well:

> A three-day debate was instituted at Pavia with Camuzio, to be held in public before the Senate. My opponent was silenced, on the first day, in the first proposition, even in the judgement of all my rivals who were present. Certain memorials of this same event are graven in letters on the monument to Camuzio: "This then, in truth, was known to all, that they debated not for a mere refutation of argument, but with a power which seemed unassailable." And I believe the memory of that debate lives to this day.[22]

Cardano wrote this in 1575 and undoubtedly it cannot be accepted entirely at face value. It may be that the clever Cardano got the best of Camuzio in debate, but it was Camuzio who published a work arguing against various *conclusiones* of Cardano, dedicating it to Danielo Barbaro.[23]

In spite of his alleged failure against Cardano, Camuzio was called to Vienna to become *protophysicus* to Maximilian II.[24] While there he published his *De amore atque felicitate* in 1574 and dedicated it to his patron.[25] This work is much indebted to Ficino and the Renaissance tradition of Platonic love treatises, making particular use of Leone Ebreo. A telling passage of the letter to Maximilian clearly shows the tenor of his work:

O poor and changeable Aristotle. Truly the Christian law preaches the law of love; of the Christians I know (if you exclude the few who have understood Plato), are there none who have hitherto attempted to define love? Rightly Plato alone among the ancient philosophers ought to be marked off by the term *divinitas* and should rightly be named *divinus*, because he treated the subject of love with care and vigor.[26]

Two years after the publication of the *De amore* the Emperor was dead and Camuzio wrote and published a work on his fatal illness.[27]

According to most reference works Camuzio died in 1578 (some giving the place as Vienna, others Milan),[28] but he was still good for another ten years of teaching at the University of Pisa, where he was *sopraordinario* in theoretical medicine from 1577 to 1587.[29] He was considered a man of eminence although he incurred the wrath of several colleagues including the irascible Girolamo Borro.[30] Among his students may have been the young Galileo, who studied medicine there in the early 1580s.[31] His death would seem to have occurred in 1587.[32]

As we have already mentioned, Camuzio's *Praefatio* was dedicated to Bishop Madruzzo, whose taste for Platonism is well known.[33] It takes the form of a preface to a disputation, that is, it can be read as a work similar to Pico's *Oratio*. Indeed, perhaps the most significant influence that is evident in Camuzio's work is that of Pico. In addition to the disputation held with Cardano, we know of at least three more public disputations in which he was involved: one held at Pavia about 1536, the one we are here concerned with, which was held at Milan in 1541, and a third held at Rome in 1544.[34] The first of these Camuzio tells us about in his *Praefatio*. Following the example of Giovanni Pico, he attempted, at the age of twenty-four, to reconcile Plato and Aristotle in a public disputation at the University of Pavia.[35] Though we do not know many details of this earlier attempt to defend the doctrines of both Plato and Aristotle, it is noteworthy that Pico's impact is still evident on a young philosopher of the 1530s. In his *De humano intellectu*, published in 1564 and dedicated to Carlo Borromeo, Pico still looms large and Camuzio's consideration of the human intellect owes as much to Pico and the Platonists as to the Aristotelians.[36]

The *Praefatio* is a straightforward apologetic work arguing that there is no essential disagreement between Greek philosophy and sacred Scripture. Though I have not been able to identify the precise reason why he was led to write on the topic when he did, it seems clear enough that there was a certain group of contemporaries to whom the work was directed as a polemical piece. Several times he speaks of those who oppose him, once saying: "I know that my adversaries (of whom there is an especially large number at Pavia) object that it is a vile thing to mouth one's own praises."[37] These opponents of his are also most notably the same ones who argue that religion and philosophy are in disagreement.

> There are some philosophers as well as professors of Scripture, who think that the study of philosophy, especially the Peripatetic variety, is very much in opposition to sacred theology and that the teachings of the philosophers are counter in every way to the decrees and saving commands of Christ.[38]

Camuzio tells us that he adhered to such an opinion before he became converted to more of a concordist position.[39] There are several reasons why he is opposed to a separation of philosophy and theology. First of all, if what the philosophers teach us is not in accord with Scripture, then they have wasted their lives in misleading us and are no more than out-and-out deceivers.[40] Such a state of affairs would be unthinkable for it would lead to a situation in which truth in philosophy would be falsehood in theology.[41]

Camuzio has no sympathy for such a "double truth" position and would prefer to follow the position of the Neoplatonists rather than the Academic Platonists.[42] Unwittingly perhaps, opposing the two main strands of the Platonic tradition one to another, he sets up a clear contrast between the Academic Scepticism known through Cicero and the Christian Neoplatonism epitomized by Ficino. We all know now, especially since Tigerstedt has put the matter forward in such clear terms,[43] that the Neoplatonic interpretation of Plato won the day during the Middle Ages and Renaissance. Camuzio is no exception to this general tendency and his Platonism is very similar to that of Ficino, even if he does not mention the Tuscan by name. The general way in which the philosophy-theology relationship is viewed is very close to that of Ficino. For example, Camuzio emphasizes that both philosophy and theology are directed towards the same end (*ad eundem finem*), and that is knowledge of God (*finis est divinae essentiae [ut philosophice dixerim] cognitio*).[44] Again, like Ficino, he emphasizes that a philosopher is capable of contemplation of the divine and that this activity is proper to him.[45] Perhaps his clearest statement of the ultimate agreement of philosophy and theology is the following:

> The professors of sacred Scripture and of philosophy may argue against it, but I am of the opinion that the doctrines of sacred theology are in no way contrary to the teachings of Aristotle and Plato, rather they agree in all ways.[46]

This, however, is not to say that philosophy and theology are not distinguishable, though it is obviously a problem for one who takes Camuzio's position. Not quite formulating the position in Ficinian terms that *Philosophia et religio germanae sunt*,[47] he does tend to see the two as parallel paths to a knowledge of God. He emphasizes that God can be known in various ways, for example, by inspired knowledge (*alii divino tantum afflati spiritu Deum agnoscunt*)[48] or through knowledge of the lower world (*per naturalium rerum speculationem*).[49] The latter method of knowledge is a gradual one and obviously Camuzio has in mind here the stepwise progression of knowledge towards God that has characterized Christian Neoplatonism. Indeed, he attributes this method of gradual ascent to a knowledge of God specifically to Plato:

> For this reason Plato has always seemed to me—in this matter, as well as in other things—to have carried out his task wisely, because he has proposed that moral reasoning has everywhere been established towards living well and happily and for the purpose of cleansing the soul of the young; next one passes through the study of natural things and hence ascends gradually to the discovery of the divine.[50]

The debt to Plato and to later Neoplatonists is evident throughout Camuzio's work. Although it is formulated in terms of a concord of Plato *and* Aristotle with sacred Scripture, the Platonic side of philosophy seems to dominate. It is true that much of the language is Aristotelian, but even that is infused with many specifically Platonic formulations. Forms, ideas, harmony, and mixture all play a central role in Camuzio's arguments. For example, there is a long passage on the importance of *harmonia* in the soul and the question of the proper balance of the constituent parts.[51] At the conclusion of the section, he states again quite clearly his preference for Plato: "In this matter Plato has always seemed to me to stand out from the others."[52]

It would distort the issue to assert that Camuzio was one of the chief representatives of Renaissance Neoplatonism, for obviously he is not a thinker of much originality. Moreover, his works must be seen in balance and we cannot call him a Neoplatonist, strictly speaking, as we might call Ficino, Pico, Steuco, or Patrizi a Neoplatonist. There is probably as much Aristotelianism in Camuzio as there is Platonism, but it is interesting to note how many Neoplatonic formulations can be detected beneath a somewhat Peripatetic exterior. What his education at Pavia was in the 1530s is not clear. His remarks indicate that there was a strong sceptical tendency there that tended to separate clearly philosophy from theology.[53] He was probably at Pavia during a transition stage when the medieval tradition of logic and natural philosophy was dying out and there was little resonance still remaining from Agrippa's short tenure there when he taught both Plato and Hermes Trismegistus.[54] Still, Camuzio got his eclectic and Neoplatonic ideas somewhere, but from where remains to be determined. Also remaining to be determined is what happened to some of his ideas in his later works, when the second phase of his publishing career started. After the publication of the *Praefatio* in 1541 nothing else from his pen appeared in print until 1563, when he began publishing various more substantial works divided between medicine and philosophy.[55]

Cassirer's contention (put forward in his book on Platonism in England)[56] that intellectual history must be studied in the foothills as well as the peaks can be well applied to the Neoplatonists of the Italian Renaissance. A figure such as Camuzio shows so well how influential the intellectual orientation of the Platonic Academy remained a couple of generations after the death of Pico and Ficino. Besides the more ambitious and more influential writings of Francesco Giorgio, Symphorien Champier, Francesco da Diaceto, and Agostino Steuco, among others, the spread of Neoplatonic teaching can be seen among minor figures such as Camuzio.

V

MODERN THOUGHT

16

Triads and Trinity in the Poetry of Robert Browning

ELIZABETH BIEMAN

First, a prefatory *apologia*. Of course the topic opened by the title is hubristically broad for development in one brief paper. Yet, in a literary critic called to explore the poetry of Browning before an audience interested in the interaction of Neoplatonism and Christian thought, a degree of rashness is preferable to the finesse, appropriate on other occasions, that would focus more narrowly.[1] Some comfort lies in the comprehensive temper of the Neoplatonic tradition, in a postlapsarian Christian consciousness of human limits, and in the robust aspiring spirit of Robert Browning that issues so candidly in his own poetic language. Heaven demands that human reach exceed the grasp, even as one acknowledges humbly that it does.

From first to last in a long and productive life Browning concerned himself with matters of psychology, theology, and epistemology: man's mind, God's mind, and exploration of the process or act of knowing that might join the two. "I have always had one lodestar," confesses the speaker of *Pauline* in 1833, "A need, a trust, a yearning after God."[2] More than five decades later the speaker of the prologue to *Asolando* (1889) offers his reader a hypothetical choice between a lens that would drape the world in varied rainbow hues and one capable of revealing the naked "inmost" truth ablaze. In the poems between these years (perhaps most strikingly in *The Ring and the Book*) lie countless instances of the search for the one Truth in a world of shifting perceptions of truth; and the records of infinite moments when Truth flashes, evanescently, upon the seeker, or of starry points beyond the world of finitude where all contraries meet.

Any student of the Neoplatonic tradition will recognize, as Browning surely did, that such epiphanic moments and centers belong to the annals of mystical experience, and that the *noesis* sought, and occasionally achieved, has at least as much to do with the dynamic of a Platonic *eros* as with the ratiocinative dialectic that may be employed to begin the pattern of ascent. But too many readers of Browning, having no prior command of the perennial wisdom of the mystic, and paying insufficient attention to the poetic dialectic through which he seeks to move them to the point of initiation, have misunderstood him grieviously.

All too often Browning has been characterized as a pious obscurantist, whether by sycophantic friends who see in him a saving prophet of some true religion bearing a resemblance to the one they themselves profess, or by hard-headed modernists who deplore his selling out what could have been a clear head in surrender to the promptings of his heart. This distorted opinion prevailed for half a century on the impetus it got in 1891, immediately after Browning's death, in Henry Jones' influential book, *Browning as a Philosophical and Religious Teacher*.[3] Few noted during that period how the vision and craft of the poet were obscured in the question-begging title.

I am far from the first to take issue with such error: it has not dominated for a few decades now, although it still finds the odd champion. But the occasion of a conference on "Neoplatonism and Christian Thought" offered the unusual course of tracing Browning's lifelong quest for God and truth through examining the triadic and trinitarian patterns so apparent in his poetry, a strategy quite appropriate to the task.[4]

Let us begin on the base of an argument from numerology. Man is propelled into a deep dyadic dilemma by his fall, whether it be understood as the fall of the soul into the body[5] or as Adam's separation from God in the primal garden. His consequent yearning turns source into goal: he longs for the world once known beyond the Platonic cave, for the Plotinian One, or for the biblical God. (Not that these are identical concepts!) He can be satisfied, however partially, only when a third term is activated to bind the separated opposites.

This truism, familiar to every Pythagorean if not to every child of Adam, led of course to the ubiquity of triadic formulations in ancient and Hellenistic philosophies. The triad can enclose a triangle, the first geometric figure in the progression generated from the monad to possess a surface, and hence the first truly visible to the senses. Thus, in the lower universe, three may be regarded as "the first *real* number."[6] In the *Timaeus,* Plato depicts triangles as the building blocks of the cosmos. It can, and will here, be argued that triadic thought patterns are equally ubiquitous in Browning's imaginative cosmos.

Although Browning was demonstrably familiar with the Neoplatonic tradition, especially as it manifested itself in the Renaissance,[7] he was at least as familiar with the triads of German idealistic thought, popular in England since the time of Coleridge. The intellectual heirs of Kant, Schelling, and Hegel are still, at some remove, heirs of Plato and the Hellenistic Neoplatonists. Triadic and dynamic thinking characterizes all periods in the tradition, but it is possible to note shifts of emphasis in the prevalent patterns.

Whereas the early Neoplatonists were concerned with a third term mediating between higher and lower, or inner and outer, poles in a dynamic eddying circuitry, Hegel characteristically visualized the third term of his triads (the synthesis) as arising logically from, but thrusting ontologically beyond, the first and second (the thesis and antithesis).[8] The Hegelian thinker, then, will still see, as did his forebears in the tradition, the world of becoming shot through with vital being from beyond; but his vision of a powerful forward thrust, as each synthesis becomes the thesis for a new triad, imposes an assumption of linear process or progress on his system that is radically different from prevailing assumptions in earlier idealism. The hypothetical absolute is still source and goal, but the post-Hegelian eye tends, in its preoccupation with process, to turn its gaze away from the top story in the three-storied universe derived from the ancients.

The contrast just drawn is simplistic, of course. For that reason alone it would be wrong-headed to attempt to pinpoint source or specific antecedent for elements in Browning's poetry that offer analogies to elements in the long Platonic tradition. An even stronger reason to resist any such temptation is this: pervasive as triadic patterns are in Neoplatonism, they are certainly not exclusive to it. Nor is every pattern of three to be assimilated to the Trinity in a Christian poet, as many an undergraduate has yet to learn. Thus, although such paradigms in the work of a poet as impressively learned as Browning are worth the examining, the process of exploration itself may have to serve as an answer to the questions we put.[9] We know better than to expect the crisp certainties sought by an earlier academic generation addicted to source-hunting; we know better than to attempt to choose Neoplatonism or Christianity as exerting exclusive domain in the Browning canon.

Disclaimer expressed, we may find nonetheless a certain clarity of insight in the realization that the world of noetic activity through which Browning's speakers seek their varieties of truth is congruent with that known to Neoplatonists of every age, and that Neoplatonists of any age would find something therein with which to feel spiritually at ease. Sometimes in the poems we find the divine forces that permeate the world of particularity discharging all differences in a mystic flash: "not a fourth sound, but a star" to quote Abt Vogler (st. VII, 4). Sometimes the moribund state of some character realized in dramatic monologue leads us to see "The central truth, Power, Wisdom, Goodness—God" (*The Ring and the Book* X, 1634) as it were by negation, in an afterimage: such is the case when the murderer, Guido, in *The Ring and the Book* characterizes himself as a bleating "shuddering sheep," helplessly judged a wolf by the shepherd, Pope Innocent, and thrust back into the hellish "quag wherein it drowns" (XI, 402, 405). Sometimes the divine creative power is best understood as that which maintains the motive thrust in an otherwise flagging human life: such in the Pope's eyes was the helpless Pompilia's instinctive compulsion to save the life of her unborn child, the "prompting of what I call God, / And fools call Nature," that moved her "To worthily defend the trust of trusts / Life from the Ever Living" (*RB* X, 1073–81).

The old Pope, more than any other character in *The Ring and the Book,* may be speaking for the older Browning. He is sceptically aware that perceptions of God's truth are very limited from man's fallen perspective, yet he accepts the limitations in sanguine good faith. In this he differs strikingly from speakers who take two other stances in Browning's poetic dialectic, each typical of a phase in the sequence of poetic attempts to bridge the gaps in human experience. Representing the first phase we can see, in 1835, the young Paracelsus: like the heroes of *Pauline* and *Sordello,* the early works that bracket the long dramatic poem bearing his name, Paracelsus seeks to ascend to realms no God-fearing son of Adam should hope to reach under his own noetic power. Forced to abandon the Promethean quest, to learn his limits through years of loss and opprobrium, Paracelsus enjoys only momentary triumphs in the course of his life, and, perhaps, a liberation of vision at the point of death. He never reaches a point at which he can make the triumphant affirmation typical of the second phase in the development of the Browning canon, "See the Christ stand!" Those words are given to David in the version of "Saul" published in 1855, ten years after the first version of the poem broke off inconclusively at a point where the loving young singer was praising the heroic power of his king in an unsuccessful attempt to heal his broken life. The incarnational assertion could not be made in the poem until Browning had himself moved to another phase in his own struggle for unified vision. The impetus came, of course, as the intensity of Elizabeth Barrett Browning's Christian faith augmented the residue of Christian fervor the youthful Browning had absorbed under his mother's influence.[10] Once experienced in maturity, the unifying incarnational vision remained a constant factor in his creative life. Yet after the death of his wife, it was rarely again articulated directly: the limits that life imposes on visionary certainties possess his imagination in later years more powerfully than vision itself.

Three phases, then, provide the schema by which I shall order the demonstrative portions of this essay. The differences are primarily those of emphasis. They are defined in dramatic voices expressing, first, strenuous aspirations towards the absolute Truth that is denied fallen man; second and centrally, proclamations of incarnational truth; third and last, awareness that moments of certainty are evanescent, but that the necessarily endless search for truth confers its own rewards. Although, as suggested, the concerns dominant in early, central, and late periods of the Browning canon may reflect the phases here defined, only the central phase—in which the "central Truth" is forcefully reiterated—applies directly to a limitable period in the life of the poet. The hunger for truth, and the recognition of the limits that deny it, are constants in the poetry of the lifetime.

In the early—the aspiring—phase, the focus is psychological, the vision is internal and subjective, in spite of the dramatic masks Browning assumes to protect the ego flayed by criticisms of his earliest publications. The reader's sympathies are not denied the thwarted aspirant, but he is led to recognize the futility of man's unaided efforts. In the central phase, the focus is theological, the vision sacramental. Affirmations of God's gracious aid to man mark the poems now so strikingly that the less than careful reader may miss the omnipresent evidences of dialectical struggle undergirding the proclamations. Scepticism is never denied, but threads through the fabric of faith. As Christian language recedes over the years to incidental dramatic occurrences, the humane concerns of the Christian—truth, goodness, justice, life here and life hereafter—never recede. The focus of the last phase is epistemological, the vision still sceptical, as it first became when events forced scepticism upon the early striver. Once again, particular truths emerge through particular voices, but the voices are more numerous in the great dramatic epic of this phase, *The Ring and the Book*. Experience is more confusing. Absolute Truth is more and more shadowy, impossible to be proclaimed in single human utterance.[11]

The disparate voices thus necessitated speak, from first to last, in paradox and metaphor, the only linguistic vehicles available for oracular and prophetic utterance.[12] Only by participating in the forward thrust of the poems themselves, focusing on the voices one by one, struggling towards a possible wholeness and holiness refracted in dramatic tensions and recalcitrant language, can we hope to experience the process of indoctrination Browning has in mind for his readers.

In *Paracelsus,* a poem of voices, the young Browning is transparently sketching out his poetic paradigms: the work claims careful attention. At the outset the protagonist is striving for power—power "to comprehend the words of God / And God himself, and all God's intercourse / With the human mind" (533–535). This fierce erotic energy asserts apparently autonomous authority within him: he boasts to Festus, his friend, that the drive comes from God, that he must trust that "God / Ne'er dooms to waste the strength he deigns impart!" (345–346). He claims, in his obsession, that the power he seeks will serve mankind, but adds, "there our intercourse must end: / I never will be served by those I serve" (612–613). Appalled by this arrogance, Festus cautions "How can that course be safe which from the first / Produces carelessness to human love?" (619–620).

The dialectic of the poem is thus established: the tensions will be generated across the gap perceived in fallen existence between the poles of power and love. That Browning's aim was allegorical—to represent an inner action "instead of having recourse to an external machinery"—he explained in the preface to the first edition, later discarded.[13] The mind of Paracelsus, actively demonstrating the stance of power-hunger, is both theater and leading actor for the psychic drama.

Love finds two chief exemplars in the action: Festus, who lives by the warmth of human love and towards whom Paracelsus expresses what little mundane affection is given him to feel; and Aprile, an etherealized Shelleyan sort of poet, whose self-characterization as he enters the action in the second canto leaves no doubt as to his function—"I would LOVE infinitely, and be loved!" (II, 385). In spite of that "infinitely," an adverb of degree, what Aprile loves as artist are the things of earth and "every passion sprung from man" (II, 433); he would capture them in art to the glory of their creator. Through this angelic presence, yearningly in love with the particulars of the world, Paracelsus comes to understand, if only partially, his own fault in unlovingly rejecting the world:[14]

> Die not, Aprile! We must never part.
> Are we not halves of one dissevered world,
> Whom this strange chance unites once more? Part? Never?
> Till thou the lover, know; and I the knower
> Love—until both are saved.
>
> (II, 633–637)

Aprile dies at the end of canto II.

The third canto, set in the middle years of the life of the Renaissance magus, gives us a humanized Paracelsus, partially successful in the university at Basel, warmer and less abstracted towards Festus, but painfully aware that his early hopes were vain and that "The truth is just as far from [him] as ever" (III, 502). He defines

> Two sorts of knowledge; one—vast, shadowy,
> Hints of the unbounded aim I once pursued:
> The other consists of many secrets, caught
> While bent on nobler prize.
>
> (III, 923–926)

Earlier, we recall, "knowledge" for him meant knowledge of absolutes, the radiant star of his youthful obsession; at midpoint now in life the adjective he applies to his "unbounded" goal—"shadowy"—underscores the change the years have brought. He sees painfully how, by contrast, the divine intelligence "casts (man's) mind / Into immeasurable shade" (III, 1026–1027). Shadows pervade this universe of loss, from top to bottom.

His fortunes have declined further by canto IV. Even scientific "knowledge" is slipping from him. Accused of quackery, he has called in dejection for Festus. In bitterness he raves of the black arts and of poetry (IV, 588–594); but admitting that he has "no julep, as men think / To cheat the grave," he consoles himself by claiming a faith in the indestructibility of the human soul (IV, 672–676). The characterization in this canto rings true to records of the historical personality, scientifically rebellious but conservative in his philosophical and religious attitudes—too strange, perhaps, to be a typical Christian Neoplatonist of his period, but participant nonetheless in the amalgamated streams.[15]

The thwarted life is near its end when the final canto opens; Festus laments at the bedside of his silent friend. Paracelsus awakes in delirium, hearing Aprile's voice, and babbling of loving and knowing. Moments of apparent lucidity alternate with flashes of arrogance towards man, or of sardonic raillery at the God who has been defeated in defeating this creature.[16] When, still delirious, he reverts to a happier past, Festus seizes the break in the black torrent to sing an Aprilean lyric of a stream meandering through a natural world inhabited by a multitude of lovely creatures (V, 418–446). Paracelsus sighs, now calmly awake, that the "dark snake that force may not expel / . . . glideth out to music sweet and low" [449–450]. The image, as we shall see, is a precise anticipation of a key moment in "Saul."

Reminiscing of Aprile's quest for God through love, and his own through the power of knowledge, Paracelsus comes to pronounce his own epitaph:

> Let men
> Regard me, and the poet dead long ago
> Who loved too rashly; and shape forth a third
> And better-tempered spirit, warned by both.
>
> (V, 885–888)

Then as death comes, another triadic pattern is implied in his last words:

> Festus, let my hand—
> This hand, lie in your own, my own true friend!
> Aprile! Hand in hand with you, Aprile!
>
> (V, 905–907)

But this triad (Paracelsus as the mean term between exemplars of mundane and etherial love) rounds to a circle in the theater of Paracelsus' mind, if we visualize the ambiguous lines in one possible way. By "this hand," he is perhaps not demonstrating his own, "my hand," in a semantic stutter, nor blurring Festus with Aprile in delirium, but is attempting to join the hand of Aprile, seen clearly as the veil of this world is parting, in the free hand of Festus, and then to take Aprile's free hand himself to close the loving circle. If so, at that moment Paracelsus triumphs by bridging in love, not power, the chasm his life's proud striving has failed to close, and rounding life's angular patterns into perfection.

The dynamic circuitry of love implied in this ending—love in, and beyond, this world of flesh—anticipates the incarnational visions of Browning's central phase in some senses, without doing so specifically. In lines at the original end of canto II, which Browning emphasized by expansion in the 1849 edition that made the incarnational suggestion explicit, Aprile voiced this insight at point of death:

> I see now. God is the perfect poet,
> Who in his person acts his own creations.
>
> (II, 648–649)

To a reader cognizant of the root meaning of "poet" and the Logos tradition in the ancient world, this came close to proclaiming the Christ, even before the expansion. The dying Aprile continued, chiding Paracelsus for the idolatrous intensity of his expressed need—and the words place him far beyond the world of flesh at this point in the fiction:

> Crown me? I am not one of you!
> 'Tis he, the king, you seek. I am not one.
>
> (II. 658–659)

More ethereal always, in his allegorical role, than the incarnate king, Aprile can speak and teach of love but is lacking in power to save. Paracelsus at his own death will call upon *men* to "shape forth [the] third" who will join the human functions expressed by knower and lover, intellectual and intuitional halves of divided humanity. But it has been given the poet of the two to hint that the saving action must come from God.

The dyadic dilemma has been expressed as operating in more than one dimension in *Paracelsus*: horizontally in the division between the two who strive for the power of forbidden knowledge and for infinite love; vertically, in the gap separating them from the creator-source who is their goal. In canto V, at the end, where Aprile is part of the eternal world of love, the vertical dimension predominates.

Power and love are opposed once again in the figures of Saul and David in the early version of "Saul," published four years before the incarnational addition to *Paracelsus*. In lonely agony, like a heavy "king-serpent," the afflicted Saul hangs motionless against a great "cross-support" in his tent (29, 31). The young singer David seeks in love to release him and restore his failed power. The song to which he progresses in the ninth stanza might have been sung by Aprile; it celebrates the same particular beauties of creation, the same passions of men. David's finale, the finale to the early version, is tonally triumphant—"The name rings—King Saul!" (96). But the narrative action is inconclusive. The image of transfixed flesh at the beginning of the poem has implied the ending Browning was presumably incapable of writing in 1845.[17]

Not until stanza X, the first of those published ten years later,[18] is Saul released to full awareness, as the dying Paracelsus had been released in response to the song Festus sang in Aprilian celebration. Yet full salvation in the poem comes not for Saul but for the young poet who will see power and love fused in the vision of Christ. The serpent image does not apply directly to Saul in the second half of the poem, yet it enters once more in the culminating lines as David makes his breathless way home through a night charged with angelic and demonic presences. Armed by his vision of Christ, he feels the fears that could beset him subside harmlessly—"the Hand still impelled me at once and supported, suppressed / All the tumult" (321–322)—and in the consequent hush he sees a serpent slide away silent, under "the new Law" of love. (The serpent image, harmless now or even benign, will be noted again in another incarnational context.)

Any tendency to see the atemporal vision of David as a pious anachronism, or as the facile imposition of a metaphysical solution upon a physical problem, should be forestalled by attention to the hand imagery in "Saul." The breakthrough whereby David sees the loving potency of Christ as the inevitable answer for a fallen and separated world comes in response to an affectionate gesture from the king, whose hand tilts the boy's head back for an intense interchange of gaze. The rush of love David then feels brings in the rush of truth. If he, mere work of God's hand, would give new life to Saul "had love but the warrant" (236), could creature possibly surpass creator in this? Love has a warrant, when love is God's, because love is a power, and grants "power to believe." "All's one gift," a dynamic process in which "all's love, yet all's law" (288, 289, 242). Ecstatically, David proclaims a truth the Neoplatonist might define as the circuitry of procession from, and return to, the lodestar, God:

As Thy love is discovered almighty, almighty be proved
Thy power, that exists with and for it, of being Beloved!
(305–306)

David then moves on to explicitly Christian utterance:

O Saul, it shall be
A Face like my face that receives thee; a Man like to me,
Thou shalt love and be loved by, for ever: a Hand like this hand
Shall throw open the gates of new life to thee! See the Christ stand!
(309–312)

David's prophetic vision is of the mediator who alone, in the Christian understanding of things, can rejoin what the fall has put asunder. And his mystical knowledge is typical of two modes of biblical "knowing"—it is felt as received from beyond but is not contrary to reason; and it is carnal knowledge too. Hands of flesh are needed to participate in the preparation for, and realization of, God's now accessible truth.

The vision of Christ in the completed "Saul" is the strongest direct declaration of its sort in the canon, direct in the sense that there is no dialectical qualification in the poetic context, although, of course, the words are dramatically distanced from Browning by ascription to David. Thereafter the incarnational "central truth" remains a given whenever Browning writes of the human dilemma. The drier tones that ensue when he explores the epistemological concerns dominant in the final phase, the inevitable resumption of sceptical ratiocination, must not be taken as evidence of denial of the peak of vision. "Infinite moments" are not susceptible of perpetuation in a finite world; to understand this is not to deny infinity.

While Browning was working his way toward the vision in "Saul" he wrote, in 1850, a long discursive double work, "Christmas Eve and Easter Day." The work is not totally successful as poetry: it reads as recall of a dialectical struggle internal to some consciousness—perhaps Browning's, perhaps by intent his reader's—punctuated by fleeting instances of more visionary mental events.

The dialectic between power and love is modified and complicated in the first and more poetic half: the speaker observes and explores his responses to the events of Christmas Eve in three imagined settings: an unlovely service in a dreary nonconformist chapel, an imposingly ritualistic service in Saint Peter's at Rome, and a lecture on Christology at Göttingen by a professor steeped in the arguments of the higher criticism. The binding thread, as the wanderer makes his imagined survey of these manifestations of contemporary response to the Christmas event, is the fleeting figure of Christ, whose flying garments serve to "suck" the speaker

along in the flying wake
Of the luminous water-snake.
(503–504)

These striking lines occur first in stanza IX as the poet is being led from the chapel to Rome, and again, in precise repetition, as he is led to Göttingen. But they have been anticipated—in brightness, in fluidity, and in the serpentine detail—in the denouement to the most mystical passage in the poem, one beginning in stanza VII and describing the vision triggered by the sight of a "moon-rainbow, vast and perfect / From heaven to heaven extending" when a "black cloud-barricade was riven" (378, 385–386):[19]

> I felt my brain
> Gutted with the glory, blazing
> Throughout its whole mass, over and under
> Until at length it burst asunder
> And out of it bodily there streamed,
> The too-much glory, as it seemed,
> Passing from out me to the ground,
> Then palely serpentining round
> Into the dark with mazy error.
>
> VIII
> All at once I looked up with terror.
> He was there.
> He Himself with His human air.
> (421–432)

The passage is logically and emotionally ambivalent. Although the vision has begun above in the moon-rainbow, "mazy error" suggests a resumption of scepticism; and the word "gutted" begins a line of suggestion that the physical brain of the speaker (note "mass") is womb for the birth of the Christmas vision. But it demonstrates a clear advance towards specifically Christian statement when compared with the unbinding of the dark snake's coils at the end of *Paracelsus*; and the "serpentining" image leads here to the sudden appearance of Christ, a Christ recognizable in the very midst of doubt and terror.

The vision of the flying Christ compels compliance in the poet, but not unthinking compliance. He debates strenuously with himself throughout the whole experience, striving to find "one way, our chief / Best way of worship" so that he might "contrive / My fellows also take their share!" (1170–1174). Once he reaches a point of recognition that

> I can but testify
> God's care for me—no more, can I—
> It is but for myself I *know*
> (1185–1187, italics added)

He feels the enfolding warmth of the flying robe, and then a passionate impulse to spring "out of the wandering world of rain, / Into the little chapel again" (1236–1237).

He is still fully aware of its ugliness. But having tested and rejected the power of the professor's searching intellect through a succinct and witty parody of the arguments by which the continental critics of Scripture were reducing the "Myth of Christ" to "vacuity"; and having earlier "feast[ed] his love" on the palpable beauties of Saint Peter's, he makes the existential choice: "I choose here!" (859, 914, 737, 1341). Having chosen, he participates freely in singing

> The last five verses of the third section
> Of the seventeenth hymn in Whitfield's Collection,
> To conclude with the doxology.
>
> (1357–1359)

The search for the universal answer has been silently dropped. The glory has faded. But the particular man has taken his stand in the dry particularity lightly mocked in lines just quoted. This nonconformism may be "an earthen vessel"; but for him it holds more accessible treasure than the "golden ewer" (1313–1314) of Rome, or the empty bell jar at Göttingen—both of which stand, he has made evident at an earlier point of transition,[20] for the dissevered halves of love and power.

"But for myself I *know*": affirmation and scepticism have become inseparably entwined in the fabric of "Christmas Eve." Knowledge has been identified with, and more importantly, conferred in, the existentially chosen Way, in this record of dialectical growth. In the process of knowing, the act of choice is all important.[21]

"How very hard it is to be / A Christian!" This opening exclamation of "Easter Day," separated from the "doxology" by merely the title of the second part, serves as much as retrospective commentary as it serves to sound the renewed theme. It is not always easy to "Praise Father, Son, and Holy Ghost."

"The whole, or chief / Of difficulties, is belief" (29–30), asserts the sceptical voice in the ensuing dialogue. Then suddenly the God of power appears in apocalyptic vision to stand in judgment over the quaking sceptic. When he sees by the light of that "One fire" (505) that knowledge of the things of earth must fail, the appellant prays for love, and reverberations of Roman 7:24 and 1 Corinthians 13:8 soften those of the book of Revelation.

> Thou Love of God! . . . .
> . . . . leave me not tied
> To this despair, this corpse-like bride!
>
> . . . .

XXXII

> Then did the Form expand, expand—
> I knew Him through the dread disguise,
> As the whole God within His eyes
> Embraced me.
>
> (992–1007)

The God of judging power, when known, is known to be loving too. The wholeness here finds expression in an embracing image that does not burst, although consciousness fades with the vision.

Power, love, and the knowledge that unites the dyadic poles through visionary experience and existential response, these terms of the Browning triad may be
fitted now to the persons of the Trinity, although the danger of overschematizing
must be resisted. The Father, the creator and judge, is shown forth usually in
Power; the Son, also creative and standard of all true judgment, is shown forth
usually in Love; but the third "person" is more elusive. This spirit is Knowledge,
but not that forbidden sort sought at first by Paracelsus. Knowledge, given in
pentecostal brilliance, communicable in the tongues of poetry, may be tenuously
sustained by the choice that brings comforting strength. The way, the truth, the
life may be willfully embraced as the visible Christ fades in the distance.

Once it is recognized that the ongoing searching and testing of knowledge
has, in the Browning scheme of things, the force of the Holy Ghost in more
traditional creeds, the epistemological concerns that dominate the final phase may
be understood in perspective. They are the interim tasting, and testing, along the
way, of the fruit that may only be assimilated in the New Jerusalem where
knowledge and the fullness of life are one.[22] The final phase in no way, then, need
be seen as marked by a falling off from faith. As the terrain through which the
fallen quester must make his way, doubt was even in 1855 for Browning the very
testing ground of faith. The Childe Roland who, after his dread passage, could
sound his slughorn still, had more courage by far than to sell out his head to his
heart or to abandon his quest. His successors in the canon can do no less.

Saint John, the disciple Jesus loved, speaks from a powerful intellect in "A
Death in the Desert" (*Dramatis Personae* 1864), offering Browning's "most closely
reasoned *apologia* for Christianity."[23]

> I saw the power; I see the Love, once weak
> Resume the Power: and in this word "I see,"
> Lo . . . the Spirit of both.
>
> (221–223)

John, on his deathbed, recognizing that his temporal witness will pass with his
temporal life, and that the poetic record of his vision on Patmos may not serve all
subsequent purposes, proceeds to argue that finite reason is not violated by the
truth, but, as agent, is incapable of comprehending the truth. He establishes his
argument on his doctrine of three souls in one (82–104), which bears an imprecise
analogy to orthodox formulations concerning the Trinity, a stronger resemblance
to the description of the tripartite soul in *The Republic* and Augustine's adapta-
tions thereof, and an even closer resemblance to the doctrine Milton's Raphael
owes to Plotinus and Plato as he instructs Adam in *Paradise Lost*.[24] John's lowest
soul, "what Does," parallels Plato's vegetative soul; his median soul, which "feel-
eth, thinketh, willeth" in an Augustinian subtriad, is seated in the brain; and "duly
tending upward" it seeks to grow into "the last soul," the one that returns to God.
Once that last soul, the "what Is," has been achieved, the finite man "ends . . . in
that dread point of intercourse." He has, hypothetically, grown into Godhead, and
hence into the world beyond death. Like the Lazarus of "An Epistle to Karshish,"

such a man can no longer be of this earth. This is why, in God's infinite wisdom, the Knowledge beyond knowledge must remain beyond man's sustained experience.

"Caliban upon Setebos," a poem from the same volume, strikes a sceptical note that also chimes with Neoplatonic doctrine. The negative theology of Dionysian mysticism is grotesquely but movingly suggested through the words of the beast-man as he struggles through the early steps of an argument from "natural theology."[25] Setebos, the god worshiped by Caliban's dam Sycorax, is a gross parody of modern man's "rational" anthropomorphic projections. Setebos is a brutish sadist, a Caliban writ large. But over him, the craven Caliban hopes wistfully, rules the hidden God, "the Quiet," who may, "some strange day . . . catch . . . Setebos" (281–282). This natural eschatology fades as soon as it is articulated: Caliban sinks back into propitiating whine. Yet an interesting triad has been suggested: worshiper, projected god, and unknowable overgod. Browning probably derived his conception of "the overgod" most immediately through Unitarian friends in his youth. Nonetheless, its remoter ancestry is Neoplatonic. Caliban's god, "the Quiet," anticipates the mystical dimensions of the discourse of the Pope, which forms the climax, Book X, of Browning's great endeavor of the late sixties, *The Ring and the Book*.

The Pope is a highly rational and humane man, engaged in his own dramatic quest for truth. His epistemological concerns set him securely in Browning's final phase. The Pope speaks of two kinds of truth, parallel to the "two sorts of knowledge" Paracelsus defined for Festus. As one who must judge the final appeal in a complex murder case, his immediate concern is with the truth he must "evolv[e] at last / Painfully" from "these dismalest of documents," the records of Guido's trial.

> Truth, nowhere, lies yet everywhere in these—
> Not absolute in a portion, yet
> Evolvible from the whole, [he must trust].
> (229–230)

"Mankind is ignorant, a man am I" (258–259), he muses, yet if he exercises his God-given judging faculty in good faith, he will be able to face Guido's ghost without fear, confident he has attained as much truth as "We men, in our degree, may know" here. But not so "There," (377–378) at "God's judgment bar" (348). There, "He, the Truth, is, too, / The Word" (376–377). The standard of absolute truth is Christ.

The Pope sees that unless, in life, "the true way" is lit by "the great glow" of faith (1816) man's movement towards eternal truth is fearfully difficult. Only at times of mortal trial, as "When in the way stood Nero's cross and stake" (1833), is true progress possible. More often "We fools dance thro' the cornfield of this life" in "ignoble confidence" (1838, 1848). The Pope's mind opens ahead to times that will "shake / This torpor of assurance from our creed" (1854), and wonders whether the Molinists currently under threat of death for heresy, recognize

> truths, obedient to some truth
> Unrecognized yet, but perceptible?—
> Correct the portrait by the living face,
> Man's God, by God's God in the heart of man?
>   (1871–1874)

The words of Innocent XII, no mystic himself as Browning draws him, link the Molinists to the visions in "Christmas Eve and Easter Day" and "Saul," the standards for existential faith in the world of doubt as the middle phase yields to the third. The Pope's sympathy towards the Molinists, first demonstrated in the first book, is juxtaposed in this second expression with his musings on the enhanced probability of finding truth at points of mortal transition.[26]

When he does finally pass the judgment on Guido, he does so with the prayer that "suddenness of fate" may open the wretch's soul to salvation:

> may the truth be flashed out by one blow,
> And Guido see, one instant, and be saved.
>   (2127–2128)

The prayer evokes John's argument that the "last soul" truly knows at the "dread point" of death. Not inconsistently, then, the Pope seems to rest his own trust in his now-secure judgment on his own impending death:

> I may die this very night:
> And how should I dare die, this man let live?
>   (2133–2134)

In the meantime, the forward thrust of living dominates the poetry of the poet's final phase. The hunger for truth that has been evident from the outset seeks, in the recognition of limits, satisfaction through discerning the evidences of God in the particulars of this world.

Unanswerable questions still trouble Browning: he ponders, for instance, arguments for and against a belief in immortality in the little volume *La Saisiaz: The Two Poets of Croisic* which was prompted by the death of a dear friend in 1877. There the poetic imagination, the "fancy" as scoffers would have it, provides truths answerable to felt need as it transmutes the hard facts of existence into truths larger than the earthly sort defined by Paracelsus and the Pope.[27]

A decade later yet, in the prologue to the *Asolando* volume published the day of his death, Browning is still playing variations on the themes of epistemology using "fact" and "fancy" as key notes.[28] "The Poet's age is sad": the first words mark the poem as personal although three voices speak its lines. The first voice laments the passing of the colors projected upon the world in youth by the "soul's iris-bow," and brought there, for one remembering Wordsworth's great ode, from the preexistent beyond. An unmasked voice responds, setting up an opposition between the effects of a lens capable of restoring such coloration, and one that would reveal "truth ablaze, / Not falsehood's fancy-haze." The apparently straightforward words are full of evocative trickery. The imagery triggers memories of "the rainbow [that] comes and goes," and also of Shelley's "dome of many-colored glass" casting its stained light on the world Platonists learn to regard as illusory, the world Victorian empiricists would call "factual." Once the reader adapts to the wavering perspectives, he realizes that a claim of exclusive truth for either lens would be quite false.

Reminiscing in tune with the opening voice the poet recalls the time, in his youth, when he found the town of Asolo "palpably fire-clothed." Now he sees Italy's "rare / O'er-running beauty" still—"But flame? The Bush is bare." Again the perspectives demand attention. Focusing one way we think of Moses, a young Moses, before a bush that like Asolo was "palpably fire-clothed," from which spoke the voice of God. The first response is to see the divine as immediate in the glowing vision. But the "palpable" fire may be a material screen, benignly protecting mere man from the "too much glory" of a hidden God. Then, from this other perspective, when "the bush is bare" the barriers to human perception of God's presence in his creation seem to be going down as the glories perceived in youth subside.

"What then?" the poet asks. From out of "Hill, vale, tree, flower" speaks a third voice, uttering a command Aprile would have been lovingly ready to obey:

> "Call my works thy friends!
> At Nature dost thou shrink amazed?
> God is it who transcends."

The words are far from one-dimensional, but one message comes clear. God can still speak through a nature that aging eyes have shrunk from as deficient—or too powerful. The world of the many does reveal the one Truth.

The epilogue to the same volume—thus, accidentally, the epilogue to a life—paints a forthright, almost blustery picture of the poet in dialogue from beyond the grave with some "you" who loved him in life. He had well-founded misgivings about publishing it—it has met with much disapproval. "It almost looks like bragging," he told his sister and daughter-in-law, "But it's the simple truth; and as it's truth it shall stand."[29] This is the self-portrait designed to forestall any possible pity at the end of a life:

> One who never turned his back but marched breast forward,
>   Never doubted clouds would break,
> Never dreamed, though right were worsted, wrong would triumph,
> Held we fall to rise, are baffled to fight better,
>   Sleep to wake.

Anyone who finds this "blustery yea-saying . . . little more than rhetoric," and untrue at that since "doubt and occasional despair run like counterpoint to his cheerfulness through all these later years"[30] is failing to take into account the primacy for Browning, ever since "Christmas Eve," of the act of choice. (He is in the company of most Christians in the Pauline, Augustinian, and existentialist tradition, of course, in making will an agency in bridging the dyadic gap.) Choosing the "here" of the existence he has been given, choosing to march "breast forward" on the Way, not in denial or even in spite of doubt, but exulting in the challenge to overcome it—this is an unabashed declaration of courage. It is also the best way discovered by one particular poet and man to move towards truth. In Christian terms, it is the continuing incorporation of, and response to, the dynamic gift of the Spirit.

> No, at noonday in the bustle of man's worktime
> Greet the unseen with a cheer!
> Bid him forward, breast and back as either should be,
> "Strive and thrive!" cry "Speed,—fight on, fare ever
> There as here."

The call to the living friend, "Greet the unseen with a cheer," is an exhortation, of course, to participation in the sort of "muscular Christianity" that left Browning open always to sneers from the genteel. But it is more than that. Until the boundaries of life are passed, "the unseen" must mean something Other to the human. In the imagined present tense of this "epilogue," "the unseen" is the speaker, seeing himself—to quote from another often strenuous Christian poet—now "made God's music."[31] Since the participant in glory is Browning, the tune must be an up-tempo march.

The vision of this last stanza erases even the qualitative boundaries between the "here" and the "there." Since Browning's existential faith has long been invested in his knowledge of the Way as the divine *persona* available to his grasping, he imagines that the nearer he comes to the real presence, the more exhilarating will be the demands upon him. Process and growth cannot possibly be seen to cease at "that dread point of intercourse":[32] they are his way of knowing God, his means of grace. Only an Hegelian heaven can attract this latter-day Neoplatonic saint.

In brief recapitulation, triadic patterns of thought mark Browning's poetry in all of its phases, and in the middle phase the median term between searching man and his God becomes specifically the Christ. The Trinity, as patristic tradition conceived it, is harder to recognize in Browning's characteristic patterns: Father and Son are abundantly clear, the Father dominating as distant goal for the Paracelsian aspirant of the first phase, and Christ the mediator standing clear to the visionary of the central phase. When, in the final phase, the vision has faded, the commitment it has occasioned and the taste it has conferred draw the *man* along his existential way. The impetus to the Way, the Truth, the Life has been the pentecostal gift; many tongues henceforth are needed in the poetry to weave out of partial truths the holy fabric of Truth.

17

The Christian Platonism of C. S. Lewis, J. R. R. Tolkien, and Charles Williams

MARY CARMAN ROSE

C. S. Lewis, J. R. R. Tolkien, and Charles Williams have had a great deal of attention as writers of fiction and poetry. In addition, Lewis is widely known as an apologist for the Christian faith and for his medieval studies; Williams' *Descent of the Dove* is accepted as a significant history of the Christian church;[1] and, Tolkien's professional work centered on Anglo-Saxon philology and literature. It has not been sufficiently recognized, however, that all three wrote as Christian Platonists. In what follows I wish to examine the Christian Platonism that informs their literary creativity. I will (1) provide evidence that these writers wished to be identified as Christian Platonists; (2) characterize Christian Platonism as it is used in this context and draw attention to some of the Christian Platonist elements in the literary work of these writers; and (3) state some conclusions pertaining to the philosophical importance of this resurgence of Christian Platonism at the present time.

   1. The establishing that Lewis, Tolkien, and Williams wished to be identified as Christian Platonists requires, first, drawing attention to their Christian faith and, moreover, to the orthodoxy of that faith and, second, establishing their

deliberate choice of Platonist concepts and beliefs for the development and illumination of Christian beliefs.

That all three intended to write as Christians is clear. In *Surprised by Joy* Lewis tells of his conversion experience.[2] In seven novels Williams explores the relation of Christianity to pagan gnostic, Jewish, and Muslim beliefs, practices, and mysticism. Also, Williams' *Taliessen through Logres* and *Descent of the Dove* express his Christian convictions.[3] Tolkien's "On Fairy-Stories" reveals the import for all his work of the explicitly Christian meaning he gives to what he sees as the important concepts of subcreativity and eucatastrophe.[4]

The thoroughgoing exploration of the Christian orthodoxy of these writers would require an extended study, including, of course, an examination of the meanings that history gives to "Christian orthodoxy" itself. Suffice it to say here that each writer has in one way or another declared himself to be a Trinitarian with no desire to demythologize the Incarnation or the Atonement. Further, no one of the three displays any tendency toward limited theism, the secularization of Christianity, or any form of Manichaeism. These points need not be argued in the case of Lewis whose orthodoxy is explicit in his theological works, while Williams states his orthodoxy in *The Descent of the Dove*.

The task of establishing Tolkien's Christian orthodoxy is more complex and presents an interesting challenge in which his concepts of subcreativity and eucatastrophe are of central importance. Tolkien's view is that to be faithful to his role as subcreator, man must work within the limits of objective truth that he did not himself create. Further, this objective truth possesses its correlative beauty, while the role of the subcreator is to be the faithful steward of truth and beauty wherever he finds them. The permanent role of steward given to man implies that man has a permanent relation to a master. This relation is not compatible with any secularized interpretation of Christianity which puts emphasis on man as independent. Further, Tolkien calls the resurrection the most important eucatastrophe.[5] (Additional exploration of this topic lies outside the scope of this paper.) I suggest, however, that any attempt to interpret the works of these three writers as informed by any view except that of Christian orthodoxy must result in a reductive, distorted view of them.

It is clear that Lewis and Williams wish to be known as Christian Platonists. In the *Chronicles of Narnia* one of Lewis' most spiritually developed and wise characters is Lord Digory.[6] The following is an account of his response to the passing of the physical world of Narnia:

> "That was not the real Narnia. That had a beginning and an end. It was only a shadow or a copy of the real Narnia, which has always been here and always will be here; just as our own world, England and all, is only a shadow or copy of something in Aslan's real world. You need not mourn over Narnia, Lucy. All of the old Narnia that mattered, all the dear creatures, have been drawn into the real Narnia. . . . And of course it is different; as different as a real thing is from a shadow or as waking life is from a dream." His voice stirred everyone like a trumpet as he spoke these words: but when he added under his breath "It's all in Plato, all in Plato. Bless me! What do they teach them at these schools?" the older ones laughed.[7]

Williams' *The Place of the Lion* relates the spiritual awakening of Damaris Tighe, a graduate student in philosophy doing a dissertation on medieval Platonism without realizing the intellectual and spiritual import of the texts she studies. Anthony, like Lewis' Lord Digory, is a spiritual leader in his community. Anthony loves Damaris and reflects on her thus:

> She would go on thoughtfully playing with the dead pictures of ideas, with names and philosophies, Plato and Pythagoras and Anselm and Abelard, Athens and Alexandria and Paris, not knowing that the living existences to which seers and saints had looked were already in movement to avenge themselves on her. "O you sweet blasphemer!" Anthony moaned, "Can't you wake?" Gnostic traditions, medieval rituals, Aeons and Archangels—they were cards she was playing in her own game. But she didn't know, she didn't understand. It wasn't her fault; it was the fault of her time, her culture, her education—the pseudo-knowledge that affected all the learned, the pseudo-skepticism that infected all the unlearned, in an age of pretense, and she was only pretending as everybody else did in this lost and imbecile century.[8]

Also, in his preface to *Essays Presented to Charles Williams,* Lewis warns against the error of taking Williams' novels as only exciting fantasies. Lewis says that Williams' novels present

> some of the most important things Williams had to say. They have, I think, been little understood. The frank supernaturalism and the frankly bloodcurdling episodes have deceived readers who were accustomed to seeing such "machines" used as toys and who supposed that what was serious must be naturalistic.[9]

Also, Lewis expresses himself on the importance of Damaris' discovery of the reality of the archetypes:

> And the frivolously academic who "do research" into archetypal ideas without suspecting that these were ever anything more than raw material for doctorate theses, may one day awake, like Damaris, to find that they are infinitely mistaken.[10]

The demonstration that Platonist convictions inform Tolkien's creativity is another matter. As a vehicle for Christian Platonism, the fiction of Lewis and Williams offers idealized situations that are not only consistent with the truth of Christian Platonism, but are to be expected if that position is true. Anyone who lived through these situations and who possessed sufficient spiritual preparation would have some experiences that would count as verification of the truth of Christian Platonism. Tolkien, on the other hand, has created a culture which, like Heidegger's *Dasein,* does not impel toward any one interpretation of reality and man, but rather is suggestive of many interpretations. Thus, while a Christian Platonist interpretation of *The Lord of the Rings* and of Tolkien's short stories is consistent with the content of these works, it is not explicitly stated by their author.[11] All doubts about Tolkien's Christian Platonist interpretation of Middle Earth are dispelled, however, with the posthumous appearance of *The Silmarillion,* the first two chapters of which provide an obviously Christian Platonist account of creation.[12] Here the divine creator puts into creation an axiological orientation toward harmony. The act of creation is accompanied by the beauty of song, and the product of this song is a metaphysically fundamental locus of beauty in the harmonious relations between creation and creator and among the various aspects of creation. The harmony is broken by the disobedience of one of the Valar, creatures analogous to the angels of the pseudo-Dionysius and to whom some of the work of creation is entrusted.

2. Platonism, Neoplatonism, and Christian Platonism are, of course, equivocal. What meanings is it legitimate and fruitful to give them in this context? And do they have the same meanings for Lewis, Williams, and Tolkien? I will try to show that there is ground for answering this latter question in the affirmative. Further, in my opinion the Christian Platonist elements shared by these three writers are too numerous to examine exhaustively in this context. I will discuss three of these elements: the reality and availability of suprasensory aspects of creation; the modes of our coming to know these aspects of creation; and the ideal copresence of truth, beauty, and goodness in all aspects of creation. I have chosen these for emphasis because I wish to show that these are of great import for the comprehension of the intention and content of the work of these three authors and also for present and future philosophical and theological creativity based on their work.

We have noted Lewis' acceptance of the reality of the archetypal realm. His eldila, or angels, which are of central importance in his Trilogy, are not perceptible to physical sight or hearing, though when they choose they can make themselves seen and heard by earth dwellers. The hero of the Trilogy is Elwin Ransom who sees and converses with the eldila:

> The faces surprised him very much. Nothing less like the "angel" of popular art could well be imagined. The rich variety, the hint of undeveloped possibilities, which make the interest of human faces were entirely absent.[13]

And in Christian Platonist fashion the eldila have work to do in respect to the physical world. One eldil tells Ransom of the former's relation to the human inhabitants of Perelandra:

> I was not sent to rule them, but while they were young I ruled all else. I rounded this ball when it first arose . . . The beasts that sing and the beasts that fly and all that swims on my breast and all that creeps and tunnels within me has been mine.[14]

Williams' character Anthony is given a vision of the archetypal realm that he immediately recognizes for what it is:

> Patterned upon the darkness he saw the forms—the strength of the lion and the subtlety of the crowned serpent, the loveliness of the butterfly and the swiftness of the horse—and other shapes whose meaning he did not understand. They were there only as he passed, hints and expressions of lasting things, but not by such mortal types did the Divine Ones exist in their own blessedness. He knew, and submitted; this world was not yet open to him, nor was his service upon earth completed. And as he adored those beautiful, serene, and terrible manifestations, they vanished from around him.[15]

One theme of *The Place of the Lion* is the development of Plato's conception of *participation*.[16] Williams writes of Anthony's knowledge of the archetypes in physical objects:

> He knew them in the spiritual intellect, and beheld by their fashioned material bodies the mercy which hid in matter the else overwhelming ardours; man was not yet capable of naked vision.[17]

Likewise, we have noted the importance Tolkien gives to the Valar who are analogous to Lewis' eldila.

All three writers see the suprasensory realm as knowable, but not by intellectual means alone. On this topic, however, there is a fundamental difference between the views of Lewis, Tolkien, and Williams, on the one hand, and, on the other hand, those of Plato as expressed in Socrates' speech in the *Symposium*; of Plotinus; and of the Jewish Platonist writers of the *Zohar*. According to all three of these last the individual who achieves direct perception of the archetypal realm of creation does so through his efforts at spiritual and intellectual development in which he is aided by a knowledgeable teacher who has walked that path of development. These efforts bring about a distinctive total maturation of the self, including the development of powers for investigation of reality. Thus, the individual becomes an instrument of metaphysical inquiry, his nature having become correlative to certain metaphysically fundamental aspects of reality.

That Lewis was cognizant of these pagan and Jewish forms of Platonist inquiry concerning suprasensory aspects of creation may be surmised from his interest in Western occultist writings, the teachings of which were in large part drawn from the *Zohar*.[18] And that Tolkien and Williams as well as Lewis were cognizant of these philosophical views may be surmised from the activities, knowledge, and powers of some of their characters. Lewis' character Uncle Andrew in *The Magician's Nephew*; Tolkien's Sauron in the *Lord of the Rings*; and Williams' Mr. Berringer and Mr. Tighe in *The Place of the Lion* and Henry Lee and his uncle in *The Greater Trumps* all represent a misuse of the Platonist and Jewish Platonist opportunity and ability to seek knowledge of suprasensory aspects of creation. That is, each wishes this knowledge for the sake of the knowledge per se; for the sake of the power that such knowledge gives; or for the sake of the contemplation of the beauty that inheres in the suprasensory.

The Jewish Platonist view, on the other hand, is that the knowledge of the suprasensory will harm the individual who does not seek it out of a willingness— an eagerness, rather—to use that knowledge for the well-being of the community. And Lewis, Tolkien, and Williams likewise draw attention to the serious results of the misuse of these Platonist modes of inquiry. Nonetheless, there is ample evidence that each was sympathetic with the legitimate use of these methods. For each has at least one character who procedes successfully along the path to the achievement and use of knowledge of the suprasensory. There is Tolkien's Gandolf who is a hero in *The Lord of the Rings*; Lewis' Hermit of the Southern March who is a kindly and honest character in *The Horse and His Boy*; and Williams' Prince Ali in *Many Dimensions* who is well-intentioned according to his own lights.

It is clear, however, that Lewis, Tolkien, and Williams are interested in contrasting all forms of non-Christian Platonism with Christian Platonism. Further, all three express the same conclusions on this topic through their characters' moral and spiritual development, as shown in words, actions, problems, aspirations, failures, and successes. This conclusion suggests the importance for these three writers of the distinction between, on the one hand, the Platonist and Neoplatonist knowledge of reality that is not Christian and, on the other hand, the way in which that knowledge is achieved. In general, Lewis, Tolkien, and Williams are agreed that these metaphysical beliefs are true. Also, they are agreed that these beliefs are desiderata for the spiritual development of some persons and their subsequent fulfilling of their roles in their communities.

The view of these three writers, however, is that these non-Christian approaches to metaphysical knowledge are not necessary for the Christian. And for the latter they may, in fact, be counterindicated. For the events of the Christian's life, together with his faith in Christian beliefs maintained through these events, takes the place of the several non-Christian disciplines. Through numerous sources come the needed insight into, convictions concerning, and experience with normally hidden depths of reality. A belief in the providential nature of these events, always important in Christianity, is a major theme in the work of these three writers.

Lewis encourages this interpretation of his work. For, on the one hand, he tells of his rejection of the non-Christian modes of inquiry;[19] yet, on the other hand, his fiction and much of his philosophical work are informed by the Platonist metaphysics. Peter, high king of Narnia, discovers that whatever knowledge of reality he requires comes to him from a variety of sources. At these times he is grateful that he has no need to use "magic." And Lewis uses "magic" to name non-Christian knowledge and the use of the laws of creation, particularly those pertaining to suprasensory aspects of creation. Also, Elwin Ransom is admitted to important knowledge of reality and of some creatures that he could never have achieved in his English university education because he had a love and reverence of the new truth he had glimpsed and because he loved those creatures whose language, knowledge, and perspective on reality he wished to learn. Lewis' description of Ransom's experience has great import for the understanding of Christian Platonism: "Through his knowledge of the creatures and his love for them he began ever so little" to hear their music "with their ears."[20]

Analogous comments are to be made of the characters of Williams and Tolkien who are spiritual leaders. Each in a distinctive way, and always in a way that is both practical and at least implicitly Christian, is an intellectual leader and provides metaphysical insight as well as spiritual leavening when and how they are needed. Thus, the unmistakable heroes of *The Lord of The Rings* are Frodo and Sam whose faithfulness and good will toward their respective tasks won for each knowledge needed for his work and the strength and wisdom to appropriate that knowledge. Also, there are Williams' characters Sybil in *The Greater Trumps,* Chloe in *Many Dimensions,* and Anthony in *The Place of the Lion.* Of great import for the comprehension of Christian Platonism are Anthony's reflections on the eve of his achieving the knowledge of reality and the determination, courage, and clarity of purpose that he needs to lead his community out of chaos:

> An intense apprehension of the danger which many . . . were in grew within him, a danger brought about by the disorder which had been introduced. He could not honestly say he loved these others, unless indeed love were partly a process of willing good to them. That he was determined to do, and perhaps this willing of good meant restoration. By order man ascended; what was it St. Francis had written? "Set love in order, thou that lovest Me."[21]

A constant theme in all the literary creativity of Lewis, Tolkien, and Williams is the fundamental roles in creation of truth, goodness, and beauty and their inextricable interdependence. This theme, which they elaborate and defend in numerous ways, may be seen as a Christian appropriation of Diotima's affirmative answer to her question, "Is not the good also the beautiful?"; of her emphasis on the "science of beauty everywhere"; and of her teaching that, since beauty is the accompaniment of truth, true beauty will be recognized by persons with a rectified spiritual nature.[22]

Lewis' character Lucy, whose name signifies her spontaneous, eager discerning of the light of truth, has a deep appreciation of natural beauty. Her cousin Eustace, however, who is totally self-centered and out of touch with the true spiritual and moral orientation of creation, finds no beauty in stars, trees, or the great Aslan, who is spiritual leader of Narnia and friend and teacher of the children whom he calls to work in Narnia.[23] Tolkien's characters who are willing, albeit grudgingly, to lend a helpful hand to others and to try to keep their promises, display in their words and actions a pleasing whimsey. And some of these characters ultimately in their very being achieve a great beauty. On the other hand, orcs, whose exploited nature suggests the Platonic understanding of evil as the nonbeing of good, have faces, music, and language that, because of their ugliness, are frightening to innocent well-intentioned creatures. Williams' acceptance of the metaphysical ground of the interdependence of truth, goodness, and beauty is implicit in *Taliessen Through Logres*.[24] And the beauty of the transcendent archetypes as well as the beauty they bestow on all that participates in them is explicit in Mr. Tighe's ecstatic discernment of the archetypal butterfly. Mr. Tighe suffers a severe lack of spiritual development, however, as seen in his failure to care sufficiently for his daughter (i.e., because of his failure to appropriate the truth and the goodness that are the correlatives of the beauty he loves).[25]

Other important aspects of the Platonist tradition, which are stressed by one or two of our writers but not predominantly featured by all three, are the Platonist psychophysical dualism; the other-worldliness that is implicit in the latter; and the Platonist ontological view of the degrees of being.

According to the Platonist psychophysical dualism, although in this life soul and body are one harmonious whole, the individual is not his body nor the combination of spirit and body. Rather, the individual is spirit, and, surviving the death of the physical body, is at home eternally in suprasensory aspects of reality. That this is Lewis' view is clear. In *Out of the Silent Planet* the Oyarsa, or archangel, can unbody anyone he likes; and the rational creatures who have been killed by evil men are said to have been unbodied and to have gone to their eternal home.[26] Further, at least three of Williams' novels—*Many Dimensions, Shadows of Ecstasy,* and *Descent into Hell*—are supportive of this psychophysical dualism.

The Platonist other-worldliness is a corollary of the Platonist psychophysical dualism. It is the belief that the mundane world is not man's true home and that during life in this world the hope for the next life provides a steadying, leavening influence. Perhaps this other-worldliness may safely be said to be at least implicit in the work of Tolkien and Williams. Tolkien's Frodo looks forward finally to unending life in the Grey Havens. It is suggested by friends of Williams' character Chloe that the latter will find fulfillment in the next life after her sacrificial acts in this life. The Platonist other-worldliness is, however, unmistakeably a major theme in the writing of Lewis. He calls the intellectually and spiritually consummatory last chapter of the last volume of the *Chronicles of Narnia* "Farewell to Shadow Lands." And, as we have seen in the quotation given above, his characters who leave the shadow lands, having passed suddenly through physical death, find themselves in the "real England." And Lewis ends *The Chronicles of Narnia* thus:

> And for us this is the end of all the stories, and we can most truly say that they all lived happily ever after. But for them it was only the beginning of the real story. All their life in this world and all their adventures in Narnia had only been cover and title page: now at last they were beginning Chapter One of the Great Story, which no one on earth has read; which goes on forever; in which every chapter is better than the one before.[27]

Finally, with Heidegger's having recalled the philosophical community to work in ontology, it is of no little import that Lewis may be interpreted as having also called our attention to ontology and having thus made a creative contribution to twentieth-century ontological thought. The basis for this statement is the last four chapters of *The Voyage of the Dawn Treader.* This novel tells how some of the characters are permitted to get very close to, yet not to enter, Aslan's country, which is the eternal home of those who die in Narnia. As they approach it they find differences in their very being and in the being of their surroundings. The characters need less food and sleep. Their eyes grow sharper and their minds clearer. The air becomes brighter, and the water is sweet. There is no explicit ontological discourse. But the children's responses, particularly those of Lucy, indicate ontological changes. Lewis describes some of their experiences thus:

> There seemed no end to the lilies. Day after day from all those miles and leagues of lilies there arose a smell which they found it very hard to describe; sweet—yes, but not at all sleepy or overpowering, a fresh, wild, lonely smell that seemed to get into your brain and make you feel that you could go up mountains at a run or wrestle with an elephant. She and Caspian said to one another, "I feel that I can't stand much more of this, yet I do not want it to stop."[28]

I suggest that here Lewis has appropriated the Platonist ontological view of degrees of being and, moreover, has revealed its existential import for those, but only for those, who are privileged to know mystically the aspects of reality where a fullness of created being is encountered.

3. To conclude: clearly the reappearance of Christian Platonism in our day is of interest to the historian of philosophy. It also has great significance for the creative and the constructively critical thinker. For Platonism has ever proved capable of harmonious synthesis of diverse philosophical views. A corollary is that Platonism has been developmental, Platonists having persuasively demonstrated the timeliness of their views in many times and places. Lewis, Tolkien, and Williams have given us clues to the present timeliness of Platonism by showing the existential import of this position.

Further, in the developmental aspect of their thought each has introduced a feature that in respect to Platonism is, perhaps, new as well as timely. This is the fact that not one of them has offered Christian Platonism as the sole path to true spiritual fulfillment. Each has characters who are appreciative of some types of beauty, truth, courage, and compassion, but who are in some respects not in total sympathy with the characters who represent the appropriation of Christian Platonism. Further, each of these characters brings to his community data, insights, and perspectives on reality and man that are possible to him only because he has walked his particular spiritual path. In fact, the view that there are several spiritual paths, each making possible the spiritual fulfillment of some, but only of some, is a central theme of all three writers. One thinks of Tolkien's hobbits, elves, dwarves, Valar, and men, each of whom in distinctive ways possesses some objective truth, enjoys some beauty and artistic creativity, and serves good causes. One thinks also of the several kinds of creatures Elwin Ransom learns from and comes to love in *Out of the Silent Planet*. And definitely this theme is dominant in Lewis' portrayal of life at Saint Anne's Manor, although it is suggested that the Christian Platonists of the community are intellectual and spiritual leaders.[29] And Williams' novels feature the tremendous importance to the philosophical enterprise not only of Christian but also of pagan, Jewish, and Islamic Platonism. I have suggested that this movement toward a philosophical ecumenism is a development within the synthetic creativity of Plato.

Further, there is in all three writers at least the suggestion of a ladder of intellectual, aesthetic, and moral development of the individual. In its totality this ladder is Platonist, Christian, and useful in our day. The first step on the ladder, however, is common to all paths that lead to peace and spiritual development. Not to take this first step is to choose one of the many paths that inevitably lead to frustration, and may lead to despair. This first step which may, but need not, lead to the spirituality of Christian Platonism has four features.

First, there is the willingness to the extent that one is able to give love to one's fellow man. *Love,* of course, is equivocal. And Lewis' analysis of love into four types serves admirably to illustrate the meaning of *love* in this context.[30] These are the appreciation of, rather than indifference to, others; willingness to share one's interests with likeminded persons; the recognition that one has need of others and the grateful appreciation of the persons who supply the need; and the charity which forgives and gives of itself for the sake of others. In this connection we have seen the importance of love in the thought of all three writers. Second, there is hope which eschews skepticisms about the feasibility and value of the search for the truth that satisfies the spirit. It is the maintaining even in times of boredom, frustration, and pain of a trust in the burgeoning of a new spring in one's life and in the affairs of one's community. This hope is seen in the Narnian's sustained hope for the end of winter and in Gandolf's and Frodo's courage maintained through intense personal misfortune.[31] And among Williams' characters there is hope in the spiritual awakening of Damaris and her effort to rebuild her life and the lives of those close to her.[32]

Third, wonder is needed. This is the wonder that Aristotle said is the source of the search for truth. And perhaps in respect to Aristotle's emphasis on wonder, we do well to reflect that Aristotle is the pupil of Plato. For in the *Dialogues* Plato continually expresses wonder before beauty and the truth which is the correlative of beauty. Wonder before objective truth, before the beauty of that truth, and before the stupendous power of rational creatures to respond to the demands of life are constant themes in the lives of the characters of these three writers. Fourth, each writer sees the individual as possessing freedom to take some responsibility for cultivating love, hope, and wonder. Although on the other hand, each writer is also realistic about the extent to which and the ways in which the individual's power of choosing these may be limited, confused, or misguided.[33]

Although, as I have suggested, the nonexclusivist view that the taking of this first step may lead to a variety of spiritually fulfilling relations to reality may be new, the theme of the philosophical import of the spiritual development that corresponds to the axiological as well as the epistemological structure of reality is not new. This view has been present in all forms of Platonism. Here is, however, a most significant type of philosophical creativity: the present-day recalling and development of philosophical truth that has been virtually forgotten but which nonetheless is full of promise. In particular, Lewis, Tolkien, and Williams have drawn our attention to the role in philosophical inquiry of the spiritual development of the thinker. The many valuable areas of the philosophical enterprise which are stressed in our day are alike in ignoring this view of the demands that philosophical work makes on the thinker. At the very least these three writers are recalling us to the unification of all aspects of our nature in the philosophical enterprise. They have pointed to a path of philosophical creativity which is really a renewal of an ancient path. And the beauty that their characters are able to find on that path and the doors of learning and service that their faithfulness opens to them are powerful final causes attracting some of us to the same path and its current philosophical promise.

18

Negative Theology, Myth, and Incarnation

A. HILARY ARMSTRONG

There are few, if any people who have done more than Jean Trouillard to open our eyes to the depth and richness of the thought of the last Hellenic Platonists, above all of Plotinus and Proclus. My own debt to him is immense, and I know others, of very different ways of thinking, who would say the same. But he has not been content simply to expound these venerable thinkers as period pieces, belonging to a past time and irrelevant to the concerns of our age. He has tried to show that they can speak to our condition, and do something to illuminate the religious and philosophical perplexities of our own time (though not, as we shall see, by providing dogmatic solutions). This has sometimes brought upon him the charge of inventing a "neo-Neoplatonism" of his own (a very Platonic thing to do). But his concern for the contemporary may be a very important reason for the depth of his insight into the ancient. And it is because of this that I dedicate in his honor this odd attempt to show the relevance of some of the late Platonic ways of thinking which he has so well explained to us to the crisis of religious thought in our own time.

It will be well to begin by explaining what this large vague phrase "the crisis of religious thought" means to me. What seems to me to have been happening for a very long time, but to have become particularly apparent recently, is the progressive breakdown of any and every sort of "absolutism." By "absolutism" I mean the making of absolute claims for forms of words and ways of thinking about God as timelessly and universally true (including, of course, the absolute claim that all God-talk is meaningless and hopelessly incoherent). These claims can be made in various ways. They can be made by prelates, preachers, and theologians asserting the absolute, unique, and universal claims of one special revelation; or by philosophers of the older style (including, of course, systematic Platonists) who claim that their metaphysical system is the one absolutely and universally true philosophy and, of course, those of their newer-style opponents who claim equally dogmatically that *their* philosophy provides the one infallible method of disposing of all this metaphysical and religious nonsense; or by the believers in a *philosophia perennis* in the Huxleyan sense, a single tradition that underlies all the great religious traditions and is uniformly confirmed by all religious experience. There are, of course, plenty of absolutists of all these varieties still with us. But their influence is generally confined to restricted circles, and outside these circles (and I think increasingly within them) absolute claims and assertions are now subjected to immediate critical questioning, and generally found wanting or dubious: historical claims are questioned historically, and dogmatic nonhistorical statements (e.g., about the personality of God or the Trinity) are questioned philosophically.

Two points must be made here, which will probably indicate to many what a conservative and old-fashioned paper this is. The first is that questioning does not mean outright rejection; that would be just another, and unpleasant, form of dogmatism. In the field of Christian theology the rejection of "absolutism" does not mean that "radical" positions are always to be preferred to "conservative" ones. Many radical positions are very silly; many conservative ones deserve serious consideration and are supported by excellent scholarship. Nor does critical questioning mean wholesale rejection of the great systematic philosophies. This paper is permeated by the deepest qualified affection and critical respect for the great late Platonists, Hellenic and Christian, who were in some ways very systematic thinkers. And even if one finds the idea of a *philosophia perennis,* in any sense, implausible, one can still agree with its exponents who insist that living tradition is necessary for any art, including the art of living. What the rejection of absolutism means is that all dogmas become hypotheses, and that one does not arrive at an unhypothetical principle of demonstration or guarantee of certainty. (God is not such a principle or guarantee.) One therefore simply continues the discussion, probably forever. One must stand away from the tradition one respects (as Aristotle stood away from Plato and Aristotle's personal pupils from Aristotle), not to propound an improved dogmatism of one's own, but to go on asking more and more questions. This paper is conceived in this spirit, as a contribution to a completely open-ended discussion, not as a final solution to anything. The second point is that when claims to possess an exclusive revelation of God or to speak his word are made by human beings (and it is always human beings who make them), they must be examined particularly fiercely and hypercritically for the honor of God, to avoid the blasphemy and sacrilege of deifying a human opinion. Or, to put it less ferociously, the Hellenic (and, as it seems to me, still proper) answer to "Thus saith the Lord" is "*Does* he?," asked in a distinctly sceptical tone, followed by a courteous but drastic "testing to destruction" of the claims and credentials of the person or persons making this enormous statement.

What are the reasons for this breakdown of absolutism? The first, and oldest, is, probably, steadily growing intellectual dissatisfaction with the arguments produced for the various and incompatible absolute positions. This springs from a very venerable element in our tradition, the sceptical in its Academic form,[1] which has revived particularly strongly in Western Europe since the Renaissance, and been powerfully reinforced in the last two centuries by the development of critical philosophy and critical history (modern critical historians and scholars are perhaps the truest spiritual descendants of the Academics in our world). The second, which is also ancient (it can be traced back to Herodotus), but which has developed very powerfully in my own lifetime, is an intense and vivid sense of our own historical limitations. We are aware, both by experience and our study of history, of the immense and irreducible diversity of human beliefs and ways of thinking. We know sufficiently well that not only our own thought but that of the founder and teachers of any religious group or philosophical tradition to which we may adhere is limited and determined by historical circumstance, by time, place, heredity, environment, culture, and education: even quite small differences in the circumstances of our education (e.g., going to a different university, or even a different college in the same university) might have made our religious and philosophical beliefs quite different by causing us to be influenced by different people, to read different books, and so on. And we think this matters—it is not to be casually dismissed with a few rude remarks about "relativism," as is still sometimes done. We should think it crudely and antiquatedly arrogant to be certain of our certitudes, especially in religious questions, without unattainable confirmation by the agreement of all those, of all beliefs and ways of thinking—saints, sages, and scholars—who are or have been competent to consider the belief for which certainty is claimed. This leads straight to the third reason for the breakdown of absolutism. This is comparatively modern (though it is anticipated to some extent in pre-Christian antiquity) and its strong and full development and increasingly wide dissemination are becoming more and more notable in our own time. It is the vast and unprecedented increase in our knowledge of other ways of faith, piety, and thought about God than our own, which has more and more both led to and been helped by a growth of understanding, respect, and sympathy for them and a willingness to learn from them. Especially if this is not merely gained by reading, but also by direct acquaintance with other ways and personal friendship with those who follow them, this produces an irrevocable change of mind and heart, which both strengthens and is strengthened by our sense of historical limitations. Our new awareness includes, of course, an awareness of the divergences, tensions, and contradictions within our own tradition and the value of many ways in it which diverge from those authoritatively accepted. We have become conscious of the folly and arrogance of "not counting" people; of simply dismissing from consideration (as some philosophers and theologians still do) those who do not conform to the official orthodoxy of the group to which we belong. We have learned at last, I think once and for all, to believe that there is no one universally true or universally saving way—that many different paths lead to the great mystery.

At this point some religious persons will no doubt want to say "But what about *real* faith? What about the Leap, the Wager, the Great Option? Throw away these rationalistic hesitations and commit yourself, if you want to know what true faith is." I am unable genuinely to accept this peremptory and dramatic invitation (I have tried hard enough), because, if one really looks around and stops "not counting" people, one finds that one is being invited to leap in altogether too many directions at once. One can only discriminate between them by returning to the probably endless and inconclusive critical discussion of claims, credentials, and arguments. And even if there was only one direction to leap in (and some Christians still talk as if this is so), it would be impossible without returning to the critical examination of the claims and credentials of the clergyman summoning me to faith (and other related matters), to distinguish faith from gross credulity, which is not religiously or morally virtuous, especially in an academician. I cannot, with regret, accept the view that our experience or awareness of God can in itself justify or guarantee one particular dogmatic and exclusive faith. This is because I hold the view that this experience (even at its lower levels) is strictly ineffable; we naturally try to interpret it, always inadequately, in the language of the religious tradition to which we belong, but the experience does not justify or guarantee the interpretations (not that we can think or say what it is "in itself" or compare it with the interpretations). Yet this whole paper is based on a faith in and dim awareness of the Unknowable Good, which I cannot and do not want to get rid of, but which remains tentative, personal, not absolute or exclusive, and making no demands on others.

What, then, has the old Neoplatonic "negative theology," and other related aspects of the later Platonic tradition—Hellenic and Christian—to give to those who have experienced the breakdown of absolutism but still want to believe in and worship God? I can only offer what I myself have found helpful. Trouillard has written most illuminatingly on this subject, and I have stumblingly tried to follow in his footsteps[2] (and have also learned very much from the Greek Orthodox Abbess Maria, who really lived the "negative theology" to its ultimate point). I will not here repeat much of what can be found better elsewhere, but it must be stressed that what seems likely to be helpful is the fully developed negative theology in which we negate our negations (which does not mean that we simply restore the original positive statement with a "super" attached, although this language is often used by the ancients because they could not find anything better); perhaps the "pre" language often used by post-Plotinian Neoplatonists ("pre-being," "preintellect," etc.) is somewhat less misleading nowadays than "super-being" or "superintellect". This leads us to the state of mind in which we are not content simply to say that God is not anything, but must say and be aware that he is not not anything either: and, in the end, not even to know that we do not know. It is a strange kind of liberation from thinkings and languages that enables us to use them freely and critically, always with a certain distance and detachment. (There are, of course, a number of kinds of human language—poetic, musical, those used in the visual arts, and mathematical, as well as the rather clumsy and limited prosaic-discursive kind normally used in philosophy and dogmatic theology, which by no means escapes metaphor.[3] Of course, if we use this last we must use it precisely, and according to the rules of the game as played in our particular environment, as the great Neoplatonists did excellently.) Having gotten this far, we can, of course, use positive terms about God as freely as negative, provided that we prefix something like the favorite *Hoion* of Plotinus ("as if" or "in a manner of speaking") to indicate their inadequacy. I can agree a great deal with what Christopher Stead says about the desirability of using "being" or "substance" terms about God, on the appropriate occasions, and could supply him with some excellent Neoplatonic texts in which they are freely and quite consistently used in a context of radical negative theology.[4] It seems that the traditional terms "beyond being," "nonbeing," or "nothing" applied to God are most significant when used in their proper Hellenic context in which being is closely correlated with intelligibility: real being is intelligible being. They mean, then, that God is not a somebody or something who can be discursively defined or discerned with intuitive precision. It is not that his intelligibility transcends our limited and fallen human intelligences, but that he has no intelligible content: Trouillard has explained this very well.[5] It is this ability to use positive terms in a peculiar way that may make the negative theologian sympathetic to "myths," as we shall see. I prefer, myself, to call what I am talking about "icons,"[6] partly for reasons of my own not unconnected with Eastern Orthodox theology and piety, and partly because "myth," since about the fifth century B.C. has had, probably for most people in the Western tradition, the rather narrow and derogatory meaning of "more or less poetic fiction." I shall, however, use "myth" (in an extended and complimentary sense) in this paper in order to relate it to contemporary theological discussions.

Before proceeding to discuss myth, it should be made clear that what has been said about "negative theology" so far is perfectly compatible with conservative Christian orthodoxy. The Eastern Christian tradition as a whole and many perfectly orthodox and traditional Western theologians insist that all our language about God is inadequate, that our statements about him are only "pointers" to or "icons" of his unknowable reality. But they hold that certain statements only are divinely revealed or authoritative, and so are privileged pointers or uniquely authorized icons, and that the Incarnate Christ is the one and only perfect icon (to use patristic language) of the supreme divinity. Reasons for disagreeing with this have nothing to do with the "negative theology" as such. They spring from the attitudes of mind discussed earlier which have led to the general breakdown of absolutism. For those in whom this breakdown has taken place, however, the "negative theology" can, I think, do something useful. It can, sometimes, prevent them from giving up the whole business of religion in disgust—the usual reaction—and help them to remain at least dimly aware that there is really somebody or something there "behind" or "beyond" (to use the inadequate spatial metaphors that we must all use in this context) the dubious stories and inadequate concepts and definitions. It may help to give some expression to a deep, obscure anonymous faith that remains untouched by the breakdown of absolutism, though as the result of this breakdown it insists on remaining anonymous. And those who arrive (not necessarily by a Neoplatonic route) at understanding that a radically apophatic faith permits the use of very positive language in a peculiar way may come to understand the expressions of their traditional religion "mythically" or "iconically" and not just as "myths" or "icons" made up by men, but as a multiple and varied revelation of images through which the Good communicates "iconically" with all of us, of all religious traditions, according to our several needs, that we may all have something through which to sense his presence and worship him.

If we understand "myth" in this way, as part of the expression of what happens when the Unknowable, so to speak, seems not content to remain aloof in his ineffable obscurity but "turns" and comes back to us as the painter of many icons not made with hands in that "outgoing" which "Dionysius" calls his "ecstatic *eros*,"[7] we may see better how we should use the term and how widely it can be extended. The sense to be given to "myth" in the context of this way of thinking will obviously be strongly positive. It will often be practically equivalent to something like "general" or natural revelation (this involves, of course, human participation, and human error and inadequacies, in expressing what God suggests). In this way it will come close to the significance of myth (and ritual) as understood by Proclus, whose accounts of the function of mythical and mathematical imagination are most illuminatingly correlated and discussed by Trouillard.[8] Myths and the rites and arts that express them can provide true ways to God, although they can also mislead. (The superbly and fruitfully ambiguous valuation of art in relation to philosophy and religion by Iris Murdoch in her very Platonic— though not Neoplatonic—book on Plato and the artists[9] should be carefully studied by anyone who wishes to understand its dangers, uses, and, in the end, inescapable indispensability.) But myth for Proclus is exclusively poetic or imaginative myth: and he would not have been at all pleased if we extended the term to cover his own (or, as he thought, Plato's) systematic philosophical theology. But the breakdown of absolutism seems to have made it necessary to see systematic theology mythically, as well as the alleged historical facts contained in some particular revelations. The most abstract and logically constructed treatments of the Henads or the Trinity can only function for us mythically, if they function at all. (One can, and should, of course criticize the logic, as one can criticize the historical evidence or the expressive quality of the images in other kinds of myth, but these separate and distinct kinds of criticism will not necessarily deprive the myths to which they are applied of all power and value.)

It may help to clarify the way in which I regard the Christian story and Christian doctrine as mythical if I compare my position briefly with those of a small selection of others. I am not conscious of any strong differences with Maurice Wiles, though our different environments and preoccupations may lead to rather different theological conclusions. I admire the scholarly caution and religious discretion with which he pursues the argument, and find his comparison between the way in which Christian thought about the Creation and the Fall has developed and the way in which Christian thought about the Incarnation might reasonably develop fruitful; and his statement (derived, like so much else in contemporary discussions, from Strauss) that a myth may have a historical element may be a very useful corrective to extremist positions.[10]

With Don Cupitt, and others who think like him, my difference is rather sharp, and may be of some general significance.[11] It is not that I object to his history—his treatment of the evidence seems to me at any rate plausible. But (to say something which, from inherited reverence, I have refrained for some time from saying), I do not find the Jesus of good critical biblical scholars very impressive or interesting. I am not even sure that the only people in the first century A.D. with whom I can conceive myself having much in common would have thought so, that is to say, Greek-speaking people with some degree of Hellenic philosophical culture, for instance in the neighboring Decapolis. This reconstructed Galilean rabbi, this Jesus (or these Jesuses) of scholarship, seems very restricted, not only in period but in place and culture.[12] It seems unlikely that the "Jesus of scholarship" can ever attain even the limited universality, even in our transitory Western culture, of the "Christ of history." (I am using here the excellent terminology of Wilfred Cantwell Smith. The "Jesus of scholarship" is the Jesus reconstructed by scholars; the "Christ of history" is the mythical or iconic Christ, the Christ who has mattered in Christian history.)

I owe a personal debt of gratitude to the biblical scholars and theologians, conservative and radical, to the demythologizers and de-Hellenizers from Bultmann onwards, and to those who, with excellent pastoral intentions, have forced the Bible so much on our attention in the non-Reformed churches in recent years. They have shown me something that I was too obtuse and traditionalist to notice before, but is of the greatest historical significance—our Inherited Conglomerate (as Gilbert Murray and E. R. Dodds would call it)[13] is breaking up. The biblical and the Hellenic elements are, apparently now finally and irrevocably, coming apart. And, if they come apart, it is not as certain as Christian theologians and preachers seem to suppose that most of those who remain at all interested in the matter will choose the biblical and reject the Hellenic. In my own case my remote forefathers (if they were ever genuinely converted to anything) were pretty certainly converted to a strongly mythical, Hellenized form of Christianity, and the succeeding generations, Roman Catholic or Anglican, retained this form, on the whole, and interpreted the Bible in its light. The faith of my fathers centered on the "Christ of history." The tradition handed down to me was the myth, and in my own religious wrigglings of earlier years I think I was, at first unconsciously, trying to get further from the Bible and nearer to the myth, in a strongly Hellenic, Mediterranean form for which I still have much affection. (Of course my Christian parents and teachers in the earlier twentieth century took very good care to see that I should be well educated in Greek poetry and philosophy, which carry Hellenic religion.) I really do not think that I have much reason for allegiance to "authentic," "truly biblical" Christianity, whether radical or conservative. And now that (because of the breakup of the Conglomerate) I have to choose between the biblical and the Hellenic, I shall choose the Hellenic, though I can only choose it as myth. And it may be that a good many other people, less well informed than I am about our own older tradition, will make the same choice: either because it has really been the strongly Hellenic elements in the theology and piety of the Conglomerate that will be discussed later which have attracted them; or because it is the myth that has inspired the great Christian visual art and music that may be doing more than anything else to keep something of Christianity alive in our own day; or because they are drawn to Indian or esoteric Islamic ways which are often (for whatever reason) very much closer to Neoplatonism than they are to Jewish-Biblical ways of faith, thought, and piety.[14]

To conclude this essay, let us attempt to see what a "mythical" treatment of the central Christian doctrine of Incarnation might look like. It must be stressed here again that there is no question of dogmatic rejection of traditional doctrines, but of well-grounded doubt, suspense of judgment, the reduction of the doctrines to endlessly discussible hypotheses. In this position one is perfectly entitled to consider as acceptable more conservative and traditional hypotheses than those just discussed, when they are well based on excellent scholarship, like those of C. F. D. Moule,[15] provided that they are still considered as hypotheses, and not used apologetically to justify a return to absolutism. And this means that, within the limits imposed by free and sound scholarship and history, a closer hypothetical linking of the "Jesus of scholarship" and the "Christ of history" might be attempted than has been suggested above. We are not bound to believe that the myth has no historical foundation or core, even if the extent of the historical element in it must probably remain forever undefinable. But it should also be made clear again that the rejection of absolutism and the questioning of claims and demands extends beyond the claim that Jesus was God Incarnate in a unique sense. It extends to all claims made that any revelation of God has unique and universal authority or that any people or community has been brought into a unique and special relationship with him. If anyone demands faith, submission, or territory as a representative of the unique "people of God," he should be taken all the way back to the covenant with Abraham and his claims tested every step of the way by the intensest criticism that can be brought to bear, for the honor of God. Criticism can be inspired by religious fervor as well as dogmatic faith.

Even if one is prepared to consider, tentatively, as tenable the hypotheses of the more conservative New Testament scholars who really are scholars and not apologists (some of course, rather bewilderingly to the layman, speak now in one capacity and then in the other), one will probably have to go fairly far in separating the fully Hellenized "Christ of history" from the "Jesus of scholarship." (It is, at least, reasonably certain that Jesus was a Jew, and this makes a difference.) I have already shown my preferences if this has to be done.[16] What then, can an irremediable gentile like myself make of the center of the Christian myth, the doctrine of Incarnation? A good deal, in fact, and some of it surprisingly traditional; and I should describe my "mythical" interpretation as "expansionist" rather than "reductionist." The method I apply here to the thought of the Greek Fathers is, of course, heretical in the strict sense, a process of *hairesis* or selection. (There is a good deal of *hairesis* in orthodox theology, especially nowadays.) For this reason I bring them in, not to claim their authority, but to acknowledge my debt to them. The characteristic that I have discovered in their thought struck me most forcibly when reading Dionysius, particularly the *Divine Names*.[17] Though it can certainly be observed over a much wider area,[18] and I do not regard it in Dionysius as an Athenian Neoplatonist deformation of Christianity, it will make for brevity and clarity—and be appropriate in a paper in honor of Trouillard—if I discuss it in a Dionysian context. The first point which impressed me was that, though the language, and I am sure the belief, of the author of the Dionysian writings about the Trinity is perfectly orthodox, *Trias* is only one of the names (all inadequate) for the Unknowable God, the Thearchy, interchangeable with others: his Trinitarian theology is rather in the background and only comes into use when required for the purposes of his simplified, and in a sense Christianized, Neoplatonism. It is not grounded in, and has not much connection with, the historic Incarnation.[19] About this, again, the author's language and faith is quite orthodox. But, as with *Trias*, "Jesus" is, in the Christological passages of the *Divine Names,* just another name for the ineffable Thearchy, whose whole function in these passages he takes over, and the details of his earthly life are interpreted entirely symbolically.[20] What this seems to mean is that what really matters to Dionysius (and perhaps to many others, in the Greek-Christian tradition especially, though individual cases need particular and careful examination)[21] is the outgoing of the Unknowable Godhead in his theophanies and ecstatic *eros,* which is creation, and his leading all things back to himself by that same *eros,* in its return, which is redemption. And both of these are cosmic and universal, not strictly tied to a particular human person or historic event, though the historic Incarnation is of course seen as the exemplar, guarantee, and center of the whole creative-redemptive process and the principal means of redemption.

When one has realized that this sort of distinction between a universal and a particularist understanding of Christian doctrine related to the Incarnation can be discovered in our Christian tradition, and that the emphasis (especially, perhaps, in the Dionysian tradition) lies sometimes more on the universal than the particular, some consequences may begin to appear to one who is conscious of the "breakdown of absolutism" and the grave doubts that must now exist about the Incarnation in its historical particularity. If one retains some sort of faith in the Unknowable Good, one may still want to be able to see not only God's creative but his saving work, as extending from everlasting to everlasting, not only to every human being, but to every being in his universe (anthropocentrism is one of the disadvantages of conservative Christianity[22]); and to hold that God so works because the cosmos is in him and he is united with it (though "inexpressibly," as the Fathers say about the Incarnation) from the beginning with an intimacy that the hypostatic union of developed Christology cannot surpass. This is part of any Platonic faith because the Platonic Good is self-diffusive, and being good means doing good.[23] And I (because of my Christian background) can think of no better way of speaking of this ineffable outgoing of the Good in his *eros* than in terms of the everlasting and universal mission of Logos and Holy Spirit. Others will legit-imately prefer other ways of speaking. I know that I only use these words because my parents and teachers, the books I have read, and perhaps most effectively of all, the great liturgies and arts of Christendom have taught me to. If I had been brought up in India, or in a Buddhist or Islamic country, I should have used different myths or icons. And even within our own traditions, many of anonymous faith—but (often with good reasons) deeply anti-Christian—will prefer other ways of speaking. But, if the negative theology carried through the double negation leads, as it often does, to this sort of belief in cosmic incarnation, then the Christian "myth" can come to have a very powerful and positive effect as a myth. It will not give us the kind of assurance possessed by all the Fathers and tradi-tional theologians who believe (as they do) in the unique Incarnation fully and completely as historical fact and the dogmas in which its meaning was explained as divinely guaranteed; we must be content with a more tentative and uncertain faith nowadays. And accepting a myth is not like accepting a creed. It leaves room for free reinterpretation, imaginative and intellectual development, and plenty of criticism of details and variation of emphasis (even the most orthodox and con-formist Christianity allows, and has always allowed, for plenty of all these, though theologians have sometimes pretended otherwise). But, in the end, I can think of no better representations of the faith I hold, if they are interpreted in the free and universal way I have suggested, than the great theological and artistic "icons" of traditional Christianity.

19

Why Christians Should Be Platonists

JOHN N. FINDLAY

In presenting this paper at the end of this distinguished conference I should like to make an apology. I am not contributing to the historic discussion of some Christian thinker influenced by Platonism or Neoplatonism in some remote epoch, but making a personal statement as to what Platonism signifies in my personal and philosophical life, and how it relates to my Christian and other interests. What I am going to say has many qualities of a sermon, a form of discourse to which I am becoming increasingly addicted, though without the talents or depth of a Meister Eckhart. I am going to ask you to see your Christianity and everything else you care for in the light of the inspiration to be derived from Plato and Plotinus. My giving this paper is also an impertinence in that I am not in any orthodox sense a Christian. I am by nature and by force of circumstances a syncretist and an ecumenist, one who has found devotional and spiritual guidance in the Tao-teh-King as much as in the New Testament, in Plotinus as much as Saint Paul, and in the Upanishads, the Gita, and the great Buddhist Sutras as much as in Christian devotional and theological works. I was unfortunate in my first contacts with Christian belief—in the form of Dutch Calvinism, that of the church of my mother—which effectively turned me off. I now realize that it represents a great intellectual structure, deeply penetrated by scriptural influences and by a type of spirituality, the Pascalian or Kierkegaardian, which, though it can never be mine, still deserves respect and reverence. It is the narrow way along which certain fine natures have to tread, even if I have the ignorance or the arrogance to think that I can well follow another course. In any case I am sufficiently a Christian not to want to leave Christianity and its transfigured Founder out of my thought and life, and with this preamble I shall proceed to business.

I regard both Christianity and Platonism as making contributions to a discipline that I prefer to call "Absolute theory," though the Aristotelian terms "theology" and "first philosophy" would be equally appropriate. Christianity, of course, does a great deal more than contribute to a philosophical discipline, but so also does Platonism. By Absolute theory I mean the elaboration of a particular sort of concept to which I shall ascribe seven demarcating characters.[1] An absolute is, in the first place, something that is credited with being in an unqualified sense, that is, it must not be thought of as existing merely in the sense that someone thinks of it or makes it the object of concern, ultimate or otherwise, or that it is merely an aspect or character or structuring form, or a dependent part of something else from which it is inseparable. What sort of thing has being in an unqualified sense will, of course, differ from ontology to ontology, and need not necessarily be individual: an absolute must, however, enjoy the prime ontological dignity in the ontology in question. An absolute must in the second place exist of necessity: it must be absolutely impossible (and not in some merely formal-logical or merely natural-scientific or merely contextual or relative sense) for such an absolute not to exist. It must not only be a fixture, but an irremovable ontological fixture. This means that, in the case of anything that *we* put forth for absolute status, its existence must cover the whole *Spielraum* of possibility and therefore be unconditionally necessary, or, if it does not and cannot do this, it can occupy no area in the *Spielraum* of possibility, and will accordingly be wholly impossible. Necessity of existence or total impossibility represent the hard choice before an absolute: it is not one of the sort of things that could either be or not be. And the ontological argument is absolutely valid provided the absolute's existence is possible, but if its nonexistence is in any way possible, then it is totally impossible that it should exist. That an absolute's being follows from its possibility is no doubt exciting, but since this very circumstance may lead us to deny its possibility, it leads to no conclusive result. An Absolute must, in the third place, be unique and can permit of no rivals and no alternatives. If *per impossibile,* there were a number of alternate absolutes, *none* of them could be *the* Absolute and there could be no absolute at all. There may be a plurality of alternative absolutes for our clouded insight, but certainly not in the nature of things. An absolute must fourthly be in the highest degree unitary: it may have many inner differentiations into aspects, members, relations, or functions, but in all of these functions it must be totally present, and can suffer no diremption into separable parts. And, since it must be a complete reality in whatever category we put it, it must, fifthly, be capable of having an inner distinction of the essential and inessential, and the inessential aspects of its nature must be ontologically dependent on its essential aspects, and be the realization of one or the other of the alternative forms of self-realization of which it is capable. And among such unessential aspects may well be a capacity to be the originative source of many dependent and derived existences that do not share its unqualified necessity of being. There must, however, be nothing in them that does not derive from the absolute, and represent the actualization of one of its essential powers. And an absolute must be credited with the power to *determine* which of the alternatives open to it will be realized by it, and must require no deciding factor beyond itself. And the sixth property of an absolute is that it must be all-comprehensive, both in regard to actual existence and also possibility. There can be nothing that exists that is not either an aspect or inseparable part of itself, or something whose being wholly depends upon it in every respect. Such all-comprehensiveness is in fact identical with its absolute necessity: there must be no possibility that it does not cover and no actuality that it does not determine. To these six qualifications of unqualified and necessary being, of uniqueness and incompositeness, and of the power to determine whatever is not necessary solely in virtue of the necessary, essential part of its nature, we may add, as a seventh character, that since Mind and its guiding values are by far the most remarkable, unique things that exist, they must both have a place in the Absolute, whether at its very center or not far from it. To banish them from the Absolute, or to give them a very marginal, derivative place in it, would make their existence unintelligible, and destroy the very nature of the Absolute itself.

I shall not attempt a detailed justification of my sevenfold delineation of an absolute. Plainly the human mind is haunted by ultimate explanatory concepts of the sort I have been sketching, and this is even the case when nothing of the sort is explicitly talked of. Matter, space-time, logical space, and the sensory continuum can be absolutes as well as the Absolute Ego or the Idea of Good or the Absolute Idea. And plainly religion builds itself around and enriches concepts of the sort I have been outlining, and would be felt to be imperfect if it did not include *all* their conditions. I shall also not attempt to deny that there are very great difficulties in the concept of an absolute. On some views, for example, those of Kant in respect to the phenomenal world, a necessity of existence is itself necessarily inapplicable and impossible, and all that exists is necessarily a brute contingency. And on other widely held views, the existence of something which is *freely* capable of realizing one or other of a set of alternatives, and which requires no further determining factor beyond the fact that it *is* so capable, is also of necessity inapplicable and impossible. And many other qualifications for absolute status can be held to be logically absurd (e.g., that an absolute can have no alternatives). I do not myself think that the conception of an absolute involves any inherent flaw, if sufficiently worked out, but I certainly do not *know* this, since the sort of insight required for determining even the *possibility* of the existence of an absolute, which involves necessary existence and the exclusion of all thinkable alternatives, exceeds my powers and could only, if at all, be enjoyed by the Absolute itself. And there is the further difficulty that some might object to the very notion of a possibility which, since it covered all alternatives, would amount to a necessity, in which case there could not be an absolute at all. Our modal concepts may be among the most important we dispose of, but they are also among the most obscure. Nonetheless, it remains profitable for us men to engage in our unreliable ventures into Absolute theory, which have not so far been shown up as invalid, and among the forms of Absolute theory that now come up before us for consideration are those of Christian belief, on the one hand, and of Platonism and Neoplatonism on the other.

How shall I attempt to characterize the Christian Absolute insofar as this is documented in the Scriptures and other representative expressions of historic Christianity? I shall do no more presently but apply my own sevenfold list of qualifications to my own general impression of Christian absolutism: everything I say will be open to countless objections which I shall not here attempt to field. The Christian Absolute I should regard as in its main traits the same as the Hebraic and the Islamic Absolutes: all have had extensive historical commerce with Platonism and Neoplatonism, but all have retained a physiognomy that is in some ways definitely non-Hellenic. They all certainly believe in an absolute that exists in no derived, dependent manner and which could not in any circumstances not exist. They also all believe in its uniqueness and its unity, even though Christianity believes in a threefoldness of personal aspect which is not posited in Judaism and Islam. The Athanasian Creed certainly rules out any suspicion of tritheism; the Christian Absolute is not divided among its constituent personae but totally present in each. The Christian Absolute is certainly also thought of as all-comprehensive as regards existence and as regards possibility. There can be nothing that exists that is not either an aspect or inseparable part of itself, or whose existence and character does not depend wholly upon and is not wholly determined by itself. And certainly the Christian Absolute is thought of as being of the nature of Mind, or as being the transcendent original of which minds, as we know them, are the dim semblances, and also as incarnating the values of knowledge, power, love, bliss, and beauty in a superlative degree, or as being something better than them all, of which they are again only the dim semblances. What, however, is distinctive of the Hebraic-Christian-Islamic Absolute, and what sets it apart from other absolutes is, in the first place, that it is thought of (at least predominantly, and by the philosophically less sophisticated) on the likeness of what is individual, of what exemplifies characters and values and activities and relationships rather than on the likeness of those characters, values, activities, and relationships themselves. The Absolute of much of Christianity exists rather than is being, is mighty rather than is might, is beautiful rather than is very beauty itself, and so on. That "God is love" is indeed a Christian utterance, and that "to live and die are alike Christ" is also a Christian utterance, but there is for the Christian a certain strain of metaphor in them, and it is more natural to say that God is superlatively loving or that living and dying alike can be Christlike. And with this rooted individualism, literal or analogical, goes a tendency to stress the contingent aspects of the Absolute, as one does in the case of an individual, and with this tendency goes the tendency—since the Absolute is the sole determinant of all that specifies or derives from it—to exalt the arbitrariness of much that the Absolute is and of all that it outwardly effects. It has generated a world but it need not have done so; it has generated such-and-such types of creaturely being conforming to such-and-such laws and having such-and-such freedoms, but it could have generated a quite different array of creaturely beings, and so on. One may of course give the Absolute an essence constituted by what one regards as the highest values (compassion, insight, etc.), but in the concrete implementation of these values there will tend to be much arbitrary selection and use of individual things and persons. The Jews are the divinely chosen people, not the Philistines; Abraham or Moses or David are their chosen leaders, Job and Saul are not; certain practices are prescribed for purification, atonement, and so on, while others are proscribed as idolatrous and vain. The Absolute does not care for Cain's pure offering of the fruits of the earth, but relishes the odors of frying lambs. Even in the New Testament there is a considerable element of the arbitrary. For while Jesus is made the embodiment of characters of boundless understanding of human need and weakness and boundless desire for human happiness and moral regeneration, which as values have nothing that is arbitrary about them, there is also something essentially arbitrary and Judaic about his role as chosen Messiah, chosen from all eternity to proclaim the gospel of the Kingdom, and to bring it about by the dreadful rite of the Passion, with its betrayal, its condemnation, and its final agonizing execution, all of which were ritually necessary for the purgation of human transgression and for the ultimate realization of God's perfect kingdom. What is further arbitrary about the whole transaction is that the Passion was *not* provoked by man's unwillingness to recognize the universal absolute values that Jesus incarnated, but by the claims to a special messianic status which were essentially part of a Jewish historicistic mythology, which has no claims to the acceptance of all men of profound insight and good will. And if one substitutes later theological language for this earlier messianism, the arbitrary element consists in the choice of a particular human nature for fusion and transfiguration by the divine, timeless Logos. Even among the beautiful parables in the New Testament there are some that sadden us with a note of arbitrariness: it was not well for those who lacked a suitable wedding garment or who arrived late for the bridegroom's feast. This large element of the arbitrary, in my view, tarnishes the Absolute's image: like Habbakuk, as Voltaire describes him, he becomes *capable de tout*. He can harden Pharoah's heart, while he reshapes and softens the heart of Paul; he has his vessels of honor and vessels of dishonor; he may even, as some late medieval philosophers opined, cause certain devout persons to have advance intimations of beatitude only to overwhelm them with final reprobation. We can then readily pass to the late medieval view, which Descartes also accepted, that the necessities of thought and the moral law are all in the last resort arbitrary, that they could and would have been otherwise had the Absolute so willed it.

These tendencies to attribute increasing arbitrariness to the Absolute are not necessary, but they spring from the strong individualism of the sort of absolute thus conceived. And with this deep individualism goes the tendency to set an unpassable gulf between dependent individuals and their absolute source, a gulf resembling that between ordinary finite individuals, only wider and deeper. The immense disparity in status and power between the Absolute and its dependents then readily relegates the latter to the rank of puppets: how they will function, what roles they will fulfil, all wholly depends upon the Absolute. They will have the further disadvantage of not feeling themselves to be puppets or wishing themselves to be such, and the conviction that they are such will be profoundly painful to them. All the agonies I have been outlining have been actually felt by Christians, mainly of post-Reformation and Calvinistic creeds, who have given their absolutes too much of that divine seasoning, contingency. Contingency is the glorious, many-colored outer icing of the ontological cake—if you will permit an irreverent simile—it is not a fit substance for its well-composed interior. It is not, as I say, necessary to conceive the Absolute as post-Reformation Christianity has so largely done, but there are strong forces always moving in this direction. This tendency has its main roots in the Hebrew scriptures, though there is, of course, much in these (particularly in the Prophets) that attentuates and ennobles it, and much too, of course, in the New Testament. It has, however, been Hellenic and (in the main) Platonic influences that have countered these tendencies in Christian absolutism.

I shall now say something about the brand of absolutism that is associated with Plato and Plotinus. This constructs an ontology in which primacy of being is given, not to particulars or individuals, but to the universal patterns that they exemplify, and in the prime case to patterns that are specific cases of intelligibility and excellence. The Platonic ontology has indeed a secondary place for patterns that merely approximate to, or fall short of, positive perfection, or which are merely relative or artificial or contingently complex, but its prime place is for the patterns of perfect substances and their essential excellences. (See, e.g., Syrianus on Aristotle's *Metaphysics,* 1078b, 32). Here we find the whole numbers of arithmetic, the celestial dynamics of a purified astronomy, and the patterns of souls that are able to cognize all patterns and direct all movements because all of these patterns are built into their structure. And beneath all these ideal structures lies the world of instances of which they are the true causes, though instantiation also involves the half-real media of empty space, on the one hand (in which indefinite multiplication and changeable combination become possible) and time, on the other hand (which is nothing but the half-real flux of sensible, instantial being, reduced to order by the regular motions that Soul and its higher exemplars impose).

Above all this complex hierarchical system, however, lies the Absolute, the Very Good itself, which is also Very Unity itself, the originative source of all the unified and excellent natures whether arithmetical, geometrical, dynamic, or psychic, and for their myriad sensible instantiations. For though Platonism sets an ineffable gulf of type between ideal patterns and their instances, and between the absolutely Good or One and all ideal patterns, this gulf of type does not prevent the lower from deriving from the higher, and throughout participating in its character, and in fact deriving all that it has by way of existence or essence from that which stands above it. Platonism, by not giving its Absolute the character of an individual instance, also enables it to communicate all that it has or is, in varying degrees, to what falls beneath it, and without sacrifice of its ontological priority which cannot be shared by anything. And the Platonic Absolute necessarily and not arbitrarily develops its inner resources in the realm of ideal patterns and in the ideal intelligence that knows and delights in them all. And it necessarily overflows into the realm of instances in which accident, deviation, mutability, and other departures from perfection necessarily have their place. But over all these confusions presides an ordering Soul or Spirit, the highest of instantial beings, which gives tone and order to the instantial cosmos, while taking its own tone and order from what lies above. And the human soul can see nothing above it that is alien or arbitrary; what can raise and guide it always enters into its deepest being since the unity that is the same as being always holds it together and enables it to exist.

All these features of Platonic absolutism may be recommended to Christians. They give God the infinite distance from and otherness than his creatures, and from their creaturely deviations and abuses, which Christians desire, but, by making this a difference of ontological type, and not of individual being, they make God something that can be genuinely participated in and communed with, which is also what Christians desire. They make whatever is contingent and that might have been otherwise deeply different from what is essential and normative and essentially subordinate to the latter. Persons, rites, books, institutions, and so on, are only authoritative to the extent that absolute patterns are exemplified in them, and never in their own right. Instances as such never can be august. At the same time the contingent and the instantial are not to be scorned, for it is of the essence of the Absolute to flow over, or to be able to flow over, into finite instances and contingencies, in which there will always be possibilities of deviation that the Absolute can help to set right. And the Trinitarian structure that was hammered out in the early church is not unacceptable from a Platonic point of view. For if the Absolute is in the first place a pure unity which transcends being because it is Very Being itself, it is also an ideal intelligence that is the timeless thought of all the ideal patterns, and also a concrete living Soul which, itself an instance, presides over the whole instantial world. I need not say, further that there is place in Platonism for Incarnation theology: if the Soul is a supreme instance presiding over the instantial world, there may also be a human instance that surpasses all other instances in its participation in the Absolute. Only on Platonic assumptions there will not be an absolute gulf between this instance and various near-incarnations of other types and degrees. And even though no one comes to the Father but through the divine Logos, the divine Logos may have other sheep that are not of a given fold, and may shepherd many who have never heard of or acknowledged his Christian manifestations. I myself speak as a vagabond among folds, and a committed member of none.

Another reason why Christians are to be recommended to become Platonists is that so many of their best members have done so. This is, of course, also true of many of the best Jews and Mohammedans. Let us start with Clement of Alexandria whose hermeneutic principle was to interpret the Scriptures so that nothing discreditable was attributed to God, which meant that the Scriptures had to be made to satisfy Platonic standards. And let me then turn to Origen whose Father is the Very Good itself, whose Son lives absorbed in his vision of the paternal depths but is surrounded by as many attendant essences, powers, and minds as in Plato and Plotinus, some of which fall into perverse ways but will for the most part return to the Father in a final restitution. Let me than mention Gregory of Nyssa who contrasts the participated goodness of finite things with the unparticipated goodness of God the Father, which includes all excellence in a wholly unsplintered, simple fashion, and contrasts with the Word which ramifies into countless distinct energies, and with the Soul which, in its higher functions, has much of the paradoxical unity-in-multiplicity of divinity. Let us also consider Augustine who, though in many of his utterances approving of the divine arbitrariness, also taught that God was Truth itself, Intelligence itself, and Unity itself, that he embodied whatever was categorial in *all* the categories, that he was good without having a quality, great without having a quantity, everlasting without having a date, and the source of all mutability without himself changing. Let us then also remember Anselm of Canterbury whose God, wrongly thought of by critical ontologists as *instance* of absolute perfection, is in his *Monologue* affirmed to be Perfection itself, Justice itself, and all other transcendental perfections, without exemplifying them as just and other good beings do. Such a being is indeed necessary as a supreme instance arguably cannot be. Finally let us consider Aquinas who, though boundlessly critical of Platonism in his explicit comments on it, is also infinitely Platonic in his actual teaching, no doubt deriving much of his Platonic inspiration from the Pseudo-Dionysius. Aquinas' God is *penitus simplex* like the One of Plato and Plotinus, and becomes many only in what derives from him and participates in him. He does not *exist* so much as *is* self-subsistent being: the gulf between him and his creatures is the ineffable gulf between what shares in being and what is the very Being in which other things only share. His existence is also one with his Essence: he is not characterized by various remarkable *properties*, but rather *is* the unified being of what in other things are only present as properties. And his perfection consists largely in this coincidence of essence and existence. God does not have to achieve the realization of anything he might have, since he already *is* whatever might be thus achieved or had, in imperfect form, by other dependent things. God's intelligence is further not at all like *our* intelligence which merely receives the pattern of external realities. God, like the supreme Unity of Neoplatonism, holds all finite existence in his power: in being himself, and thus inclusive of all possibilities, he is something that our cognitive intentionality only distantly imitates. His will also is a mere expression of his essence, the external actualization of an infinitesimal fragment of what in his timeless essence he is. The three Persons of the Trinity are somewhat dimly distinguished in the divine simplicity: they are outward-facing aspects rather than inner differences. Aquinas is so Platonic in his theology that he is almost a Unitarian. I shall not proceed further in my analysis: I approach Thomas as an interested outsider who perhaps sees things in him that his ultraorthodox supporters fail to discern. Certainly I see a much stronger vein of Neoplatonism in him than his orthodox expositors would countenance. He is acceptable to such as myself since the mere tantrums of will play a very small part in his Absolute: his God simply is the systematic unity of all the values that I venerate, which I rejoice to see treated as more absolutely real than the botched things I see around me or that I know of through history.

I have, I may say in conclusion, given you a number of reasons why Platonic and Neoplatonic reinterpretations of Christianity are to be preferred to versions that are less revisionary, and that adhere more closely to the original Hebraic deposit. There is nothing impious in holding that, while the Jews may have provided the basic energies which make for the kingdom of heaven, it was the Greeks that gave them an intellectually acceptable and beautiful form. The Jews themselves, since the time of Philo, have admitted as much, and so have the adherents of Islam. Providence, the Absolute in action, works through many instruments, and is as capable of influencing Western spirituality through the subtle frauds of a Dionysius as through the narrow zeal of Tertullian. And I believe, as I have said, that the present syncretic confluence of many religious traditions also represents the Absolute in action: it deepens our understanding of what is invariant and necessary and what is contingent and variable in our belief and our devotion. Many of you will not agree with me at all, and you are quite at liberty to hold that Christians should resist the persuasive lures of Platonism.

Notes

INTRODUCTION

1. See A. H. Armstrong and R. A. Markus, *Christian Faith and Greek Philosophy* (New York, 1960), chapter 10.
2. Known as "Middle Platonism"; see J. M. Dillon, *The Middle Platonists 80 b.c. to a.d. 220* (Ithaca, New York, 1977).
3. The Platonism of Plotinus and his followers is known as "Neoplatonism"; for a good survey see R. T. Wallis, *Neoplatonism* (New York, 1972). These historians' labels are potentially misleading. Plotinus could well be described as a very original and outstanding Middle Platonist, and non-Plotinian Middle Platonism (!) continued to affect the Platonic movement after Plotinus' death. All, in any case, would have described themselves simply as "Platonists."
4. See, for example, C. Fabro, *La nozione metafisica di partecipazione secondo S. Tommaso d'Aquino* (Turin, 1950).
5. The treatment in, for example, C. Elsee, *Neoplatonism in Relation to Christianity* (Cambridge, 1908), is no longer adequate. Albert Camus' dissertation for the Diplôme d'études supérieures, *Métaphysique chrétienne et Néoplatonisme* in *Essais*, ed. R. Quilliot and L. Faucon (Paris, 1965), contains some valuable insights, but is of most interest, it seems, for the study of Camus. A recent useful survey of Neoplatonism in relation to Patristic thought can be found in E. P. Meijering, *God Being History* (Amsterdam, 1975), pp. 1–18. See also H. Dörrie, "Die Andere Theologie," *Theologie und Philosophie* 56 (1981), pp. 1–46.

6. See H. Dehnhard, *Das Problem der Abhängigkeit des Basilius von Plotin* (Berlin, 1964); D. Balas, *Metousia theou* (Rome, 1966) (on Gregory); P. Hadot, *Porphyre et Victorinus* (Paris, 1968); P. Hadot, P. Courcelle, and A. Solignac (on Ambrose) in *Revue des Etudes Latines* 34 (1956), 202–239, and *Archives de Philosophie* 29, 3 (1956), 148–156; on Augustine's sources, see above, p. 35.

7. In a paper presented at the Conference on "Platonism and Christianity, the Fourth Century: Some Problems that Remain," Professor John Rist also gave a cautionary critique of various attempts to find Neoplatonic influences in Arius, Athanasius, and some Neo-Arians. This paper is part of a larger project to be published in the *Proceedings* of the Toronto Saint Basil Symposium.

8. On this triad see P. Hadot, in *Entretiens Hardt* 5 (1960), 107–141. On the *Liber de causis*, see Mahoney's bibliography below, p. 275, n. 45; p. 278, n. 56.

9. See McGinn's comments, above, p. 138.

10. The antidogmatic character of language about God in Neoplatonism and its religious value were also stressed by Professor Werner Beierwaltes in his paper "Image and Counterimage? Reflections on Neoplatonic Thought with Respect to Its Place Today" presented at the Conference and to be published in *Neoplatonism and Early Christian Thought*, ed. H. J. Blumenthal and R. A. Markus (Liverpool, 1981).

THE PLATONIC AND CHRISTIAN ULYSSES

1. 'Ο Φιλόσοφος 'Οδυσσεύς, "the philosopher Ulysses," is an expression used by the twelfth century Byzantine exegete Eustathius, *Comm. ad Hom. Odysseam* I 51, vol. I (Leipzig, 1825), p. 17, 10; X 241, p. 379, 1, etc.

2. See the two antithetical declamations *Ajax* and *Ulysses*, ed. F. Decleva Caizzi, *Antisthenis fragmenta* (Testi e docum. per lo studio dell' Antichità 13) (Milano-Varese, 1966), pp. 24–28, with fragments 51, 52A, and 54, pp. 43–45 and the corresponding notes, pp. 105–108. See also R. Höistad, *Cynic Hero and Cynic King. Studies in the Cynic Conception of Man* (Diss. Uppsala, 1948), pp. 94–102.

3. Cf. *testim.* 2B and 12, and fragment 15 in J. F. Kindstrand, *Bion of Borysthenes. A Collection of the Fragments with Intro. and Comment.* (Acta Univ. Upsal., Studia Graeca 11) (Uppsala, 1976), pp. 106, 108, and 116, with the corresponding commentary, pp. 134, 155, and 204.

4. Thus *Diogenis epist.* VII 2 and XXXIV 2–3, ed. Hercher pp. 237 and 248; cf. W. Capelle, *De Cynicorum epistulis* (Diss. Göttingen, 1896), pp. 23–24; H. W. Attridge, "The Philosophical Critique of Religion under the Early Empire," in *Aufstieg und Niedergang der römischen Welt* II 16, 1 (Berlin-New York, 1978), pp. 64–65 dates the pseudepigraphic Cynic letters to the first century A.D. One will note that later Ulysses ceased to be an *exemplum* for the Cynics, as can be seen in *Cratetis epist.* XIX, pp. 211–212; cf. W. Capelle, *op. cit.* pp. 52–53. The same change is found in "Un recueil de diatribes cyniques, Pap. Genev. inv. 271," edited by V. Martin, *Museum helveticum* 16 (1959), col. XIV 42–57, pp. 104–105, trans. pp. 82–83. On the Cynic Ulysses, see also W. B. Stanford, *The Ulysses Theme. A Study in the Adaptability of a Traditional Hero* (Oxford, 1954), pp. 96–100; F. Buffière, *Les mythes d'Homère et la pensée grecque* (Thèse Paris, 1956), pp. 367–374.

5. Cf. W. B. Stanford, *op. cit.*, pp. 121–127; F. Buffière, *op. cit.*, pp. 374–380.

6. Plutarch *Quaest. conviv.* IX 14, 6, 745DF. A probable reminiscence, as noted by F. Buffière, *op. cit.*, p. 480 (cf. pp. 476–481), of Plato *Phaedrus* 249B–250A, on the quasi-amourous emotion of the soul which remembers the former sights.

7. Thus Theo of Smyrna, *Expos.* ed. Hiller, p. 147, 3–6, credits the Pythagoreans with having meant by the Sirens the harmony of the spheres. Furthermore, two famous Pythagorean *akousmata* (in Iamblichus *De vita pythag.* 18, 82, = 58 C 4 Diels-Kranz, I, p. 464, 6–7) seem to testify, the one to a belief in a planetary sojourn of the souls after death (the Sun and Moon as the Islands of the Blessed), the other to the symbolic equation Sirens = cosmic harmony (the harmony in which the Sirens ‹sing›). See finally the attribution to Pythagoras of a theory of the Milky Way as the resting place of the souls that have left their bodies (Porphyry *De antro nymph.* 28, ed. Westerink *et al.*,

p. 28, 1–2; Proclus *In Plat. Rempubl. comment.* ed. Kroll II, p. 129, 24–26; Macrobius *Comment. in Somn. Scip.* I 12, 3; all three authors depend on Numenius: cf. *Testim.* 42, 44, 47 Leemans and pp. 151–152 of his collection), on which see P. Boyancé, *Études sur le Songe de Scipion* (Biblioth. des Univ. du Midi 20) (Bordeaux-Paris, 1936), pp. 136–137. There are, however, some reservations about this; see most recently I. P. Culianu, "'Démonisation du cosmos' et dualisme gnostique," *Revue de l'Hist. des religions* 196 (1979), pp. 4–10.

8. On this exegesis see A. Delatte, *Études sur la littérature pythagoricienne* (Biblioth. de l'École des Hautes Études, Sciences histor. et philol. 217) (Paris, 1915), pp. 133–134, 259–264, 276; F. Cumont, *Recherches sur le symbolisme funéraire des Romains* (Biblioth. archéol. et histor. des Antiquités de Syrie et du Liban 35) (Paris, 1942), pp. 23 and 328–331; E. Kaiser, "Odyssee-Szenen als Topoi," *Museum helvet.* 21 (1964), pp. 114–115. P. Boyancé, "Études philoniennes," *Revue des études grecques* 76 (1963), pp. 76–77, draws attention to a similar exegesis of the same origin (it is in fact simply a literary rapprochement, and not an allegory) in Philo *Quaest. in Gen.* III 3. The Pythagoreans also developed a more banal interpretation in which the murderous songs of the Sirens represent sensual pleasures; cf. Porphyry *Vita Pythag.* 39 and Clement of Alexandria *Strom.* I 10, 48, 6.

9. Cf. A. Delatte, *op. cit.*, pp. 128ff., 129: "Il semble que tous les mythes et toutes les légendes de l'*Odyssée* en particulier furent traités par l'interprétation symbolique." We must admit that we lack sufficiently well-established facts about this Pythagorean Ulysses, despite the efforts of M. Detienne, "Ulysse sur le stuc central de la Basilique de la Porta Maggiore," *Latomus* 17 (1958), pp. 270–286, and especially *Homère, Hésiode et Pythagore. Poésie et philosophie dans le pythagorisme ancien* (Collection Latomus 57) (Bruxelles, 1962), pp. 52–60.

10. See the discussion between Socrates and Hippias in Plato *Hippias min.* where we meet again with Antisthenes' preoccupations. The discussion in fact has to do with a quotation from *Iliad* IX 308-314 (365AB).

11. Notably in the episodes of Calypso (*Od.* v 55–269; vii 241–267), Circe (x 210–574; xii 8–143), the Sirens (xii 39–54 and 158–200), Charybdis and Scylla (xii 73–126 and 222–262).

12. Proclus *In Plat. Rempubl.* ed. Kroll, I, p. 131, 7–8 thus mentions those who "transpose to other deeper meanings (ἐπ' ἄλλας ὑπονοίας) what is called the wandering" of Ulysses.

13. This difference impressed I. Heinemann, "Die wissenschaftliche Allegoristik der Griechen," *Mnemosyne* IVa ser., 2 (1949), pp. 15–16 who opposes Numenius to Heraclitus *Quaest. homer.* 70 (note that this last text contains several instances of the word "allegory", but it relates to a moral allegory on the surface of the text).

14. *Enn.* I 6 [1] 8, 16–21, ed. Henry-Schwyzer², p. 102; the first words Φεύγωμεν . . . φίλην ἐς πατρίδα come from *Iliad* II 140 = IX 27 where they are spoken by Agamemnon, but φίλην ἐς πατρίδα is also found, in relation to Ulysses, in *Od.*, v 37. There is a possible allusion to the return of Ulysses to his fatherland after much wandering in *Enn.* V 9 [5] 1, 20–21.

15. *In Plat. Parmen.* V, ed. Cousin², col. 1025, 33–37; the mention of Ulysses is induced by the word πλάνη in *Parm.* 136E2.

16. *Ibid.*, col. 1025, 1–33.

17. *In Plat. Crat.* 158, ed. Pasquali, p. 88, 20–23; the passage commented on is *Crat.* 403DE, which has to do with the Sirens of Hades (Proclus distinguishes them from those of *genesis*). There are comparable texts, including the reference to the *Phaedrus*, in Proclus *In Rempubl.* II, p. 68, 3–16 and especially p. 238, 23–26: ". . . τῶν γενεσιουργῶν . . . Σειρήνων, ἃς δὴ καὶ αὐτὸς (Plato) ἀλλαχοῦ συμβουλεύει κατὰ τὸν Ὁμηρικὸν ἐκεῖνον Ὀδυσσέα παραπλεῖν." See Festugière's notes *ad loc.*, vol. III, p. 195. Proclus' word θέλγειν, "to bewitch," is already applied to the Sirens at *Od.* xii 40 and 44. On the sea as image of coming-to-be, see Proclus *In Plat. Tim.* ed. Diehl, I, p. 113, 30–31: τὴν εἰς τὸν πόντον τῆς γενέσεως . . . τῆς ψυχῆς φοράν; Julian *Orat.* VIII *In Matrem deor.* 9, 169D: the soul flees γένεσιν καὶ τὸν ἐν αὐτῇ κλύδωνα; F. Cumont, *op. cit.*, p. 66 n. 1 and p. 326.

18. *Comment. ad Hom. Odysseam* I 51, 1389, Leipzig ed. (Weigel, 1825) I, p. 17, 9–16; see for more details F. Buffière, *op. cit.*, pp. 461–464. The most remarkable aspect of this passage is its skill in combining Homeric and Platonic themes: the body as "envelope" (ἔλυτρον) comes from *Republ.* IX 588E; but the assimilation of the enveloped soul to a pearl (μάργαρον) connects with the

comparison with the oyster in *Phaedrus* 250C; the island surrounded by currants (νήσῳ ἐν ἀμφιρύτῃ) of *Od.* i 50 evokes for the commentator *Timaeus* 43A on the body which receives and excretes a liquid flux (ἐπίρρυτον σῶμα καὶ ἀπόρρυτον), etc.

19. 259AB: παραπλέοντάς σφας ὥσπερ Σειρῆνας ἀκηλήτους, ὃ γέρας παρὰ θεῶν ἔχουσιν ἀνθρώποις διδόναι ταχ᾽ ἂν δοῖεν.

20. Hermias *In Plat. Phaedrum schol.* 259A, ed. Couvreur, p. 214, 4–24; the words between square brackets give mostly the restitutions or clarifications in Couvreur's apparatus. For the idea that the true fatherland of the souls is the intelligible world, see already *ad* 230CD, p. 32, 26.

21. *In Crat.* p. 88, 20–23 and *In Rempubl.* II, p. 238, 23–26; cf. *supra* p. 5 and note 17.

22. This is the case for Proclus himself, *In Rempubl.* II, p. 68, 11 παραπλεύσεται; the verb here is intransitive, as it often is; it can also have an object in the accusative as we have seen in Hermias and in Proclus following *Phaedrus* 259A: παραπλέοντάς σφας.

23. Thus H. Dunbar, *A Complete Concordance to the Odyssey of Homer* (Oxford, 1880; Hildesheim², 1962 ed. B. Marzullo), p. 293B; A. Gehring, *Index homericus* (Leipzig, 1891–1895; Hildesheim-New York², 1970 ed. U. Fleischer), col. 656.

24. In xii 69, where the ship Argo alone sailed past (παρέπλω) the Wandering Rocks. Yet here the verb is used in its Ionian form παραπλώω.

25. Porphyry *De antro nymph.* 34, ed. Westerink, p. 32, 13–21. The two verses quoted are *Od.* xi 122–123. The reference to Numenius is *Testim.* 45 Leemans, pp. 103, 25–104, 2, = Fragment 33 des Places, p. 84. The word ἀποκαθισταμένου, which denotes a reestablishment in a former state, has been studied by W. Theiler, *Forschungen zum Neuplatonismus* (Quellen und Studien zur Geschichte der Philos. X) (Berlin, 1966), p. 27 and n. 48, and *Untersuchungen zur antiken Literatur* (Berlin, 1970), p. 536: he attempts to show that the well-known *apocatastasis* doctrine in Origen derives to some degree from Numenius, via Ammonius Saccas.

26. *Ibid.* 35, pp. 32, 29–30 and 34, 4–7. Ulysses' "audacity" is to have blinded the Cyclops, hence Poseidon's hate (*Od.* i 68–75), which is to say: one does not free oneself of the life of the senses by blinding it in one blow. P. 34, 5 ἐν ψυχαῖς ἀπείροις, "with people who do not know . . .", is Westerink's correction of the MS reading ἔμψυχος ἀπείρων and of the reading ἄπειρος given by Hercher followed by Nauck; it has the advantage of harmonizing better with *Od.* xi 122–129 and with ch. 34 of the *De antro*, where it is the people among whom Ulysses must arrive, and not obviously Ulysses himself, who know so little of the sea as to make the mistake in question.

27. Thus, in the geographical myth toward the end of the *Phaedo*, we find a devaluation of the sea, a place of corruption, imperfection, ugliness, decay (110A and E); in *Republ.* X 611B–612A the soul, joined to the body, is disfigured like the submerged statue of Glaucus, and will only show her true nature by leaving the sea (ἐκ τοῦ πόντου) in which she is; in *Laws* IV 704D–705A the proximity of the sea (θάλαττα) ruins morals; etc.

28. 273D: εἰς τὸν τῆς ἀνομοιότητος ἄπειρον ὄντα πόντον (τόπον codd.); the whole context is ostensibly nautical: the Demiurge is described at length as a pilot who moves between the tiller and his observation post. One can understand then why πόντον would have been substituted for the supposedly authentic τόπον, whereas the reverse change would be harder to explain. The Neoplatonists in any case generally read πόντον. For the comparison, see J. B. Skemp, *Plato's Statesman* (London², 1961), pp. 95–97. For the relation with *De antro* 34, see F. Cumont, *op. cit.*, p. 500.

29. Thus Proclus *In Tim.* I, p. 179, 25–26: . . . ὕλη, ἣν ἀνομοιότητος πόντον ἐν τῷ Πολιτικῷ προσείρηκε [sc. Plato], and pp. 174, 10–11; 175, 18–20 (178, 15–16), etc.

30. We must note here a very similar image in a text which, by all accounts, is important to Porphyry. It is the alleged oracle of Apollo which he quotes in his *Life of Plotinus*. If Ulysses is not named in this text, his figure can be read between the lines, for in this text victory over corporeal subjection is assimilated to a swift swim to the coast; the nausea and dizziness produced by carnal food are compared to sea sickness. Plotinus' striving for salvation is presented as an escape from the bitter waves, in the midst of the billows (ἐν μεσάτοισι κλύδωνος) (*Vita Plot.* XXII 25–27 and 31–33).

31. Numenius Fr. 27 L., pp. 141, 16–142, 2 = Fr. 18, 2–10 des Pl., pp. 58–59, = Eusebius *Prae. evang.* XI 18, 24, in particular *in fine*: "The Demiurge resides over her (i.e., matter) as if above a ship on that sea which is matter" (thus I think one should translate, in the light of the reference to

Plato in the preceding fragment and keeping the received text: αὐτὸς μὲν ὑπὲρ ταύτης ἵδρυται, οἷον ὑπὲρ νεὼς ἐπὶ θαλάττης, τῆς ὕλης). This is an actual quotation from Book VI of Numenius' treatise *On the Good.*

32. As thinks J. F. Kindstrand, *Homer in der Zweiten Sophistik. Studien zu der Homerlektüre und dem Homerbild bei Dion von Prusa, Maximos von Tyros und Ailios Aristeides* (Acta Univ. Upsal., Studia Graeca 7) (Uppsala, 1973), pp. 179–180.

33. ὑποβαλοῦσα, a reading proposed with reason by J. F. Kindstrand, *op. cit.*, p. 179 n. 81 instead of Hobein's ὑπολαβοῦσα.

34. Maximus of Tyre *Philos.* XI 10 h (= XVII 10 Dübner), ed. Hobein, p. 142, 8–12.

35. J.Huskinson, "Some Pagan Mythological Figures and their Significance in Early Christian Art," *Papers of the British School at Rome* 42 (1974), pp. 80–81 has shown, à propos of the scene of Ulysses and the Sirens in early Christian art, that in most cases it is a re-use of pagan images by Christians in decorating their churches. For the same scene in early Christian art and its interpretation in the light of pagan and Christian literary documents, see T. Klauser, "Studien zur Entstehungsgeschichte der christlichen Kunst," VI, in *Jahrbuch für Antike und Christentum* 6 (1963) pp. 71–100.

36. The principal work on the Christian allegories of this episode is H. Rahner, *Symbole der Kirche. Die Ekklesiologie der Väter* (Salzburg, 1964), pp. 247–267; see also, by the same author, "Antenna crucis, I: Odysseus am Mastbaum," *Zeitschrift für katholische Theologie* 65 (1941), pp. 123–152. See also, especially for the Latin Fathers, P. Courcelle, "Quelques symboles funéraires du néo-platonisme Latin. Le vol de Dédale.—Ulysse et les Sirènes," *Revue des études anciennes* 46 (1944), pp. 73–91 (he gives also many details about pagan Neoplatonic exegesis); and again, by the same author, "L'interprétation evhémériste des Sirènes—courtisanes jusqu'au XIIᵉ siècle," in *Mélanges L. Wallach* (Monographien zur Geschichte des Mittelalters 11) (Stuttgart, 1975), pp. 33–48.

37. Clement of Alexandria *Protrept.* XII 118, 1–4, ed. Stählin, p. 83, 8–30. I have profited by Mondésert's translation in the "Sources chrétiennes" series, 2. The prose quote at the end of the text comes from I Cor. 2:9. The last of the three poetical quotes is pure ornament and comes from Hesiod *Works* 373–374. The first two, on the other hand, are taken from *Od.* xii 219–220 and 184–185 (at 185 θειοτέρην, a "more divine" voice, is substituted for the νωιτέρην of the text, "our" voice). There is furthermore an allusion to verses 45–46 (the island crowded with human bones) and 178 (Ulysses tied to his mast). This is good confirmation that Clement is really developing an exegesis of the Homeric episode.

38. *Protrept.* X 109, 1, p. 77, 29–30; same opposition at X 89, 2 and 99, 3, as well as at XII 118, 1. On the word as applied to the cult of idols, see IV 46, 1; X 99, 1; 101, 1 and 3. These texts are referred to by H. Rahner, *op. cit.*, pp. 254–255.

39. L. Alfonsi, "La *Consuetudo* nei *Protrettici*," *Vigiliae christ.* 18 (1964), pp. 32–36 gives several examples of this; let us make note of Cicero *Hortensius* Fr. 63 Ruch p. 134 (*consuetudo vitiosa*), Seneca *De ira* II 20, 2: plurimum potest consuetudo, quae si gravis est alit vitium.

40. *Protrept.* IX 86, 2, p. 64, 27–37. This text has been very well analyzed by M. L. Amerio, "Su due similitudini del *Protrettico* di Clemente Alessandrino (*prot.* 9, 86, 2)," *Invigilata lucernis* (Bari), 1 (1979), pp. 7–37.

41. I have drawn in this analysis from M. L. Amerio, *art. cit.*, especially pp. 12, 21–24 and 28–32 where a complete study may be found.

42. *Strom.* VI 11, 89, 1–3, ed. Stählin, p. 476, 14–26; the quotation in brackets is from Psalm 23, 1, = I Cor. 10:26; it expresses at the same time the fact that Christian recruitment does not have ethnic limitations and that all knowledge is at the service of the faith. See the commentary on this text in A. Méhat, *Étude sur les 'Stromates' de Clément d'Alexandrie* (Patristica sorbonensia 7) (Paris, 1966), pp. 67, 132–133, 287, 327.

43. Thus Paulinus of Nola (fourth to fifth century) *Epist.* XVI (*ad Jovium philosophum*) 7, ed. Hartel, pp. 121, 6–122, 2, cited by P. Courcelle, *art. cit.*, p. 89.

44. Like [Justin] *Cohort. ad gentiles* (date uncertain) 36, ed. Otto, pp. 116–118: Plato and Aristotle seduce only by their δοκιμότης φράσεως and their εὐγλωττία; let us stop our ears with wax so as to escape the sweet death produced by these Sirens. One will note that Clement himself had

recourse to the Sirens in order to denounce the magic of Sophists and the leading of the soul based on the charm of language; let us not repeat the trial of Ulysses, "it is quite enough for one man to have had to sail past the Sirens (Σειρῆνας δὲ παραπλεύσας)" (*Strom.* I 10, 48, 6, p. 32, 8–10). On these texts see H. Rahner, *op. cit.*, pp. 255–256.

45. Hippolytus *Elenchus* VII 13, 1–3, ed. Wendland, pp. 190, 21–191, 11.

46. Cf. *supra* p. 11 and V. Buchheit, "Homer bei Methodios von Olympos," *Rheinisches Museum* 99 (1956), pp. 19–23.

47. Methodius *De autexusio* I 1-5, ed. Bonwetsch, pp. 145, 3–147, 1.

48. Ambrose *Expos. in Lucam* IV 2-3, ed. Schenkl, pp. 139, 12–141, 3; the connection with the text of Luke seems very loose.

49. Isaiah 13:21; there are thus "Sirens" in the Septuagint and in the Latin translation of the Old Testament read by Ambrose, but Jerome dared to use the word only once in the Vulgate, as Is. 13:22; cf. P. Antin, "Les Sirènes et Ulysse dans l'oeuvre de saint Jérôme, "*Revue des études lat.* 39 (1961), pp. 232–234; E. Kaiser, *art. cit.*, p. 126.

50. *Sermo* XXXVII 1-3, lines 1-43, ed. Mutzenbecher, pp. 145–146, = *Homilia* 49, Migne *Patrologia latina* 57, 339B–340B.

51. This is the case in Augustine; see my work "*Ex Platonicorum persona*". *Études sur les lectures philosophiques de saint Augustin* (Amsterdam, 1977), p. xiii.

52. Besides *Protrept.* XII 118, 3, see *Strom.* I 10, 48, 6, quoted *supra* note 44.

53. *Nigrinus* 19: one must, imitating Ulysses, sail past (παραπλεῖν) the seductions of Roman life, but without binding one's hands or stopping one's ears with wax, so as to hold them, in full knowledge and liberty, in contempt. Every opinion on this point is of course full of uncertainty, given the lack of any collection of references which is near being exhaustive. I base myself on the rich repertory in E. Kaiser, *art. cit.*, where one finds seven instances of παραπλεῖν applied to the Sirens (pp. 128, 130, 131, 132, 134, 135, 136). If we eliminate the instances where this verb means "sail beside," and not "avoid," there remain only four texts of which two only are early enough to be of interest to our inquiry, one in Philostratus (*Heroicus* 11), who must be a little later than Clement, and that in Lucian, who must be a little earlier.

54. For the connection of the theme of flight with that of the return to the fatherland, see H. Merki, ʹΟΜΟΙΩΣΙΣ ΘΕΩ *Von der platonischen Angleichung an Gott zur Gottähnlichkeit bei Gregor von Nyssa* (Paradosis VII) (Freiburg/Schweiz, 1952), p. 127. Hermias, *loc. cit.*, p. 214, 22 does not have φεύγωμεν, but has ἐκφεύγοντα τὴν Κιρκην, etc.

55. Clement, *loc. cit.*, p. 83, 21: πάριθι τὴν ἡδονήν; Hermias, p. 214, 9–10: παρερχόμεθα τὸν ἐνταῦθα βίον.

56. See on this theme the classic article by C. Bonner, "Desired Haven," *Harvard Theological Review* 34 (1941), pp. 49–67.

57. *In Parmen.* V, col. 1025, 36–37.

58. See the title of the article by I. P. Culianu cited *supra* p. 235, n. 7.

59. Cf. P. Reymond, *L'eau, sa vie et sa signification dans l'Ancien Testament* (Supplements to *Vetus Testamentum* VI) (Leiden, 1958), pp. 123–124 and 182–198.

60. Thus Origen *Hom. in Gen.* I 10; *Hom. in Levit.* VIII 3; *In Epist. ad Rom.* 5, 10; Ambrose *De fide* V 2, 31; *Expos. in Lucam* IV 40. I take these references from H. Rahner, *op. cit.*, pp. 291–292.

61. *Op. cit.*, p. 253, where indeed no reference is made to Hermias.

62. Origen Fr. 95–96 *In Thren.* 4, 3, ed. Klostermann p. 270, 2–12: τὰς κατὰ Σύμμαχον Σειρῆνας ἀκούσει τὰ πονηρὰ πνεύματα . . . Κατὰ γὰρ τὸν ἔξω μῦθον αὗται διὰ τῆς ἡδονῆς τοὺς προστυχόντας ἀπώλλυον.

63. P. Boyancé, "Écho des exégèses de la mythologie grecque chez Philon," in *Philon d'Alexandrie. Actes du colloque de Lyon 1966* (Paris, 1967), p. 170.

64. Hippolytus *Elenchus* VI 15, 4–16, 2, ed. Wendland, pp. 141, 22–142, 5; this concerns *Od.* x 286–306.

65. *Ibid.*, V 7, 30–32, pp. 85, 23–87, 3, on which see H. Leisegang, *La gnose*, French trans. (Biblioth. histor.) (Paris, 1951), pp. 89–90; the Homeric passage is *Od.* xxiv 1–5; ἀνεμνησμένων, a word-play with μνηστῆρες, "suitors."

66. Proclus *In Rempubl.* II, p. 351, 7–17, a reference given by the editor Wendland, p. 86.
67. J. Carcopino, *De Pythagore aux Apôtres. Études sur la conversion du monde romain* (Paris, 1956), especially pp. 177, 188, 211–213.
68. As thinks W. Foester, intro. to *The Exegesis on the Soul*, in R. McL. Wilson (ed.), *Gnosis* vol. II (Oxford, 1974), p. 103.
69. *The Exegesis on the Soul* ed. M. Krause and P. Labib, *Gnostische und Hermetische Schriften aus Codex II und Codex VI* (Glückstadt, 1971), pp. 85–86, = p. 136, 26–35 of the Codex. What is given as a quotation from Homer is based on a compilation of several passages from *Od.* i 55–59 (Ulysses weeps and wants to see again the smoke of Ithaca), iv 555–558 (on Calypso's island, Ulysses weeps at not being able to return to his fatherland), v 82–83 and 151–158 (each day Ulysses weeps sitting on the cape), v 219–220 (Ulysses wants to return), xiii 299–301 (Athena never stopped helping Ulysses), etc.
70. Epictetus *Discourses* III 24, 18–21, notably: "if Ulysses cried and lamented, he was not a noble man."
71. See the excellent article by M. Scopello, "Les citations d'Homère dans le traité de *L'exégèse de l'âme*," in M. Krause (ed.), *Gnosis and Gnosticism* (Nag Hammadi Studies VIII) (Leiden, 1977), p. 3: the treatise is "une exposition du mythe gnostique de l'âme déchue dans le monde"; the purpose of the biblical and Homeric quotations is to "justifier le thème gnostique de la remontée de l'âme au Plérôme."

ORIGEN'S DOCTRINE OF THE TRINITY AND SOME LATER NEOPLATONIC THEORIES

1. *Ep. ad Menam*, p. 208, 26–32 Schw. = Fr. 9 Koetschau.
2. *Ep.* 124, 2, p. 98, 1–6 Hilberg.
3. Ἐκ τοῦ πρώτου λόγου τοῦ Περὶ ἀρχῶν βιβλίου. Ὅτι ὁ μὲν θεὸς καὶ πατὴρ συνέχων τά πάντα φθάνει εἰς ἕκαστον τῶν ὄντων, μεταδιδοὺς ἑκάστῳ ἀπὸ τοῦ ἰδίου τὸ εἶναι ὅπερ ἐστίν, ἐλαττόνως δὲ παρὰ τὸν πατέρα ὁ υἱὸς φθάνων ἐπὶ μόνα τὰ λογικά (δεύτερος γάρ ἐστι τοῦ πατρός), ἔτι δὲ ἡττόνως τὸ πνεῦμα τὸ ἅγιον ἐπὶ μόνους τοὺς ἁγίους διικνούμενον ὥστε κατὰ τοῦτο μείζων ἡ δύναμις τοῦ πατρὸς παρὰ τὸν υἱὸν καὶ τὸ πνεῦμα τὸ ἅγιον, πλείων δὲ ἡ τοῦ υἱοῦ παρὰ τὸ πνεῦμα τὸ ἅγιον, καὶ πάλιν διαφέρουσα μᾶλλον τοῦ ἁγίου πνεύματος ἡ δύναμις παρὰ τὰ ἄλλα ἅγια.
4. "Filium quoque minorem a patre eo quod secundus ab illo sit, et spiritum sanctum inferiorem a filio in sanctis quibusque versari, atque hoc ordine maiorem patris fortitudinem esse quam filii et spiritus sancti, et rursum maiorem filii fortitudinem esse quam spiritus sancti, et consequenter ipsius sancti spiritus maiorem esse virtutem ceteris, quae sancta dicuntur."
5. "Arbitror igitur operationem quidem esse patris et filii tam in sanctis quam in peccatoribus, in hominibus rationabilibus et in mutis animalibus, sed et in his, quae sine anima sunt, et in omnibus omnino quae sunt; operationem vero spiritus sancti nequaquam prorsus incidere vel in ea, quae sine anima sunt, vel in ea, quae animantia quidem sed muta sunt, sed ne in illis quidem inveniri, qui rationabiles quidem sunt sed 'in malitia positi' nec omnino ad meliora conversi. In illis autem solis esse arbitror opus spiritus sancti, qui iam se ad meliora convertunt et 'per vias Christi Iesu' incedunt, id est qui sunt 'in bonis actibus' et 'in deo permanent.'"
6. The former question is well discussed in an article by Manlio Simonetti, "Sull' interpretazione di un passo del *De Principiis* di Origene (I 3, 5–8)," in *Riv. di Cult. Class. e Med.*, 6 (1964), pp. 15–32, but he does not concern himself with possible Platonic analogies.
7. Πᾶν αἴτιον καὶ πρὸ τοῦ αἰτιατοῦ ἐνεργεῖ καὶ μετ' αὐτὸ πλειόνων ἐστὶν ὑποστατικόν.
   εἰ γάρ ἐστιν αἴτιον, τελειότερόν ἐστι καὶ δυνατώτερον τοῦ μετ' αὐτό. καὶ εἰ τοῦτο, πλειόνων αἴτιον· δυνάμεως γὰρ μείζονος τὸ πλείω παράγειν, ἴσης δὲ τὰ ἴσα, καὶ τῆς ἐλάττονος ἐλάττω· καὶ ἡ μὲν τὰ μείζονα ἐν τοῖς ὁμοίοις δυναμένη δύναμις καὶ τὰ ἐλάττονα δύναται, ἡ δὲ τὰ ἐλάττονα δυναμένη οὐκ ἐξ ἀνάγκης τὰ μείζω δυνήσεται. εἰ οὖν δυνατώτερον τὸ αἴτιον, πλειόνων ἐστὶ παρακτικόν.

ἀλλὰ μὴν καὶ ὅσα δύναται τὸ αἰτιατόν, μειζόνως ἐκεῖνο δύναται. πᾶν γὰρ τὸ ὑπὸ τῶν δευτέρων παραγόμενον ὑπὸ τῶν προτέρων καὶ αἰτιωτέρων παράγεται μειζόνως. συνυφίστησιν ἄρα αὐτῷ πάντα ὅσα πέφυκε παράγειν.

εἰ δὲ καὶ αὐτὸ πρότερον παράγει, δῆλον δήπουθεν ὅτι πρὸ αὐτοῦ ἐνεργεῖ κατὰ τὴν παρακτικὴν αὐτοῦ ἐνέργειαν. ἅπαν ἄρα αἴτιον καὶ πρὸ τοῦ αἰτιατοῦ ἐνεργεῖ καὶ σὺν αὐτῷ καὶ μετ᾽ αὐτὸ ἄλλα ὑφίστησιν.

ἐκ δὴ τούτων φανερὸν ὅτι ὅσων μὲν αἰτία ψυχή, καὶ νοῦς αἴτιος, οὐχ ὅσων δὲ νοῦς, καὶ ψυχὴ αἰτία· ἀλλὰ καὶ πρὸ ψυχῆς ἐνεργεῖ, καὶ ἃ δίδωσι ψυχὴ τοῖς δευτέροις, δίδωσι καὶ νοῦς μειζόνως, καὶ μηκέτι ψυχῆς ἐνεργούσης νοῦς ἐλλάμπει τὰς ἑαυτοῦ δόσεις, οἷς μὴ δέδωκε ψυχὴ ἑαυτήν. καὶ γὰρ τὸ ἄψυχον, καθόσον εἴδους μετέσχε, νοῦ μετέχει καὶ τῆς τοῦ νοῦ ποιήσεως.

καὶ δὴ καὶ ὅσων νοῦς αἴτιος, καὶ τὸ ἀγαθὸν αἴτιον· οὐκ ἔμπαλιν δέ. καὶ γὰρ αἱ στερήσεις τῶν εἰδῶν ἐκεῖθεν (πάντα γὰρ ἐκεῖθεν). νοῦς δὲ στερήσεως ὑποστάτης οὐκ ἔστιν, εἶδος ὤν.

8. τὸ γὰρ ἓν καὶ ὕπερ τὸ ὂν καὶ σὺν τῷ ὄντι καὶ ἐπὶ τάδε τοῦ ὄντος, ὡς ἐπὶ τῆς ὕλης καὶ τῆς στερήσεως.

9. *Did.* ch. X, 2: τούτου δὲ (sc. the Active Intellect) καλλίων ὁ αἴτιος τούτου καὶ ὅπερ ἂν ἔτι ἀνώτερω τούτων ὑφέστηκεν. οὗτος ἂν εἴη ὁ πρῶτος θεός, . . .

10. *Fr.* 15 Des Places: ὁ μὲν πρῶτος θεὸς . . . ἐστώς. The πρῶτος νοῦς is also termed αὐτόον in Fr. 17, as being an object of contemplation for the Demiurge.

11. Alex. Aphrod. *In Metaph.* p. 59, 1 Hayduck, *ad Met.* 988a10–11.

12. *Fr.* 34 Des Places: Ἔνθεν ἀποθοώσκει γένεσις πολυποικίλου ὕλης. Matter is also described as πατρογενής by Psellus in his *Hypotyposis*, sect. 27, p. 201 Des Places.

13. *In Alc.* p. 110, 13ff. Creuzer = Iambl. *In Alc.* Fr. 8 Dillon.

14. Amelius, e.g., *In Tim.* Fr. 39; Fr. 54; Fr. 57 (with Numenius); Porphyry, Fr. 16; Fr. 70, Dillon.

15. *Expos. Chald.* 1153a10–11; p. 191 Des Places: συμπαθῆ δὲ τὰ ἄνω τοῖς κάτω φασὶ καὶ μάλιστα τὰ ὑπὸ σελήνην.

A NEOPLATONIC COMMENTARY ON THE CHRISTIAN TRINITY: MARIUS VICTORINUS

1. Augustine, St., *Confessions* VIII. 2.
2. P. Hadot, *Marius Victorinus* (Paris: Etudes Augustiniennes, 1971), p. 239.
3. *Ibid.*, p. 237
4. H. Dörrie, "Une Exégèse Néoplatonicienne du prologue de l'Evangile de Saint Jean," in *Epektasis* (Paris: Beauchesne, 1972), pp. 75–87.
5. M. Victorinus, *Adversus Arium* I. 26 in *Traités Théologiques sur la Trinité* (Paris: Editions du Cerf ["Sources chrétiennes" series], 1960). All translations of Victorinus' words are my own.
6. Plotinus, *Ennead* III. 2.9.
7. Victorinus, *Adv. Ar.* III. 14. 20.
8. *Ibid.*, III. 6. 20; I. 4. 20–25.
9. Victorinus, *Ad Cand.* 29, 16–19; *Adv. Ar.* III. 17. 2; III. 15. 1.
10. Victorinus, *Adv. Ar.* III. 18.
11. Victorinus, *Hymn* I, 15–16.
12. Victorinus, *Adv. Ar.* I. 48. 21.
13. *Ibid.*, III. 8. 33.
14. *Ibid.*, III. 11. 13.
15. *Ibid.*, IV. 33. 21.
16. Jn. I. 18; *Adv. Ar.* III. 6. 20; I. 4. 20–25.
17. Jn. 14. 9–11.
18. P. Hadot, *Porphyre et Victorinus* II (Paris: Etudes Augustiniennes, 1968).
19. D. O'Meara, review of A. Smith, *Porphyry's Place in the Neoplatonic Tradition*, in *Erasmus* 29(1977), pp. 628–630.

20. T. E. Pollard, "Marcellus of Ancyra, a Neglected Father" in *Epektasis,* pp. 187–196.
21. Plotinus, *Enn.* V. 4. 2; *Enn.* VI. 2. 6; *Enn.* II: Victorinus, *Adv. Ar.* I. 32. 32.
22. *Anonymous Commentary on the Parmenides* XII. 22–29 in Hadot, *Porphyre et Victorinus* II.
23. Victorinus, *Adv. Ar.* III. 4. 6–46; IV. 5. 41–45; IV. 22. 10–14.
24. Plotinus, *Enn.* V. 4. 2.
25. Augustine, St., *De Trinitate,* VI. 10. 11; X. 10. 13.
26. *Christlicher Platonismus* (Zürich: Artemis Verlag, 1967), p. 15.
27. Plotinus, *Enn.* VI. 8. 13.
28. Victorinus, *Ad Cand.* 30, 1–26; *Adv. Ar.* I. 43, 34–43; IV. 21. 19–25; *De hom. rec.* 3. 11.
29. Victorinus, *Adv. Ar.* I. 23, 1–40.
30. *Ibid.,* I. 30.
31. *Ibid.,* II. 3. 34.
32. Victorinus, *Hymn* III.
33. Victorinus, *Adv. Ar.* IV. 22.
34. *Ibid.,* III. 3 and 4.
35. *Ibid.,* I. 61. 13; I. 56. 7–15; cf. Aug. *Conf.* VII. 9. 13; *City of God* X. 2.

THE NEOPLATONISM OF SAINT AUGUSTINE

1. "Ancient Christian Writers" series vol. 12 (Washington, D.C., 1950), p. 23.
2. "St. Augustine's '*notitia sui*' related to Aristotle and the early Neoplatonists," *Augustiniana* 27 (1977), p. 102.
3. A. Ernout, *Lucrèce* (Paris, no date), p. 26: "même si l'explication était fausse, elle est bonne du moment qu'elle procure le résultat cherché."
4. *Contra Acad.* III. 43.
5. *Ibid.* 396f.
6. *Revue internat. de Philos.* 92 (1970), pp. 321–337.
7. *Recherches sur les Confessions de saint Augustin* (Paris, 1950), pp. 157 ff.
8. Augustine, *Conf.* 7. 23 (slightly rearranged).
9. *Ibid.,* 9. 25.
10. *Ciu. Dei* XIV. 28.
11. Plotinus, *Enn.* V. 2. 1 (Henry-Schwyzer).
12. *Ciu. Dei* XIX. 23.
13. *Ibid.,* X. 32 (Loeb translation).
14. *Kleine patristische Schriften,* herausgegeben von Günter Glockmann (Texte und Untersuchungen 83) (Berlin, 1967).
15. P. Agaësse and A. Solignac, "Bibliothèque Augustinienne" series, volumes 48 and 49 (Paris, 1972).
16. In the *Saint Augustine Lecture 1977,* Villanova University, Pennsylvania (Villanova, 1981).
17. Plotinus, *Enn.* V. 3. 13 (MacKenna translation).
18. *Sententiae* XXV. 11, 4 (Mommert).
19. *De ordine* II. 16. 44.
20. *De gen. ad. litt.* V. 16. 34.
21. *Ciu. Dei* XXII. 29.

SOME LATER NEOPLATONIC VIEWS ON DIVINE CREATION AND THE ETERNITY OF THE WORLD

1. W. Wieland, "Die Ewigkeit der Welt," in *Die Gegenwart der Griechen im neueren Denken* (Tübingen, 1960), p. 293: "Noch bei seinem Übertritt zum Christentum macht er den Vorbehalt, es sei ihm unmöglich, in allen Punkten der christlichen Lehre zuzustimmen: zu denjenigen Punkten, die er von seiner bisherigen philosophischen Überzeugung auf keinen Fall aufgeben zu können glaubt, gehört die Lehre von der Ewigkeit der Welt."

2. L. G. Westerink, *Anonymous Prolegomena to Platonic Philosophy* (Amsterdam, 1962), pp. xv–xx.

3. L. G. Westerink, *op. cit.*, pp. xxiii–xxiv. According to Westerink, Elias "is clearly unwilling to abandon the old belief (viz., the eternity of the world)," whereas David and Stephen mention this doctrine without dismissing it. According to A. Cameron ("La fin de l'Académie," in *Le Néoplatonisme* [Paris, 1971], p. 282), the influence of Philoponus' teaching on the Alexandrian school was rather weak: "Olympiodore qui enseignait encore à Alexandrie dans les années 560, était en effet païen, et ses successeurs Élie, David, Étienne, bien que chrétiens, continuèrent à enseigner des doctrines comme l'éternité du monde et la divinité des corps célestes, qui avaient déjà été depuis longtemps réfutées par Philopon."

4. H. D. Saffrey, "Le chrétien Jean Philopon et la survivance de l'École d'Alexandrie au VIe siècle," *Revue des études grecques* LXVII (1954), p. 406.

5. H. D. Saffrey, *art. cit.*, p. 397. After the death of Proclus there was some contention between Marinus who represented the Aristotelian trend and Isidorus who sided with the Platonic tendency.

6. H. D. Saffrey, *art. cit.*, p. 400; L. G. Westerink, *Anonymous Prolegomena*, p. xi.

7. W. Wieland, *art. cit.*, p. 300.

8. L. G. Westerink, *Anonymous Prolegomena*, p. xii.

9. Simplicius, *In Phys.* VIII, 10, p. 1363, 8 (*Commentaria in Aristotelem graeca* [CAG], vols. IX–X).

10. L. G. Westerink, *Anonymous Prolegomena*, pp. xv–xx.

11. H. D. Saffrey, *art. cit.*, p. 403.

12. H. D. Saffrey, *art. cit.*, p. 401.

13. Cf. W. Wieland, *art. cit.*, p. 303. The sentence in question (*nihil ex nihilo*) is considered to be well known, notorious among physicists (πολυθρύλητον ἀξίωμα).

14. This position was firmly maintained by Proclus: in his view whatever comes to be must proceed from prime matter; cf. Philoponus, *De aeternitate mundi contra Proclum*, ed. H. Rabe (Leipzig, 1899), p. 455, 26.

15. Philoponus, *In Phys.* I, 3, p. 54, 8ff. (CAG XVI–XVII); cf. *De aeternitate mundi*, p. 458, 7ff.

16. Simplicius, *In Phys.* VIII, 1, pp. 1141–1142; cf. *De aeternitate mundi*, p. 344, 18.

17. Cf. *De aeternitate mundi*, pp. 64, 22; 367, 16; 368, 1.

18. Philoponus, *In Phys.* I, 9, p. 191, 9ff.; in his *De aeternitate mundi* also Philoponus endeavors to clarify the notion of divine creation: the author emphasizes the fact that God does not use any instrument when performing his creative activity (p. 76, 21) and that the divine substance does not become more perfect by producing the world; the cosmos does not contribute to the perfection of the Creator (p. 21, 1 and 21, 14). Both views are very interesting from a metaphysical viewpoint: they are clearly intended to show how creation has to be considered as an integral or transcendental causation.

19. Philoponus, *In Phys.* III, 5, p. 428, 23ff.

20. Philoponus, *In Phys.* III, 5, p. 429.

21. Philoponus, *In Phys.* III, 5, p. 458, 30; IV, 13, p. 762, 5–9.

22. E. Évrard, "Les convictions religieuses de Jean Philopon et la date de son commentaire aux 'Météorologiques.'" Acad. royale de Belgique, *Bulletin de la Classe des Lettres*, 39 (1953), pp. 300–301; cf. W. Wieland, *art. cit.*, p. 301.

23. Simplicius, *In Phys.* VIII, 1, p. 1130, 7ff.

24. Simplicius, *In Phys.* VIII, 1, p. 1133.

25. One of the arguments developed by Proclus in order to prove the eternity of the world starts from the Platonic definition of the soul. By its very nature the soul is a principle of movement and because it always exists, it necessarily causes an eternal movement; consequently the world must be constantly in movement, without beginning and without end. Philoponus however disagrees on this Platonic definition of the soul: the very essence of the soul could not be self-movement (*De aeternitate mundi*, p. 248, 19). If it belonged to the nature of the soul to move corporeal reality, then the psychic principle would depend on something lower and could not exist independently of the body. Moreover, the fact that the soul is able to move does not entail that it actually always moves (*De aeternitate mundi*, pp. 252ff.).

26. Simplicius, *In Phys.* VIII, 1, p. 1178, 9ff.
27. Simplicius, *In Phys.* VIII, 1, p. 1179.
28. Simplicius, *In Phys.* VIII, 1, p. 1179.
29. According to the *Timaeus* (32C and 41AB) of Plato, the Demiurge will never destroy the world; it would undoubtedly be wrong to pull down such a harmonious whole as the cosmos.
30. Simplicius, *In Phys.* VIII, 10, p. 1327.
31. Simplicius, *In Phys.* VIII, 10, p. 1329. According to Philoponus even the heavenly bodies are perishable by nature; they may however continue to exist indefinitely as a result of a divine decision; cf. *De aeternitate mundi,* p. 598, 7.
32. Simplicius, *In Phys.* VIII, 1, p. 1167.
33. Simplicius, *In Phys.* VIII, 1, p. 1163; Proclus contends that time must be eternal because it has been made according to an eternal pattern. In Philoponus' view the world could not reproduce in a perfect way the model according to which it has been made; there is always some distance between a perfect pattern and its imitation (*De aeternitate mundi,* p. 551, 8). As to the use of temporal terms, Philoponus points to the fact that we often use such words without implying any temporal meaning; we use them even when speaking about God (*De aeternitate mundi,* p. 117, 13).
34. Simplicius, *In Phys.* VIII, 1, pp. 1157–1158.
35. Simplicius, *In Phys.* VIII, 1, p. 1158.
36. Simplicius, *In Phys.* VIII, 1, p. 1164.
37. Simplicius, *In Phys.* VIII, 1, pp. 1141–1142; cf. *De aeternitate mundi,* p. 367, 16.
38. Simplicius, *In Phys.* VIII, 1, p. 1142; cf. *De aeternitate mundi,* p. 458, 7.
39. Simplicius, *In Phys.* VIII, 1, p. 1141; cf. *De aeternitate mundi,* p. 76, 21ff.
40. A. Cameron, *art. cit.,* p. 289.
41. Simplicius, *In Phys.* VIII, 1, p. 1166.
42. Simplicius, *In Phys.* VIII, 1, p. 1164. According to Simplicius all philosophers, except Plato, accept movement as eternal.
43: Simplicius, *In Phys.* VIII, 1, p. 1131.
44. Simplicius, *In Phys.* VIII, 1, p. 1135.
45. Simplicius, *In Phys.* VIII, 1, p. 1136.
46. Simplicius, *In Phys.* VIII, 1, p. 1180.
47. Simplicius, *In Phys.* VIII, 1, pp. 1180–1181.
48. Simplicius, *In Phys.* VIII, 1, p. 1165. Proclus already contends that, the pattern of the world being eternal, the world itself must be eternal too (*De aeternitate mundi,* pp. 24, 14; 550, 18). The reply of Philoponus is twofold: he firstly points to the fact that the Platonic doctrine of the Ideas is rather controversial and has actually been opposed by Aristotle. Moreover, the very essence of the Ideas is not that they are the patterns of sensible reality. In Philoponus' view the Ideas are self-sufficient and could perfectly exist without any relation to something else (*De aeternitate mundi,* p. 35, 6).
49. Simplicius, *In Phys.* VIII, 1, p. 1163.
50. Simplicius, *In Phys.* VIII, 1, p. 1168.
51. Simplicius, *In Phys.* VIII, 1, p. 1151. According to Philoponus the starting of creation does not involve any change in the divine perfection: it is not situated in a temporal dimension and is consequently not a movement; besides it is not a passage from potency to act, but a transition from an habitual (ἕξις) disposition to act, which can occur without being produced by something else (*De aeternitate mundi,* pp. 51ff.).
52. Simplicius, *In Phys.* VIII, 1, pp. 1159–1161.
53. Simplicius, *In Phys.* VIII, 1, p. 1161.
54. Simplicius, *In Phys.* VIII, 1, p. 1177.
55. Simplicius, *In Phys.* VIII, 1, p. 1173.
56. Simplicius, *In Phys.* VIII, 1, p. 1174.
57. Simplicius, *In Phys.* VIII, 1, p. 1177.
58. Simplicius, *In Phys.* VIII, 1, p. 1150.
59. Simplicius, *In Phys.* VIII, 1, p. 1327.
60. Muhsin Mahdi, "Alfarabi against Philoponus," *Journal of Near Eastern Studies* 26 (1967), p. 352.

61. W. Wieland, *art. cit.*, p. 315: "Denn das zeichnet ja Philoponus von den anderen Christen der Spätantike aus, dass er die zeitliche Endlichkeit der Welt nicht als Glaubenssatz hinnimmt, sondern sie gerade im Rahmen der *aristotelischen* Begrifflichkeit zu beweisen versucht."

JOHN PHILOPONUS AND STEPHANUS OF ALEXANDRIA: TWO NEOPLATONIC CHRISTIAN COMMENTATORS ON ARISTOTLE?

Note: All references to the Greek commentaries on Aristotle are by page and line of the Berlin Academy edition, (CAG), and to the *de Anima* commentary unless otherwise stated; references to the Latin version of Philoponus' commentary on Book 3 of the *de Anima* are to G. Verbeke's edition, *Jean Philopon. Commentaire sur le de Anima d'Aristote. Traduction de Guillaume de Moerbeke* (Louvain/ Paris, 1966).

1. Cf. S. van Riet, "Fragments de l'original grec du 'de Intellectu' de Philopon dans une compilation de Sophonias," *Rev. Philosophique de Louvain* 63 (1965) 5–40.
2. On the relation of our texts to the original courses, cf. M. Richard, "ΑΠΟ ΦΩΝΗΣ," *Byzantion* 20 (1950) 191–199.
3. The authenticity of the commentary usually ascribed to Simplicius has recently been questioned, and its authorship assigned to Priscian, by F. Bossier and C. Steel, "Priscianus Lydus en de 'in de Anima' van Pseudo(?) Simplicius", *Tijdschrift voor Filosofie* 34 (1972) 761–782: their reasons do not seem to me entirely convincing. For another view cf. now I. Hadot, *Le Problème du Néoplatonisme Alexandrin. Hiéroclès et Simplicius* (Paris, 1978), 193–202.
4. Themistius, by contrast, wrote roughly the same on all three books.
5. Cf. A. J. Festugière, "Mode de composition des commentaires de Proclus," *Mus. Helv.* 20 (1963) 81ff. The presence of this arrangement in Book 3 only of Philoponus' commentary was already noted by the CAG editor, M. Hayduck, preface p. v.
6. Cf. 432a 26.
7. Cf. H. Blumenthal, "Neoplatonic interpretations of Aristotle on *Phantasia*," *Rev. of Metaphysics* 31 (1977) 251–252.
8. Simplicius refers to his (lost) commentary on *Metaphysics Lambda* for a discussion of *nous khōristos*, cf. 217. 23–28.
9. Philoponus 2. 13–27.
10. Stephanus 516. 8–15.
11. *Ibid.* 516. 8–517. 32.
12. Cf. above, p. 56, and n. 6.
13. On this cf. H. Blumenthal, "Neoplatonic elements in the *de Anima* commentaries," *Phronesis* 21 (1966) 72–83.
14. Cf. *ibid.*, 84–86, and Philoponus 215. 4ff., 224. 12ff.
15. Philoponus 2. 33ff.
16. Stephanus 518. 8ff.
17. Stephanus 520. 21ff.
18. Philoponus 3. 54–4. 69
19. Stephanus 518. 8–520. 20.
20. Philoponus 4. 70–75.
21. Stephanus 521. 11ff.
22. He was summoned to the capital to become *oikoumenikos didaskalos* under Heraclius (610–634), cf. H. Usener, *De Stephano Alexandrino* (Bonn, 1880), in *Kleine Schriften* 3 (Leipzig, 1914) 248ff.
23. E.g., Stephanus 527. 29–32: on this cf. above, p. 61.
24. Cf. L. G. Westerink, *Anonymous Prolegomena to Platonic Philosophy* (Amsterdam, 1962) xxiv–xxv.
25. Some of these are, of course, publications by Philoponus of courses given by Ammonius, who was not a Christian.
26. A. Gudeman, "Ioannes Philoponus," Pauly-Wissowa, *Real-Encyclopädie* 9.i (1916) 1769, 1771,

followed, e.g., by Schmid-Staehlin, *Geschichte der Griechischen Literatur*[6] 2.ii (Munich, 1924) 1067, and M. Meyerhoff, "Joannes Grammatikos (Philoponos) von Alexandrien und die Arabische Medizin," *Mitteilungen des Deutschen Instituts für ägyptische Altertumskunde in Kairo* 2 (1931) 2–3.

27. *Les derniers commentateurs alexandrins d'Aristote* (Mémoires et Travaux des Facultés Catholiques de Lille) (Lille, 1941) 55–56. Cf., too, H. D. Saffrey, "Le chrétien Jean Philopon et la survivance de l'Ecole d'Alexandrie au VIe siècle," *Rev. des études grecques* 67 (1954) 402.

28. "Les convictions religieuses de Jean Philopon et la date de son Commentaire aux 'Météorologiques,'" Académie R. de Belgique, *Bulletin de la Classe des Lett., Sc. Mor. et Pol.* sér. 5. 39 (1953) 299–357.

29. Cf. the article cited in note 13, 73–74.

30. *Commentary on de Anima* 734.

31. On this question cf. E. R. Dodds, *Proclus. The Elements of Theology*[2] (Oxford, 1963) 313–321. Philoponus discusses it in his preface, cf. especially 18. 7–33.

32. For a history of the question, cf. Proclus *in Tim.* I. 276. 10ff. For modern accounts, from opposing points of view, cf. F. M. Cornford, *Plato's Cosmology* (London, 1937) 34ff., and G. Vlastos, "The disorderly Motion in the *Timaeus*" (1939) reprinted with an updating postscript, "Creation in the *Timaeus*: is it a fiction?" (1964), in R. E. Allen (ed.) *Studies in Plato's Metaphysics* (London, 1965) 379–399 and 401–419.

33. Philoponus 229. 31–33.

34. Cf. *Topographia Christiana* 7. 1 (340A), and the notes *ad loc.* in the edition of W. Wolska-Conus, vol. 3, Sources Chrétiennes 197 (Paris, 1973) 56. Cf. also *eadem, La Topographie Chrétienne de Cosmas Indicopleustes* (Paris, 1962), chap. 5, especially 183ff.

35. Verbeke, in the introduction to his edition of Philoponus, lxx, suggests that a belief in preexistence and reincarnation may not have been regarded as incompatible with Christianity even at this period.

36. The Origenist belief in man's resurrection without a body, as well as preexistence, had been rebutted by Gregory of Nyssa a century and a half before Philoponus; cf. e.g., *de Hom.Opif.* 28, Migne, *Patrologia graeca* (*PG*) 44. 229B ff., and J. Daniélou "La résurrection du corps chez Grégoire de Nysse," *Vig. Chr.* 7 (1953) 155ff. It should however be noted that Origenism was not yet dead in Philoponus' time; cf. e.g., Justinian's letter to the patriarch Menas, 534 A.D.

37. Cf. *Contra Christianos* fragment 94 Harnack.

38. As opposed to the view that man approaches God by grace, encapsulated in Gregory's *ei gar hoper autos esti tēn physin, toutou tēn oikeiotēta kharizetai tois anthropois . . .*: "if he *gives* to men *by grace* assimilation to what he himself is by nature . . .," *de Beat.* 7, *PG* 44. 128OD.

39. Philoponus 5. 26–32.

40. *Ibid.* 12. 15ff.

41. *Ibid.* 2. 12–14, 18.16–24.

42. *De Opificio Mundi* 6. 23 = 276. 22–278. 13 Reichardt.

43. Simplicius 86. 17ff.

44. 413a 6–9.

45. Cf. Simplicius 95. 24–33.

46. Philoponus 25. 8.

47. Moerbeke, *op. cit.*, 6. 10–12.

48. Stephanus 527. 27–33.

49. *Op. cit.*, (n. 24) xxiv.

50. For this cf. e.g., Paul the Silentiary, *Hagia Sophia* 126–27.

51. Cf. Lampe, *Patristic Greek Lexicon* s.v. *Pronoia* B. 2. iv., for this use.

52. Stephanus 511. 26, 521. 6.

53. *Ibid.* 547. 12–14.

54. Cf. Westerink, *The Greek Commentaries on Plato's Phaedo* vol. 1. *Olympiodorus* (Amsterdam/Oxford/New York, 1976) 20.

55. Cf. the comments of Proclus, *PT* i.i = I. 6. 16ff. Saffrey-Westerink and Plotinus, *Enn.* 5. 1. 8.10–14.

56. On these conditions cf. A. D. E. Cameron, "The last days of the Academy at Athens," *Proceedings of the Cambridge Philological Society* n.s. 15 (1969), and, on the arrangements made, Saffrey, *op. cit.* (n. 27) 400–401.
57. Cf. Cameron, *ibid.*, 7–8 and H. Blumenthal, "529 and its sequel: what happened to the Academy?" *Byzantion* 48 (1978) 369–385.
58. Cf. the article "Fragments . . ." by S. Van Riet cited in note 1.
59. The eleventh century manuscript Vaticanus 268, is defective for the last two-thirds of Stephanus: Parisinus 1914, from the twelfth century, is the first complete manuscript.
60. I should like to thank those members of the conference whose comments have enabled me to make improvements to this paper.

NEW OBJECTIVE LINKS BETWEEN THE PSEUDO—DIONYSIUS AND PROCLUS

1. H. D. Saffrey, "Un lien objectif entre le Pseudo-Denys et Proclus," in *Studia Patristica* IX (Texte und Untersuchungen, Bd. 94) (Berlin, 1966), 98–105.
2. *Ibid.*, 104–105.
3. Ammonius Saccas according to E. Elorduy; Damascius according to R. F. Hathaway; Peter the Iberian according to E. Honigmann; Peter the Fuller according to U. Riedinger. The various studies relative to these identifications were surveyed and reviewed by J. M. Hornus, "Les recherches récentes sur le pseudo-Denys l'Aréopagite," in *Revue d'Histoire et de Philosophie religieuses* 35 (1955), 404–448 and 41 (1961) 22–27. See also the very suggestive table in R. F. Hathaway, *Hierarchy and the Definition of Order in the Letters of Pseudo-Dionysius* (The Hague, 1969), 31–35.
4. H. Urs von Balthasar, "Das Scholienwerk des Johannes von Scythopolis," in *Scholastik* 15 (1940), 16–38, reproduced with corrections in appendix to *Kosmische Liturgie*, 2nd. ed. (Einsiedeln, 1962), 644–672, under the title: "Das Problem der Dionysius-Scholien."
5. At the present time one is obliged to read these scholia in the edition of Cordier (Paris, 1634), reproduced in Migne, *Patrologia Graeca (PG)*, tome 4 (Paris, 1857).
6. *PG* 4, col. 264B–C. Cf. H. Ch. Puech, "Liberatus de Carthage et la date de l'apparition des écrits dionysiens," in *Annuaire de l'École pratique des Hautes Études*, Section des Sciences religieuses, 1930–1931 (Melun, 1930), 3–39; and R. F. Hathaway, *op. cit.*, 11–12.
7. *PG* 4, col. 368D–369A.
8. Proclus, *Theol. plat.* I 29, 124. 12–125. 2 Saffrey-Westerink.
9. Proclus, *In Crat.*, 18.27–19.17 Pasquali. Cf. J. Trouillard, "L'activité onomastique selon Proclus," in *De Jamblique à Proclus* (Entretiens de la Fondation Hardt, tome XXI) (Vandoeuvres-Genève, 1975), 239–251.
10. Proclus, *In Parm.* IV, col. 851. 8–10 Cousin. See also *In Tim.* I, 99. 1–4.
11. Cf. A. Bielmeier, *Die neuplatonische Phaidrosinterpretation* (Paderborn, 1930), 29–39.
12. Hermias, *In Phaedr.* 70. 4–5 Couvreur.
13. On Hierocles, see most recently, Ilsetraut Hadot, *Le problème du néoplatonisme alexandrin, Hiéroclès et Simplicius* (Paris, 1978), 17–20.
14. Hierocles, *In Aur. Pyth. Carmen*, XXV 2, 105. 19–23 Koehler.
15. Plato, *Phil.* 12C 1–3.
16. Damascius, *In Phil.* §24.4, p. 15 Westerink, and note.
17. Damascius, *In Phaed.* I, §503.3 Westerink, and note.
18. Iamblichus, *De myst.* VII 4–5, 254–260 des Places.
19. Julian, *Ep.* 89, 160.23–161.16 Bidez.
20. Marinus, *Vita Procli* 30. Cf. H. D. Saffrey and L. G. Westerink, Proclus, *Theol. plat.* I (Paris, 1968), Introduction, Life of Proclus, pp. xxii–xxiii and notes. On the devotion of Proclus to Athena, see A. J. Festugière, "Proclus et la religion traditionnelle," in *Mélanges Piganiol* (Paris, 1966), 1581–1590, reproduced in *Études de philosophie grecque* (Paris, 1971), 575–584.
21. Unless John of Scythopolis is making an allusion to the telestic rite of the animation of statues, which consisted in introducing into the figurine symbols of the divinity through whom one wished

to animate the statue. On this rite, cf. Hans Lewy, *Chaldaean Oracles and Theurgy*, new edition by Michel Tardieu (Paris, 1978), 495–496. See also Proclus, *In Tim.* I, 273. 11–13: "In the statues erected by the telestic art, certain characters are visible, others, hidden inside like symbols of the presence of the gods, and these are known only to the initiates . . ." and *ibid.*, III, 4.18–5.4.

22. Plato, *Symposium* 215A7–B3.

23. *Ibid.*, 216D3–7.

24. *Ibid.*, 215B1.

25. Plutarch, *De genio Socratis* 10, 580E.

26. Synesius, *Ep.* 154, p. 275, 7–9 Garzya.

27. John M. Dillon, *Iamblichi Chalcidensis in Platonis dialogos commentariorum fragmenta* (Philosophia Antiqua 23) (Leiden, 1973), p. 22. The quite incidental reference to the Platonic doctrine on demons in the *Symposium*, used by Iamblichus to support his interpretation of the third hypothesis of the *Parmenides*, cannot in any case be considered as an indication of a commentary by Iamblichus on the *Symposium*, see Dillon, *ibid.*, 222–223 (text of Damascius) and 400–401 (commentary). The implications of the position of Iamblichus have been admirably elucidated by Carlos G. Steel, *The Changing Self. A Study on the Soul in later Neoplatonism: Iamblichus, Damascius and Priscianus* (Bruxelles, 1978), p. 85.

28. Proclus, *In Remp.* II, 381. 14 Kroll.

29. Proclus, *In Alc.*, 89. 3–10 Westerink.

30. Plato, *Symposium*, 218A5.

31. *Ibid.*, 216E6.

32. *PG* 3, col. 589D–592B.

33. St. Paul, Titus 3:4.

34. *PG* 3, col. 592B.

35. Willy Theiler, in *Theol. Literaturzeitung* 69 (1944), col. 71–72.

36. *PG* 4, col. 197A.

37. Cf. A. Van den Daele, *Indices Pseudo-Dionysiani* (Louvain, 1941), s.vv.

38. Pseudo-Dionysius, *Letter IX*, §1, *PG* 3, col. 1108A.

39. Proclus, *Theol. plat.*, IV 9, p. 31, 14–16 Saffrey-Westerink.

40. *PG* 3, col. 645B. Cf. H. Koch, *Pseudo-Dionysius Areopagita in seinen Beziehungen zum Neuplatonismus und Mysterienwesen* (Forschungen zur christlichen Literatur und Dogmengeschichte, Bd. 1) (Mainz, 1900), 162–163, and W. Theiler, *Die chaldäischen Orakel und die Hymnen des Synesios* (Schriften der Königsberger Gelehrten-Gesellschaft, 18, 1) (Halle, 1942), p. 20, reproduced in *Forschungen zum Neuplatonismus* (Berlin, 1966), p. 275.

41. In John 4:14, it is the Christian who becomes a source of living water through which he never again thirsts, and it is always the Christians who are the buds on the tree of the people of God.

42. Proclus, *De malorum subsistentia*, II §11, 23–24, p. 192 Boese.

43. Werner Beierwaltes and Richard Kannicht, "Plotin-Testimonia bei Iohannes von Skythopolis," in *Hermes* 96 (1968) 247–251. W. Beierwaltes returned to the borrowings of John of Scythopolis from Plotinus in another article: "Johannes von Skythopolis und Plotin," in *Studia Patristica* XI (Texte und Untersuchungen, Bd. 108) (Berlin, 1972), 3–7.

44. *PG* 3, col. 820A.

45. Proclus, *Theol. plat.*, I 3, p. 14. 1–4 Saffrey-Westerink.

46. *Ibid.*, II 3, p. 23, 15–19.

47. Plato, *Parm.*, 144B1–2.

48. *PG* 3, col. 824C.

49. *PG* 4, col. 329B.

50. I. P. Sheldon-Williams, "Henads and Angels: Proclus and the ps.-Dionysius," in *Studia Patristica* XI (Texte und Untersuchungen, Bd. 108) (Berlin, 1972), 65–71.

51. H. D. Saffrey and L. G. Westerink, *Proclus, Théologie platonicienne*, tome III (Paris, 1978), ix–lxxvii.

52. To the examples of the use of the word "henad" before Proclus must be added: Aristides Quintilianus, *De musica* I 3, p. 4.8 Winnington-Ingram.

53. Cf. *Indices Pseudo-Dionysiani*, s.v. ἑνάς.

54. *Divine Names*, VIII §5, 892D.
55. *Ibid.*, I §1, 588B.
56. Proclus, *Theol. plat.* II 11, p. 65.12 and note 10 (p. 124 of Complementary Notes), and III 7, p. 30.4 and note 2 (p. 119 of Complementary Notes).
57. Th. Whittaker, *The Neo-Platonists*, 2d ed. (Cambridge, 1918), p. 187.
58. C. Steel, *The Changing Self . . .*, p. 155.

THE PROBLEM OF GENERAL CONCEPTS IN NEOPLATONISM AND BYZANTINE THOUGHT

1. See n. 3.
2. Ed. L. Benakis, *Philosophia* (Athens) 3 (1973), 361–379.
3. See L. Benakis, "The Study of Byzantine Philosophy: Critical Survey 1949–1971," (in Greek) *Philosophia* (Athens) 1 (1971), 390–433. H. Hunger, *Die hochsprachliche profane Literatur der Byzantiner* 1 (A. Philosophie) (München, 1978), 3–62.
4. My main source is K. Kremer's important contribution to the problem: "Die Anschauung der Ammonius (Hermeiou)-Schule über den Wirklichkeitscharakter des Intelligiblen," *Philosophisches Jahrbuch* 19 (1961–1962), 46–63. This article has not so far been given the attention it deserves.
5. It must be noted that the term "Platonism" is used here and subsequently in accordance with its established usage in many of today's logicians and specialists in the theory of knowledge, such as Quine, Goodman, Stegmüller, and others. That is, it is not an exact characterization of Platonic teaching, but is a recognition that today also it is a question of scientific significance whether or not abstract objects exist besides the concrete in the natural world. It is also generally accepted that if we remove the metaphysical and mythical appendages that have surrounded the Platonic theory of the Forms and which today have historical rather than theoretical interest, the Platonic "discovery" of ideal beings emerges even more as the great contribution of Plato to philosophy. Kant's important view on this point is not very well known; see *The Critique of Pure Reason* B, 370–371.
6. From a contemporary perspective on the problem of general concepts and given the content that the terms "Platonism" and "nominalism" assume today, there does not seem to be any room for theoretical support for this traditional conceptualism (conceptual realism), and particularly for psychological conceptualism (formation of general concepts by abstraction from experience, e.g., Locke: "to frame abstract ideas"). The latter, starting from the failure of the nominalistic interpretation of language, also ends up as a form of nominalism—this time at least without internal contradictions.

   That which certainly appears of great interest today in the theory of knowledge is so-called constructive conceptualism or constructionism, which reliable scholars consider to be an "unorthodox Platonism" to the extent that it involves an ontological questioning of the existence of ideal constructions. Perhaps in fact it is a variation of it, but free of contradictions which it avoids by its renunciation of "nonpredicative conceptual constructions" (nonpredicative concepts and definitions) and of "unpredicative conceptual constructions." We have in mind several such systems in the area of mathematics and mathematical logic of which the most known are those of Quine, Hao Wang, Kleene, Church, Turing, and other more recent systems. On the whole subject of the *universalia* problem, see now *Das Universalien-Problem*, ed. W. Stegmüller (Darmstadt: Wissenschaftliche Buchgesellschaft [Wege der Forschung 83] 1978): papers by B. Russell, F. P. Ramsey, P. Bernays, O. Quine, A. Church, N. Goodman, L. Henkin, Hao Wang, N. Chomsky, A. Ross Anderson, R. Carnap, and others.
7. Porphyry *Isagoge*, ed. A. Busse, *Commentaria in Aristotelem Graeca* (CAG) vol. IV, 1, p. 1, 9–13.
8. Ammonius *In Porph. Isagogen*, ed. A. Busse, CAG IV, 3, p. 87, 19–20.
9. It is clear that we have here a mixing of two different problems without, curiously, the substance of the matter being altered.

10. Ammonius *In Porph. Isagogen* 39–42 and 104–105; Philoponus *In Categorias*, CAG XIII, 9 and 167.

11. With this transfer of the Forms to the mind of the God-Creator, the primary significance of the Form as creative cause of the sensible weakens, of course, but the Form does not cease to have its defining role in relation to sensible particulars. The difference is that it becomes an intermediate cause between the God-creator and the creature.

In Christian writers and in Byzantium, the exemplary character of the Forms ("exemplarism") is utterly rejected: God has no need of models, especially those existing before him. The Forms will be reduced still further to simple thoughts of the demiurge (Psellos: "thoughts of the Creator," "the first concepts of the creative Mind"; Symeon Seth: "existing kinds in the creative Mind," etc.) and their self-existence is rejected even more categorically (τὸ αὐθύπαρκτον, τὸ ἀπόλυτον, τὸ ἐνυπόστατον, τὸ μένειν καθ' ἑαυτάς). In the most positive formulation they give, the Forms are the creative causes of the sensible, disseminated by the Creator in the natural world as instruments of his power.

12. Photius *Amphilochia* 76, p. 131ff.

13. P. Joannou, "Eustrate de Nicée. Trois pièces inédites de son procès (1117)," *Revue des Études Byzantines* 10 (1952), 34.

14. See L. Benakis, "The Problem of General Concepts and the Conceptual Realism of the Byzantines" (in Greek) *Philosophia* (Athens) 8–9 (1978–1979), 311–340 (especially 327–336).

THE PRIMACY OF EXISTENCE IN THE THOUGHT OF ERIUGENA

1. In this connection, one should consult, among others, the important studies of P. Hadot, *Porphyre et Victorinus* (Paris, 1968), vols. I and II, particularly pages 270ff., 280ff., 488ff.; also S. Gersh, *From Iamblichus to Eriugena* (Leiden, 1978).

2. That is, the word "creator" (Eriugena, *Expositiones* (*Exp.*) XIII, 607). The other terms, *creare, creaturae, ex nihilo,* are absent from the text of Dionysius.

3. R. Roques has already illustrated this working method of Eriugena with the aid of other examples; see *Libres sentiers vers l'érigénisme* (Rome, 1975), pp. 99–130. E. Jeauneau likewise dealt with this question in a lecture entitled "Les traductions de Jean Scot" at Dumbarton Oaks, Washington, D.C. (May 1977).

4. See R. Roques, *L'univers dionysien* (Paris, 1954), p. 41.

5. *Ibid.*, p. 79ff.

6. E. Gilson, in his book *L'Etre et l'essence* (Paris, 1948), has clearly shown that the question of origin raises that of existence, particularly on page 93 and the following pages.

7. Migne, *Patrologia graeca* (*PG*) III, 817, 816; see also *Celestial Hierarchy* ("Sources chrétiennes" series), IV, 1; XIII, 4.

8. *PG* 816; *Celestial Hierarchy* XIII, 4.

9. M. de Gandillac, in his translation of the *Celestial Hierarchy* (above note 7), has in my opinion interpreted this passage very well (p. 93).

10. *De divisione naturae* (*DDN*); Migne, *Patrologia latina* CXXII, 682; *Exp.* XIII, 405.

11. Column (Col.) 643.

12. Col. 682.

13. *Exp.* XIII, 607.

14. *DDN* 553.

15. *DDN* 453–454.

16. *DDN* 443, 644; *Exp.* IV, 133.

17. I accept the excellent translation of M. de Gandillac, *op. cit.,* p. 94, who writes: "La divinité sur-essentielle (i.e., au delà de l'être) est l'être de toute chose."

18. *Exp.* IV, 132. Eriugena here suspects the scribe of having written ΖΩΑ instead of ΟΝΤΑ; it matters little as these terms would be synonymous, if not for all the Greeks at least for Dionysius. It was a fine opportunity for him to translate ΟΝΤΑ by *entia* or *essentiae*. Why then *existentiae*?

19. *DDN* 462.

20. *DDN* 490, 776. See the analysis by B. Stock in *Actes du Colloque de Laon,* éd. CNRS (Paris, 1977), p. 327.
21. *DDN* 487.
22. *De Praedestinatione,* Migne, *Patrologia latina* CXXII, 390.
23. *Exp.* VIII, 76.
24. *DDN* 455.
25. *DDN* 759. That is to say that the term *"entia"* is known; there is already an attestation for it in the *Inst. Orat.* of Quintilian, VIII, 3[33].
26. *Exp.* IV, 132.
27. See the commentary by M. de Gandillac, *Actes du Colloque de Laon,* éd. CNRS (Paris, 1977), p. 398.
28. A metaphor analysed by E. Jeauneau, *Quatre thèmes érigéniens* (Montréal, 1978), p. 36ff.
29. *DDN* 470, 471, 472.
30. *Exp.* IV, 62.
31. *DDN* 471.
32. *DDN* 445.
33. *DDN* 444.
34. *DDN* 867. It was doubtless for that reason that Eriugena wrote a *De divisione naturae* and not a *De divisione essentiae.*
35. *DDN* 481.
36. *DDN* 482.
37. *DDN* 482.
38. *DDN* 445
39. *DDN* 443.
40. *DDN* 443.
41. *DDN* 444.
42. *DDN* 482, 639.

THE OVERCOMING OF THE NEOPLATONIC TRIAD OF BEING, LIFE, AND INTELLECT BY SAINT THOMAS AQUINAS

1. The Proclean authenticity of the *Elements of Theology,* which some had placed in doubt (namely, Bardenhewer and Geyer), is by now beyond discussion. On this point, see E. R. Dodds, *Proclus: The Elements of Theology* (Oxford, 1933), p. xiv, n. 3. Another problem is that of the dating of this work within the total literary output of Proclus. Its affinity with *The Platonic Theology* leaps to the eye of any reader, even in the edition of the entire text published by Portus (Hamburg, 1618). Instead of being a youthful work, as is commonly believed, could not the *Elements of Theology* perhaps derive from *The Platonic Theology* as a sort of compendium?

   I shall on occasion refer to William of Moerbeke's translation of the *Elements of Theology* in the edition of C. Vansteenkiste, "Procli Elementatio Theologica translata a Guilelmo de Moerbeke," *Tijdschrift voor Filosofie,* 13 (1951), pp. 263–302 and 491–531.

2. Dodds, p. xxv. On "absolute realism," see my *Tomismo e pensiero moderno* (Rome, 1969), pp. 440–441.

3. Saint Thomas Aquinas, *Super librum de causis expositio,* ed. H. D. Saffrey, Textus Philosophici Friburgenses, 4 / 5 (Fribourg and Louvain, 1954), lect. XVI, p. 94, lines 13–19; Pera, n. 318, p. 97a (since the edition of C. Pera [Turin, 1955] usually has a more accurate text, we shall follow it here):

   > Secundum autem Platonicas positiones, omne quod in pluribus invenitur oportet reducere ad aliquod primum quod per suam essentiam est tale, a quo alia per participationem talia dicuntur. Unde secundum eos virtutes infinitae reducuntur ad aliquod primum quod est essentialiter Infinitas virtutis; non quod sit virtus participata in aliqua re subsistente, sed quia est subsistens per seipsam.

4. See *De causis*, prop. II, in Otto Bardenhewer, *Die pseudo-aristotelische Schrift 'Ueber das reine Gute' bekannt unter dem Namen 'Liber de causis'* (Freiburg, 1882), p. 165. See also lect. II in Saint Thomas' commentary (Saffrey, p. 11).
5. Saint Thomas, *Super librum de causis expositio*, lect. XVI, Saffrey, p. 94, 11. 16–29.
6. Proclus, *Elements of Theology*, prop. 138, ed. Vansteenkiste, p. 505. For the Greek text, see Dodds, p. 122.
7. See Proclus, *Elements of Theology*, prop. 138, ed. Vansteenkiste, p. 505. The original Greek reads: πάντων, μετεχόντων τῆς θείας ἰδιότητος καὶ ἐκθεομένων πρωτιστόν ἐστι καὶ ἀκρότατον τὸ ὄν (ed. Dodds, p. 122).
8. See Saint Thomas, *Super librum de causis expositio*, lect. IV, Saffrey, p. 29, 11. 8–16; Pera, n. 102, p. 28b.
9. *De causis*, prop. IV, ed. Bardenhewer, p. 166, 11. 19–25.
10. "De hoc igitur esse in intelligentiis participato, rationem assignat quare sit maxime unitum: dicit enim quod hoc contingit propter propinquitatem suam primae causae, *quae est esse purum subsistens*, et est vere unum non participatum, in quo non potest aliqua multitudo inveniri differentium secundum essentiam: quod autem est propinquius ei quod est per se unum, est magis unitum quasi participans unitatem. Unde intelligentia, quae est propinquissima causae primae, habet esse maxime unitum" (Saint Thomas, *Super librum de causis expositio*, lect. IV, Saffrey, p. 29, 11. 16–24).
11. It is not easy to decipher a text as difficult as that of the *De causis* in regard to what it preserves and what it lets drop of the complicated Proclean derivations. The key, it seems to me, is indicated in prop. II, which simplifies the triadic process by dividing *esse superius*, which is the sphere of the divine (τὸ Θεῖον) into *ante aeternitatem, cum aeternitate*, and *post aeternitatem et supra tempus*, which are respectively the First Cause, Intelligence, and Soul. The three propositions of Proclus to which Saint Thomas refers do not speak of the First Cause at all but treat of the sphere of the real as such, namely τὸ ὄντως ὄν. The Angelic Doctor himself understands the ". . . *enter ens* per oppositum ad mobiliter ens, sicut esse stans dicitur per oppositum ad moveri" and such is then the *esse superius* (lect. 2, Saffrey, p. 13, 11. 9–11). In the commentary on prop. 86, in which τὸ ὄντως ὄν appears for the first time in the technical sense, Dodds (p. 245) denotes it by *the One* while he translates (and does so better) *in loco* by *the true Being* (p. 79). The fact then that Proclus qualifies τὸ ὄντως ὄν as ἄπειρον . . . κατὰ δύναμιν μονήν does not at all demonstrate that it is the One, not only because πέρας and ἄπειρον are proper determinations of the sphere of οὐσία, but also because Proclus himself affirms the existence of a πρῶτον πέρας and of a πρώτη ἀπειρία (prop. 90) as principles of every composite. It is not a matter here of a simple nuance. The Platonic One and Good is ἐπέκεινα τῆς οὐσίας while τὸ ὄντως ὄν of Proclus, on the other hand, is composed of the finite and the infinite (prop. 89) and is said to be placed the "closest" and "most like" to the One, and therefore cannot itself be the One.

    It is Saint Thomas' merit to have given a metaphysical content to the *Sum, qui sum* of Exodus (3:14) by means of the concept of intensive *esse*. Neoplatonism certainly noticed the break between the One, the Forms or Ideas (the "participations"), and the concrete things (the things which participate), but it did not succeed in bridging this gap. The One always remains isolated because there is lacking free creation.
12. Cf. Emile Bréhier, *La philosophie de Plotin* (Paris, 1928), p. 38; idem, *The Philosophy of Plotinus*, trans. Joseph Thomas (Chicago, 1958), p. 46.
13. *The Platonic Theology* III, c. 7; ed. Portus, p. 135. Proclus explains the relations of appendage by way of a *circle* (III, 9, p. 135). Further on the dependence of the three hypostases on the first divinity is expressly affirmed (IV, c. 3, p. 185). This triad is then in its turn the source and cause of everything which comes after it (III, c. 21, p. 172). It should be noted that in all these complex schemes of metaphysical phylogenesis, of which *The Platonic Theology* is so extraordinarily rich, the fundamental triad is always stated in this order: οὐσία, ζωή, νοῦς, and this is also to be noted in the *Elements of Theology*. On the probable origin of this latter doctrine, which sets forth life as the dynamic bond between οὐσία and νοῦς, see the commentary of Dodds, p. 252ff. and C. Fabro, *Partecipazione e causalità* (Turin, 1960), p. 412ff.
14. According to the Platonic conception of "vertical falling," as it has been called.

15. Saint Thomas, *Super librum de causis expositio,* lect. III, Saffrey, p. 18, 11. 14–23; Pera, n. 66, p. 20a:

> Inter has tamen formas hunc ordinem ponebat: quod quanto aliqua forma est universalior, tanto est magis simplex et prior causa: participatur enim a posterioribus formis. Sicut si ponamus animal participari ab homine et vita ab animali, et sic de aliis. Ultimum autem quod ab omnibus participatur, et ipsum nihil aliud participat, est ipsum Unum et Bonum separatum quod dicebat summum Deum et primam omnium causam. Unde et in libro Procli inducitur propositio CXVI talis: *Omnis Deus participabilis est, . . . excepto uno.*

The passage cited from Proclus is: πᾶς Θεὸς μεθεκτός ἐστι, πλὴν τοῦ ἑνός (ed. Dodds, p. 102; ed. Vansteenkiste, p. 497). On Proclus' oscillation regarding this principle, see Dodds' commentary, p. 262.

16. *Ibid.,* p. 18, 1. 23 to p. 19, 1.9; Pera, n. 67, p. 20a.
17. *Ibid.,* p. 19, 11. 21–28; Pera, n. 70, p. 20b. Saint Thomas here quotes Proclus, *Elements,* prop. 129 (ed. Dodds, p. 114, 1. 11).
18. *Ibid.,* p. 19, 1. 28 to p. 20, 1. 4; Pera, n. 68–71, p. 20ab.
19. *Ibid.,* p. 21, 11. 9–24; Pera, n. 78, p. 21b.
20. *Ibid.,* p. 22, 1. 13 to p. 23, 1. 20.
21. *De causis,* prop. XVII, ed. Bardenhewer, p. 179, 1. 23 and p. 180, 11. 2–5.
22. Saint Thomas, *Super librum de causis expositio,* lect. XVIII, Saffrey, p. 104, 11. 1–9; Pera, n. 345, pp. 103b–104a.
23. *Ibid.,* p. 104, 11. 9–14; Pera, n. 345–347, pp. 103b–104b:

> Quia ergo intelligere praesupponit vivere, et vivere praesupponit esse, esse autem non praesupponit aliquid aliud, inde est quod primum ens *dat esse omnibus per modum creationis. Prima autem vita,* quaecumque sit illa, non dat vivere per modum creationis sed *per modum formae* scilicet informationis. Et similiter dicendum est de intelligentia.

24. *Ibid.,* p. 104, 11. 14–16; Pera, n. 348, p. 104b:

> Ex quo patet quod cum supra dixit intelligentiam esse causam animae, non intellexit quod esset eius causa per modum creationis, sed solum per modum informationis.

25. *Ibid.,* lect. V, Saffrey, p. 38, 11. 1–9; Pera, n. 139, p. 36b. See *De causis,* prop. IV; ed. Bardenhewer, p. 167,1. 24 to p. 168, 1. 2.
26. *Ibid.,* p. 38, 11. 9–20. Modern historiography, especially under the influence of the studies of Werner Jaeger, accepts the "continuity of development" among Plato, Aristotle, and Neoplatonism. See Philip Merlan, *From Platonism to Neoplatonism* (The Hague, 1953), p. 169. Merlan remarks at the conclusion of his book: "It is perfectly legitimate to speak of an *Aristoteles Neoplatonicus*" (p. 195). Whatever be the case regarding the historic Aristotle, this statement can also hold for the Thomistic Aristotle.
27. It is instructive to compare this chapter with the *De spiritualibus creaturis,* a. 5, which has the identical scheme for the same argument, but which completely lacks the Neoplatonic theory of the intermediaries. That theory constitutes the principal part of the *De substantiis separatis.* The other sporadic allusions to the Platonists in the *De spiritualibus creaturis* are also somewhat vague. See a. 8, ad 10 and a. 9, ad 2.
28. Saint Thomas, *De substantiis separatis,* c. 1, n. 4; ed. Perrier, p. 125:

> Una quidem secundum quod apprehendit numeros mathematicos et magnitudines et figuras mathematicas sine materiae sensibilis intellectu. . . . Alia vero abstractione utitur intellectus noster intelligendo aliquod universale absque consideratione alicuius particularis

29. *Ibid.,* c. 1, n. 5; ed. Perrier, p. 126 (trans. Lescoe, modified):

> In ipsis etiam speciebus ordinem quemdam ponebat: quia secundum quod aliquid simplicius in intellectu, secundum hoc prius erat in ordine rerum. Id autem quod primo est in intellectu, est unum et bonum: nihil enim intelligit qui non intelligit unum et bonum. Unum autem et

bonum consequuntur se: unde ipsam primam ideam unius, quod nominabat secundum se unum et secundum se bonum, primum rerum principium esse ponebat, et hunc summum Deum esse dicebat.

Perrier accepts the reading "summum bonum" instead of the other reading of "summum Deum," which I think should be preferred. In fact, the latter appears in the same context further on, namely in c. 16, and also in the commentary on the *De coelo et mundo*, II, lect. 4, cited below in note 36.

30. Further on in c. 16 (n. 94; ed. Perrier, p. 185), Saint Thomas praises Dionysius on this subject for his notion of intensive *esse*: "In quo removet opinionem Platonicorum, qui ponebant quod ipsa essentia bonitatis erat *summus Deus,* sub quo erat alius Deus qui est ipsum esse, et sic de aliis."

31. In the *Super librum de causis expositio,* lect. III, Saffrey, p. 19, 1. 2, and lect. XVIII, Saffrey, p. 103, 1. 18, mention is made of an *intellectus idealis*. This position is quickly corrected by Saint Thomas with Dionysius.

32. Saint Thomas, *De substantiis separatis,* c. 1, nn.5–6:

> Sub hoc autem uno diversos ordines participantium et participatorum instituebat in substantiis a materia separatis: quod quidem omnes ordines secundos deos esse dicebat, quasi quasdam unitates secundas post primam simplicem unitatem.
>
> Rursus, quia omnes aliae species participant uno, ita etiam oportet quod intellectus ad hoc quod intelligat, participet entium speciebus. Ideo sicut sub summo Deo, qui est unitas simplex et imparticipata, sunt aliae species quasi unitates secundae et dii secundi, ita sub ordine harum specierum et unitatum ponebat ordinem intellectuum separatorum, quia partici- pant supradictas species ad hoc quod sint intelligentes in actu: inter quos tanto unusquisque est superior, quanto propinquior est primo intellectui, qui plenam habet participationem specierum, sicut in diis seu unitatibus tanto unusquisque est superior, quanto perfectius participat unitatem primam.
>
> Separando autem intellectum a diis, non excludebat quin dii essent intelligentes; sed volebat quod superintellectualiter intelligerent, non quidem quasi participantes aliquas species, sed per se ipsos; ita tamen quod nullus eorum esset bonus et unus nisi per participationem primi et unius boni.

33. *Ibid.,* c. 1, n. 6; ed. Perrier, p. 126:

> Rursus, quia animas quasdam intelligentes videmus, non autem hoc convenit animae ex eo quod est anima (alioquin sequeretur quod omnis anima esset intelligens, et quod anima secundum totum id quod est esset intelligens), ponebat ulterius, quod sub ordine intellectuum separatorum esset ordo animarum, quarum quaedam, superiores videlicet, participant intellec- tuali virtute; infirmae vero ab hac virtute deficiunt.
>
> Rursus, quia corpora videntur non per se moveri . . ., ponebat corporibus accidere in quantum participabant animam: nam illa corpora quae ab animae participatione deficiunt, non moventur nisi ab alio. Unde ponebat animabus proprium esse quod se ipsas moverent secundum se ipsas.

34. *Ibid.,* c. 1, n. 7; ed. Perrier, p. 127.

35. *Ibid.,* c. 9, n. 60:

> His autem rationibus moti Platonici posuerunt quidem omnium immaterialium substantiarum et universaliter omnium existentium Deum esse immediate causam essendi secundum praedictum productionis modum, qui est absque mutatione vel motu; posuerunt tamen secundum alias participationes bonitatis divinae ordinem quemdam causalitatis in praedictis substantiis.

As we have seen, this affirmation, which is of major import in Thomism, goes beyond the Neoplatonic dialectic. It also constitutes the innovation in Thomas' turning things upside down in his comparison of Plato and Aristotle.

36. Saint Thomas, *De substantiis separatis,* c. 9, n. 61; ed. Perrier, p. 162ff. The following synthetic

exposition in a commentary on Aristotle which is contemporaneous with the *De substantiis separatis* should be noted:

> Considerandum est quod Platonici ponebant unum *Deum summum,* qui est ipsa essentia boni-tatis et unitatis, sub quo ponebant ordinem superiorum *intellectuum* separatorum, qui apud nos consueverunt intelligentiae vocari; sub hoc ordine ponebant ordinem *animarum,* sub quo ordine ponebant ordinem corporum. Dicebant ergo quod inter intellectus separatos superiores, primi dicuntur *intellectus divini,* propter similitudinem et propinquitatem ad Deum; alii vero non sunt divini, propter distantiam ad Deum; sicut etiam animarum supremae sunt intellectivae, infimae autem non intellectivae sed irrationales. *Corpora* etiam suprema et nobiliora dicebant esse *animata,* alia vero inanimata. Rursus dicebant quod *supremae animae* propter hoc quod dependent ex intelligentiis divinis, sunt *animae divinae:* et iterum corpora suprema propter hoc quod sunt coniuncta animabus divinis, sunt corpora divina (Saint Thomas, *In librum II De coelo et mundo expositio,* lect.4, *Opera omnia,* XIX [Parma, 1866], p. 87b).

It is satisfying to note that in his mature commentaries Saint Thomas frequently sees Aristotle in agreement with Plato on this point.

37. Saint Thomas, *De substantiis separatis,* c. 17, n. 111; ed. Perrier, p. 198. Cf. Proclus, *Elements of Theology,* prop. 196, ed. Vansteenkiste, p. 525; Dodds, pp. 170 and 300. The meaning of this proposition from Proclus is that only the unparticipated Soul is wholly lacking in corporeity, since every other soul has a relationship with the "first body" (πρῶτον σῶμα) and the "first vehicle" (πρῶτον ὄχημα). See again Dodds, p. 313ff.: "The Astral Body in Neoplatonism."

38. Saint Thomas points out the agreement of the two schools on this point. See *Super librum de causis expositio,* lect. II, Saffrey, p. 12; lect. XI, Saffrey, pp. 73–75, with appropriate discussion; lect. XXX, Saffrey, p. 137, for the eternal motion of the heavens.

39. According to Saint Thomas, the *De causis* is divided into the following general sections: prop. I, general theorem; prop. II–XV, the distinction of the causes; prop. XVI–XXXII, the coordination or dependence or comparison of the causes to one another. On the structure of the *Elements,* see Dodds, pp. 187, 193, 200–201, 212, 223, 227, 230, 236, 240, 246, 250, 257, 284, and 294.

40. The superiority of the *Parmenides* over the other dialogues of Plato, which even involves the reduction of the latter to the former, is the point of departure for the dialectical method of Proclus. One aspect of that dialogue's superiority is its reference to Parmenides himself. See *The Platonic Theology,* I, c. 9; ed. Portus, p. 17ff. See also c. 10, p. 23, and earlier c. 7, p. 16. In c. 10, p. 21, Proclus cites his commentary on the *Parmenides.*

41. *De causis,* prop. I, ed. Bardenhewer, p. 163, 1. 3.

42. We observe something similar a century earlier in Nicholas of Methone or Messene, who often appeals to Dionysius. See his *Institutionis Theologiae Procli Refutatio,* ed. J. Th. Voemel (Frankfurt, 1825), pp. 6, 9, 17, 25, and 31. In the commentary on prop. LXXVI, p. 102ff., Dionysius is cited for having placed the "Ideas" of things in God.

43. In like fashion, there are many secondary universal causes. However, Saint Thomas still leaves out the "universalis" and it is not by chance that he does so.

44. Saint Thomas, *Super librum de causis expositio,* lect. I, Saffrey, pp. 5–6; Pera, n. 21, p. 6a.

45. *Ibid.,* lect I, Saffrey, p. 7, 11. 11–16; Pera, n. 24, p. 6a;

> Ergo hoc ipsum quod causa secunda sit causa effectus, habet a prima causa: esse ergo causam effectus inest primo primae causae, secundo autem causae secundae. Quod autem est prius in omnibus, est magis, quod perfectiora sunt priora naturaliter; ergo prima causa est magis causa effectus quam causa secunda.

46. *De causis,* prop. I, ed. Bardenhewer, p. 164, 11. 3–6 and 12–16:

> Iam ergo manifestum est et planum quod causa prima longinqua est plus comprehendens et *vehementius* causa rei quam causa propinqua, et propter hoc fit eius operatio *vehementioris adhaerentiae* cum re quam operatio causae propinquae . . ., et quando removetur causa secunda a causato suo non removetur causa prima, quoniam *causa prima est maioris et vehementioris adhaerentiae cum re quam causa propinqua* et non figitur causatum causae secundae nisi per virtutem causae primae.

For "vehementius" the German version of Bardenhewer has "in hoheren Grade" (p. 59), which is certainly weaker. Proclus has μειζόνως (prop. 56; p. 54, lines 5 and 16), which Dodds (p. 55) translates as "in greater measure." The Latin version is far more effective.

47. Saint Thomas, *Super librum de causis expositio,* lect. I, Saffrey, p. 8, 11. 21–26; Pera, n. 34, p. 6b:

> Manifestum est enim quod quanto aliqua causa efficiens est prior, tanto eius virtus ad plura se extendit; unde oportet quod proprius eius effectus communior sit; causae vero secundae proprius effectus in paucioribus invenitur, unde et particularior est. Ipsa enim causa prima producit vel movet causam secundam agentem et sic fit ei causa ut agat.

48. Proclus, *Elements of Theology,* prop. 56, ed. Vansteenkiste, p. 286:

> Omne quod a secundis producitur et a prioribus et causalioribus producitur eminentius . . . . Si enim secundum totam habet substantiam ab eo quod ante ipsum, et potentia sibi producendi inde est. Et enim potentiae productivae secundum substantiam sunt in producentibus et complent ipsorum substantiam. Si autem potentiam producendi a superiori causa sortita sunt, ab illa habent quod sint causa quorum sunt causa, mensurata inde secundum hypostaticam potentiam.

Identical terminology is to be found in the following proposition, namely, prop. 57. There "producere" is used to translate the Greek παράγειν which on other occasions is expressed by "derivare" (cf. Dodds, p. 54). We can observe that the problem of "producere" is discussed much earlier in the *Elements.* Following after the prologue, which contains the general doctrine of participation, the term appears explicitly in prop. 7: "Omne *productivum* alterius melius est quam natura eius quod producitur" (ed. Vansteenkiste, p. 267). Cf. especially prop. 25–30, which prepare for the doctrine of ἐπιστροφή.

49. Saint Thomas, *Super librum de causis expositio,* lect. I, Saffrey, p. 8, line 8 to p. 9, line 1:

> Inveniuntur igitur praedicta tria quae tacta sunt [causa prima *plus influit* . . . , *tardius recedit, prius advenit!*] primordialiter quidem in causis efficientibus et ex hoc manifestum est quod derivatur ad causas formales: unde et hic ponitur verbum *influendi,* et Proclus utitur verbo *productionis* quae exprimit causalitatem causae efficientis.

50. *Ibid.,* lect. I, Saffrey, p. 9, 11. 14–19; Pera, n. 38, p. 7a:

> Comparatur autem prima omnium causa ad totam naturam sicut natura ad artem. Unde id quod primo subsistit in tota natura est a prima omnium causa quod appropriatur singulis rebus officio secundarum causarum.

Since Proclus expressly holds to this doctrine in the *Elements of Theology,* prop. 72 (ed. Vansteenkiste, p. 292), it is strange that Saint Thomas does not appeal to it here. However, the principle is present in an implicit form in prop. 57, which was cited by Saint Thomas. This extension of the causality of the One to prime matter is a post-Platonic development which is already found expressly in Syrianus (cf. Dodds, p. 231).

In *The Platonic Theology,* the creation or production of matter is the work of some one of the gods situated above the demiurge, while the demiurge of the whole places order and arrangement in the complex. The term used most frequently to indicate creation is ἀπογεννᾶν and it seems to be a question of total production, though not from nothing in the biblical sense. In fact, Proclus uses the term πρόεισιν (see especially V, c. 17; ed. Portus, p. 281) both for the origin of matter and also for bodies.

51. Saint Thomas, *Super librum de causis expositio,* lect. I, Saffrey, p. 9, 11. 19–25; Pera, n. 39, p. 7a:

> Nam propter ultimum finem, qui est universalis, alii fines appetuntur, quorum appetitus advenit post appetitum ultimi finis, et ante ipsum cessat. Sed et huius ordinis ratio ad genus causae efficientis reducitur: nam finis in tantum est causa in quantum movet efficientem ad agendum, et sic prout habet rationem moventis pertinet quodammodo ad causae efficientis genus.

THE PROBLEM OF THE REALITY AND MULTIPLICITY OF DIVINE IDEAS IN CHRISTIAN NEOPLATONISM

1. Cf. Plato's famous description of the ideas as "the really real" (*to ontos on*) in *Phaedo* 65–66 and other classic discussions of the ideas.
2. Cf. *Parmenides* 132b–c (trans. Cornford):

   "But Parmenides, said Socrates, may it not be that each of these forms is a thought, which cannot properly exist anywhere but in a mind? In that way each of them can be one and the statements that have just been made would no longer be true of it.

   Then, is each form one of these thoughts and yet a thought of nothing?

   No, that is impossible.

   So it is a thought of something?

   Yes.

   Of something that is, or of something that is not?

   Of something that is."
3. Cf. *Enneads* VI, 7, 15–16 (trans. MacKenna-Page), and occasionally through V, 1–2. In these passages the Ideas are spoken of as the product of the Intellectual-Principle.
4. *Enneads* V, 9, 7–8. Cf. also V, 3, VI, 6, 7–8, and off and on throughout V, 1–2. The essence of the position is that *Nous* and its objects constitute a single interdependent relational unity, neither properly prior to the other, nor constituted together as a unitary life *simultaneously* by the overflow of the Good. But see VI, 6, 8 for a priority of being over *Nous*: "First, then, we take Being as first in order; then the Intellectual Principle. . . . Intellectual Principle as the Act of Real Being, is a second." The Greek texts here are entirely clear, the terms used being *pro, proteron*, etc.
5. This doctrine is clear, explicit, and constant throughout the *Enneads*. Cf. V, 1, 4; V, 6; V, 3, 10–15; V, 6; V, 9, 6; VI, 6, 9; VI, 7, 13 and 17. The intellectual realm is always a one-many, both because Being as object is distinct from the act that knows it and because each Being-Idea is distinct from every other, though not divided from it.
6. Anton Pegis has admirably summed up the dilemma posed to Christian thought by the Platonic world of ideas: "St. Augustine . . . thought to baptize the Platonic Forms and to make them ideas in the mind of God. But this was easier to assert than to accomplish philosophically. For the perplexing mystery of the Platonic Forms is that in a Christian world they can be neither God nor creatures. They cannot be creatures because they are immutable and eternal; and they cannot be God because they are a real plurality of distinct and distinctly determined essences. Yet they rose before the minds of Christian thinkers again and again, and they hovered somewhere on the horizon between God and creatures, strange aliens both from heaven and from earth, and yet aliens whose message proved so enduringly dear to Christian thinkers that, rather than forget it, they exhausted their energies in pursuing it." "The Dilemma of Being and Unity," in R. Brennan, *Essays in Thomism* (New York: Sheed and Ward, 1942), pp. 158–159. The whole article, in fact, is a brilliant example of a truly philosophical study in depth of the history of philosophy.
7. Cf. for example his famous brief treatise on the ideas, *De Diversis Quaestionibus LXXXIII*, Qu. 46 (Migne, *Pat. Lat*, XL, 29–31), and other standard references.
8. Cf. F. J. Thonnard, "Ontologie augustinienne," *L'Année théologique augustinienne* 14 (1954), 39-52, esp. pp. 42–43. Clear texts are in Augustine *De Trin*. V, 2, 3: "Ab eo quod est esse dicta est essentia," and *De Immortalitate Animae* XII, 19: "Omnis enim essentia non ob aliud essentia est, nisi quia est."
9. *De Trinitate* V, 2, 3.
10. *Sermo* VII, n. 7.
11. *De Moribus Manichaeorum* VII, 7
12. *Contra Manichaeos*, c. 19 (*PL*, XLII, 557). On the above texts see V. Bourke, *St. Augustine's View of Reality* (University of Villanova Press, 1965), and J. Anderson, *St. Augustine and Being* (The Hague: Nijhoff, 1966).
13. It has been called to my attention, however, by the Augustinian scholar, Robert J. O'Connell, that

Augustine, in *Confessions* X, c. 9–12, when speaking about memory, distinguished between the *sensible images* of past contingent events, such as going to the Tiber river, and the *intellectual intuition* of numbers and their relations, which intuition puts us in contact with the *very things themselves* (*res ipsae*), with the very reality of numbers, which *truly are* (*valde sunt*), hence buried deep in our intellectual memory, which is always in contact with the immutable and eternal truths of the intelligible world through divine illumination. Now since, as *rationes aeternae*, numbers are certainly on a par with all the other *rationes aeternae*, it would seem necessary to conclude by analogy that all the *rationes aeternae* are also *res ipsae, et valde sunt* (c. 12). Yet Augustine never quite seems to go this far or work out the implications.

14. On John Scottus Eriugena's doctrine, see M. Cappuyns, *Jean Scot Erigène* (Paris: Desclée, 1933); H. Bett, *Johannes Scotus Erigena* (New York: Russell & Russell, 1964); J. Trouillard, "Erigène et la théophanie créatrice," in J. O'Meara and L. Bieler, eds., *The Mind of Eriugena* (Dublin: Irish Univ. Press, 1973), 98–113; T. Gregory, *Giovanni Scoto Eriugena* (Florence: Felice Le Monnier, 1963), ch. I: "Dall' Uno al Molteplice"; and the standard histories of Gilson, etc.

15. Cf. *De Divisione Naturae* II, c. 36 (I, ed. Sheldon-Williams, *Johannis Scotti Eriugenae Periphyseon*, Dublin Inst. for Advanced Studies, 1972, pp. 205ff.). See also other main discussions of the primordial causes, *De Div. Nat.* III, c. 1–17 (M. Uhlfelder and J. Potter, *John the Scot: Periphyseon—On the Division of Nature*, Indianapolis: Bobbs Merrill, 1976).

16. *De Div. Nat.* II. c. 4–9. Thus material things exist more perfectly even in the mind of man, as spiritual, than in themselves.

17. *De Div. Nat.* III, c. 1 (trans. Uhlfelder and Potter, p. 129): "The first causes themselves are, in themselves, one, simple, defined by no known order, and unseparated from one another. Their separation is what happens to them in their effects. In the monad, while all numbers subsist in their reason alone, no number is distinguished from another; for all are one and a simple one, and not a one compounded from many. . . . Similarly the primordial causes while they are understood as stationed in the Beginning of all things, *viz.*, the only-begotten Word of God, are a simple and undivided one; but when they proceed into their effects, which are multiplied to infinity, they receive their numerous and ordered plurality, . . . all order in the highest Cause of all and in the first participation in it is one and simple distinguished by no differentiae; for there all orders are indistinguishable, since they are an inseparable one, from which the multiple order of all things descends."

18. Thus in *Enneads* VI, 6, 9 in the order of Being in the *Nous* number is declared to be already *unfolded, not* as it is in the Monad or One. In V, 3, 15, all the ideas are unfolded as distinct in the *Nous*, which thus becomes a one-many, whereas the One should not be said to contain all things as in an indistinct total. See the other texts in note 5. Thus what Eriugena describes as the mode of the primordial causes in the Word is explicitly denied by Plotinus of the divine *Nous* and could be applied only to the One, in which the ideas could in no way be said to be present.

19. *De Div. Nat.* II, c. 20 (ed. Sheldon-Williams, p. 77).

20. *Ibid.*, II, 8 (ed. Sheldon-Williams, p. 29). For this identity of the being of things with the thought of them, see Bett, *op. cit.*, in n. 14, pp. 51, 145; Gregory, *op. cit.*, in n. 14, p. 12: "Gli essere nella mente di Dio si risolvono nell'atto con cui elgi li conosce."

21. Cf. E. Gilson, *History of Christian Philosophy in the Middle Ages* (New York: Random House, 1954), ch. III: "Platonism in the Twelfth Century"; N. Häring, *Life and Works of Clarembald of Arras* (Toronto: Pontifical Institute of Medieval Studies, 1965).

22. Clarembald of Arras, *Tractatus super Librum Boetii De Trinitate* (ed. Häring, *op. cit.* in n. 21), II, 41, p. 123.

23. *Ibid.*, II, 29–30, p. 118: "Forma sine materia est ens a se, actus sine possibilitate, necessitas, aeternitas. . .et ipsa Deus est."

24. Thierry of Chartres' commentary on Boethius' *De Trinitate*, called *Librum Hunc* (ed. W. Janssen, *Der Kommentar des Clarembaldus von Arras zu Boethius De Trinitate*; Breslau, 1926, p. 18): "Omnium formae in mente divina consideratae una quodammodo forma sunt, in formae divinae simplicitatem inexplicabili quodam modo relapsae."

25. See note 21.

26. *Tract. super Lib. Boet. De Trin.* I, 34 (Häring, p. 99): "Omnis multitudo in simplicitate unitatis

complicata latitat, et cum in serie numerandi post unam alterum et post alterum tercium numeratur, et deinceps tunc demum certa pluralitatis ab unitate profluentis forma cognoscitur, sicque sine alteritate nulla potest esse pluralitas."

27. *De Scientia Christi*, q. 2, c, Responsio (*Obras de S. Buenaventura*, Bibl. de Autores Christianos, Madrid, 1957), p. 138. Cf. also q. 3.

28. Cf. the standard treatments on the "Thomistic existentialism," introduced by St. Thomas: E. Gilson, *The Christian Philosophy of St. Thomas Aquinas* (New York: Random House, 1956), the famous chapter 1 on "Existence and Reality"; J. de Finance, *Etre et agir* (Rome: Gregorian University Press, 1960, 2nd ed.); and my own summaries: "What is Really Real?" in ed. J. Williams, *Progress in Philosophy* (Milwaukee: Bruce, 1955), pp. 61–90, and "What is Most and Least Relevant in the Metaphysics of St. Thomas Today?" *Internat. Phil. Quart.* 14 (1974), 411–434.

29. For Thomas' treatments on the divine ideas, see *Sum. c. Gentes* IV, c. 13, no. 10; *Sum. Theol.* I, q. 15 entire; I, q. 44, a. 3; I, q. 18, a. 4: "Whether All Things are Life in God"; *De Veritate*, q. 3, q. 4, a. 6 and 8. The description of the divine ideas as "invented" by God is in *De Ver.*, q. 3, a. 2 *ad* 6 m; as *rationes quasi excogitatas* is in *De Potentia*, q. 1, a. 5, *ad* 11 m.

30. For Thomas' fundamental criticism of the Platonic realism of ideas, see *In I Metaph.*, *lectio* 10; *In I De Anima*, *lect.* 4, and the general discussion with texts in R. Henle, *St. Thomas and Platonism* (The Hague: Nijhoff, 1956), part II, ch. 4: "Basic Principles of the *Via Platonica*."

31. *De Trinitate* VI, c. 8.

32. Cf., for example, the great Flemish mystic, Jan Ruusbroec. "According to the Flemish mystic, man's true essence (*wesen*) is his superessence (*overwesen*). Before its creation the soul is present to God as a pure image; this divine image remains its superessence after its actual creation." Louis Dupré, *Transcendent Selfhood* (New York; Seabury, 1976), p. 103–104.

33. See the texts in note 29, in particular *Sum. Theol.* I, q. 18, a. 4; *De Ver.*, q. 4, a. 8; *Sum. c. Gentes* IV, c. 13, n. 10 (Pegis trans.), and the special article just on this point, *De. Ver.*, q. 4, q. 6: "Whether Things are More Truly in the Word than in Themselves." *In I Sent.*, d. 36, q. 1, q. 3 *ad* 2 m (M837): four modes of *esse creaturae*.

St. Thomas' point is that if one looks at the mode of being of the thing in itself and in an idea (God's or man's), the *mode of being* in an idea, especially the divine idea, is a *spiritual* mode, identical with the being of the mind thinking it, hence from this point of view higher than the material being of a thing in itself; but if one considers the *proper mode* of a thing's *own being* as this thing, this is found only in the thing's own material being and not in its idea. Properly speaking, a thing's own being is not found in its idea. Thus Thomas is able to preserve intact the traditional formulas about the existence of things in the Word as more perfect, but the meaning he gives to them is notably different from their original intention, where his distinctions were not yet made.

34. Henry of Ghent, *Quodlibeta* IX, 2, cited in the fine study by Jean Paulus, *Henri de Gand* (Paris: Vrin, 1938), p. 91, n. 1.

35. *Summa*, 68, 5, 7-14, cited in Paulus, *loc. cit.*

36. *Loc. cit.* Cf. the illuminating remarks on Henry and his place in the history of our problem by Anton Pegis, *art. cit.* in note 6 above, esp. pp. 172–176.

37. *In I Sent.*, d. 35, q. 5; cited in Pegis, *art. cit.*, p. 170.

38. Gabriel Biel, *In I Sent.*, d. 35, q. 5C (Tübingen, 1501); cited in Pegis, p. 159.

39. *In I Sent.*, d. 17, q. 1, a. 3K; Pegis, p. 171.

40. *Art. cit.* in note 6, pp. 168–172.

MEISTER ECKHART ON GOD AS ABSOLUTE UNITY

1. *Meister Eckhart. Die deutschen und lateinischen Werken* (Stuttgart and Berlin: Kohlhammer, 1936ff.), hereafter abbreviated as *DW* and *LW*. The passage discussed may be found in *LW* V, pp. 37–48. The most complete study of this text is that of R. Imbach, *Deus est Intelligere* (Studia Friburgensia, N. F. 53. Freiburg, Sweiz, 1976). See also J. Caputo, "The Nothingness of the Intellect in Meister Eckhart's 'Parisian Questions,'" *The Thomist* 39 (1975), pp. 85–115.

2. "Dico nihilominus quod, si in deo est aliquid, quod velis vocare esse, sibi competit per intelligere" (*LW* V, p. 45. lines 4–5). The translation is that of A. Maurer, *Master Eckhart. Parisian Questions and Prologues* (Toronto: Pontifical Institute of Mediaeval Studies, 1974), p. 48.

3. E.g., R. Klibansky, *Magistri Eckhardi Opera Latina XIII* (Leipzig-Rome: Santa Sabina, 1936), p. xix.

4. For an outline of some of these positions, see Imbach, p. 290, n. 42.

5, E.g., *Predigt* (hereafter *Pr.*) 52 "Beati pauperes spiritu" (*DW* II, p. 492). I have examined this problem in greater detail in my paper "The God Beyond God: Theology and Mysticism in the Thought of Meister Eckhart" *The Journal of Religion* 61 (1981), pp. 1–19.

6. See, e.g., D. T. Suzuki, *Mysticism Christian and Buddhist. The Eastern and Western Way* (New York: MacMillan, 1957), pp. 18–21. For a nuanced discussion of the implications of the breakthrough to the Godhead in Eckhart, see R. Schürmann, *Meister Eckhart Mystic and Philosopher* (Bloomington: University of Indiana Press, 1978), pp. 114–118, 156–165, and 213.

7. E.g., V. Lossky, *Théologie négative et connaissance de Dieu chez Maître Eckhart* (Paris: Vrin, 1960), pp. 342–345 and 363–367; and J. Loeschen, "The God Who Becomes: Eckhart on Divine Relativity," *The Thomist* 35 (1971), pp. 417–419. The problem is also raised by M. de Gandillac, "La 'dialectique' du Maître Eckhart," *La mystique rhénane* (Colloque de Strasbourg, 1961; Paris: Presses universitaires, 1963), pp. 73–75.

8. *In agro dominico*, art. 22: "Pater generat me suum filium et eundem filium. Quidquid Deus operatur, hoc est unum; propter hoc generat ipse me suum filium sine omni distinctione" (Denzinger, *Enchiridion Symbolorum*[32] #972, olim 522). The excerpt is based on a passage in *Pr.* 6 "Iusti vivent in aeternum" (*DW* I, pp. 109.7–110.1). Eckhart's teaching on this point is also condemned in articles 11, 12, 13, 20, and 21, as well as being implied in appended article 1 concerning the uncreated element in the soul.

9. The *Defense* has been edited both by A. Daniels and G. Théry. I make use of Théry's edition here, "Edition critique des pièces relatives au procès d'Eckhart contenues dans le manuscrit 33b de la bibliothèque de Soest," *Archives d'histoire doctrinale et littéraire du moyen âge* 1 (1926), pp. 129–268. See, e.g., pp. 197–199, 241–244 for a rebuttal on the birth of the Word in the soul, and pp. 188, 209–215, for one on the uncreated part of the soul.

10. K. Kertz comes close to this in his article "Meister Eckhart's Teaching on the Birth of the Divine Word in the Soul," *Traditio* 15 (1959), pp. 327–363.

11. *LW* I, pp. 131–132, 166–170, 181.

12. E.g., *In Ex.* n. 15 (*LW* II, p. 21); *In Sap.* n. 20 (*LW* II, pp. 341–342); *In Io.* nn. 97 and 347 (*LW* III, pp. 83–84, and 321); and the *Defense* (ed. Théry, p. 195).

13. *In II Periherm.* lectio 2, #2–5, commenting on *Periherm.* 10 (19b20–25).

14. *LW* I, p. 167. 2–8: "Cum igitur dico aliquid esse, aut unum, verum seu bonum praedico, et in praedicato cadunt tamquam secundum adiacens praemissa quattuor et formaliter accipiuntur et substantive. Cum vero dico aliquid esse hoc, puta lapidem, et esse unum lapidem, verum lapidem aut bonum hoc, scilicet lapidem, praemissa quattuor accipiuntur ut tertium adiacens propositionis nec sunt praedicata, sed copula vel adiacens praedicati" (trans. Maurer, p. 94).

15. *LW* I, pp. 169. 6; 172. 6–9; 175. 12–176. 2.

16. *LW* I, p. 132. 4–5: "quod solus deus proprie est et dicitur ens, unum, verum et bonum" (trans. Maurer, p. 79). See also *LW* I, pp. 167. 9–10; and 181. 15.

17. ". . . quaedam copula" (*LW* I, p. 181. 14).

18. E.g., *Prologus* n. 3 (*LW* I, pp. 166.12–167.2); *In Io.* n. 60 (*LW* III, pp. 49. 13–50. 1); *Collatio in Sent.* n. 3 (*LW* V, p. 20. 2). The importance of the distinction has been underlined by K. Albert, "Der philosophische Grundgedanke Meister Eckharts," *Tijdschrift voor Filosofie* 27 (1965), pp. 320–39.

19. Almost all the major studies of Eckhart contain a treatment of his doctrine of analogy. In addition there are the valuable articles of M. de Gandillac, "La 'dialectique'," especially pp. 83–86; J. Koch, "Zur Analogielehre Meister Eckharts," *Mélanges offerts à Etienne Gilson* (Paris: Vrin, 1959), pp. 327–50; and F. Brunner, "L'analogie chez Maitre Eckhart," *Freiburger Zeitschrift für Philosophie und Theologie* 16 (1969), pp. 333–49.

20. *LW* V, p. 45. 1–2.

21. *LW* V, p. 54. 1–2.

22. *LW* II, pp. 280–83. Eckhart's starting point in Thomas Aquinas is *In I Sent*. d. 22, q.1, a.3, ad 2.
23. *LW* II, p. 282.1–5: ". . . analogata nihil in se habent positive radicatum formae secundum quam analogantur. Sed omne ens creatum analogatur deo in esse, veritate et bonitate. Igitur omne ens creatum habet a deo et in deo, non in se ipso ente creato, esse, vivere, sapere positive et radicaliter."
24. The term is that of Brunner, *op. cit.*, p. 341–342.
25. *LW* V, pp. 37–48. For other examples of this denial, see *In Io*. nn.5, 182–83 (*LW* III, pp. 7, 150–51).
26. *DW* V, pp. 8–61 *passim*, especially p. 30. 5–19. See also *Pr*.30 "Praedica Verbum" (*DW* II, pp. 93–109).
27. *History of Christian Philosophy in the Middle Ages* (New York: Random House, 1955), pp. 440–441.
28. "Zur Analogielehre," pp. 341–345. Brunner seems to agree when he detects traces of an analogy of intrinsic attribution (*op. cit.*, pp. 344–46).
29. See Lossky, *op. cit.*, pp. 315, 322–323, and 356–357 on this reversal. If I read him aright, the same is suggested by C. F. Kelley, *Meister Eckhart on Divine Knowledge* (New Haven: Yale University Press, 1977), p. 170.
30. See Koch, *op. cit.*, pp. 336–337, and Brunner, *op. cit.*, 347, for the contrast with analogy in Aquinas.
31. *Meister Eckhart on Divine Knowledge*, pp. 167–171.
32. *In agro dominico* art. 26 (D 976): "Omnes creaturae sunt unum purum nihil: non dico, quod sint quid modicum vel aliquid, sed quod sint unum purum nihil." The proposition is taken from *Pr*. 4, "Omne datum optimum" (*DW* I, pp. 69. 8–70. 1).
33. R.Schürmann, *op.cit.*, pp. 176–180, 185–192, has rightly emphasized the radical insufficiency of traditional notions of analogy to grasp the distinctive character of Eckhart's doctrine of God.
34. *LW* II, p. 482. 4–5: "Est igitur sciendum quod li unum idem est quod indistinctum. Omnia enim distincta sunt duo vel plura, indistincta vero omnia sunt unum."
35. Especially *LW* I, p. 172. 6–9. Slightly earlier in the *Prologus* Eckhart even seems to give priority to *unum* when he says: "Praeterea Boethius De Consolatione docet quod, sicut bonum et verum fundantur et finguntur per esse et in esse, *sic et esse fundatur et figitur in uno et per unum*" (p. 171.3–5). On *unum* as the *nomen super omne nomen*, see *In Gen* I, n. 84 (*LW* I, p. 64. 7–10).
36. *LW* II, pp. 482. 10–483. 1: "Dicens ergo deum esse unum vult dicere deum esse indistinctum ab omnibus, quod est proprietas summi esse et primi et eius bonitas exuberans."
37. These are found in *LW* II, pp. 484. 1–485. 2.
38. *LW* II, p. 485. 5–7: "Sciendum igitur ad praesens quod li unum primo est voce quidem negativum, sed re ipsa affirmativum. Item est negatio negationis, quae est purissima affirmatio et plenitudo termini affirmati." The two poles identified here are similar to the two functions of unity discussed by Lossky, *op. cit.*, p. 68–72: *l'identité exclusive* or *puritas* (my second pole), and *l'identité inclusive* or *plenitudo* (my first pole).
39. *LW* II, p. 486. 3–5: "Propter quod immediatissime se tenet ad esse, quin immo significat puritatem et medullam sive apicem ipsius esse, quam nec li esse significat."
40. Macrobius, *Comm. in Somn. Scip.* I. 6. 7; Boethius, *De Trin.* 2; Proclus, *Elementatio theologica*, prop. 1.
41. *LW* II, p. 489. 7–8: "Iuxta quod notandum quod nihil tam distinctum a numero et numerato sive numerabili, creato scilicet, sicut deus, et nihil tam indistinctum." For what follows, see also the excellent discussion in Lossky, *op.cit.*, pp. 261–263.
42. *LW* II, p. 490. 4–7: "omne quod indistinctione distinguitur, quanto est indistinctius, tanto est distinctius; distinguitur enim ipsa indistinctione. Et e converso, quanto distinctius, tanto indistinctius, quia distinctione sua distinguitur ab indistincto. Igitur quanto distinctius, tanto indistinctius; et quanto indistinctius, tanto distinctius, ut prius." Eckhart concludes by citing the authority of Aquinas and John Damascene.
43. I wish to thank Richard Kieckhefer and his seminar group for helpful suggestions regarding these paraphrases.
44. *LW* II, p. 491. 7–10: "nihil tam indistinctum ab aliquo quam ab illo, a quo distinctione ipsa

indistinguitur. Sed omne numerosum sive creatum sua distinctione indistinguitur a deo, ut dictum est supra. Ergo nihil tam indistinctum et per consequens unum. Indistinctum enim et unum idem. Quare deus et creatum quodlibet indistincta." The minor of the syllogism depends on the doctrine of *esse* advanced in n. 145 (p. 483. 4–7). This was the side of Eckhart's doctrine of God as Absolute Unity (taken in isolation, something which would have been anathema to the Meister) that was condemned in the Bull *In agro dominico* art. 10 (D960). The other two articles that attack his denial of distinction in God (arts. 23, 24) seem to be directed against the implications of the doctrine for faith in the Trinity.

45. Cited at *LW* II, p. 492. 3: "quanto quid est simplicius et unitius, tanto est potentius et virtuosius, plura potens."

46. This is logically distinct from the notion of identity that in its positive form lacks the dialectical character of *indistinctum*. *Sermo* XXIX n. 303 (*LW* IV, p. 269. 11–13) views *identitas* as one of the *consequentiae* of *unitas*.

47. The following list of examples is not exhaustive: *In Ex.* nn. 59–60, 102, 104, 107, and 117 (*LW* II, pp. 65–66, 104, 106, 107 and 112); *In Sap.* n. 52 (*LW* II, p. 379); *In Io.* nn. 99, 197, and 562 (*LW* III, pp. 85, 166, 489); *Sermones* II n. 7, X n. 105, XXIX n. 298, and XLIV. 1 n. 438 (*LW* IV, pp. 9, 100, 265, 368); and *Prol. gen.* n. 10 (*LW* I, p. 155).

48. See the note in *DW* I, pp. 361–362. Cf. B. Schmoldt, *Die deutsche Begriffssprache Meister Eckharts* (Heidelberg: Quelle, 1954), p. 37.

49. *Quod.* X, q. 1, a. 1, *ad* 3; and *In I Sent.* d. 24, q. 1, a. 3, *ad* 1.

50. *Procli Commentarium in Parmenidem*, eds. R. Klibansky and C. Labowsky in *Plato Latinus*, vol. III (London: Warburg Institute, 1953). On the question of the *negatio negationis* in Proclus and its possible influence on Eckhart, see W. Beierwaltes, *Proklos. Grundzüge seiner Metaphysik* (Frankfurt: Klostermann, 1965), pp. 361–366, 395–398.

51. *In Ex.* nn. 110–117 (*LW* II, pp. 109–117) centers on the analysis of three axioms: (a) "nihil tam dissimile quam creator et creatura quaelibet," (b) "nihil tam simile quam creator et creatura quaelibet," and (c) "nihil tam dissimile pariter et simile alteri cuiquam, quam deus et creatura quaelibet sunt et dissimilia et similia pariter" (p. 110. 3–6). The dialectical parallel of this text to that in the *Wisdom* commentary comes out most strongly on p. 112. 7–15. See the discussion of this text in Lossky, *op. cit.*, pp. 265–274.

52. E.g., *In Sap.* nn. 38–39 (*LW* II, pp. 359–360), stressing opposition more than dialectic; *In Io.* nn. 99, 103, 151, 206–208 (*LW* III, pp. 85, 88, 125, 174–176); *Sermones* VI. 1 n. 53, X n. 103, XXXIV. 2 n. 344, XXXVII n. 375, and XLIV. 1 n. 438 (*LW* IV, pp. 52, 98, 299, 320–321, 367–368).

53. *Sermo* IV. 1 n. 28 (*LW* IV, p. 28. 5–9): "quia sicut deus est in se indistinctissimus secundum naturam ipsius, utpote vere unus et propriissime et ab aliis distinctissimus, sic et homo in deo indistinctus ab omnibus, quae in deo sunt—nam *in ipso sunt omnia*—et simul distinctissimus ab omnibus aliis."

54. *Pr.* 52 "Beati pauperes" (*DW* II, p. 502. 5–9). The translation is that of R. Schürmann, *op. cit.*, pp. 218–219.

55. See K. Albert, *Meister Eckharts These vom Sein* (Saarbrücken: Universtäts-und Schulbuchverlag, 1976).

56. *In Io.* n. 360 (*LW* III, pp. 304–306).

57. *In Io.* nn. 511–513 (*LW* III, pp. 442–445). The same position can be found in nn. 516–518, and throughout the commentary on John 14:8 in nn. 546–565 (*LW* III, pp. 446–448, 477–493). See especially n. 562 (pp. 489–490).

58. This is clear from the discussion of *unum* in n. 513 (p. 444. 1–5). Here Eckhart approves the appropriation of *unum* or *unitas* to the Father, whereas in n. 360 he had distinguished between the *unitas* that signifies origin and is therefore proper to the Father and the hidden *li unum* which is proper to the divine ground and does not bear this positive connotation (p. 305. 9–306. 2).

59. *In Io.* n. 562 (*LW* III, p. 489. 3–10): "ratio enim entis est quid abiectum et indistinctum et ipsa sua indistinctione ab aliis distinguitur. Quo etiam modo deus sua indistinctione ab aliis distinctis quibuslibet distinguitur. Hinc est quod ipsa essentia sive esse in divinis ingenitum est et non gignens. Ipsum vero unum ex sui proprietate distinctionem indicat. Est enim unum in se indistinc-

tum, distinctum ab aliis et propter hoc personale est et ad suppositum pertinet cuius est agere. Propter quod sancti unum sive unitatem in divinis attribuunt primo supposito sive personae, patri scilicet."

60. Even presumably late texts maintain the priority of *intelligere* over *esse* in God when *esse* is conceived of as God's first external work innermost to all things, e.g., *In Io.* n. 34 (*LW* III, pp. 27–28).

61. *Sermo* XXIX n. 300 (*LW* IV, pp. 266–267).

62. See n. 301 (*LW* IV, p. 267. 10).

63. N. 304 (pp. 269. 15–270. 3): "Intellectus enim proprie dei est, *deus* autem *unus.* Igitur quantum habet unumquodque de intellectu sive de intellectuali, tantum habet dei et tantum de uno et tantum de esse unum cum deo. Deus enim unus est intellectus, et intellectus est deus unus." On this Sermon, see Lossky, *op. cit.*, pp. 165–173, Imbach, *op. cit.*, pp. 173–174.

64. *Théologie négative*, especially pp. 60–64, 86–96, 200–207, 218, and 254–276. See the treatment of God as *unum* in Imbach, *op. cit.*, pp. 188–194.

65. *Art. cit.*, especially pp. 87–94.

66. E.g., H. Hof, *Scintilla animae* (Lund: Gleerup, 1952), pp. 105–112, 152–158, who has Hegel in mind; and J. Loeschen, *art. cit.*, pp. 416 and 422, who never gives the reader any hint of what he understands by dialectic. For an introduction to the variety of ways in which dialectic has been understood in the history of philosophy, see R. Hall, "Dialectic," *Encyclopedia of Philosophy* vol. II (New York: MacMillan, 1967), pp. 385–389.

67. *Hegel's Dialectic. Five Hermeneutical Studies* (New Haven, Conn.: Yale University Press, 1976), pp. 20–22.

68. Gadamer argues for the latter on pp. 22–27.

69. *From Iamblichus to Eriugena* (Leiden: Brill, 1978), pp. 153–167, 283–288. In terms of the exegetical background to this shift, Gersh (pp. 11, 155, and 166, note 181) follows E. Corsini in seeing it as involving the application of both the First Hypothesis (negative) and the Second Hypothesis (positive) of the *Parmenides* to the Christian God.

70. E.g., *Enneads* V. 5. 1, V. 5.9, and VI. 4–5. On this dialectic of immanence and transcendence in Plotinus, see R. Arnou, *Le désir de Dieu dans la philosophie de Plotin* (Rome: Gregorian University Press, 1967²), pp. 148–185; and E. Bréhier, *The Philosophy of Plotinus* (Chicago: University of Chicago Press, 1958), p. 159.

71. Indicative of this new dimension in Christian thought are the differences that W. Beierwaltes discerns between the Proclean and the Eckhartian understandings of the *negatio negationis*, especially concerning the positive and personalistic dimensions in Eckhart (*Proklos*, pp. 395–398).

72. *Dialogus de substantiis separatis physicis* (Strasbourg: Grataroli, 1567, reprint: Frankfurt: Minerva, 1967, p. 306).

73. Especially in #209, 213–215.

74. This has recently been pointed out by B. Gerrish, *Tradition in the Modern World. Reformed Theology in the Nineteenth Century* (Chicago: University of Chicago Press, 1978), pp. 46–47. "Codetermination" is Gerrish's term, not Schleiermacher's.

75. "Dialektik und Analogie des Seins," *Scholastik* 26 (1951), pp. 57–86.

76. *Art. cit.*, p. 82.

77. *Art. cit.*, pp. 83–86.

78. Lossky discusses Coreth in *op. cit.*, pp. 260–261, note 42; and p. 322, note 313.

79. *Théologie négative*, p. 275.

NEOPLATONISM AND CHRISTIAN THOUGHT IN THE FIFTEENTH CENTURY (NICHOLAS OF CUSA AND MARSILIO FICINO)

1. *Nikolaus von Cues und die griechische Sprache* (Heidelberg, 1938).

2. The Letter to Paul II is quoted in the partial critical edition in Honecker, *op. cit.*, 70–73.

3. Cf. F. Masai, *Pléthon et le platonisme de Mistra* (Paris, 1956), p. 306ff.

4. *Ein Proklosfund* (Heidelberg, 1929), p. 29, n. 2.

5. *De venatione sapientiae* (1463), ch. 20.

6. *Ibid.*, ch. 22.

7. *Directio speculantis*, or *De non aliud* (1462), ch. 20.

8. *De venatione*, ch. 21.

9. *Directio*, ch. 20.

10. Strasbourg ed. 1488, p. 76, Basel ed., 1565 p. 66; cf. *De venatione*, ch. 21: *Dionysius in hoc Platonem imitatur*; ch. 36: *ut recte dicebat Dionysius, quod et Plato prius viderat*.

11. *De venatione*, ch. 39.

12. *Ibid.*, ch. 17.

13. *Ibid.*, ch. 39.

14. In fact, the text of *Cel. Hier.* II 3, 140d to which Wilpert-Senger refer in their bilingual edition (Hamburg, 1970, p. 122) indicates only that the "revelatory sayings" of the "Thearchy" offer "images" that "signify what it is not, not what it is."

15. Strasbourg ed., p. 144; Basel ed., p. 127.

16. Strasbourg ed., p. 147; Basel ed., p. 130.

17. Strasbourg ed., pp. 148–151; Basel ed., p. 131–134.

18. *Directio*, ch. 21.

19. *De beryllo*, chaps. 5 and 36.

20. *De venatione*, ch. 21; cf. ch. 8.

21. Cf. Prov. 1:29.

22. Anonymous here, but Wilpert, in his bilingual edition of Book II (Leipzig, 1965, p. 127), easily recognizes, on the basis of allusions in the text, the reference to be to Augustine, John Scottus Eriugena, Thierry of Chartres, and Meister Eckhart.

23. *De conjecturis* (1441–1445), I 19.

24. *Vier Predigten im Geiste Eckharts*, J. Koch ed. (Heidelberg, 1937), p. 84ff.

25. *Cribratio Alchorani*, preface and II 12.

26. *De venatione*, ch. 30.

27. *Apologia*, Strasbourg ed., p. 74; Basel ed., pp. 64–65.

28. *De venatione*, ch. 8.

29. *Le Problème de l'être chez Aristote* (Paris, 1962, 2d ed. 1966).

30. *De beryllo*, ch. 24.

31. *De venatione*, ch. 1.

32. Basel ed., p. 355.

33. Migne, *Patrologia latina* LIV, 226c.

34. Cf. notably the sermon *Nos revelate* given at Brixen November 1, 1456 (Basel ed., pp. 610–611): "Speculantes transformantur continue in imaginem objecti. . . . Sed haec transformatio est semper nova. . . . Quare speculantes illi sunt transeuntes semper et aeternaliter a claritate in claritatem, cum absoluta maximitas uti est semper incompraehensibilis praecedat et attrahat."

35. *Opera* (Basel, 1561), II, p. 1537.

36. Letter to Barbaro, December 6, 1484, quoted and commented on by R. Marcel, *Marsile Ficin* (Paris, 1958), p. 472.

37. Saffrey-Westerink eds., I, p. 5.

38. *Ibid.*, pp. 6–7.

39. Letter of September 6, 1469, *Opera* I, p. 616.

40. Cf. his *Summary of the Doctrines of Zoroaster and of Plato*, Alexandre ed., trans. Pellissier (Paris, 1858), pp. 262–269.

41. On this see the contrast, in parallel columns and in relation to some significant examples, of texts from Saint Thomas and from Ficino in the short study by E. Gilson, which is part of a course of lectures and is much earlier than the studies by Kristeller and Marcel, "Marsile Ficin et le *Contra Gentiles*," *Archives d'Histoire Littéraire et Doctrinale du Moyen Age* XXIV (1958), pp. 101–113.

42. On this text and its date, cf. Marcel, *op. cit.*, p. 309.

43. *Opera* I, p. 875.

44. To Pierleone, *Opera* I, p. 920.

45. To Poliziano, *Opera* I, p. 958.

46. *Opera* I, p. 871.
47. Cf. also *Plat. Theol.* XII, 1.
48. To Pannonius, *Opera* I, p. 872; cf. the *Proemium* to the *Enneads*, *Opera* II, p. 1557.
49. Commentary on the *Timaeus, Opera* II, p. 1438.
50. *Confirmatio christ., Opera* I, p. 868.
51. *Opera* I, p. 866.
52. *In Epist. Pauli*, ch. 12, *Opera* I, p. 461.
53. *Opera* I, p. 956.
54. In *Plat. Theol.* IV, 1, one is surprised at the misinterpretation made by Raymond Marcel who, in order to justify an erroneous translation, modifies the text of the manuscripts by writing (p. 165 of his edition, vol. I [Paris, 1964]) *et mundum vita carere volunt et sensu qui tamen vitam dant . . .,* where one must clearly read *dat*, the subject of that verb being *mundus*, certainly not the opponents of Platonism, who refused to acknowledge life and feeling in the world, while rightly for them—the reference is, of course, to the Aristotelians—the heat of the sun and the humidity of the earth make plants grow without sowing and give a sensitive soul to animals born by *generatio aequivoca*, which Ficino is far from denying but in which he sees an additional reason for admitting cosmic animation.
55. Letter of June 25, 1490, *Opera* I, p. 911.

NEOPLATONISM, THE GREEK COMMENTATORS, AND RENAISSANCE ARISTOTELIANISM

1. We shall treat both Themistius and also Simplicius as sources of Neoplatonic doctrines for the Renaissance Aristotelians. Since various scholars simply deny that Themistius is a Neoplatonist, some comment is in order. He is categorically denied to be a Neoplatonist by Wilhelm Von Christ, Wilhelm Schmid, and Otto Stählin, *Geschichte der Griechischen Literatur*, 6th ed., II, 2 (Munich, 1961), p. 1011: "Denn so viel er den Platon im Mund führt und sein Handeln durch Berufung auf ihn rechtfertigt, so ist er sich doch genau bewusst, dass er eigentlich kein Platoniker, am wenigstens ein Neuplatoniker ist." They do go on, however, to point out that while Themistius is an Aristotelian and wants to be one, he also believed Platonism can be reconciled with Aristotelianism. On the other hand, they point out (p. 1011, n. 8) that although there are Neoplatonic ideas in some of Themistius' orations, the latter also contain criticism of Neoplatonism and an emphasis on a practical, political direction lacking in Neoplatonism. Fritz Schemmel, in his "Die Hochschule von Konstantinopel im IV. Jahrhundert P. Ch. N.," *Neue Jahrbücher für Pädagogik* 22 (1908), pp. 147–168, discusses Themistius' paraphrases of Aristotle, dating their composition between 337 and 355 (pp. 152–155). He emphasizes their pedagogical purpose (p. 157) and the primacy of ethics and practise in Themistius' conception of philosophy (pp. 155 and 160–161). He too denies that Themistius is a Neoplatonist, though he admits that Themistius agrees with the Neoplatonists in the conviction that Plato and Aristotle teach essentially the same thing (p. 155). In like fashion, Eduard Zeller, *Die Philosophie der Griechen in ihrer geschichtlichen Entwicklung*, 5th ed., III, 2 (Leipzig, 1923; repr. Hildesheim, 1963), pp. 799–801, argues that the distinctive traits of Neoplatonism are not prominent in Themistius. Indeed, Themistius himself expressly indicates that he does not approve the innovations of Neoplatonism since these go beyond the older Platonic-Aristotelian philosophy. In turn, Karl Praechter, *Die Philosophie des Altertums*, 12th ed. (Berlin, 1926), pp. 657–658, admits that if Themistius also wrote commentaries on Plato, this would agree with Themistius as a Neoplatonist, but he then emphasizes that Themistius had taken Aristotle as his model. The tendency to reconcile Plato and Aristotle is seen as self-evident in Themistius' day and not limited to Neoplatonism. G. Faggin sees Themistius as belonging to Aristotelianism, not Platonism, and suggests that if he believed in the doctrinal unity of Platonism and Aristotelianism, he opposed it to the novelties of the Neoplatonists. See his article "Temistio," in *Enciclopedia filosofica*, 2nd ed., VI (Florence, 1967), col. 370–371. Willy Stegemann also follows the view that Themistius was not a Neoplatonist. See his article on Themistius in Paulys-Wissowa, *Real-Encyclopädie der classischen Altertumswissenschaft, Zweite*

Reihe, V (Stuttgart, 1934), col. 1642-1680, at col. 1648-1649. In a recent and important article, H. J. Blumenthal appears to deny or at least to minimize any Neoplatonism in Themistius and in the paraphrases on the *De anima* in particular. In his "Neoplatonic Elements in the *De anima* Commentaries," *Phronesis* 21 (1976), pp. 64–87, he remarks (p. 82) that Neoplatonism was already the dominant philosophy in the time of Themistius, who was "trying to be an Aristotelian." He admits that Themistius did not exclude Platonic or Platonist ideas and then adds (p. 83): "But his orientation was certainly different from that of the Neoplatonists." As to Themistius' comments on *De anima*, III, c. 5, Blumenthal remarks: "The vocabulary is Peripatetic, and the thought shows no signs of the Neoplatonic multiplication of entities: there are no participated and unparticipated transcendent intellects, no distinction between intelligible and intellectual life, no members of triads." Blumenthal does not appear to exclude completely the possible influence of Neoplatonism on Themistius when he refers in his article, "Neoplatonic Interpretations of Aristotle on *Phantasia*," *The Review of Metaphysics* 31 (1977), pp. 242–257, p. 253 to "Themistius, who, if not always a profound interpreter of Aristotle, is to some extent free from the Neoplatonic influences which in his time already dominated Greek philosophy." See also Blumenthal's *Plotinus' Psychology, His Doctrines of the Embodied Soul* (The Hague, 1971), pp. 11–13, nn. 10 and 13, where he indicates specific remarks of Plotinus which Themistius may be discussing. Stuart B. Martin makes no mention of Plotinus or Neoplatonism in his article, "The Nature of the Human Intellect as it is Expounded in Themistius' *Paraphrasis in libros Aristotelis De anima*," in *The Quest for the Absolute*, ed. Frederick J. Adelmann, Boston College Studies in Philosophy, I (Boston and The Hague, 1966), pp. 1–21, though he is careful to bring out Themistius' tendency to reconcile Plato and Aristotle (p. 2, n. 3). And while he recognizes that the agent intellect is "both transcendently one and yet immanent in many" and that Themistius tries to account for this by the analogy of light and its source, the sun, Martin concludes that there really is only one agent intellect. His assumptions appear to be that Themistius cannot have it both ways and that analogy is insufficient as an explanation (pp. 14–16 and 20–21).

On the other hand, Pierre Duhem relates Themistius' explication of Aristotle's psychology to Neoplatonism and to Plotinus in particular. See Duhem's *Le système du monde*, IV (Paris, 1916), pp. 379–380, 387, and 395–397. It seems an exaggeration, however, simply to refer to Themistius as a Neoplatonist, as does Johannes Geffcken, *Der Ausgang des griechische-römischen Heidentums* (Heidelberg, 1920), p. 168. Perhaps the most accurate way to express the situation is to point to those elements in Themistius' paraphrases on the *De anima* which are Neoplatonic without claiming that he is a thoroughgoing Neoplatonist. As Augusto Guzzo and Vittorio Mathieu express the matter: "Nell'interpretazione di Temistio si trovano tracce della concezione neoplatonica, senza tuttavia che egli possa esserne considerato un portavoce fedele." See their joint article, "Intelletto", in *Enciclopedia filosofica*, 2nd ed. III (Florence, 1967), col. 963. See also Paul O. Kristeller's review of Philip Merlan's *Monopsychism, Mysticism, Metaconsciousness* (The Hague, 1963), which appeared in *The Journal of Philosophy* 64 (1967), pp. 124–125. Kristeller clearly connects Themistius to Plotinus. One example of Neoplatonic influence appears to be Themistius' conception of a plurality of hierarchically arranged souls in man, each of which serves as "matter" or subject to the soul superior to it. See Themistius, *In libros de anima paraphrasis*, ed. Richard Heinze, Commentaria in Aristotelem graeca, V, 3 (Berlin, 1899), p. 100, line 31 to p. 101, line 1. The notion that each level in the hierarchy of being is related to the level immediately above it as matter to form is Plotinian. See Plotinus, *Enneads* II, 4, 3; III, 4, 1; and III, 9, 15. For discussion see A. H. Armstrong, *The Architecture of the Intelligible Universe in the Philosophy of Plotinus* (Cambridge, 1940), pp. 76 and 86. Another apparent example of Neoplatonic influence occurs in Themistius' discussion regarding the question whether the agent intellect is one or many. In a celebrated passage, he says that the intellect that primarily illuminates (πρώτως ἐλλάμπων) is one, while those that are illuminated and illuminate (ἐλλαμπόμενοι καὶ ἐλλάμποντες) are many, just like light, for while the sun is one, light is in some way divided in regard to the different powers of sight. Themistius underscores that Aristotle compares the intellect to light, while Plato, who makes it similar to the Good, compares it to the sun. He then adds that all of us have our being from this one intellect. See Themistius, *In libros de anima paraphrasis*, ed. R. Heinze, p. 103, lin. 32–39, and p. 100, lin. 31–32 and lin. 35 to p. 101, lin. 1. I suggest that those scholars are mistaken who hold that there is something faulty with the text here, arguing that Themistius could not have meant that the agent intellect is one and yet also many. Such a view is put forth by Hans Kurfess, *Zur Geschichte der Erklärung der Erklärung der Aristotelischen Lehre vom sog.* ΝΟΥΣ ΠΟΙΗΤΙΚΟΣ *und* ΠΑΘΗΤΙΚΟΣ (Tübingen, 1911), p. 23, n. 26, who is followed by Philip Merlan, *Monopsychism, Mysticism, Metaconsciousness: Problems in the Neoaristotelian and Neoplatonic Tradition* (The Hague, 1963), p. 50–51, n. 3. Rather than correct the text of Themistius, we might do well to note that Plotinus' *Enneads* contain terminology and ideas that help make sense of Themistius' remarks about the intellect just cited and which seem to indicate the Neoplatonic background of those remarks. Plotinus tells us that the sun, which is a center for the light dependent upon it, serves as a model of the Good (I, 7, 1, 25–26). The act emanating from the One is like the light emanating from the sun. While remaining itself immobile, the One illuminates the intelligible realm (V, 3, 12, 40–45). The One is simply light, whereas *Nous* is illuminated in its very substance by the light which the One provides it. In turn, the Soul is made intelligent by *Nous* (V, 6, 4, 18–22). *Nous* provides light for the Soul just as the One does in regard to *Nous* (VI, 7, 17, 36–37). Soul illuminates because it is always illuminated (II, 9, 2, 17–18). Since it is illuminated and possesses light in an uninterrupted fashion, it gives light to the things that follow after it (II, 9, 3, 1-2; see II, 3, 17, 15-16 and IV, 3, 17, 18-31). Soul is a certain light coming from *Nous*, on which it depends (V, 3, 9, 15-16). There is an illuminating light that shines in Soul and makes it intelligible and like the light that is above it. Soul takes hold of intelligible light, which is an image of the life of *Nous* itself. The life of *Nous* is activity, namely, a first light which primarily illuminates (λάμπον πρώτως) by itself, a light to itself, at once illuminating and being illuminated (λάμπον ὁμοῦ καὶ λαμπόμενον), a true intelligible, which both knows and is known (V, 3, 8, 24-40). For discussion regarding Plotinus' use of the metaphor of light and his concept of the higher illuminating the lower, see A. H. Armstrong, "Emanation," *Mind* 46 (1937), pp. 61–66; H. R. Schwyzer, "Plotinos," in Paulys-Wissowa, *Real-Encyclopädie der classischen Altertumswissenschaft*, XXI (Stuttgart, 1951), col. 570; Paul Aubin, "L' 'image' dans l'oeuvre de Plotin," *Recherches de science religieuse* 41 (1953), pp. 351ff. and n. 6; Joseph Moreau, "L'idée d'univers dans la pensée antique," *Giornale di metafisica* 8 (1953), pp. 332–334 and 337; *idem*, "L'un et les êtres selon Plotin," *Giornale di metafisica* 11 (1956), pp. 218 and 221–222; *idem*, *Plotin ou la gloire de la philosophie antique* (Paris, 1970), pp. 92–95; Émile Brehier, *The Philosophy of Plotinus*, trans. Joseph Thomas (Chicago, 1958), pp. 48, 96–97 and 114–115; Werner Beierwaltes, "Die Metaphysik des Lichtes in der Philosophie Plotins," *Zeitschrift für philosophische Forschung* 15 (1961), pp. 334–362; Cleto Carbonara, *La filosofia di Plotino*, 3rd ed. (Naples, 1964), pp. 318–320; J. M. Rist, *Plotinus: The Road to Reality* (Cambridge, 1967), pp. 68, 72–73, 96, 114–117 and 197; John H. Fielder, "*Chorismos* and Emanation in the Philosophy of Plotinus," in *The Significance of Neoplatonism*, ed. R. Baine Harris, Studies in Neoplatonism: Ancient and Modern, I (Norfolk and Albany, 1976), pp. 106–115. The significance of the higher illuminating the lower within the individual soul is brought out by Blumenthal, "Neoplatonic Elements," pp. 68–69. However, Blumenthal himself in a recent article, "Themistius, the Last Peripatetic Commentator on Aristotle?" in *Arktouros: Hellenic Studies Presented to Bernard M. W. Knox*, eds. G. W. Bowersock, W. Burkert, and M. C. J. Putnam (Berlin and New York, 1979), pp. 391–400, especially pp. 396–398, seems to exclude any Platonic or Neoplatonic influence on Themistius' doctrine regarding the unity of the agent intellect. I am indebted to Professor Kristeller for having pointed out to me many years ago the apparent Neoplatonic aspects of Themistius' remarks about whether the agent intellect is one or many.

2. Paul of Venice, *Scriptum super librum de anima* (Venice, 1481). For discussion see Felice Momigliano, *Paolo Veneto e le correnti del pensiero religioso e filosofico nel suo tempo* (Turin, 1907); Bruno Nardi, *Saggi sull'aristotelismo padovano dal secolo XIV al XVI* (Florence, 1958), pp. 75–93; Eugenio Garin, *Storia della filosofia italiana* (Turin, 1966), pp. 436–446; Alan R. Perreiah, "A Biographical Introduction to Paul of Venice," *Augustinianu* 17 (1967), pp. 450–461.

3. Cajetan of Thiene, *Super libros de anima* (Venice, 1493). The basic study on Thiene remains Silvestro da Valsanzibio, *Vita e dottrina di Gaetano di Thiene filosofo dello Studio di Padova (1387–1465)* (Padua, 1949). There is a copy of the first edition of Thiene's *De anima* (Padua, 1475; Hain 15502) in the Biblioteca Universitaria at Padua which contains notations apparently in

more than one hand. However, many of these notations are clearly in the hand of Nicoletto Vernia. The shelf-mark of this volume is Sec. XV. 724. I identified this volume as belonging to Vernia in June, 1973.

4. On Vernia see Pietro Ragnisco, *Nicoletto Vernia: Studi storici sulla filosofia padovana nella seconda metà del secolo decimoquinto* (Venice, 1891); Nardi, *Saggi*, pp. 95–126; Paolo Sambin, "Intorno a Nicoletto Vernia," *Rinascimento* 3 (1952), pp. 261–268; Garin, *Storia della filosofia italiana*, pp. 450–454; idem, *La cultura filosofica del Rinascimento italiano* (Florence, 1961), pp. 293–299; Cesare Vasoli, "La scienza della natura in Nicoleto Vernia," in *La filosofia della natura nel medioevo* (Milan, 1966), pp. 717–729.

5. On Nifo see Pasquale Tuozzi, "Agostino Nifo e le sue opere," *Atti e memorie della R. Accademia di scienze, lettere ed Arti* (Padua), n. s. 20 (1904), p. 63–86; Giuseppe Tommasino, *Tra umanisti e filosofi* (Maddaloni, 1921), I, 123–147; Nardi *Saggi*, passim; idem, *Sigieri di Brabante nel pensiero del Rinascimento italiano* (Rome, 1945), passim; Garin, *Storia della filosofia italiana*, pp. 523–527, 535–538 and 572–573; idem, *La cultura filosofica*, pp. 114–118 and 295–303; Etienne Gilson, "Autour de Pomponazzi, Problématique de l'immortalité de l'âme en Italie au début du XVIe siècle," *Archives d'histoire doctrinale et littéraire du moyen âge* 28 (1961), pp. 236–253; William A. Wallace, *Causality and Scientific Explanation, I: Medieval and Early Classical Science* (Ann Arbor, 1972), pp. 139–153; Edward P. Mahoney, "A Note on Agostino Nifo," *Philological Quarterly* 50 (1971), pp. 125–132; idem, "Agostino Nifo," *Dictionary of Scientific Biography*, X (New York, 1974), pp. 125–132; idem, "Agostino Nifo's Early Views on Immortality," *Journal of the History of Philosophy* 8 (1970), pp. 451–460; idem, "Agostino Nifo's De sensu agente," *Archiv für Geschichte der Philosophie* 53 (1971), pp. 119–142; idem, "Antonio Trombetta and Agostino Nifo on Averroes and Intelligible Species: A Philosophical Dispute at the University of Padua," in *Storia e cultura nel Convento del Santo a Padova*, ed. Antonino Poppi (Vicenza, 1976), pp. 289–301; Antonino Poppi, *Introduzione all'aristotelismo padovano* (Padua, 1970), passim. Nifo is presented from other points of view in three recent and interesting articles. See Paola Zambelli, "I problemi metodologici del necromante Agostino Nifo," *Medioevo* 1 (1975), pp. 129–171; E. J. Ashworth, "Agostino Nifo's Reinterpretation of Medieval Logic," *Rivista critica di storia della filosofia* 31 (1976), pp. 354–374; Lisa Jardine, "Galileo's Road to Truth and the Demonstrative Regress," *Studies in History and Philosophy of Science* 7 (1976), pp. 277–318, especially pp. 290–295. Jardine brings out well the impact of the Greek Commentators, especially Themistius, in her discussion. What is surprising is that she does not mention Wallace's treatment of Nifo cited above. Nifo's interest in Themistius and Simplicius is noted in another context by Paolo Galluzzi, *Momento: Studi galileiani* (Rome, 1979), pp. 138–143. The only secondary literature on Nifo that he appears to cite is Zambelli's article just mentioned. However, he does state (p. 142, n. 105) that she has argued effectively against the thesis of Nifo's noteworthy philological competence supposedly sustained by Wilhelm Risse, F. Edward Cranz, Charles B. Schmitt, and myself. Although I have, on more than one occasion, drawn attention to the significance of Nifo's deliberately learning Greek, I am unaware that I have given him any grades for his ability at the language. Moreover, that he may have lightly revised an already existent translation does not appear to be unique to him (p. 94, 122–123) nor that he misunderstood a passage in Aristotle (p. 142). Galluzzi is to be praised, however, for presenting sections on the views of the Greek Commentators, notably, Themistius, Simplicius, and Philoponus (pp. 98–106 and 125–134), and for admitting the drawbacks of Ermolao's translation of Themistius (p. 98).

6. Themistius, *Paraphrasis in Aristotelem*, trans. Ermolao Barbaro (Treviso, 1481). See Hain *15463. I have examined copies of this edition at the Newberry Library, Chicago, and at the Beinecke Library, Yale University. This translation was reprinted on several occasions in the sixteenth century. For discussion see Arnaldo Ferriguto, *Almorò Barbaro, l'alta cultura del settrione d'Italia nel '400* Miscellanea di Storia Veneta, 3rd ser., XV (Venice, 1922), pp. 133–150. A new translation of the paraphrases on *De anima* III was made by Ludovico Nogarola and published as a supplement to a printing of Ermolao's translation. See *Themistii peripatetici lucidissimi Paraphrasis in Aristotelis Posteriora . . . Hermolao Barbaro patricio Veneto interprete . . .* (Venice, 1554), pp. 104–119. See p. 103 for the dedicatory letter to Cardinal Giulio da Montefeltro-Della Rovere in which Nogarola criticizes Ermolao's translation. I have examined a

copy of this edition at the Biblioteca Vallicelliana, Rome. Yet another translation of the third book of Themistius' paraphrases on the *De anima* was made by Federico Bonaventura and published as the second volume of his *Opuscula* (Urbino, 1627). See *Themistii Euphradae Paraphrasis in tertium librum Aristotelis De anima Federico Bonaventura Urbinate interprete* (Urbino, 1627), pp. 10–11 for an attack on Ermolao and Nogarola as translators. I have examined a copy of this work at the Bibliothèque Nationale, Paris. See also Nardi, *Saggi*, pp. 365–368. Vernia's own copy of the 1481 edition of Ermolao's translation of Themistius is today in the Biblioteca Universitaria at Padua. I identified this volume in July, 1973. It bears the shelf-mark Sec. XV. 96 and contains a statement on sig. ii7v that it had been his. The marginal notations are without doubt in his hand. I discovered another copy of the 1481 edition of Ermolao's translation in the Biblioteca San Marco Marciana, Venice, which also appears to have marginal annotations in Vernia's hand. It has the shelf-mark Inc. 447 and is bound with Inc. 448, which is a copy of Thomas Aquinas' *De unitate intellectus* (Treviso, 1476). The latter contains many marginal annotations that are clearly in Vernia's hand. Vernia was already citing Ermolao's translation in his preface regarding the *Physics* and in *Quaestio est, an medicina nobilior atque praestantior sit iure civili*, both of which are to be found in Vernia's edition of Walter Burley, *Super octo libros physicorum* (Venice, 1482). In the preface (sig. A2rb), Vernia praises Ermolao for his translation. See also sig. A3rb and A4rb for other references to Themistius. The question on medicine and law has been edited and republished by Eugenio Garin in *La disputa delle arti nel quattrocento* (Florence, 1947), pp. 111–123.

There are allusions to Themistius and also to Simplicius in the marginal annotations that Vernia made in his copy of John of Jandun, *Quaestiones super tres libros de anima* (Venice, 1473; Hain 7458). I discovered this volume at the Biblioteca Universitaria, Padua, in July 1974. It carries the shelf-mark Sec. XV. 717. Vernia himself indicates at the end of Book II (f. 48rb) that he had completed Book II on August 6, 1487. A few folios later (bottom margin of f. 51v) there is a long annotation in which he dismisses Scotus for saying Aristotle was in doubt whether the soul is bodily. He goes on to cite Averroes as saying that while the intellect remains after death, it has no memory. He then adds that Themistius and Simplicius expound the text in the same way. In another annotation (left margin of f. 74v), he addresses Jandun, telling him that he has not understood Aristotle's *Posterior Analytics* because he has not seen the *Doctor lucidus*, that is, Themistius. There is also a copy of Jandun's *Quaestiones in libros physicorum Aristotelis* (Venice, 1488; Hain 7457) in the same library which once belonged to Vernia. Its shelf mark is Sec. XV. 665. I identified this volume in June, 1972. My attention was called to the existence of Vernia's copies of Jandun's *Physics* and Themistius' paraphrases in the Biblioteca Universitaria at Padua by a remark of Ragnisco, *Nicoletto Vernia*, p. 35 (= p. 625), n. 1.

In his lectures on Aristotle's *Posterior Analytics*, which are to be found in Bodleian Library, Oxford, Canonici Miscell. Latini Cod. 506, ff. 224r–241r, Vernia makes constant reference to Themistius. At one point he tells his students: "Nemo enim fuit doctior illo, proinde adorate verba Themistii" (f. 234). Much from these lectures reappears to the word in Vernia's treatise against Averroes, cited in the following note 7. That a conciliating approach to Aristotle and Plato was taught at Padua is, of course, not in itself a surprise. That it was taught by Vernia is. I am editing this work for future publication.

7. See Nicoletto Vernia, *Contra perversam Averrois opinionem de unitate intellectus et de animae felicitate* (Venice, 1505), which was also reprinted in *Acutissimae quaestiones super libros de physica auscultatione ab Alberto de Saxonia editae* (Venice, 1516), ff. 83r–91rb. The first edition appeared in the Venice 1504 printing of Albert of Saxony's *Physics*, ff. 84ra–92rb. I have examined a copy of the first edition in the Biblioteca Nazionale Vittorio Emanuele, Rome. I shall cite the 1505 and 1516 editions in the present paper. For Vernia's references to Simplicius' *Physics*, see f. 5ra (1516 ed.: ff. 85vb–86ra), f. 9ra (f. 89ra), f. 10vab (f. 90rb–90va); for Simplicius' *De coelo*, see f. 4ra (f. 85ra); and for his *De anima*, see f. 4vb (f. 85va). There is discussion regarding the second of these commentaries in D. J. Allen, "Mediaeval Versions of Aristotle, *De caelo*, and of the Commentary of Simplicius," *Mediaeval and Renaissance Studies* 2 (1950), pp. 82–120. Vernia refers to Simplicius' *De anima* several times in his *Proemium in libro*

de anima, Bodleian Library, Oxford, Canonici Miscell. Latini Cod. 506, ff. 319r, 321r, 321v. There are also several references to Themistius' *De anima* in this work.

The classic study on Simplicius' influence on late fifteenth-and sixteenth-century philosophy in Italy is Bruno Nardi's fine essay, "Il commento di Simplicio al *De anima* nelle controversie della fine del secolo XV e del secolo XVI," which was reprinted in his *Saggi*, pp. 365–442. Regrettably, Nardi nowhere discusses Vernia in his essay. On the other hand, he draws attention to the fact that Giovanni Pico della Mirandola had a copy of Simplicius' *De anima* in his library and also to the fact that he lists basic theses of Simplicius' own psychology in his "conclusiones." See Giovanni Pico della Mirandola, *Conclusiones sive theses DCCCC Romae anno 1486 publice disputandae, sed non admissae*, ed. Bohdan Kieszkowski (Geneva, 1973), p. 39, and Pearl Kibre, *The Library of Pico della Mirandola* (New York, 1936), pp. 29 and 179 (entry 447). For discussion see Garin, *Storia della filosofia italiana*, pp. 463–464 and 470–471; Paul Oskar Kristeller, "Giovanni Pico della Mirandola and His Sources," in *L'opera e il pensiero di Giovanni Pico della Mirandola nella storia dell'umanesimo, Convegno internazionale (Mirandola: 15-18 Settembre 1963)*, I (Florence, 1965), pp. 54–55 and 62; Giovanni Di Napoli, *Giovanni Pico della Mirandola e la problematica dottrinale del suo tempo* (Rome, 1965), pp. 87, 125 and 218. The latter two scholars bring out in particular the connection between Pico's conciliation of Plato and Aristotle and his interest in Simplicius. There are also references to Simplicius in Pico's oration on the dignity of man. See Pico della Mirandola, *De hominis dignitate*, ed. Eugenio Garin, Edizione Nazionale dei Classici del Pensiero Italiano, I (Florence, 1942), pp. 140 and 144. In the latter text he mentions Simplicius along with Boethius as predecessors who proposed to show the conciliation of Plato and Aristotle but did not live up to their promises. However, it should be added that it is regrettable that modern historians have contrasted the interest in Neoplatonism and the conciliation of Plato and Aristotle to be found in Pico with the supposedly rigid Averroism of Vernia. The latter's own interests in Simplicius have been wholly overlooked, as have his attempts to conciliate Plato and Aristotle. Vernia is presented as a strict Averroist by Bohdan Kieszkowski, *Studi sul platonismo del Rinascimento in Italia* (Florence, 1936), pp. 138–143, and Tullio Gregory, "Aristotelismo," in *Grande antologia filosofica*, VI, ed. M. F. Sciacca (Milan, 1964), p. 614.

The attribution of the *De anima* traditionally ascribed to Simplicius has been challenged by two recent scholars, F. Bossier and C. Steel, in their article, "Priscianus Lydus en de *In de anima* van Pseudo(?)-Simplicius," *Tijdschrift voor Filosofie* 34 (1972), pp. 761–821 (French summary: pp. 821–822). Their thesis that the work is in fact by Priscianus Lydus and not Simplicius has been submitted to a critical but sympathetic analysis by Ilsetraut Hadot in her book, *Le problème du néoplatonisme Alexandrin: Hiéroclès et Simplicius* (Paris, 1978), pp. 193–202. While she appears to grant their thesis probability, she calls on them to remove all doubts by a more detailed examination of the style of Priscianus. One of the authors has returned to the thesis in a book which he has authored by himself. See now Carlos G. Steel, *The Changing Self, A Study on the Soul in Later Neoplatonism: Iamblichus, Damascius and Priscianus*, Verhandelingen van de Koninklijke Academie voor Wetenschappen, Letteren en Schone Kunsten van Belgie, Klasse der Letteren, Jaargang XL, Nr. 85 (Brussels, 1978), p. 7–11 and 123–154. In the present paper, I shall continue to refer to this *De anima* commentary as Simplicius' and I do so simply for the sake of convenience. However, I do not intend to question the plausibility of the thesis of Bossier and Steel. For useful summaries of the doctrine of this *De anima* commentary, see A. Ed. Chaignet, *Histoire de la psychologie des grecs*, V (Paris, 1893), pp. 357–375; O. Hamelin, *La théorie de l'intellect d'après Aristote et ses commentateurs*, ed. Edmond Barbotin (Paris, 1953), pp. 44–57. I very much regret that Steel's book became available to me only as I was completing the notes for this article. Given the theme of the present paper, it is interesting to note that Simplicius' authorship of the *De anima* commentary had already been questioned in the Renaissance and the possibility of Priscianus Lydus being the true author had been proposed. See Nardi, *Saggi*, pp. 431–432, who draws attention to a discussion in Francesco Piccolomini. See the latter's "Capita sententiae Simplicii ex commentariis librorum de anima deprompta," in his *In tres libros Aristotelis de anima lucidissima expositio* (Venice, 1602), f. 216r. I have examined a copy of this work in the Biblioteca Nazionale Vittorio Emanuele at Rome. Bossier and Steel pay credit (p. 762) to their Renaissance forerunner. On the dating of the commentaries regarded by all as genuinely Simplician, namely, those on the *De caelo* and *Physics*, see Alan Cameron, "The Last Days of the Academy at Athens," *Proceedings of the Cambridge Philological Society* 195 (1969), pp. 7–30, at pp. 22–24.

8. *Alexandri Aphrodisei enarratio de anima ex Aristotelis institutione interprete Hieronymo Donato patritio veneto* (Brescia, 1495). See *GKW*, #859. For discussion of Alexander and his influence in the Renaissance see F. Edward Cranz, "Alexander Aphrodisiensis," in *Catalogus Translationum et Commentariorum: Mediaeval and Renaissance Latin Translations and Commentaries* I, ed. P. O. Kristeller (Washington, D.C., 1960), pp. 77–135, especially pp. 85–86 and 111–112; *idem*, "Alexander Aphrodisiensis: Addenda et corrigenda," in *Catalogus Translationum et Commentariorum* . . . II, eds. P. O. Kristeller and F. E. Cranz (Washington, D.C., 1971), pp. 411–422, especially pp. 417–418; Nardi, *Saggi*, pp. 369–372 and *passim;* P. O. Kristeller, *Renaissance Thought II: Papers on Humanism and the Arts* (New York, 1965), pp. 111–118; E. P. Mahoney, "Nicoletto Vernia and Agostino Nifo on Alexander of Aphrodisias: An Unnoticed Dispute," *Rivista critica di storia della filosofia* 23 (1968), pp. 268–296.

9. See Martin Grabmann, *Mittelalterliche lateinische Übersetzungen von Schriften der Aristoteles-Kommentatoren Johannes Philoponos, Alexander von Aphrodisias und Themistios*, Sitzungsberichte der Bayerischen Akademie der Wissenschaften, Philosophisch-historische Abteilung, 1929, heft 7, pp. 63–68; Marcel de Corte, "Thémistius et Saint Thomas d'Aquin," *Archives d'histoire doctrinale et littéraire du moyen âge* 8 (1932), pp. 47–83, especially pp. 65–83; G. Verbeke, introduction to *Thémistius, Commentaire sur le traité de l'âme d'Aristote, Traduction de Guillaume de Moerbeke*, Corpus Latinum Commentariorum in Aristotelem Graecorum, I (Louvain and Paris, 1957), pp. ix–lxii; E. P. Mahoney, "Themistius and the Agent Intellect in James of Viterbo and Other Thirteenth Century Philosophers (Saint Thomas, Siger of Brabant, and Henry Bate)," *Augustiniana* 23 (1963), pp. 422–467. For an analysis of Moerbeke as a translator, see Gérard Verbeke, "Guillaume de Moerbeke et sa méthode de traduction," in *Medioevo e Rinascimento, Studi in onore di Bruno Nardi* II (Florence, 1955), pp. 779–800. See also Verbeke's "Guillaume de Moerbeke, traducteur de Jean Philopon," *Revue philosophique de Louvain* 49 (1951), pp. 222–235. For scholarly literature on Moerbeke as a translator of Proclus, see below note 56. It must be added that Verbeke's remarks on the influence of Themistius on Thomas have been challenged by C. Vansteenkiste in his review of Verbeke's edition. See Vansteenkiste's review in *Revue d'histoire ecclésiastique* 53 (1958), pp. 514–526, especially pp. 524–526. However, he does not appear to question that influence in regard to Thomas' *De unitate intellectus*.

10. "Utrum anima intellectiva humano corpore unita tamquam vera forma substantialis dans ei esse specificum substantiale aeterna atque unica sit in omnibus hominibus," (Biblioteca Nazionale San Marco [Marciana], Venice, Cod. Lat. VI, 105 [= 2656], ff. 156ra–160va). I have prepared an edition of this treatise that will be published by Editrice Antenore, Padua under the title *Nicoletto Vernia's Early Treatise on the Intellective Soul: Introduction and Critical Text*. Vernia's authorship of this treatise has been established by a carefully documented and well-argued essay of Giulio F. Pagallo, "Sull'autore (Nicoletto Vernia?) di un'anonima e inedita quaestio sull'anima del secolo XV," in *La filosofia della natura nel medioevo* (Milan, 1966), pp. 670–682.

11. See my study, "Nicoletto Vernia on the Soul and Immortality," in *Philosophy and Humanism: Renaissance Essays in Honor of Paul Oskar Kristeller* (New York and Leiden, 1976), pp. 144–163. On Vernia's "Albertism," see my essay, "Albert the Great and the *Studio Patavino* in the Late Fifteenth and Early Sixteenth Centuries," in *Albertus Magnus and the Sciences: Commemorative Essays 1980*, ed. James A. Weisheipl (Toronto, 1980), pp. 537–563.

12. Vernia, *Contra perversam Averrois opinionem*, f. 4rb–4va (f. 85rab). For identification of Vernia's sources in Albert, see my article, "Nicoletto Vernia on the Soul," p. 151. Cf. Leopold Gaul, *Alberts des Grossen Verhältnis zu Plato*, Beiträge zur Geschichte der Philosophie des Mittelalters, XII, 1 (Münster, 1913), pp. 12–21; Pierre Michaud-Quantin, "Les 'Platonici' dans la psychologie de S. Albert le Grand," *Recherches de théologie ancienne et médiévale* 23 (1956), pp. 194–207, especially pp. 198–201 and 204–206.

13. *Ibid.*, f. 6ra (f. 87ra). See also f. 8rb (f. 88va).

14. *Ibid.*, f. 5va (f. 86rb). Vernia adds arguments from the discussion in Plotinus' *Enneads* IV, 9, regarding the question whether all souls are one.
15. *Ibid.*, f. 10vb (f. 90va).
16. Themistius, *In libros de anima paraphrasis*, ed. R. Heinze, p. 103, lin. 32–36. For the literature on the debate regarding this passage in the late thirteenth century, see note 9 above. The Neoplatonic aspects of the passage were discussed in note 1 above.
17. "Hoc idem in capitulo 32 ubi solvendo quaestionem an plures sint agentes intellectus inquit an intellectum illustrantem unum oportet esse, illustratos vero plures, sicut unus sol, et tamen lumen divellitur" (Vernia, *Contra perversam Averrois opinionem*, f. 9ra [f. 89rb]). See Themistius, *Paraphrasis de anima* III, c. 32, in *Paraphrasis in Aristotelem*, trans. Ermolao Barbaro, sig. ff2v, lin. 28–30: "An primum quidem intellectum illuminantem credi unum oportet. Illuminatos vero et subindeo illuminantes multos, quemadmodum quamquam sol est unus, tamen lux quae de sole prodit et mittitur quasi abiungitur ab eo et divellitur atque ita in multos obtutus distrahitur distribuiturque." It is noteworthy that Vernia refers to the many intellects only as "illuminated" and not also as "illuminating." He does not integrate this passage very well with his overall presentation of Themistius. The single illuminating intellect is not further identified.
18. *Ibid.*, f. 6va (f. 87rb) and f. 7ra (f. 87va). Vernia denies that Themistius intended to say that Aristotle condemned Plato regarding reminiscence. The text in question is Themistius, *Analyticorum posteriorum paraphrasis*, ed. Maximilian Wallies, Commentaria in Aristotelem graeca, V, 1 (Berlin, 1900), I, c. 1, p. 4, lin. 27–32. See Themistius, *Paraphrasis in posteriora analitica*, I, c. 3, in *Paraphrasis in Aristotelem*, trans. Ermolao Barbaro, sig. A4r, lin. 30–34.
19. On Vernia's use of Simplicius' *Physics* to defend his extraordinary claim that Alexander of Aphrodisias held to human immortality, see my article, "Nicoletto Vernia and Agostino Nifo," pp. 276–277 and note 34.
20. For a contrast between Simplicius' *Physics* and the *De anima* traditionally attributed to him, see Bossier and Steel, *op. cit.*, pp. 798–815. But see also the comments by I. Hadot, *Le problème*, pp. 196–199. Vernia's difficulty in reconciling the two commentaries may be a persuasive argument in favor of the Bossier-Steel thesis.
21. Vernia, *Contra perversam Averrois opinionem*, f. 5ra (f. 85vb). See Simplicius, *In Aristotelis physicorum libros quattuor posteriores commentaria*, ed. Hermann Diels, Commentaria in Aristotelem graeca, X (Berlin, 1895), VIII, p. 1249, lin. 30 to p. 1250, lin. 4. Vernia does not give a wholly accurate report of what Simplicius says.
22. *Ibid.*, f. 5ra (f. 85vb) and f. 9ra (f. 88ra). See Simplicius, *In Aristotelis physicorum libros quattuor posteriores commentaria*, V, p. 965, lin. 29–30. See also Vernia, f. 10va (f. 90rb).
23. Vernia, *Contra perversam Averrois opinionem*, f. 7rab (f. 87vab). This discussion is also to be found in Vernia's lectures on the *Posterior Analytics*, f. 240v. If it is in fact based on the *De anima* attributed to Simplicius, it is a roughly accurate presentation of some of its doctrines. We can give here only a few remarks to indicate how Vernia agrees with the text. All references will be to Simplicius, *In libros Aristotelis de anima commentaria*, ed. Michael Hayduck, Commentaria in Aristotelem graeca, XI (Berlin, 1882). The intellect in us is divided into the theoretic and practical intellects (p. 5, lin. 6–8; p. 61, lin. 11–13). The former is divided into the actual and the potential intellects—distinct "faculties" are not involved but the one soul as operating in various ways (p. 223, lin. 28–33). The potential intellect is the intellect as it proceeds forth to the outside, turning as a whole to the sensibles and in no way perceiving the intelligible forms that are apprehended by the actual intellect. It is then imperfect. However, when it turns away from sensation back within itself and is united with the actual intellect, it is perfected by the intelligible forms and is thus the perfect or habitual intellect. These forms are within the soul and bring about the perfecting of the potential intellect (p. 229, lin. 3–14). The intelligible forms are within, and it is from these forms as from causes that the intellect knows lower things (p. 124, lin. 28–30). That is to say, our intellect can sometimes operate along with sensation and so attend to sensibles, but it can also operate alone by itself and grasp inferior things from their causes, since it can know the very essences of physical forms (p. 276, lin. 16–27). Sense and imagination are aware of the accidental, not the substantial or essential (p. 277, lin. 34–37). Judgment, self-consciousness and comprehension of the intelligible forms are all reserved to the intellect as it operates independently

of the body (p. 46, lin. 8–9; p. 124, lin. 28–30; p. 196, lin. 16–20; p. 203, lin. 35–36; p. 218, lin. 36–39; p. 223, lin. 33–34; p. 264, lin. 26–27; p. 277, pp. 29–30; p. 279, lin. 26–29; p. 281, lin. 29–30; p. 321, lin. 28). Besides the potential intellect and the habitual intellect there is also in the soul the active intellect, which Aristotle compares to light and habit (p. 223, lin. 9–11). The actual intellect turns into itself and is in no way in potentiality (p. 228, lin. 6–7). It draws its actuality into the unity and permanence within itself (p. 5, lin. 14–15). This intellect abides wholly in itself and unlike the potential intellect is united to higher beings, namely, the intellect above it which perfects it. In turn, the active intellect perfects the potential intellect (p. 243, lin. 21–26 and 34–35).

24. "Istum etiam triplicem modum operandi animae habes a Proculo propositione tertia *de causis* et decimaquinta. In tertia: 'Omnis anima nobilis triplices habet operationes, animalem, intellectivam et divinam.' In decimaquinta: 'Omnis sciens qui scit essentiam est rediens ad eam reditione completa'" (*Ibid.*, f. 7rb [f. 87vb]). The numbering of propositions agrees with that found in Saint Thomas Aquinas, *Super librum de causis expositio*, ed. H. D. Saffrey (Fribourg and Louvain, 1954), p. 17 and p. 88. Perhaps Vernia is simply following his own understanding of Thomas' remark that the *Liber de causis* was excerpted by some Arab philosopher from the *Elements of Theology* by Proclus. See the *Proemium* in Saffrey's edition, p. 3. For scholarly literature on the *Liber de causis* and Proclus' *Elements*, see note 56 below.

25. Above the human soul and its intellect there are two separated intellects that are distinguished according as to whether or not human intellects participate in them. Simplicius refers to them respectively as the unparticipated intellect and the participated intellect. See Simplicius, *In libros Aristotelis de anima commentaria*, p. 49, lin 37 to p. 50, lin. 1, and p. 245, 38 to p. 246, lin. 1. For discussion regarding the two intellects above the human soul and intellect, see Chaignet, *Histoire de la psychologie des grecs*, V, p. 364; Kurfess, *Zur Geschichte*, p. 32; Steel, *The Changing Self*, pp. 123–132.

26. *Destructiones destructionum Averrois cum Augustini Niphi de Suessa expositione* (Venice, 1497), XIII, dub. 4, f. 112ra and f. 115va; XIV, dub. 1, ff. 119ra, 120ra, 121rb and 121vb–122ra. There is perfect agreement between Nifo's citation at XIII, dub. 4, f. 115va of Plotinus, *Enneads* II, 2, 1 and Marsilio Ficino's translation. Nifo even quotes the chapter title.

27. See I, dub. 11, f. 13vab; VII, dub. 3, f. 87rb; X, dub. 3, f. 103va for references to Simplicius' *De coelo*. His *Physics* is mentioned at VIII, dub. 1, f. 92vab and X, dub. 2, f. 101vb.

28. The first edition is *Augustini Niphi super tres libros de anima* (Venice, 1503). For the sake of convenience, we shall cite the later edition: *Suessanus super libros de anima: Augustini Niphi Medices philosophi suessani, Collectanea ac commentaria in libros de anima* (Venice, 1522). See II, coll. 37, ff. 93vb–94ra. See Themistius, *In libros Aristotelis de anima paraphrasis*, ed. R. Heinze, Commentaria in Aristotelem graeca, V, 3 (Berlin, 1899), p. 25, lin. 35 to p. 27, lin. 7. For Ermolao's translation, see Themistius, *Paraphrasis de anima*, I, c. 23, in *Paraphrasis in Aristotelem*, sig. bb2v, lin. 7–50.

29. See Marsilio Ficino, *Argumentum* to Ennead I, l, c. 1, 7 and 8 in his *Opera omnia* (Basel, 1576), pp. 1548–1549 and 1551–1552. See *Opera Plotini*, trans. M. Ficino (Florence, 1492), ff. 11–12 and 14–14v. On one occasion Nifo compares the Plotinus who emerges from Ficino's commentary to the position of Averroes. He inquires whether they both believe man is always united by cognition with higher beings. See Nifo, *In libros de anima*, III, comm. 36, ff. 61vb–62ra. Nifo is obviously dependent on Ficino. See Ficino, *Argumentum* to Ennead I, 1, c. 11, in *Opera omnia*, p. 1553 (*Opera Plotini*, f. 15r–15v). See the relevant remarks of Eugenio Garin, *La cultura filosofica del Rinascimento italiano* (Florence, 1961), p. 118.

30. Nifo, *In libros de anima*, II, text. comm. 11, f. 66ra; comm. 21, f. 76va; comm. 26, f. 80rb; III, text. comm. 6, f. 26rb–26va. See Simplicius, *In libros Aristotelis de anima commentaria*, ed. Michael Hayduck, Commentaria in Aristotelem graeca, XI (Berlin, 1882), p. 94, lin. 28 to p. 95, lin. 7; p. 102, lin. 12 to p. 103, lin. 8; p. 105, lines 6–13; p. 227, lin. 6–17. Nifo's presentation of Simplicius in *In libros de anima*, text. comm. 19, f. 40rb omits all reference to the notion of "lives" found in the text in question. (See Simplicius, p. 243, lin. 10–32.) On the other hand, when he refers to "lives" in *In libros de anima*, III, text, coll. 1, f. 1va, he assumes incorrectly that the vegetative and sensitive parts form but one life for Simplicius. On Simplicius' doctrine of "lives,"

see Chaignet, *Histoire de la psychologie des grecs,* V, pp. 362–363. Limits of this essay prevent us from analyzing passages from the *De anima* attributed to Simplicius relating to "lives."

31. Nifo, *In libros de anima,* III, text. comm. 19, f. 40rb. However, he appears to take the third intellect to be one for all men when in fact Simplicius held that the third intellect was individual in each man's soul. Nifo's Averroist leanings at this point in his career may have led him to misread Simplicius. See Simplicius, p. 254, lin. 31–35 and 258, lin. 14–17. For discussion regarding the three levels of intellect according to Simplicius, see Chaignet, *Histoire de la psychologie des grecs,* V, pp. 364–370. Although Nifo was later attacked by such philosophers as Marcantonio Genua and Federico Pendasio for having misunderstood Simplicius, his interpretation regarding the unity of the intellect was widely accepted. Bruno Nardi points out that Flaminio Nobili, Francesco Piccolomini, Giacomo Zabarella, and even Genua himself believed that Simplicius held to one intellect for all men. See Nardi, *Saggi,* pp. 389, n. 52, 416–417, 420, 435–437 and 452. Even Nardi himself seems to believe that there is only one intellect for all men according to Simplicius (p. 450). Nifo also presents his interpretation of Simplicius' three levels of intellect in his *Liber de intellectu* (Venice, 1503), I, tr. 4, c. 13, f. 41rb–41va, where he is discussing his own interpretation of Averroes, namely, that there are three agent intellects, the first of which is God. For discussion see my article, "Pier Nicola Castellani and Agostino Nifo on Averroes' Doctrine of the Agent Intellect," *Rivista critica di storia della filosofia* 25 (1970), pp. 387–409, especially pp. 397–407. Nifo's interpretation of Simplicius as holding to the unity of the intellect stands in sharp contrast to Vernia's interpretation. The divergence between Averroes' doctrine of the unity of the intellect and Simplicius' belief that each human being had an intellectual and immortal soul which was proper to him is underscored by Léon Gauthier, *Ibn Rochd (Averroès)* (Paris, 1948), pp. 248–249. Nifo's tendency to interpret Simplicius from an Averroist perspective has been emphasized by Gregory, "Aristotelismo," p. 627 as well as by Nardi.

32. I should like to emphasize that Nifo should not be given sole credit for initiating that tradition. Surely Vernia and also Pico must be kept in mind. It is surprising that there is no mention of Vernia's contribution to the development of interest in Simplicius and Themistius during the Renaissance in Charles B. Schmitt's essay for the Garin Festschrift, "Filosofia e scienza nelle università italiane del XVI secolo," in *Il Rinascimento, Interpretazioni e problemi* (Bari, 1979), pp. 355–398, especially at pp. 358–359 and 361–362. Dr. Schmitt appears to have overlooked my article, "Nicoletto Vernia on the Soul and Immortality." See note 11 above.

33. Nifo, *In libros de anima,* III, text. comm. 1, f. 1rab. See Simplicius, p. 217, lin. 23–37. Cf. Ficino, *Argumentum* to *Ennead* I, 1, c. 8, in *Opera omnia,* pp. 1551–1552. In his *Saggi,* pp. 378–379, Nardi identifies some of the passages from Simplicius that Nifo is here quoting, but he does not indicate Ficino's influence. Compare also Nifo, *In libros de anima,* III, comm. 23, f. 47va to Simplicius, p. 124, lin. 18–35; p. 126, lin. 29–30; and p. 252, lin. 5–7, and Ficino, *Argumentum* to *Ennead,* I, 3, c. 1 and that to I, 1, c. 11 in *Opera omnia,* p. 1560 and pp. 1553–1554.

34. Agostino Nifo, *Liber de intellectu* (Venice, 1503), I, tr. 2, c. 7, ff. 18vb–19ra. See Ficino, *Argumentum* to *Ennead* I, 1, c. 7–8, in *Opera omnia,* pp. 1551–1552. Ficino uses the terms *vita* and *animatio* in *Argumentum* to *Ennead* I, 1, c. 1, p. 1549, and *imago* in I, 1, c. 8, p. 1552. For *vestigium* see Ficino, *Theologia platonica,* XV, c. 5, in *Opera omnia,* p. 338. It should be added that the terms "*vita*" and "*animatio*" are also used by Ermolao Barbaro in his translation of Themistius' paraphrases on the *De anima.* See Themistius, *Paraphrasis de anima,* in *Paraphrasis in Aristotelem,* trans. E. Barbaro, I, c. 23, sig. bb2v, lin. 7–8, 17 and 20 (Heinze: p. 25, lin. 34, p. 26, lin. 7, 12–13) for examples. See also Nifo's discussion of the concept of "animations" and "lives" attributed to Plotinus, Iamblichus, and Proclus in *De intellectu,* I, tr. 3, c. 12, which draws on Ficino, *Argumentum* to *Ennead* I, 1, c. 2, 4, 7, 8, 10 and 12. For discussions regarding Plotinus' own doctrine, see Gaetano Capone Braga, "Il problema del rapporto tra le anime individuali e l'anima dell'Universo nella filosofia di Plotino," *Rivista di filosofia* 23 (1932), pp. 106–125, especially p. 111, where the comparison to light and rays is mentioned; H. J. Blumenthal, "Soul, World-Soul and Individual Soul in Plotinus," in *Le Néoplatonisme* (Paris, 1971), pp. 55–63, especially p. 60.

35. *Ibid.,* I, tr. 2, c. 21, ff. 26vb–27rb. Nifo is relying on Themistius, *In libros Aristotelis de anima*

paraphrasis, ed. R. Heinze, p. 26, lin. 8–21; *Paraphrasis de anima*, trans. E. Barbaro, I, c. 23, sig. bb2v, lin. 17–28. For discussion see my articles, "Agostino Nifo and Saint Thomas Aquinas," *Memorie Domenicane* 7 (1976), pp. 195–226 at pp. 207–208, and "Themistius and the Agent Intellect," pp. 434–438.

36. *Ibid.*, I, tr. 3, c. 20, ff. 33vb–34ra.

37. *Ibid.*, I, tr. 3, c. 27, f. 36rb. See Ficino, *In Timaeum commentarium*, c. 4, in *Opera omnia*, p. 1439. In the same chapter, Nifo had appealed to John the Evangelist, Paul, Moses, Augustine, and other theologians to argue for personal immortality. A few chapters later (I, tr. 3, c. 32, f. 37vb), he discusses the views of Plotinus and Proclus on the individuation of the soul. He is in fact borrowing almost to the word from Ficino, *Theologia platonica*, XV, c. 13, p. 354. See also *Argumentum* to *Ennead* IV, 3, c. 3, pp. 1732–1733. Nifo then attacks this position. For discussion see Bruno Nardi, *Sigieri di Brabante nel pensiero del Rinascimento italiano* (Rome, 1945), pp. 162–163; Mahoney, "Agostino Nifo and Saint Thomas Aquinas," pp. 208–209. The "Platonic" theory of the soul and intellect which Nifo presents in *De intellectu*, I, tr. 4, c. 2, f. 38va is taken from Ficino's *Argumentum* to *Ennead* I, 1, c. 9 and 11, pp. 1552–1553. His summary contains a quotation from Ficino's translation of *Ennead* I, 1, 11.

38. For a discussion of the one-and-many in regard to Soul, see Bréhier, *The Philosophy of Plotinus*, pp. 64–73. Schwyzer alludes to the same theme in regard to *Nous*. See his article, "Plotinos," col. 556.

39. Agostino Nifo, *De immortalitatae animae libellus* (Venice, 1518), c. 5, f. 2rab. There is frequent reference to Themistius and Simplicius in Crisostomo Marcello's *Universalis de anima traditionis opus* (Venice, 1508). See especially V, c. 6–7, ff. 209r–210v and c. 23, ff. 227v–228v. Nifo again makes use of Simplicius and Themistius in his later, Pisan commentary on the *De anima*, but he also makes heavy use of Philoponus. He again says that the Greek commentators, notably Themistius and Simplicius, hold there to be one intellect for all men, but he insists that Aristotle held no such thing. What is more important for our discussion here is that Nifo attacks Vernia for having taught that Plato and Aristotle both held to the preexistence of the human soul and to knowledge as a reminiscence. He argues that Aristotle held neither doctrine. See Nifo, *In libros de anima*, III, comm. 5, ff. 23ra, 23vb, 25rab and 26rb. Earlier in the commentary, he had noted that intelligible and sensible species are concreated with the soul according to Plotinus and the Plato-nists, for whom sensing and thinking are active and not passive. Nifo separates both Themistius and Aristotle from this position, thereby rejecting Vernia's interpretation of Aristotle and that Com-mentator. See Nifo, *In libros de anima*, III, comm. 2, f. 4ra–4vb.

40. See Nardi, *Saggi*, pp. 383–442. Vernia's position is apparently ignored by Nardi.

41. "Utor expositoribus graecis, latinis, arabibus; praecipue vero graecis, unde omnis et excitata et consummata philosophiae cognitio est, Iamblicho, Porphyrio, Alexandro, Themistio, Simplicio, Philopono, caeteris huius modi; post hos Averroi, quem ut multis ante se ita nemine post se inferiorem fuisse comperio. Et, hercule, si conferas eius viri scripta cum graecis, invenies singula eius verba singula esse furta ex Alexandro, Themistio, Simplicio. Sed de hoc alias" (Ermolao Barbaro, *Epistolae, orationes et carmina*, ed. Vittore Branca, I [Florence, 1943], p. 92, letter to Arnoldo di Bost, dated 1485). Ermolao and Vernia were in correspondence with one another. See Ermolao's letter to Vernia, dated 1484, in *Epistolae*, I, pp. 79–80. In a letter to Pico, dated 1485 (*ibid.*, I, pp. 84–87, at p. 86), Ermolao cites Simplicius to argue that no one can understand Aristotle if he doesn't also study Plato.

42. The most striking examples of the concern of church authorities regarding these two topics are the relevant propositions condemned by Stephen Tempier at Paris in 1277, Pietro Barozzi's 1489 edict forbidding public discussion of the unity of the intellect at Padua and the decree of the Fifth Lateran Council regarding the unity and mortality of the soul which was issued in 1513.

43. Proclus, *The Elements of Theology*, ed. E. R. Dodds, 2nd ed. (Oxford, 1963). For discussion see E. Vacherot, *Histoire critique de l'école d'Alexandrie*, II (Paris, 1846; rep. Amsterdam, 1965), pp. 227–234, 242, 247–252, 270–280 and 307ff. Laurence Jay Rosan, *The Philosophy of Proclus* (New York, 1949), pp. 66–80, 101–105, 127, 134–135 and 190–192; Hampus Lyttkens, *The Analogy between God and the World: An Investigation of its Background and Interpretation of Its Use by Thomas of Aquino* (Uppsala, 1952), pp. 66–77; Giuseppe Martano, *Proclo di Atene*.

L'ultima voce speculativa del genio ellenico (Naples, 1974), pp. 128–129 and 155–158, which is a reprint of his *L'uomo e Dio in Proclo* (Naples, 1952); Jean Trouillard, "La monadologie de Proclus," *Revue philosophique de Louvain* 57 (1959), pp. 310–315; Klaus Kremer, *Die neuplatonische Seinsphilosophie und ihre Wirkung auf Thomas von Aquin* (Leiden, 1966), pp. 119–281, especially pp. 208–233; Annick Charles, "Analogie et pensée sérielle chez Proclus," *Revue internationale de philosophie* 23 (1969), pp. 69–88, especially pp. 69–77. It seems extraordinary that there is no reference to the scheme of ascent-descent and hierarchical gradation in H. F. Müller, *Dionysios, Proklos, Plotinos: Ein historischer Beitrag zur neoplatonischen Philosophie*, BGPM, XX, 3–4 (Münster, 1926).

For a valuable and careful analysis of Plotinus' own doctrine of hierarchy, see Dominic J. O'Meara, *Structures hiérarchiques dans la pensée de Plotin*, Philosophia Antiqua, XXVII (Leiden, 1975), pp. 4–6, 44–47, 79–85, 89–90, 97–98, 101–108, 111, 114 and 120–123. Dr. Salvatore R. C. Lilla has pointed out to me that the conceptual scheme is only suggested in Plotinus but becomes hardened in Syrianus, Iamblichus, Proclus, and Damascius. A precise comparison between Plotinus and these other thinkers is out of place here, but a survey of some of the relevant texts in Plotinus does seem appropriate. Plotinus thus speaks of the One as a measure which is itself not measured (*Enneads* V, 5, 4), as the measure and limit of everything else (I, 8, 2), and as the principle of all things (III, 8, 9; VI, 9, 3). All things imitate the One, but some do so in a distant manner, while others do so in a closer manner. Things are thus arranged in a series of priority and posteriority according as they have more or less unity (VI, 2, 11). That is to say, things exist and are unities according as they participate in the One and are closer to or more distant from the One (V, 3, 15–16). Plotinus discerns a diminution downwards through the realms of living things and of natural things (II, 9, 13; III, 2, 3). In the case of souls, they are ranked according as they are nearer to or further away from the intelligible world (IV, 3, 6), that is, according as they descend more or less from *Nous* (IV, 3, 12 and 17). A fuller treatment of Plotinus' doctrine regarding hierarchy in the living and natural realms would of course have to examine the roles played by Soul and the Logos. For discussion, see O'Meara, p. 89–95. Also relevant to the topic of this essay are Plotinus' remarks about the One that it has no place but is everywhere and yet nowhere (VI, 9, 6; VI, 8, 16; see also VI, 5, 4).

44. Dionysius Areopagita, *De divinis nominibus*, c. 2, #10, c. 4, #4 and c. 5, #6, in *Patrologia Graeca*, III (Paris, 1889), cols. 648C, 697C, 700A, 820–821A; *idem, De coelesti hierarchia*, c. 8, #2, col. 240B–C and c. 10, #1, cols. 272D–273B. For discussion see V. Lossky, "La notion des 'Analogies' chez Denys le Pseudo-Aréopagite," *Archives d'histoire doctrinale et littéraire du moyen âge* 5 (1930), p. 292–293 and 298–300; Endre von Ivánka, "Zum Problem des christlichen Neuplatonismus. II. Inwieweit ist Pseudo-Dionysius Areopagita Neuplatoniker?" *Scholastik* 31 (1956), pp. 387–393; Michele Schiavone, *Neoplatonismo e Cristianismo nello Pseudo Dionigi* (Milan, 1963), pp. 76–90, 115–120, 124–133, 198–202 and 215–220. Especially important is René Roques, *L'univers dionysien, Structure hiérarchique du monde selon le Pseudo-Denys* (Paris, 1954), pp. 53–54, 72–81 and 96–106. For a good analysis of the scholarly literature regarding the Pseudo-Dionysius' dependence on Neoplatonism, see Salvatore R. C. Lilla, "Alcune corrispondenze tra il 'De divinis nominibus' dello pseudo-Dionigi l'Areopagita e la tradizione platonica e patristica," in *Studi in memoria di Carlo Ascheri*, Differenze, IX (Urbino, 1970), pp. 149–177. Several scholars have underscored the difference between the Pseudo-Dionysius and the Neoplatonic tradition. See Endre von Ivánka, "'Teilhaben,' 'Hervorgang,' und 'Hierarchie' bei Pseudo-Dionysius und bei Proklos (Der 'Neuplatonismus' des Pseudo-Dionysios)," in *Actes du XIème Congrès International de Philosophie*, XII (Brussels, 1953), pp. 153–158, and also his earlier "La signification du Corpus Areopagiticum," *Recherches de science religieuse* 36 (1949), pp. 5–24, especially pp. 15–18. See also F. Edward Cranz, "The Transmutation of Platonism in the Development of Nicolaus Cusanus and of Martin Luther," in *Nicolò Cusano agli inizi del mondo moderno* (Florence, 1970), pp. 76–77; John M. Rist, "In Search of the Divine Denis," in *The Seed of Wisdom: Essays in Honour of T. J. Meek*, ed. W. S. McCullough (Toronto, 1964), pp 137–138.

45. For editions of the *Liber de causis*, see Otto Bardenhewer, *Die pseudo-aristotelische Schrift Ueber das reine Gute bekannt unter dem Numen Liber de causis* (Freiburg, 1882); ed. Robert Steele in

Roger Bacon, *Quaestiones supra librum de causis, Opera hactenus inedita Rogerii Baconis*, XII (Oxford, 1935), pp. 161–187; Adriaan Pattin, "Le Liber de Causis. Édition établie à l'aide de 90 manuscrits avec introduction et notes," *Tijdschrift voor Filosofie* 28 (1966), pp. 90–203, which was published separately as *Le Liber de Causis*, ed. A. Pattin (Louvain, 1966). For discussion see Pierre Duhem, *Le système du monde*, IV (Paris, 1916), pp. 329–347; Leo Sweeney, "Doctrine of Creation in *Liber de Causis*," in *An Etienne Gilson Tribute*, ed. Charles J. O'Neil (Milwaukee, 1959), pp. 274–289; Henri-Dominique Saffrey, "L'état actuel des recherches sur le *Liber de causis* comme source de la métaphysique au moyen âge," in *Die Metaphysik im Mittelalter, Miscellanea Mediaevalia*, II (Berlin, 1963), pp. 267–281.

46. For discussion regarding the scheme in Augustine, see John Burnaby, *Amor Dei: A Study of the Religion of St. Augustine* (London, 1938 and 1947), pp. 36–41, 90 n. 5, 149–150, 162, 174 and 193–194; Olivier Du Roy, *L'intelligence de la foi dans la Trinité selon saint Augustin* (Paris, 1966), pp. 185–190, 324, 334–337 and 477–478; Robert J. O'Connell, *St. Augustine's Early Theory of Man, A. D. 386–391* (Cambridge, Mass., 1968), pp. 41, 45–49, 114, 117–120 and 143–144; *idem, St. Augustine's Confessions: The Odyssey of Soul* (Cambridge, Mass., 1969), pp. 80–88, 146–149 and 178–181; Émilie Zum Brunn, *La dilemme de l'être et du néant chez saint Augustin* (Paris, 1969); *eadem*, "La dialectique du 'magis esse' et du 'minus esse' chez saint Augustin," in *Le Néoplatonisme* (Paris, 1971), pp. 373–380.

47. See my study, "Metaphysical Foundations of the Hierarchy of Being according to Some Late Medieval and Renaissance Philosophers," which will appear in *Ancient and Medieval Philosophies of Existence*, ed. Parviz Morewedge, to be published by the Fordham University Press in 1981.

48. Albert the Great, *Super Dionysium De divinis nominibus*, ed. Paul Simon, *Opera omnia*, XXXVII, 1 (Aschendorff, 1972), especially c. 1, 4, 5, and 7. See also *De causis et processu universitatis*, ed. A. Borgnet, *Opera omnia*, X (Paris, 1891), II, tr. 1, c. 8, p. 447b; tr. 2, c. 6, p. 488a; tr. 2, c. 15, pp. 500b–501a, c. 22, p. 512ab, c. 24, pp. 514b–515a; tr. 3, c. 4–5, pp. 553a–554a; *Metaphysica: Libros VI-XIII*, ed. Bernhard Geyer, *Opera omnia*, XIV, 2 (Aschendorff, 1964), X, tr. 1, c. 3, pp. 434–435 and 437–438; *Commentarium in primum sententiarum*, ed. A. Borgnet, *Opera omnia*, XV (Paris, 1893), d. 8, A, a. 7–8, pp. 228–230. For discussion see Rudolf Kaiser, "Die Benutzung proklischer Schriften durch Albert den Grossen," *Archiv für Geschichte der Philosophie* 45 (1963), pp. 1–22; Bernhard Geyer, "Albertus Magnus und die Entwicklung der scholastischen Metaphysik," in *Die Metaphysik im Mittelalter*, pp. 9–10.

49. Thomas Aquinas, *Commentum in primum librum sententiarum, Opera omnia*, VII (Paris, 1873), Prol., q. 1, a. 2, ad 2, p. 6; d. 8, q. 4, a. 1, pp. 115–116, and a. 2, ad 3, p. 118; q. 5, a. 1, p. 120; *Quaestiones disputatae de potentia Dei*, in *Quaestiones disputatae*, II, ed. P. Bazzi, et al. (Turin, 1953), q. 3, a. 5, p. 49; *Summa contra Gentiles*, I (Paris, 1959), c. 28, pp. 224–226; *Super librum De causis expositio*, ed. H. D. Saffrey (Fribourg and Louvain, 1954), prop. 4a, pp. 29–32. The basic study on God as a "measure" according to Aquinas is Gaston Isaye, *La théorie de la mesure et l'existence*, Archives de philosophie, XVI, 1 (Paris, 1940). But see also the important essays of Vincent de Couesnongle, "La causalité du maximum. L'utilisation par saint Thomas d'un passage d'Aristote," *Revue des sciences philosophiques et théologiques* 38 (1954), pp. 433–444; "La causalité du maximum. Pourquoi Saint Thomas a't-il mal cité Aristote?", *ibid.*, pp. 658–680; "Mesure et causalité dans la 'quarta via'," *Revue thomiste* 58 (1958), pp. 55–75 and 244–284. On the topic of transferring a proportion from a quantitative relationship to any relationship and on analogy in general, see George P. Klubertanz, *St. Thomas on Analogy* (Chicago, 1960), pp. 27, 31–32, 46–49, 83–84 and 88–92; Bernard Montagnes, *La doctrine de l'analogie de l'être d'après Saint Thomas d'Aquin*, Philosophes médiévaux, VI (Louvain and Paris, 1963), pp. 75–89. There are scattered remarks regarding the scheme in Pierre Faucon, *Aspects néoplatoniciens de la doctrine de saint Thomas d'Aquin* (Lille and Paris, 1975), but no specific analysis of it. On the connection of the scheme to Thomas' doctrine of participation see my article cited above in note 47.

50. Thomas Aquinas, *Quaestiones disputatae de veritate*, q. 2, a. 3, ad 16, and a. 11, ad 4; q. 23, a. 7, c. and ad 9, in *Quaestiones disputatae*, I, ed. R. Spiazzi (Turin, 1953), pp. 34, 51 and 427–429.

51. Thomas Aquinas, *Summa theologiae*, ed. P. Caramello (Turin, 1952), I, q. 8, a. 1, c. and ad 3, p. 36; q. 9, a. 1, ad 3, p. 40; q. 67, a. 2, ad. 3, p. 328. On the metaphorical manner of speaking

involved, see Montagnes, *La doctrine*, pp. 88–89; M. T. L. Penido, *Le rôle de l'analogie en théologie dogmatique*, Bibliothèque Thomiste, XV (Paris, 1931), p. 103.

52. Siger of Brabant, *Questions sur la Métaphysique*, ed. C. A. Graiff, Philosophes médiévaux, I (Louvain, 1948), I, q. 7, pp. 11–22; III, q. 7, pp. 95–96; q. 12, pp. 109–110; q. 8, p. 99 and p. 103. See also Joachim Vennebusch, "Die *Questiones metaphysice tres* des Siger de Brabant," *Archiv für Geschichte der Philosophie* 48 (1966), pp. 182–183. For discussion see Fernand Van Steenberghen, "La composition constitutive de l'être fini," *Revue néoscolastique de philosophie* 41 (1938), pp. 489–518, especially pp. 510–518; *idem, Maître Siger de Brabant*, Philosophes médiévaux, XXI (Louvain and Paris, 1977), pp. 289–293 and 297–301; Armand Maurer, "*Esse* and *Essentia* in the Metaphysics of Siger of Brabant," *Mediaeval Studies* 8 (1946), pp. 68–86. The scheme is also to be found in Siger's late questions on the *Liber de causis*. See *Quaestiones super Librum de causis*, ed. Antonio Marlasca, Philosophes médiévaux, XII (Louvain and Paris, 1972), q. 46, pp. 163–164.

53. Henry of Ghent, *Summae quaestionum ordinariarum*, I (Paris, 1520; repr. St. Bonaventure, 1953), a. 1, q. 6, f. 27; a. 25, q. 2, f. 148v–150r; a. 26, q. 2, f. 159v; *Summae quaestionum ordinariarum*, II, q. 1, f. 4r and f. 5r; a. 42, q. 2, ff. 6r–8r; *Quodlibeta* (Paris, 1518; repr. Louvain, 1961), Quodl. III, q. 5, f. 53r; IV, q. 15, ff. 124r–124v, 129r and 130r; V, q. 1, f. 152r and f. 143r; q. 3, f. 155v and f. 157r; q. 11, f. 169v; q. 12, f. 171r; VI, q. 1, f. 215r–215v; q. 2, f. 220r; q. 3, f. 221v; IX, q. 1, f. 393v and q. 2, ff. 346r–347r; XI, q. 11, f. 465v, f. 466v and f. 477r. There is no explicit treatment of the scheme in the classic work of Jean Paulus, *Henri de Gand: Essai sur les tendances de sa métaphysique* (Paris, 1938), but see p. 302 n. 2 and pp. 308–309 n. 2. See also José Gómez Caffarena, *Ser participado y ser subsistente en la metafísica de Enrique de Gante* (Rome, 1958), p. 153–158.

54. Giles of Rome, *Quaestiones metaphysicales super libros metaphysicae Aristotelis* (Venice, 1501; repr. Frankfurt, 1966), X, q. 1, ff. 35va–36ra; q. 3, ff. 36vb–37ra; q. 4, f. 37vab; q. 6, f. 38rb–38vb; XI, q. 1, f. 39rb; *Primus Sententiarum* (Venice, 1521), dist. 8, par. 1, prin. 2, q. 1, a. 2, ff. 47vb–48ra; a. 3, f. 48va; *In secundum librum sententiarum quaestiones*, I (Venice, 1581; repr. Frankfurt, 1968), dist. 1, q. 3, a. 3, pp. 40a–41a; dist. 2, q. 1, a. 2, pp. 109b–110a; dist. 3, pars 1, q. 2, a. 2–5, pp. 195b–197b, 200ab and 206a; dist. 3, pars 2, q. 2, a. 2, p. 245ab; a. 4, pp. 256a–257b. Girolamo Trapè has written a number of highly informative articles on Giles' metaphysics. See for example his "Causalità e partecipazione in Egidio Romano," *Augustinianum* 9 (1969), pp. 91–117. However, there is no explicit discussion of the scheme. In like fashion, William E. Carlo presents texts containing the scheme in Giles' writings, but he too does not explicitly study it. See Carlo's *The Ultimate Reducibility of Essence to Existence in Existential Metaphysics* (The Hague, 1966).

55. Godfrey of Fontaines, Quodl. I, q. 3, in *Les quatre premiers Quodlibets*, ed. M. De Wulf and A. Pelzer, Les philosophes belges, II (Louvain, 1904), pp. 242–247; Quodl. VII, q. 1, q. 7, q. 8, q. 12, in *Les Quodlibet cinq, six et sept*, ed. M. De Wulf and J. Hoffmans, Les philosophes belges, III (Louvain, 1914), pp. 265–266, 359–360, 364 and 388–389; Quodl. X, q. 1, in *Le deuxième quodlibet*, ed. J. Hoffmans, Les philosophes belges, IV, 3 (Louvain, 1931), pp. 298-299. It should be emphasized that Godfrey makes very tentative use of the scheme and does not appear to give wholehearted endorsement to it. For discussion see John F. Wippel, "The Dating of James of Viterbo's Quodlibet I and Godfrey of Fontaines' Quodlibet VIII," *Augustiniana* 24 (1974), pp. 348–386, especially pp. 350–362; Maurice De Wulf, *Étude sur la vie, les oeuvres et l'influence de Godefroid de Fontaines* (Brussels, 1904), pp. 116–118 and 122–123.

56. On the Pseudo-Dionysius and his influence in the Middle Ages, see Paul Lehmann, "Zur Kenntnis der Schriften des Dionysius Areopagita im Mittelalter," *Revue Bénédictine* 35 (1923), pp. 81–97, especially for earlier period; H. F. Dondaine, *Le Corpus Dionysien de l'Université de Paris au XIIIe siècle* (Rome, 1953); Josef Koch, "Augustinischer und dionysischer Neuplatonismus und das Mittelalter," *Kant-Studien* 48 (1956/1957), pp. 117–133, reprinted in his *Kleine Schriften*, I (Rome, 1973), pp. 3–25; Joseph Turbessi, "L'influence du Pseudo-Denys en Occident," in *Dictionnaire de spiritualité*, III (Paris, 1957), cols. 343–356; M. Cappuyns, "Le Pseudo-Denys l'Aréopagite en occident au moyen âge," in *Dictionnaire d'histoire et de géographie ecclésiastique*, XIV (Paris, 1960), col. 290–295; Piero Scazzoso, *Ricerche sulla struttura del linguaggio*

dello pseudo-Dionigi Areopagita (Milan, 1967), pp. 193–200. For his influence on Albert, see Francis Ruello, *Les noms divins et leurs "raisons" selon saint Albert le Grand, commentateur du "De divinis nominibus"*, Bibliothèque Thomiste, XXXV (Paris, 1963). The classic study for Thomas is, of course, J. Durantel, *Saint Thomas et le Pseudo-Denis* (Paris, 1919).

On the *Liber de causis*, see Saffrey, "L'état actuel des recherches sur le *Liber de causis*," cited above in note 45. Its influence on Thomas has been studied by various scholars. Among them are C. Vansteenkiste, "Il *Liber de causis* negli scritti di San Tommaso," *Angelicum* 35 (1958), pp. 325–374; Daniel A. Callus, "Les sources de Saint Thomas," in *Aristote et Saint Thomas d'Aquin* (Louvain and Paris, 1957), pp. 149–153; and Werner Beierwaltes, "Der Kommentar zum 'Liber de causis' als neuplatonisches Element in der Philosophie des Thomas von Aquin," *Philosophische Rundschau* 11 (1963), pp. 192–215. The influence of Dionysius and the *Liber de causis* on Giles of Rome is brought out by Girolamo Trapè, "Il platonismo di Egidio Romano," *Aquinas* 7 (1964), pp. 309–344. See also Carlo, *The Ultimate Reducibility*, especially pp. 57–86.

Translations of the *Elements of Theology* and other works of Proclus by William of Moerbeke made him directly accessible to the Christian medievals. See Clemens Baeumker, *Witelo*, BGPM, III, 2 (Munster, 1908), p. 261–271; Martin Grabmann, *Mittelalterliches Geistesleben*, II (Munich, 1936), pp. 413–423; *idem, Guglielmo di Moerbeke O. P. il traduttore delle opere di Aristotele* (Rome, 1946), pp. 147–160; Gérard Verbeke, "Guillaume de Moerbeke traducteur de Proclus," *Revue philosophique de Louvain* 51 (1953), pp. 349–373. Moerbeke's translation of the *Elements* has been edited by C. Vansteenkiste in *Tijdschrift voor Filosofie* 13 (1951), pp. 263–302 and 491–531. For influence on Albert in particular, see, among others, Rudolf Kaiser, "Die Benutzung proklischer Schriften durch Albert den Grossen," *Archiv für Geschichte der Philosophie* 45 (1963), pp. 1–22. On Moerbeke's own sympathies for Neoplatonism, see Maurice de Wulf, *Histoire de la philosophie médiévale*, 5th ed., II (Louvain and Paris, 1925), p. 110, Grabmann, *Guglielmo di Moerbeke*, pp. 57–61 and 147–160.

57. On the doctrine of intension and remission of form in medieval philosophy, see Anneliese Maier, *Zwei Grundprobleme der scholastischen Naturphilosophie*, 2nd ed. (Rome, 1951), pp. 1–109; Marshall Clagett, "Richard Swineshead and Late Medieval Physics," *Osiris* 9 (1950), pp. 131–161. There is a good general survey of fourteenth-century developments regarding the latitude of forms in John E. Murdoch, "*Mathesis in philosophiam scholasticam introducta*: The Rise and Development of Mathematics in Fourteenth-Century Philosophy and Theology," in *Arts libéraux et philosophie au moyen âge* (Montreal and Paris, 1969), pp. 215–254, especially pp. 238–249. See also Edith D. Sylla, "Medieval Concepts of the Latitude of Forms. The Oxford Calculators," *Archives d'histoire doctrinale et littéraire du moyen âge* 40 (1973–1974), pp. 223–283, especially pp. 252–256.

58. On Swineshead's influence in Italy during the fifteenth and sixteenth centuries, see Marshall Clagett, *The Science of Mechanics in the Middle Ages* (Madison, 1961), pp. 644–652 and 659–671; John E. Murdoch and Edith Dudley Sylla, "Swineshead, Richard," in *Dictionary of Scientific Biography*, XIII (New York, 1976), pp. 184–213, at pp. 209–210 and 212. See also Carlo Dionisotti, "Ermolao Barbaro e la fortuna di Suiseth," in *Medioevo e Rinascimento: Studi in onore di Bruno Nardi*, I (Florence, 1955), pp. 217–253; Garin, *Storia della filosofia italiana*, pp. 444–449 and 456–457.

59. Paul of Venice, *Scriptum super librum de anima* (Venice, 1481), II, tr. 1, c. 3, t. c. 2, sig. e7rb; *Expositio super octo libros physicorum Aristotelis necnon super commento Averrois cum dubiis eiusdem* (Venice, 1499), V, tr. 1, c. 3, t. c. 19, sig. B5rb.

60. See Paul O. Kristeller, *The Philosophy of Marsilio Ficino*, trans. V. Conant (New York, 1943), pp. 74–84 and 98–109; *idem, Il pensiero filosofico di Marsilio Ficino* (Florence, 1953), pp. 66–77 and 93–105. The general conception of the scheme was accepted by Ficino in his early *Tractatus de Deo, natura et arte*, written in 1454 or 1455. See Kristeller, *Studies in Renaissance Thought and Letters* (Rome, 1956), pp. 44–46 and 64–65. The joint influence of Neoplatonism and Thomism on Ficino's metaphysics has been well highlighted by Kristeller, *Medieval Aspects of Renaissance Learning*, ed. and trans. E. P. Mahoney, Duke Monographs in Medieval and Renaissance Studies, I (Durham, N.C., 1974), pp. 76–77.

61. See Kristeller, *The Philosophy*, p. 14 and p. 160; *idem, Il pensiero*, p. 27 n. 4 and p. 169 n. 1.

62. Marsilio Ficino, *The "Philebus" Commentary*, ed. and trans. Michael J. B. Allen (Berkeley, Los

Angeles and London, 1975), I, c. 27, pp. 251–257, c. 36, pp. 359–365; II, c. 1, pp. 387–393. For discussion regarding whether God is transcendent to or included within the ascending hierarchy of things, see Walter Dress, *Die Mystik des Marsilio Ficino* (Berlin and Leipzig, 1929), pp. 34–35 and 55, and Giuseppe Anichini, *L'Umanesimo e il problema della salvezza in Marsilio Ficino* (Milan, 1937), pp. 34–37. See also Kristeller, *The Philosophy*, pp. 82–83; *idem*, *Il pensiero*, pp. 75–77; Ardis Collins, *The Secular is Sacred: Platonism and Thomism in Marsilio Ficino's "Platonic Theology"* (The Hague, 1974), pp. 18–19, 44–45, and 55–56.

63. Marsilio Ficino, *Theologia Platonica*, II, c. 2 and c. 3, in *Opera omnia*, pp. 93 and 95. For Ficino's commitment to the scheme see *ibid.*, X, c. 3, p. 226 and XI, c. 6, pp. 259–260. Kristeller brings out Ficino's adoption of the scheme. See ch. IX of *The Philosophy*, entitled "Primum in Aliquo Genere," especially pp. 147, 150–153 and 159–166 (*Il pensiero*, pp. 154–155, 157–161 and 167–175). For discussion on the way in which Ficino's philosophy reflects both the Plotinian and medieval conceptions of hierarchy, the one emphasizing a few general spheres and the other accepting only grades or species, see Kristeller, *The Philosophy*, pp. 75–76 and 80–82 (*Il pensiero*, pp. 67–68 and 72–75); Michael J. B. Allen, "The Absent Angel in Ficino's Philosophy," *Journal of the History of Ideas* 36 (1975), pp. 219–240. See also A. K. Lloyd, "Primum in genere: The Philosophical Background," *Diotima* 4 (1976), pp. 32–36, who emphasizes the background of Aristotle, Plotinus, and Proclus. It should perhaps be noted that, while Ficino does accept the two poles of the scheme, he especially emphasizes the role of God as a measure.

64. Ficino, *Theologia Platonica*, XI, c. 4, pp. 247–249 and 252–253.

65. See George of Trebizond, *Comparationes [sic] philosophorum Aristotelis et Platonis* (Venice, 1523; repr. Frankfurt, 1965), II, c. 2, sig. D4v5 and E7v, who argues that all creatures are equally distant from God inasmuch as all are infinitely distant from him. In his *In calumniatorem Platonis libri IV*, III, c. 6, in Ludwig Mohler, *Kardinal Bessarion als Theologe, Humanist und Staatsmann*, II (Paderborn, 1927; repr. Aalen, 1967), pp. 238–239, Cardinal Bessarion escapes from George's criticism by suggesting that that relation of creatures to God can be understood either as to an infinite God or as to a being that is more perfect than any other being and which is the highest being. He uses texts from Aquinas and Augustine in arguing for his general position.

66. Gabriele Zerbo adopts the scheme in his *Quaestiones metaphysicales* (Bologna, 1482), I, q. 1, sig. A3vb–A4ra; XII, q. 10, sig. ee5ra–ee6rb. He rejects the position and arguments of the "Calculator," that is, Swineshead, in X, q. 3, sig. aa3rb–aa4rb.

67. See Pearl Kibre, "Cardinal Domenic Grimani, 'Questio de Intensione et Remissione Qualitatis': A Commentary on the Tractate of that Title by Richard Suiseth (Calculator)," in *Didascaliae: Studies in Honor of Anselm M. Albareda*, ed. Sesto Prete (New York, 1961), pp. 187–194.

68. Pietro Pomponazzi, *Corsi inediti dell'insegnamento padovano, vol. I: "Super libello de substantia orbis expositio et quaestiones quattuor" (1507)*, ed. Antonino Poppi (Padua, 1966), c. 2, pp. 110–111; q. 1, pp. 195 and 210; *idem*, *Tractatus de intensione et remissione*, in his *Tractatus acutissimi, utillimi et mere peripatetici* (Venice, 1525), Proemium and Sectio prima, c. 1, f. 2rab; c. 5–7, ff. 3ra–3vb; Sectio quinta, c. 6–7, ff. 15vb–17vb. For a discussion of the latter work, see Curtis Wilson, "Pomponazzi's Criticism of Calculator," *Isis* 44 (1953), pp. 355–363.

69. Antonio Trombetta, *Opus in Metaphysicam Aristotelis Padue in thomistas discussam cum quaestionibus perutilissimis antiquioribus adiectis* (Venice, 1502), f. 84rb. See also f. 77vb and 94rb. On Trombetta see Antonino Poppi, "Lo scotista patavino Antonio Trombetta (1436–1517)," *Il Santo* 2 (1962), pp. 349–367.

70. Thomas de Vio, *In De ente et essentia D. Thomae Aquinatis commentaria*, ed. M. H. Laurent (Turin, 1934), c. 5, #103, pp. 162–163, and c. 6, #131, pp. 210 and 212–213; Iacobus Brutus, *Corona Aurea* (Venice, 1496), sig. i7r–i8v. Cajetan's commentary was finished at Padua in 1495. A few years later, in a question finished at Pavia in 1499, he faced the problem of how God could be infinitely distant from creatures and yet measure them by their approach to him. See his "Utrum Deus gloriosus sit infinitae virtutis," in his *Opuscula omnia* (Venice, 1588), p. 193a and p. 205b. For discussion see Antonino Poppi, *Causalità e infinità nella scuola padovana dal 1480 al 1513* (Padua, 1966), pp. 170–185.

71. See *Destructiones destructionum Averrois cum Augustini Niphi de Suessa expositione*, cited above in note 26.

72. For references to the *Liber de causis*, see *ibid.*, III, dub. 12, f. 35vb; VII, dub. 3, f. 84vab; VII,

dub. 5, f. 89ra; XIV, dub. 1, f. 122rb. Albert's commentary on the work is cited at XIV, dub. 1, f. 119ra. On the possible influence of Thomas, see my article, "Agostino Nifo and Saint Thomas Aquinas," pp. 197–198.

73. *Ibid.,* III, dub. 12, ff. 35rb–36vb; dub. 16, ff. 42vb–43ra; VIII, dub. 1, f. 92ra. See also III, dub. 14, f. 14vb; dub. 19, f. 52ra; V, dub. 3, f. 70rb. The scheme also appears in Nifo's *De intellectu* and his commentaries on Aristotle's *De anima* (1503) and Averroes' *De beatitudine animae* (1508). For further discussion see my article, "Pier Nicola Castellani and Agostino Nifo on Averroes' Doctrine of the Agent Intellect," especially pp. 397–405.

74. Marcantonio Zimara, *Annotationes in Joannem Gandavensem super quaestionibus Metaphysicae,* in John of Jandun, *Quaestiones in duodecim libros Metaphysicae* (Venice, 1505), f. 174rb–174va and f. 175va; *Theoremata seu memorabilium propositionum limitationes* (Venice, 1539), prop. 10, f. 6ra; prop. 12, f. 9ra; prop. 13, f. 9vab. On Zimara see Antonio Antonaci, *Ricerche sull'aristotelismo del Rinascimento: Marcantonio Zimara* I (Lecce-Galatina, 1971); Nardi, *Saggi,* pp. 321–355.

75. On Achillini see Herbert Matsen, *Alessandro Achillini (1463–1512) and His Doctrine of "Universals" and "Transcendentals"* (Lewisburg, 1974); Nardi, *Saggi,* pp. 179–279; Garin, *Storia della filosofia italiana,* pp. 502–504 and 563–564.

76. Zimara, *Theoremata,* prop. 13, ff. 9vb–10ra.

77. Alessandro Achillini, *De intelligentiis quodlibeta* (Bologna, 1494), Quodl. I, q. 1, sig. A2ra; Quodl. II, q. 1, sig. B6ra; q. 4, sig. C4vb; Quodl. V, q. 1 and q. 2, sig. F3ra–F3va and F4ra–F5ra. For discussion, see Nardi, *Saggi,* pp. 200–202 and 220–221.

78. Zimara, *Theoremata,* prop. 13, f. 10ra.

79. Giovanni Crisostomo Javelli, *Epitome super propositionibus libri de causis* (Venice, 1567), prop. IV, ff. 28r–30r.

80. Gaspare Contarini, *Primae philosophiae compendium,* in his *Opera* (Paris, 1571), II, pp. 106–107, 110, and 117; III, p. 123; IV, pp. 141–143; VI, pp. 161–162 and 167.

81. Francesco Buonamici, *De motu libri decem* (Florence, 1591), X, c. 17, p. 928; c. 40, pp. 975–976; c. 42, pp. 979–980; c. 43, pp. 981–982. For further analyses of this work see Alexandre Koyré, *Études galiléennes,* I (Paris, 1939), pp. 18–41; William A. Wallace, "Buonamici, Francesco," *Dictionary of Scientific Biography,* II (New York, 1970), pp. 590–591. Professor Wallace was kind enough to draw my attention to these passages. I shall examine the thought of Contarini, Buonamici, Galileo, Mazzoni, and Cremonini regarding hierarchy in greater detail on another occasion.

82. *Ibid.,* X, c. 42, pp. 980–981. He explicitly attacks the "Calculator" (that is, Swineshead) and Achillini for taking the zero grade of being as the sole measure of hierarchy. See X, c. 41, p. 977.

83. Galileo Galilei, "Juvenilia," q. 5, in *Le opere di Galileo Galilei,* ed. Antonio Favaro, I (Florence, 1890), p. 78, lin. 14–25 and p. 95, lin. 32 to p. 96, lin. 4. However, Galileo does not discuss in these passages whether the zero grade of being can be taken as the measure of all things. The *Juvenilia* are early notebooks apparently based on the lecture notes of various Jesuit professors at the Collegio Romano and other writers. See William A. Wallace, "Galileo and the Thomists," in *Saint Thomas Aquinas, 1274–1974: Commemorative Studies,* I (Toronto, 1974), pp. 293–330, especially pp. 325–330; *idem, Galileo's Early Notebooks: The Physical Questions* (Notre Dame, 1977), pp. v–viii, 12–24 and 270–274; *idem,* "Galileo Galilei and the Doctores Parisienses," in *New Perspectives on Galileo,* eds. Robert E. Butts and Joseph C. Pitt (Dordrecht and Boston, 1977), pp. 87–138; A. C. Crombie, "The Sources of Galileo's Early Natural Philosophy," in *Reason, Experiment, and Mysticism in the Scientific Revolution,* eds. M. L. Righini Bonelli and William R. Shea (New York, 1975), pp. 157–175 and 303–305.

84. Jacopo Mazzoni, *In universam Platonis et Aristotelis philosophiam praeludia sive de comparatione Platonis et Aristotelis* (Venice, 1597), p. 16 and pp. 47–48. Professor Wallace and Professor Frederick Purnell, Jr. brought these passages to my attention and discussed them with me. Mazzoni rests much of his argument on Contarini's *Primae philosophiae compendium,* but he also makes some use of Aquinas. On Galileo's relations with Mazzoni, see Frederick Purnell, Jr., "Jacopo Mazzoni and Galileo," *Physis* 14 (1972), pp. 273–294. Both Mazzoni and Cremonini are mentioned by Alexander Koyré in his *Metaphysics and Measurement* (Cambridge, Mass., 1968), pp.

35–36; *Études d'histoire de la pensée scientifique* (Paris, 1966), pp. 12, 149, 152, 167–168 and 197; "Galileo and Plato," *Journal of the History of Ideas* 4 (1943), pp. 402 and 420–421.

85. Cesare Cremonini, *Disputatio de coelo in tres partes divisa* (Venice, 1613), Part III, Section 2, c. 2, pp. 320–321; c. 3, pp. 321–322; c. 4, pp. 323–326; c. 5, pp. 327–330; and c. 6, pp. 330–331 and 333. He cites in the first text (pp. 320–321) Nifo's *De intellectu* (Venice, 1503), I, tr. 4, ff. 43vb–44va and Zimara's *Theoremata*, prop. 40, ff. 25vb–26rb. For Galileo's acquaintance with Cremonini, see Antonio Favaro, *Galileo Galilei e lo studio di Padova,* 2 vols. (Florence, 1883), I, pp. 282–283, 392–394 and 466; II, pp. 29–30, 36–42, 87 and 283. On the thought of Cremonini, see among others Léopold Mabilleau, *Étude historique sur la philosophie de la Renaissance en Italie (Cesare Cremonini)* (Paris, 1881), especially pp. 191–264, 349–355, and 357–366; Giuseppe Saitta, *Il Rinascimento,* 2nd ed., II (Florence, 1961), pp. 436–454, who discusses Cremonini's *De coelo* but not the scheme; Maria Assunta Del Torre, *Studi su Cesare Cremonini, Cosmologia e logica nel tardo aristotelismo padovano* (Padua, 1968), especially pp. 53–88; Stillman Drake "Galileo and the Career of Philosophy," *Journal of the History of Ideas* 38 (1977), pp. 12–32, especially pp. 21–28. In his *Storia della filosofia italiana,* p. 559, Eugenio Garin appears to attribute the scheme to Cremonini, but the matter is not wholly clear. In any case, he does not mention the passages in Cremonini's *De coelo* which we have cited.

86. See *Enneads* V, 5, 10; V, 8, 9; VI, 5, 11; VI, 7, 32; VI, 8, 9; VI, 9, 6. On the One as infinite and on Plotinus' general doctrine of infinity see Joseph Moreau, "L'un et les êtres selon Plotin," *Giornale di metafisica* 11 (1956), pp. 209–213 and 221; Leo Sweeney, "Infinity in Plotinus," *Gregorianum* 38 (1957), pp. 515–535 and 713–732; *idem,* "Another Interpretation of *Enneads* VI, 7, 32," *The Modern Schoolman* 38 (1960–1961), pp. 289–303; *idem,* "Basic Principles in Plotinus' Philosophy," *Gregorianum* 42 (1961), pp. 506–516; W. Norris Clarke, "Infinity in Plotinus: A Reply," *Gregorianum* 40 (1959), pp. 75–98; Rist, *Plotinus,* pp. 24–37. Of particular note are two essays of A. H. Armstrong, "Plotinus' Doctrine of the Infinite and its Significance for Christian Thought," *The Downside Review* 73 (1955), pp. 47–58, especially p. 53, and "God's Transcendence and Infinity" in A. H. Armstrong and R. A. Markus, *Christian Faith and Greek Philosophy* (New York, 1960), pp. 8–15, especially p. 12. He comments that when Plotinus calls the One the measure, he does not refer to him as infinite. I hope to return to this point on another occasion.

87. See *Enneads,* VI, 8, 9 and 20. For comment see A. H. Armstrong, *An Introduction to Ancient Philosophy* (Boston, 1963), pp. 155 and 182; O'Meara, *Structures hiérarchiques,* pp. 58–59, n. 22 and p. 98, nn. 12–13.

88. For bibliography on Proclus, see note 43 above. In his commentary on the *Elements of Theology* (p. xxi), Dodds notes that Proclus hardens into a "law" what Plotinus expresses only in a tentative fashion. See also my essay, "Metaphysical Foundations," n. 2.

89. See William R. Schoedel, "'Topological' Theology and Some Monistic Tendencies in Gnosticism," in *Essays on the Nag Hammadi Texts in Honour of Alexander Böhlig,* ed. Martin Krause (Leiden, 1972), pp. 88–108; *idem,* "Enclosing, Not Enclosed: The Early Christian Doctrine of God," in *Early Christian Literature and the Classical Intellectual Tradition; In Honorem Robert M. Grant* (Paris, 1979), pp. 75–86. I am endebted to my colleague at Duke, Professor Robert C. Gregg, for bringing these essays to my attention.

90. On the contrary, Gregory rejects the notion of degrees of "more" and "less" being, appears to consider all creatures to be an equal distance from God, and maps out major divisions in the metaphysical hierarchy rather than a gradually ascending scale of degrees or species. Indeed, he appears to reserve the notions of degrees of perfection and of "more" and "less" participation for the human being's striving for greater and greater perfection and likeness to God, a God who by reason of his infinity will never be reached. See the clear and helpful study of David L. Balás, *ΜΕΤΟΥΣΙΑ ΘΕΟΥ: Man's Participation in God's Perfections according to Saint Gregory of Nyssa,* Studia Anselmiana, IV (Rome, 1966), pp. 44, 51, 55, 62, 77–78, 114–115, 130–135 and 154–155. See also Endre Ivánka, *Hellenisches und Christliches im frühbyzantinischen Geistesleben* (Vienna, 1948), pp. 43–49 and Ekkehard Mühlenberg, *Die Unendlichkeit Gottes bei Gregor von Nyssa* (Göttingen, 1966), especially pp. 147–165. For a sample of Gregory's notion of the soul's unending ascent upwards toward an infinite God who can never be reached, see his *De vita*

Moysis, ed. Herbert Musurillo, *Gregorii Nysseni Opera*, vol. VII, pars 1 (Leiden, 1964), Book II, pp. 110–117.

91. This essay was completed in its final form during the tenure of a fellowship from the John Simon Guggenheim Foundation for 1979–1980. Many friends and colleagues have discussed with me various of the topics which it covers. However, I must thank in particular Robert C. Gregg, Paul O. Kristeller, Dominic O'Meara, and Frederick Purnell for helpful advice and information which enabled me to complete the essay.

ANDREAS CAMUTIUS ON THE CONCORD OF PLATO AND ARISTOTLE WITH SCRIPTURE

Note: Research for this paper was facilitated by grants from the Harvard University Center for Renaissance Studies, The American Philosophical Society, and the John Simon Guggenheim Memorial Foundation. I am also indebted to the Biblioteca Trivulziana of Milan for providing a microfilm of Camuzio's *Praefatio*. B. P. Copenhaver and P. O. Kristeller made various helpful suggestions while I was preparing the final draft for publication.

1. See esp. J. Soudek, "The Genesis and Tradition of Leonardo Bruni's Annotated Latin Version of the (Pseudo-)Aristotelian *Economics*," *Scriptorium* 12 (1958), 260–8; "Leonardo Bruni and His Public: a Statistical and Interpretative Study of the Annotated Latin Version of the (Pseudo-) Aristotelian *Economics*," *Studies in Medieval and Renaissance History* 5 (1968), 51–136; "A Fifteenth-Century Humanistic Bestseller: the Manuscript Diffusion of Leonardo Bruni's Annotated Latin Version of the (Pseudo-)Aristotelian *Economics*," in *Philosophy and Humanism: Renaissance Essays in Honor of Paul Oskar Kristeller* (Leiden, 1976), 129–143; H. Goldbrunner, "Durandus de Alvernia, Nicolaus von Oresme und Leonardo Bruni. Zu den Übersetzungen der pseudo-aristotelischen Ökonomik," *Archiv für Kulturgeschichte* 50 (1968), 200–39; "Leonardo Bruni's Kommentar zu seiner Übersetzung der pseudo-aristotelischen Ökonomik: ein humanistischer Kommentar," in eds. A. Buck and O. Herding, *Der Kommentar in der Renaissance* (Bonn-Bad Godesberg, 1975), 99–118. In general see E. Garin, "Le traduzioni umanistiche di Aristotele nel secolo XV," *Atti dell'Accademia fiorentina di scienze morali "La Colombaria"* N.S. 2 (1947–50), 55–104.

2. M. Flodr, *Incunabula classicorum* (Amsterdam, 1973).

3. See F. E. Cranz, *A Bibliography of Aristotle Editions, 1501–1600* (Baden Baden, 1971), which is far from complete.

4. This is true for essentially all of Aristotle's works. The documentation for this will appear in the section on Latin translations of Aristotle which I am preparing for *Catalogus translationum et commentariorum*. One typical example is the pseudo-Aristotelian *De virtutibus et vitiis* of which there is a single thirteenth-century translation, three fifteenth-century translations, eight versions from the sixteenth century, and two from the early seventeenth century. See my "Aristotle's Ethics in the Sixteenth Century: Some Preliminary Considerations" in *Ethik im Humanismus*, eds. W. Ruëgg and D. Wuttke (Boppard, 1979), 87–112.

5. Fabro, *La nozione metafisica di partecipazione secondo S. Tommaso d'Aquino* (Milan, 1939) and later editions and translations.

6. The terms *"generatio"* and *"corruptio"* were used in all the medieval translations to render γένεσις and φθορά. The same usage continued through the fifteenth century with the translations of Georgius Trapezuntius and Andronicus Callistus and into the sixteenth century with the new rendering of Agostino Nifo, who in this matter might be called the last of the medievals. The other sixteenth-century translations by Vatable (1519), Alcionio (1521), Périon (1550), Grouchy's revision (1552), and Nobili (1567) wavered between the titles of *De ortu et interitu* (Vatable, Périon, and Grouchy) and *De generatione et interitu* (Alcionio and Nobili). The new usage gradually won the day at the end of the sixteenth century with Vatable's translation getting into both the Casaubon and Duval editions. For further details and documentation see my "Some Observations on the Renaissance Translations of Aristotle" to appear in the proceedings of the Colloquium on the Transmission and Reception of Knowledge held at Dumbarton Oaks (Washington) in May, 1977.

7. For one example see E. J. Ashworth, "Agostino Nifo's Reinterpretation of Medieval Logic," *Rivista critica di storia della filosofia* 31 (1976), 354–374.
8. This has yet to be worked out in detail, but see E. Garin, *Rinascite e rivoluzioni. Movimenti culturali dal XIV al XVIII secolo* (Bari, 1975), 316.
9. D. P. Walker, *The Ancient Theology* (London, 1972), incorporating papers written in the early 1950s.
10. See the references given in my "Reappraisals in Renaissance Science," *History of Science* 16 (1978), 200–214, at 212n26.
11. See C. B. Schmitt, *A Critical Survey and Bibliography of Studies on Renaissance Aristotelianism, 1958–1969* (Padua, 1971) and "Towards a Reassessment of Renaissance Aristotelianism," *History of Science* 11 (1973), 159–193.
12. On this see the literature cited in *Storia di Milano* (Milan, 1953–1966) XI, 353n5.
13. The full title of the work is *Andreae Camutii ad reverendissimum et illustrissimum episcopum et principem Tridentinum dominum D. Christophorum Matrucium, in Sacrarum Literarum cum Aristotele et Platone concordiam, Praefatio*. At the end we read: "Ex Academia Ticinensi pridie nonas Decembreis, anno virginei partus M.D.XLI. Sacrarum Literarum placita, neque Aristoteli neque Platoni aliqua ex parte adversari, et fatemur, et asserimus. Disputabitur Mediolani, die et hora alias publicanda. Excudebat Ticini Io. Maria Simoneta." The only copy known to exist is in the Biblioteca Trivulziana and is described in *Le cinquecentine della Biblioteca Trivulziana. Il Le edizioni lombarde,* ed. G. Bologna (Milan, 1966), 131 (no. 283) and *Index aureliensis* VI, 382 (no. 130. 936). My citations will be to my photocopy which I have paginated from the beginning and it is hereafter referred to simply as *Praefatio*.
14. I have used the following sources: Zedler, *Grosses Universal Lexicon* (Halle-Leipzig, 1732–1754) V, 491; Supplementband IV, 1367; C. G. Joecher, *Allgemeines Gelehrten-Lexicon* (Leipzig, 1750–1751) I, 1617; J. C. Adelung, *Fortsetzung und Ergänzungen* (Leipzig, 1784–1897; repr. Hildesheim, 1960–1961) II, 72; F. Argelati, *Bibliotheca scriptorum Mediolanensium* (Milan, 1745; repr. Farnborough, 1966), 2076–2077; G. B. Giovio, *Gli uomini della Comasca* (Modena, 1784), 326; A. Fabroni, *Historia Academiae Pisanae* (Pisa, 1791–1795; repr. Bologna, 1971) II, 281–284; *Dictionnaire historique, critique et bibliographique* (Paris, 1821–1823) V, 418; Michaud, *Biographie universelle,* nouv. éd. (Paris, 1854) VI, 524; Hoefer, *Nouvelle biographie générale* (Paris, 1855–1866), VIII, 431–432; *Dictionnaire historique et biographique de la Suisse* XII (1924), 396; *Biographisches Lexikon der hervorragenden Ärzte* (Berlin-Vienna, 1929–1935) I, 816; M. E. Cosenza, *Biographical and Bibliographical Dictionary of the Italian Humanists* (Boston, 1962) I, 815. A. L. Albanese, "The Theory of Love and Happiness of Andrea Camuzio" (Ph.D. thesis, Columbia University, 1973 = *Dissertation Abstracts* 34 (1973), p. 2544A [order no. 73–28 180] adds little which is new. Of these Argelati and Fabroni are probably the most helpful. I have not been able to see G. A. Oldelli, *Dizionario storico-ragionato degli uomini illustri del Canton Ticino* (Lugano, 1807–1811) and G. Ghilini, *Alcune biografie di medici illustri* [per nozze Tecchio-Sardi] (Venice, 1880).
15. See the material cited in note 12 and C. Salzmann, "Francesco Camuzios Consilium über das Steinleiden," *Gesnerus* 8 (1951), 168–176 and "Der Luganersee. Betrachtung zu einem Brief des Humanisten Francesco Cicereio aus Mailand an den Luganeser Arzt Girolamo Camuzio aus den Jahr 1539," *Gesnerus* 10 (1953), 69–76.
16. Argelati (note 14), 2076.
17. "Neque enim me praeterit multos esse, qui me plus iusto audacem dicant et temerarium, quod iuvenis adhuc utpote novem et viginti vix natus annos, de altissimis philosophiae locis (nam et theologiam eandem esse cum philosophia contendimus) de sublimibus naturae mysteriis, quae nemo hactenus ne olfacere quidem ausus est nedum adgredi, in amplissimo doctissimorum hominum coetu saepe disputationes promulgare non dubitem" (*Praefatio,* 19).
18. See note 34 below.
19. The secondary works agree on this and it seems to be the implication of various indirect statements in the *Praefatio*.
20. *Memorie e documenti per la storia dell'Università di Pavia* (Pavia, 1877–1878; repr. Bologna, 1970) I, 121, 169.
21. *Ibid.,* 169: "Dal 1538 al 1559 non insegnò, cessò affatto dal 1568, nel qual anno credesi morto."

22. Jerome Cardan, *The Book of My Life* (*De vita propria liber*), trans. J. Stoner (New York, 1930; reprint New York, 1962), 44. For the original text see Jérôme Cardan, *Ma vie*. Texte présenté et traduit par Jean Dayre (Paris, 1936), 30.

23. *Andreae Camutii disputationes quibus Hieronymi Cardani magni nominis viri conclusiones infirmantur, Galenus ab eiusdem iniuria vindicatur, Hippocrates praeterea aliquot loca diligentius multo, quam unquam alias explicantur* (Paris, 1563) [copy used: British Library 774.b.9(3)]. According to the table of contents in volume I of Cardano's *Opera* (Lyon, 1663) this work should appear in volume VIII, but I have been unable to locate it in the reprint (Stuttgart-Bad Cannstatt, 1966).

24. This presumably happened in 1568 when he left Pavia. See above note 21. According to Hoefer (note 14) he was called to Vienna in 1564.

25. *Andreae Camutii Serenissimae Imperatricis physici de amore atque felicitate libri novem* (Vienna, 1574) [copy used Vatican Library Barb. L.IX.25]. There is a manuscript of this work which I have not seen in Milano, Biblioteca nazionale Braidense A. G. IX. 31 [see P. O. Kristeller, *Iter Italicum* (London-Leiden, 1963f.) I, 358]. The manuscript version is in six books.

26. *Ibid.*, fol.)(iii[r.] The letter is dated July 1, 1574.

27. *Andreae Camutii . . . excussio brevis praecipue morbi nempe cordis palpitationis Maximiliani secundi Caesaris invictissimi simul ac aliorum aliquot virorum illustrium praeter naturam affectuum* (Florence, 1578) [copy used British Library 1187. a. 1(1)]. I have not seen the reprint of the same work issued at Florence in 1580 [Index Aureliensis 130. 942]. There is a substantial literature on the illness and death of Maximilian II. See H. Schöppler, "Über den Tod Kaiser Maximilians II," *Mitteilungen zur Geschichte der Medizin und der Naturwissenschaften* 9 (1910), 219–225, which cites the earlier literature.

28. E.g., *Dictionnaire . . . de la Suisse* (note 14) XII, 396 and *Biographisches Lexikon der . . . Ärzte* (note 14) I, 816. See note 21 for a death date as early as 1568.

29. Fabroni (note 14). His presence there is corroborated by Pisa, Archivio di Stato, Univ. G. 77, fols. 155–165 and Univ. 178–179, during which time he was the highest paid professor in the Faculty of Arts at Pisa, earning more than twice the salary of his nearest rival.

30. Fabroni (note 14) II, 341–344. Cf. Schmitt, "Girolamo Borro's *Multae sunt nostrorum ignorationum causae* (Ms. vat. Ross. 1009)" in *Philosophy and Humanism: Renaissance Essays in Honor of Paul Oskar Kristeller* (Leiden, 1976), 462–476, at 463–464.

31. Camuzio is listed in the *rotulo* published in *Le opere di Galileo Galilei,* ed. A. Favaro (Florence, 1929–1939), XIX, 33.

32. I have thus far uncovered no information regarding the precise date of his death. He is not listed in the Pisa *rotulo* for the academic year 1587–1588, cited above in note 29.

33. H. Jedin, *A History of the Council of Trent,* trans. F. Graf (London, 1957f.) I, 570n6.

34. MS Vat. lat. 3725 [s. XVI, 22 fols., on vellum, well written in a neat italic hand; see Kristeller, *Iter* II, 323]. *Andreas Camutius contra Martinum Lut[h]erum. Ad S.D.N. Paulum III Pontificem Max. in ecclesiae catholicae defensionem contra haeresiarchas nostrae tempestatis Andreae Camutii, praefatio.* The MS is dated "Lucani pridie Kalendas Iulias anno virginei partus 1544." At the end is written: "Disputabitur Romae die et hora alias publicanda." This formula is the same as that used in *Praefatio,* cited above in note 13.

35. "Huius monitis alias Aristotelis et Platonis dogmata pro viribus publica disputatione conciliavi, quod caeteri utriusque interpraetes ne somniarunt quidem, tantum abest ut praestiterint: Ioannem Picum Mirandulam excipio, qui in epistola quadam ad Angelum Politianum, pollicitus est quidem Aristotelis et Platonis concordiam, sed morte praeventus quod pollicitus fuerat, conficere non potuit. Porro quam strenue aut (si quibus potius arridet) quam male me gesserim hoc in negotio, testes sunt viri Bononienses nobilissimi, quorum incredibilem expertus sum humanitatem nullo aevo posthabendam: testis est clarissima Patavinorum et Ticinensium Academia. Deffendi et seorsum prius cuncta Platonis dogmata: adhaec genii eiusdem instinctu priusquam publice profiteret, quartum et vigesimum vix natus annum, omnes pene dignas Aristotelis interpraetum controversias collegi summo cum labore, deffendique in utranque partem in clarissimo Ticenensium Gymnasio" (*Praefatio,* 19–20). For Pico's letter to Poliziano (i.e., *De ente et uno*) see G. Pico della Mirandola, *De hominis dignitate, Heptaplus, De ente et uno,* ed. E. Garin (Florence, 1942),

385–441. Camuzio then goes on to quote at length Gianfrancesco Pico's account of his uncle's attempt to reconcile Plato and Aristotle. Cf. G. F. Pico, *Opera quae extant omnia* (Basel, 1601), 486 [*Examen vanitatis* I,2].

36. *Andreae Camutii theoricam in Gymnasio Ticinensi primo loco publice profitentis, de humano intellectu libri quatuor* (Pavia, 1564) [copy used Florence, Biblioteca nazionale 5. 9. 56]. The prefatory letter, dated June 1564, reads in part: "Verum enimvero profusa Dei benignitas interim credentibus ultro nobis, affatim sapientiae latices effundit, humanam certitudinem (quam scientificae demonstrationes parturiunt) longo intervallo superantes. Adeo constat experientia (quanquam humanae cognitionis fineis egreditur) fidei habitum, ei quem scientiae gignunt, anteire: quod adpositissime summi vir ingenii Mirandulanus ille Ioannes Picus aetatis suae decus adnotavit" (fol. *₃ᵛ).

37. "Obiicient (dico) mei adversarii (quorum Ticini praecipue maximus numerus viget) laudes in ore proprio sordescere" (*Praefatio*, 21).

38. "Eo nanque animo sunt, cum philosophi, tum Sacrarum Literarum professores, ut existiment philosophiae studium peripatheticum praecipue, Sacrae Theologiae plurimum adversari, philosophorumque placita theologorum sanctionibus, salutaribusve Christi praeceptis omni ex parte reluctari" (*Praefatio*, 1).

39. Following on from the text quoted in the previous note, he says: "Horum sententiae quae vulgo probatur dudum subscripsi, favique adeo, ut interea puderet pigeretque studiorum meorum" (*Ibid.*).

40. "Etenim si istud donemus, inficiari non possumus philosophiam nihil aliud agere praeterquam decipere, circumvenire, praestigiari, veluti magicis machinamentiis siderare homines, ac pro arbitrio (ut rhetores) in candida quod aiunt nigrum vertere, in nigra candidum. Nunquid igitur philosophiae professores rerum caussas non docent, sed tanquam argumentosi homines rerum puritatem ludicris veluti, et calamistris dehonestant, ac in quam libuerit faciem habitumque transformant, ut non quales suape natura res naturales ac divinae, sed quales voluerint, non fiant quidem, sed cum non sint, esse tamen audientibus appareant?" (*Ibid.*, 1–2).

41. "Proh Deum atque hominum fidem, si philosophus talis tantusque impostor est, qui publice in doctissimorum coetibus profiteri passim permittitur? Quid? Quod quidam ultro obstrepunt idem apud philosophos verum esse, quod in theologia mendacium sit, quasi unius rei multiplex possit esse veritas?" (*Ibid.*, 2).

42. The roots of two quite different tendencies are to be found in the intellectual tradition stemming from Plato. One is the synthetic, metaphysical, dogmatic, and constructive side which developed into Neoplatonism. The other is the critical, negative, antidogmatic, and destructive side that developed into Academic scepticism. See my discussion in *Cicero scepticus* (The Hague, 1972), 51–53, 160.

43. E. N. Tigerstedt, *The Decline and Fall of the Neoplatonic Interpretation of Plato* (Helsinki, 1974).

44. "Quod variis ratiociniis aucupari humana ratio contendit, id lex divina severa quadam maiestate sancitur, quo facile liquidove videatur utranque [i.e., philosophiam et theologiam] ad eundem finem dirigi, utrius siquidem finis est divinae essentiae (ut philosophice dixerim) cognitio" (*Praefatio*, 3). Cf. Ficino, *Opera* (Basel, 1561), 668.

45. "Philosophus nanque, cum divino propter contemplationem atque decoro frequenter adhaereat, ob idque divinus ipse decorus, quoad homini possibile est, efficiatur, ea quae in superna illa mente intuetur, ad mores hominum iure optimo et privatim et publice transferat, oportet" (*Praefatio*, 10). Ficino adopts a similar position, for example in the *Quaestiones quinque de mente* in *Opera*, 675–682.

46. "Obstrepant licet sacrarum literarum philosophiaeque professores, ego sum huius sententiae, ut existimem sacrosanctae theologiae praecepta Aristotelis atque Platonis placitis nulla ex parte reluctari, quinetiam conspirare in omnibus" (*Praefatio*, 18).

47. Ficino, *Opera*, 853–854.

48. *Praefatio*, 4.

49. *Ibid.*

50. "Quamobrem cum aliis in rebus, tum hoc in negotio praecipue mihi semper visus est Plato

sapienter laborasse, quod disputationes ubique morales ad bene beateque vivendum institutas proposuerit ad purgandum adolescentum animos. Mox ad naturalia investiganda perexit, hinc ad divina indaganda paulatim ascendit" *(Ibid.).*

51. "Ac cum ex naturalium contemplatione abunde didicerit animam quandam esse harmoniam, pro viribus nititur, ut fortitudinem cum temperantia misceat, harmoniamque in moribus constituat compositioni animae quae harmonia dicitur, si fieri possit, maxime conformem. Quod harmonia quaedam sit animus, coelestique harmoniae aliquando (ut Platonice dixerim) assuetus, vel illud evidentissimum argumentum esse potest, quod nullum animal praeter hominem rhithmi et harmoniae sensum habet. Quinetiam corpus nostrum teste Platone harmonia quadam consistit: vegetant et harmonia quadam plantarum partes, omnium denique mixtorum temperaturae harmonia vigent, praecipue primum animae instrumentum spiritus. Huiusce rei argumentum est, quod si vindictae cupiditate nonnunquam (ut fit) exarserit, per consonantiam vocum aëream, aëreum spiritum motu penetrantem, praesertim si tanta fuerit consonantia, ut affectum canentis et animam secum transferat: tunc praecipue audientis affectum movet affectu, et animum afficit animo, sensimque mentem in pristinum habitum restituit, iramque propulsat. Hinc sit, ut animus pulchra et consona, propterea quod natura suae conformia sint et cognata, semper desyderet. Hinc nimirum Academici passim inculcant optimum id esse ingenium, quod ex temperantia et fortitudine mixtum sit, utpote docile, memor, ad divina propensum, cumque eiusmodi ingenia recte educata sunt, religionis cultum ab iis in alios proficisci verissimum, civitatisque omnium utilissimum asserunt. Tantum potest in hominum mentibus miscella fortitudinis cum temperantia, quam philosophus ex rerum naturalium divinarumque contemplatione primum invexit" *(Praefatio,* 7–9).

52. "Atque hoc in negotio praecipue Plato mihi semper visus est caeteris praestare, cum de musica passim disserat atque gymnastica, quod magni sint momenti, plurimumque conferant ad fortitudinis temperantiaeque mixtionem consequendam aut conservandam" *(Ibid.,* 9).

53. Further investigation is required to determine the cultural *ambiente* at Pavia during those years. Among those teaching philosophy at Pavia during Camuzio's time are Branda Porro (who was also subjected to abuse by Cardano), Arcangelo Lanfranconi (a Carmelite), Giulio Ferrari, and Filippo Marchesi (a Franciscan).

54. See C. B. Schmitt, "L'Introduction de la philosophie platonicienne dans l'enseignement des universités à la Renaissance," in *XVIe Colloque international de Tours: Platon et Aristote à la Renaissance* (Paris, 1976), 93–104, at 99, and the literature cited there.

55. In addition to the works listed above in notes 13, 23, 25, 27, 34, and 36, there are also the following two published works: (1) *Rationes adductae in articulos duos . . . de sacramento ordinis . . .* (Pavia, 1563) [not seen: Index aureliensis 130. 938] and (2) *Andreae Camutii . . . de nobilitate libri octo hactenus in lucem nusquam editi* (Milan, 1641) [copy used: Florence, Biblioteca nazionale 22. 6. 13]. Besides the manuscript works already mentioned, there are various letters scattered through various collections of manuscripts.

56. E. Cassirer, *Die platonische Renaissance in England und die Schule von Cambridge* (Leipzig-Berlin, 1932), Einleitung (1–5).

TRIADS AND TRINITY IN THE POETRY OF ROBERT BROWNING

1. A prefatory footnote, also, is essential. I am conscious that, in thus surveying the Browning canon, I have drawn on the wisdom of many critics read over the years whose names will not appear in the ensuing notes. To all such, my gratitude is here expressed. I thank also my colleagues and friends, Thomas J. Collins, Donald S. Hair, Cory Bieman Davies, and Linda Dowler, with all of whom I have conversed, fruitfully from my point of view, during the evolution of this paper.

2. *The Works of Robert Browning,* ed. F. G. Kenyon, Centenary Edition (London, 1912; rpt. New York: Barnes and Noble, 1966), "Pauline," pp. 292, 295. All further line references will be drawn from this edition and incorporated in the text.

3. New York: MacMillan, 1891.

4. Boyd Litzinger, in *Time's Revenges: Browning's Reputation as a Thinker, 1889–1962* (Knoxville: University of Tennessee Press, 1964), documents the decline in Browning's reputation and calls for reassessment.

   Jones is answered most directly by Philip Drew in "Henry Jones on Browning's Optimism," *Victorian Poetry* 2 (1964), pp. 29–41. He expands his arguments in *The Poetry of Browning: A Critical Introduction* (London: Methuen, 1970); a long note on p. 186 gives examples of the "incalculable" and misleading influence of Jones' work. Drew's sane discussions are representative of good modern criticism on the issues here raised. He is not directly concerned with triadic or trinitarian formulations.

5. To speak of birth as the "descent" of the soul was commonplace in Plato and his followers, and in ancient Gnosticism; the philosophers usually showed themselves conscious of using metaphor, the Gnostic mythmakers less so. Two brief references: "The Descent of the Soul" in *The Essential Plotinus,* trans. and ed. Elmer J. O'Brien (Toronto: Mentor, 1964), 59–71; Hans Jonas, *The Gnostic Religion* (Boston: Beacon, 1958), pp. 62–64.

6. Christopher Butler, *Number Symbolism* (London: Routledge and Kegan Paul, 1970), p. 3.

7. In notes to a previous essay, "An *Eros Manqué*: Browning's 'Andrea del Sarto'," *Studies in English Literature* 10 (Autumn, 1974), pp. 252–254, I cite evidence and confirming opinion concerning Browning's familiarity with the Platonic tradition. More recently, Curtis Dahl and Jennifer L. Brewer have written on "Browning's 'Saul' . . . A Neoplatonic-Hermetic Approach," *Browning Institute Studies* III (1975), pp. 101–118. John Maynard, in *Browning's Youth* (Cambridge: Harvard University Press, 1977), pp. 85–96, describes the encyclopedic nature of Browning's father's library. *Curiosa* and standard works of all kinds, in Greek, Latin, Hebrew, and many modern languages were available, both directly, and as filtered through the elder Browning's retentive memory. Thurman Los Hood, in *Browning's Ancient Sources* (Cambridge: Harvard, 1922), offers exhaustive lists of analogues and sources for specific passages in Browning: Plato, Suetonius, Plutarch, Cicero, and Iamblichus are among those cited. Judith Berlin-Lieberman, in *Robert Browning and Hebraism* (Jerusalem: n.p., 1934) demonstrates Browning's familiarity with rabbinical sources, without being concerned directly with their possible use as vehicle of Neoplatonic commonplaces.

8. A brief description of Hegel's dynamic system is available in most encyclopedias and histories of philosophy: see, for example, *New Encyclopedia of Philosophy,* eds. J. Grooten and G. Jo Steenbergen (New York: Philosophical Library, 1972), pp. 180–183.

9. At the risk of anticipating key arguments in this paper: the process of critical discovery, as the revealing of the desired end, bears a precise analogy to Browning's understanding of the poetic process as his means of reaching towards his Answer.

10. The stages in Browning's development that culminate in the completed "Saul" have been described by such critics as F. E. L. Priestley, Thomas J. Collins, William Whitla, and David Shaw. Notes to my article, "The Ongoing Testament in Browning's 'Saul'," *University of Toronto Quarterly* 43 (Winter, 1974), pp. 151–168, give particulars.

11. I indicate at this point some fairly recent publications that bear on matters here addressed. H. B. Charlton's "Browning as Poet of Religion," first published in the *Bulletin of the John Rylands Library* (June, 1943), was given fresh currency in 1970 in a Folcroft Library Edition. It all but ignores Jones' adverse charges in providing an outline of Browning's more positive assertions concerning faith, and misses the constant presence of scepticism in the scheme of things. William Whitla's *The Central Truth: The Incarnation in Robert Browning's Poetry* (Toronto: University of Toronto Press, 1963) recognizes the continuing importance of scepticism in Browning, seeing the movement through doubt and the recognition of love to acceptance of the incarnate Christ; but Whitla does not deal with the differences in emphasis I find important between early, central, and late periods, as defined by my awareness of such differences. (His organization is thematic, without, of course, ignoring chronology.) He finds Browning's "trinitarian" position a good deal more readily definable than I do. He equates the Holy Spirit with Knowledge, without underscoring the radical necessity of the act of choice in knowing, itself dependent upon the fruitful scepticism. Norton B. Crowell in *The Triple Soul: Browning's Theory of Knowledge* (University

of New Mexico Press, 1963) is not as concerned with triadic formulations as his title suggests. He offers, primarily, a series of readings of individual poems that are chosen to demonstrate Browning's view of man's quest for knowledge.

12. In "The Ongoing Testament . . . ." I develop more fully the easily recognized evidence that Browning sees himself in a prophetic role.

13. W. C. DeVane, *A Browning Handbook* (New York: Appleton-Century-Crofts, 1955), p. 55.

14. F. E. L. Priestley, in "The Ironic Pattern of Browning's *Paracelsus,*" *University of Toronto Quarterly* 34 (1964) pp. 68–81, and Collins, in *Robert Browning's Moral-Aesthetic Theory, 1833–55* (Lincoln: University of Nebraska Press, 1967), p. 30, emphasize the degree to which Aprile's aspiration to love "infinitely" misleads Paracelsus at this point. I agree that Aprile's words feed Paracelsus' passion for infinity, but find the Priestley and Collins arguments not at all incompatible with mine, that Paracelsus glimpses the partial truth here that "love" and "power" belong together. For suggestions as to how I will have it both ways, see the paragraph on vertical and horizontal dimensions of the dyadic dilemma on page 194.

15. C. G. Jung's two essays on Paracelsus, accessible in *The Spirit in Man, Art, and Literature* (Princeton: Bollingen, 1966), give an interesting and concise impression of the life, with enough historical particulars to substantiate Browning's characterization.

16. Paracelsus, like most Renaissance mages, dabbled in cabalistic lore. Some method is suggested in his madness if we recall the prominence of the occult commonplace "as above, so below" in Cabala with the suggestion therein of a reciprocal dynamic between spiritual and mundane realms. A passage in *Zohar* on the creation of man (ed. G. G. Scholem, New York: Schocken, 1963 pp. 31–33) witnesses to the close interrelationship between upper and lower worlds in rabbinical lore, a devout mystical awareness pushed towards manipulative magic in Renaissance occultism. See also Keith Thomas, *Religion and the Decline of Magic* (Harmondsworth: Penguin, 1971), pp. 264–274.

17. See note 10, and works therein cited.

18. Collins, p. 122, points to evidence in the "Essay on Shelley" which implies that the movement of conversion for Browning was essentially complete by 1852, in which case the stanzas in question may have been written at least that long before publication.

19. They have been anticipated, too, in the luminous watersnakes that provide release for Coleridge's ancient mariner from the stagnation that has bound him.

20. In stanza xii.

21. The dissenters' chapel of the speaker's choice should not be too closely identified with the York Street Congregational Chapel attended by the youthful Browning with his mother, which was more pretentious than the one the poem presents. See Maynard, pp. 51–62, and Hoxie N. Fairchild, *Religious Trends in English Poetry* IV (New York: Columbia, 1957), p. 139.

22. Images from Genesis 2:9 and Revelation 22:2 underlie these words of course. Fallen life itself becomes the median term stretching between primal innocence and *eschaton.*

23. DeVane, p. 298.

24. *Enneads* III, 8 (available in O'Brien, 163–175); *Paradise Lost* V, 469–505.

25. The poem is subtitled "Or, Natural Theology in the Island."

26. The usage of the term "Molinists," in multiple occurrences throughout *The Ring and the Book,* is curious. Browning clearly intends it to refer to the followers of Miguel de Molinos, who are mentioned only once in the Old Yellow Book that serves as his major source; these "heretics" espoused, in the late seventeenth century, a form of contemplative mysticism known usually as "Molinosism," or as "Quietism." "Molinism," in church history, is not regarded as a heresy: it is a legitimate doctrine on the freedom of the will established in the sixteenth century by Luis de Molina. Helen M. Loschky, in "Free Will Versus Determinism in *The Ring and the Book,*" *Victorian Poetry* 6 (1968), pp. 333–352, reviews the criticism to that point, and finds as I do, against the majority of earlier discussants, that Browning is not at all confused in his usage. (The thrust of her argument is towards the earlier term, of mine towards both.) Browning's conflation serves to provide appropriate historical coloring to his narrative, a purpose for which "Molinosism" would have done at some strain to the metrics; the term serves, through evidences that a mystical heresy is being indicated, to point to the apprehensions of eternal truth by inner means while

avoiding the term "Quietism" which would be quite foreign to the active encounters with spiritual truth Browning is interested in presenting; and it serves to suggest the dimensions of willful choice that are central to Browning's own evolved theology. It is doubtful that he would have expected many readers to catch the play upon terminology, but in a poet whose applications of erudition impressed his incompatible contemporary Swinburne with their precision (see Clyde de L. Ryals, *Browning's Later Poetry*, Ithaca: Cornell, 1975, p. 245), such density in the function of obscure detail is not surprising.

27. See F. E. L. Priestley, "A Reading of 'La Saisiaz'," *University of Toronto Quarterly* 25 (1955), pp. 47–59; and Cory Bieman Davies, "From Knowledge to Belief in *La Saisiaz: The Two Poets of Croisic*," *Studies in Browning and his Circle* 6 (1978), pp. 7–24.

28. Donald S. Hair, in "Exploring Asolando," *Browning Society Notes* 8 (1978), pp. 3–6, finds in the volume's subtitle "Fancies and Facts" a useful focus for ranging through the volume.

29. DeVane, p. 553.

30. Ryals, p. 238.

31. John Donne, "A Hymn to God my God, in my Sickness," available in many anthologies as well as in *John Donne, The Complete English Poems*, ed. A. J. Smith (Harmondsworth: Penguin, 1971) p. 347.

32. "A Death in the Desert," 1. 101.

THE CHRISTIAN PLATONISM OF C. S. LEWIS, J. R. R. TOLKIEN, AND CHARLES WILLIAMS

1. *Descent of the Dove* (Grand Rapids, Mich.: William B. Eerdmans Publishing Co., 1974) copyright date is 1939.

2. *Surprised by Joy* (London, England: Fontana Books, 1959) copyright date is 1955, chapters XIII, XIV, and XV.

3. *Taliessin Through Logres* in Charles Williams and C. S. Lewis, *Taliessin Through Logres, The Region of the Summer Stars*, and *Arthurian Torso* (Grand Rapids, Mich.: Eerdmans Publishing Co., 1974) copyright date of *Taliessin Through Logres* is 1938. Six of Williams' novels are currently published by Eerdmans Publishing Co.: *Shadows of Ecstasy, War in Heaven, Many Dimensions, The Greater Trumps, The Place of the Lion,* and *Descent into Hell*. The seventh novel, *All Hallows' Eve*, is published by Noonday Press.

4. "On Fairy Stories" in *The Tolkien Reader* (New York: Ballentine Books, 1966).

5. *Ibid.*, p. 72.

6. *The Chronicles of Narnia* are currently published by Collier Books: *The Lion, The Witch, and The Wardrobe; Prince Caspian; The Voyage of the Dawn Treader; The Silver Chair; The Horse and His Boy; The Magician's Nephew;* and *The Last Battle*.

7. *The Last Battle*, p. 170.

8. p. 73.

9. *Essays Presented to Charles Williams*, ed. C. S. Lewis (Eerdmans Publishing Co., 1966), p. 8.

10. *Ibid.*, p. 9.

11. *The Lord of the Rings* consists of *The Fellowship of the Ring, The Two Towers,* and *The Return of the King* (New York: Ballentine Books, 1965) copyright date is 1963.

12. *The Silmarillion* (London, England: George, Allen, and Unwin, 1977).

13. The Trilogy is currently published by Macmillan: *Out of the Silent Planet; Perelandra;* and *That Hideous Strength*. The quotation is from *Perelandra*, p. 199.

14. p. 195.

15. *The Place of the Lion*, p. 116.

16. *Sophist* 248C in the *Dialogues of Plato*, trans. B. Jowett (New York: Random House, 1892).

17. *Ibid.*, p. 190.

18. *Surprised by Joy*, chap. XI. Also, *The Abolition of Man* (New York: MacMillan, 1947), pp. 86–90.

19. *The Abolition of Man*, loc. cit.

20. *Out of the Silent Planet*, p. 131.
21. p. 189.
22. *Symposium* 201D–212A in *The Dialogues of Plato*, trans. B. Jowett.
23. *The Voyage of the Dawn Treader*, chap. VII.
24. In my opinion, Williams' desire to express this philosophico-religious position in literary art is firmly within the Platonist tradition. Here the beauty of the material is expressed in the beauty of poetry.
25. *The Place of the Lion*, chap. XI.
26. chap. 18.
27. *The Voyage of the Dawn Treader*, p. 184.
28. p. 206.
29. *That Hideous Strength*, chap. XVII.
30. C. S. Lewis, *The Four Loves* (New York: Harcourt Brace and World, 1960).
31. *The Lion, The Witch, and The Wardrobe*, chap. X.
32. *The Place of the Lion*, chap. XI.
33. *The Last Battle*, chap. XV.

NEGATIVE THEOLOGY, MYTH, AND INCARNATION

1. The Academic rather than the Pyrrhonian is, I think, the strongest sceptical element in our tradition. It differs from the Pyrrhonian in admitting degrees of probability, and so leaving room for enthusiasm, and even a degree of commitment (though not absolute commitment). See the generally excellent statement of the difference between the two traditions by the Pyrrhonian Sextus Empiricus (*Outlines of Pyrrhonism* 226–231): though it does not seem to be true that, as Sextus asserts, the Academics fell into the elementary mistake of stating dogmatically that they knew that they did not know, or that Carneades in any way illegitimately smuggled certainty as an ultimate norm into his theory of probability: see A. A. Long, *Hellenistic Philosophy* (London, 1974) pp. 94–99.

2. J. Trouillard, "Valeur critique de la mystique Plotinienne" in *Revue philosophique de Louvain* 59 (August, 1961) pp. 431–434: "Raison et Mystique chez Plotin" in *Revue des études augustiniennes* 20 (1974) pp. 3–14: "Théologie négative et autoconstitution psychique chez les néoplatoniciens" in *Savoir, faire, espérer: les limites de la raison* (Publications des Facultés Universitaires Saint-Louis, Brussels, 1976) pp. 307–321: A. H. Armstrong "The Escape of the One" in *Studia Patristica XIII* (Berlin, 1975) pp. 77–89: "Negative Theology" in *Downside Review* vol 95, no 320 (July, 1977) pp. 176–189.

3. "Of course he [Plato] used metaphor, and metaphor is basic; how basic is the most basic philosophical question." Iris Murdoch, *The Fire and the Sun* (Oxford, 1977) p. 88.

4. See Christopher Stead, *Divine Substance* (Oxford, 1977) ch. x, *Conclusion*. Plotinus uses a great deal of positive "substance" language about God, in the way described, in VI 8 [39] where in my view, which I propose to develop in another paper, he is arguing, patiently though not without irritation, with a Christian theist much concerned about the free will of God. But the Neoplatonic work that uses substance and knowledge-language most strikingly (and quite coherently) of God in a context of extremely radical negative theology is the anonymous commentary on the *Parmenides* so admirably studied and edited by P. Hadot in his *Porphyre et Victorinus* (Paris, 1968: text of the Commentary in vol. II), especially IV and V (pp. 74–83, Hadot: fol. 94ᵛ and fol. 64ᵛ), It is not quite as certain as Hadot supposes that the commentary is by Porphyry. I hope that my pupil Dr. G. Adolf will publish his reasons for questioning the identification of the author. But it is a most original Neoplatonic work, of great importance for the development of negative theology.

5. In "Théologie négative et autoconstitution psychique . . ." (see note 2) pp. 312–313: "Dès lors, la notion de "Dieu caché" change de sens. Le Dieu de saint Augustin et de saint Thomas est caché parce que, étant la plénitude infinie de l'intelligibilité, sa trop grande clarté nous éblouit, comme le soleil regardé en face offusque nos yeux. L'Un néoplatonicien est nocturne parce qu'il refuse tout contenu intelligible et toute pensée. Il est au-delà l'ordre de connaissance. Il n'a donc pas de

secret, c'est-à-dire d'essence qui se déroberait au regard. Cela ne veut pas dire qu'il ne peut se communiquer et qu'il reste muré dans une transcendance inaccessible." What follows, on the immanent interior transcendence of the One as an "inexhaustible starting-point," always before, never attained by, thought is very relevant to a proper understanding of what I mean by "myth" in its extended and positive sense.

6. For my curious use of "icon," cf. "Negative Theology" (see note 2) pp. 188–189.

7. *Divine Names* 4. 13 (712A–B).

8. In "Le Merveilleux dans la vie et la pensée de Proclos," in *Revue philosophique de la France et de l'Etranger*" (1971) pp. 439–452; section 3 "La fonction de l'imagination," pp. 447–452. The principal source for the views of Proclus on poetic myth is *In Rempublicam* I 368–407, 69–205 Kroll, especially 368–378, 71–86 Kroll.

9. *The Fire and the Sun* (see note 3), especially pp. 69–89.

10. I refer particularly to his "Does Christology Rest on a Mistake" in *Religious Studies* 6.1. (March, 1970) pp. 69–76 and his second essay in *The Myth of God Incarnate* (London, 1977) "Myth in Theology," pp. 148–166. I also find very satisfying his treatment, both historical and theological, of a most important and difficult theme in the "myth," that of resurrection, in the appendix to his *Remaking of Christian Doctrine* (London, 1974) pp. 125–146. I find this much more satisfying than the summary dismissal of the resurrection by both sides in the older controversy between Jaspers and Bultmann (originally published in book form as *Die Frage der Entmythologisierung*: English translation (*Myth and Christianity*) first printed in paperback New York, 1958 and frequently reprinted since). In many ways, however, my position is fairly close to that of Jaspers', and I agree with much in his defense of liberalism and his appreciation of the religious value of myth.

11. I have in mind particularly his essay in *The Myth of God Incarnate* (see note 10) "The Christ of Christendom," pp. 133–147, and his numerous and vigorous defenses of his position since, generally on radio or television.

12. On the historical Jesus I am at present in general agreement with the position of Dennis Nineham in his somewhat devastating *Epilogue* (pp. 186–204) to *The Myth of God Incarnate* (see note 10), which shows clearly what very awkward questions a serious critical study of the evidence can raise.

13. Cf. Gilbert Murray *Greek Studies*, pp. 66f and E. R. Dodds, *The Greeks and the Irrational* (University of California Press, 1951) pp. 179–180.

14. I have discovered this by experience in dialogue with an Indian and an Isma'ili friend. If they spoke the language of their own traditions and I spoke the language of Neoplatonism, we understood each other without much need of interpretation. P. Hadot, in his profound interpretation of Hellenic philosophy as a whole, *Exercices Spirituels* (*Annuaire de l'École Pratique des Hautes Études*, 5ᵉ Section, T. *LXXXIV*, pp. 25–70) has demonstrated that we have in our own Western tradition a rich and varied store of the sort of wisdom for which many people now look to the East.

15. In *The Origins of Christology* (Cambridge, 1977). The excellent hypotheses—clearly presented as such—of the chapters devoted to a scholarly consideration of the New Testament evidence do not, unfortunately, seem to me, even if they are taken as certain conclusions from that evidence, to support sufficiently the apologetic conclusion.

16. Those of others will, of course, be different. It is perfectly possible to make a "Jesus of scholarship," even before he goes out of fashion, the historical foundation of a myth: and for very many people a Semitic rather than a Hellenic form of myth, incarnational or nonincarnational, Jewish, Christian, or Muslim, will be the right and necessary one. My own reasons for especially disliking un-Hellenic or de-Hellenized Western Christian or post-Christian biblical myths would take too long to explain adequately: it would be necessary to deal with such subjects as the disjunctiveness of biblical monotheism, the "meaning of history," and the harm done in real history by the idea of an elect or chosen people in its various forms. (Of course, in many of them the gentiles of the myth will include or be Jews).

17. My belief that what I had noticed in Dionysius was really there was strengthened by discovering that Dr. Bernhard Brons had noticed the same phenomena and forcibly described them in his

scholarly studies of the Dionysian writings, *Gott und die Seienden* (Göttingen, 1976) and "Pronoia und das Verhältnis von Metaphysik und Geschichte bei Dionysius Areopagita" in *Freiburger Zeitschrift für Philosophie und Theologie* 24 (1977) 1–2, pp. 165–186. Of course, as the theological position of Dr. Brons seems to be almost the exact opposite of my own, he notes these characteristics of Dionysian thought with disapproval.

18. It has often been observed that the Fathers of the Alexandrian tradition, in particular, seem more interested in the "incarnability" of the Logos and the universal theandric union of God with humanity as a whole than in the particular historic Incarnation, and something of this persists in Greek-Christian theology and theology influenced by it in the West. E. P. Meijering's "Cyril of Alexandria on the Platonists and the Trinity" in *God Being History* (Amsterdam-Oxford-New York, 1975) pp. 114–127 is of much interest in this connection.

19. For the way in which Dionysius speaks of the Trinity see, e.g., *Celestial Hierarchy* VII 4 (212C); *Ecclesiastical Hierarchy* I 3 (373C–D); *Divine Names* I 4 (592A); 5 (593B); II 7 (645B–C); III 1 (680B); XIII 3 (980D–981A); *Mystical Theology* III (1033A) and V (1048A; cf. Letter II). On the way in which Dionysius, as is generally supposed, adapts Athenian Neoplatonism to Christian purposes by a certain conflation of the Neoplatonic One and the Neoplatonic *Nous*, see the most recent discussion by S. Gersh *From Iamblichus to Eriugena* (Leiden, 1978). It is agreed that Dionysius is not a "hierarchical" thinker in the sense of Proclus (cf. my "Negative Theology"—see note 2—pp. 181–184) and that he uses very positive language about God's being, knowledge and action while strongly maintaining an extreme apophatic theology. But there are unsolved, and possibly insoluble, questions as to the precise relative importance of the contributions made to this Dionysian Christian Platonism by the distinctively Christian side of the theology which he inherited (especially from the Cappadocians), by the predominantly pre-Plotinian Platonism which was the philosophy most used by fourth-century theologians, and, possibly, by a return, which might have been deliberate, to a more Plotinian-Porphyrian kind of Neoplatonism (see p. 217 and note 4).

20. The principal Christological passage is *Divine Names* II 9–10 (648A–649A): cf. XI 1–2, 948D–953B where *Eirene* and "Jesus" or "Christ" seem to be interchangeable divine names.

21. In view of his great influence, the universal sweep of his vision of creation and salvation, and his intense devotion to the Incarnate Lord (who is much more than a symbol to him, however allegorically he interprets the details of his earthly life), Origen deserves particularly careful investigation on this point. And I do not wish to lump together the great thinkers, from Maximos onwards, who have more or less followed the Dionysian tradition under any superficial generalization.

22. See my "Man in the Cosmos" in *Romanitas et Christianitas* (Amsterdam-London, 1973) pp. 5–14.

23. The main Platonic authority for this conviction for later Platonists has of course been *Timaeus* 29D–30B, though it pervades the theology of the *Dialogues*. My way of putting it is a summary paraphrase of Proclus, *Elements of Theology,* Proposition 122 (especially p. 128, lines 19–21 Dodds).

Note: I had written this paper before the publication of Dr. E. P. Meijering's excellent book, *Theologische Urteile über die Dogmengeschichte: Ritschl's Einfluss auf von Harnack* (Leiden, 1978). This does a very great deal to clarify the nature, origin, and much of the development of what I have described as "biblical" theology, and in the author's final critique of Harnack suggests approaches to the Bible, Greek philosophy, and the theology of the Christian Fathers which, if they were widely followed, might lead to the transformation rather than the disintegration of our Inherited Conglomerate.

WHY CHRISTIANS SHOULD BE PLATONISTS

1. On Absolute theory, see also my *Ascent to the Absolute* (New York, 1970), *The Discipline of the Cave* (New York, 1966) and *The Transcendence of the Cave* (New York, 1967).

Index of Names
and Subjects

Absolute, The, 224ff.
Absolutism, 214ff.
Achillini, A., 175
Albertus Magnus, 122, 170, 173–4
Albinus, 22
Alcibiades, 70–1, 162
Alexander of Aphrodisias, 55, 57–8, 83, 170
Alexandria, School of, 45ff., 54ff., 77ff.
Alfarabi, 52
Alfaric, P., 35
Algazel, 175
Altaner, B., 39
Ambrose, Saint, 13–14
Amelius, 23
Ammonius of Alexandria, 43ff., 57, 77ff.
Ammonius Saccas, 23, 65
Analogy, 131ff.
Angels, 61, 161ff., 206ff.
Anima mundi, 99, 155ff.
Anonymous Commentary on the Parmenides, 28ff.

Anselm, 230
Antisthenes, 3
Anthropocentrism, 221
Apophasis. See "Negative theology"
Apuleius, 159
Aquinas, Thomas, 40, 59, 96ff., 122ff., 130–1, 134, 158, 163, 166, 170, 172–4, 230
Archetypes, 206ff. *See* "Forms"
Aristotle, 45–63 (*passim*), 77ff., 97–8, 106–7, 130, 152, 155, 157ff., 169ff., 178ff.
Arius, 29
Asceticism, 41
Asclepius, 77, 81
Astrology, 157ff.
Athanasius, Saint, 32–3, 39
Athanasius II (Patriarch), 46
Athena, 70
Athens, School of, 22, 45ff., 66ff.
Augustine, Saint, 24, 29, 34ff., 104, 114–5, 149, 158ff., 163, 166, 173, 175, 177, 198

Averroes, 152, 164, 170ff., 175ff.
Avicenna, 124, 147, 167

Barbaro, D., 131
Barbaro, E., 170, 172
Basil of Ancyra, 29–30
Basil, Saint, 39
Beauty, 160, 209ff.
Beierwaltes, 73
Being, 29ff., 47ff., 81ff., 89ff., 98ff., 114ff., 122f., 129ff., 224ff.
Being-Life-Intellect, 23, 28, 97ff.
Being, degrees of, 118ff., 173ff., 210ff.
Bessarion, 83, 144–5, 157, 162
Bible, 25ff., 181ff.
  Genesis, 39, 91
  Wisdom 7:27, 132
  Gospel of Saint John, Prologue, 25
    1:18, 27
    5:26, 27
    14:9–11, 28
    14:25–6, 27
  Epistles of Saint Paul, Romans 1:19, 148
    7:24, 197
    8:30, 73
    1 Corinthians 13:8, 197
    Philippians 2:5–7, 27
    Colossians 1:17, 73
    Titus 3:4, 71
  Epistle of Saint James 1:17, 149
Biel, G., 125–6
Bion, 3
Blemmydes, N., 85
Boese, H., 72
Boethius, 80, 133, 159
Bonaventure, Saint, 122
Booth, E., 36
Borro, G., 182
Bossier, G., 35
Boyer, C., 35
Brons, B., 66
Browning, E. Barrett, 190
Browning, R., 187ff.
Bruni, L., 146, 179
Bruno, G., 153, 178
Brutus, J., 175
Bultmann, R., 219
Buonamici, F., 176
Bussi, G. A., 144ff.

Cabbala, 163
Cajetan of Thiene, 170
Cameron, A., 50
Camuzio, A., 178ff.
Camuzio, F., 181
Carcopino, J., 17
Cardano, G., 181ff.
Cassirer, E., 152, 184
Castellani, G., 173

Causation, 20ff., 47ff., 90ff., 100ff., 114ff., 123ff.
Chaldaean Oracles, 22ff., 71ff., 158–9
Champier, S., 184
Chartres, School of, 120–1, 149
Chatillon, F., 35
Chorismos (separation), 78, 100, 105
Choumnos, N., 76, 84
Christ, 10, 14, 20ff., 119, 126, 165, 190ff., 219ff. *See* "Word"
Cicero, 179, 183
Clarembald of Arras, 120
Clement of Alexandria, 10–13, 15–18, 229
Conceptualism, 77ff.
Consubstantiality, 28ff.
Contarini, G., 175–6
Continuous procreation, 76
Conversio, 37ff.
Coreth, E., 138
Corsini, E., 65
Cosmas Indicopleustes, 60
Courcelle, P., 34
Creation, 25, 47ff., 77, 90ff., 101ff., 122ff., 221ff.
Cremonini, C., 176
Cumont, F., 34
Cupitt, D., 219
Cynics, 3

Damascius, 46, 64–5, 69
David of Alexandria, 46, 77, 86
De causis, Liber, 97ff., 134, 145, 173ff.
Demiurge, The, 9, 22, 77, 86, 90ff., 110ff., 155
Democritus (the Platonist), 69
Demons, 16, 68, 161ff.
Descartes, 125, 151, 227
Diaceto, F. da, 184
Dialectic, 132ff., 152
Dillon, J. M., 71
Dionysius the Areopagite, 64ff., 90ff., 97ff., 121, 137, 146ff., 173ff., 221ff., 230
Dodds, E. R., 21, 219
Donato, G., 170
Dörrie, H., 25
Dualism, 41, 161, 209ff.

Ebreo, L., 181
Eckhart, 128ff., 149, 152, 154
Eclecticism, 36, 180ff.
Ecstasy, 37
Elias of Alexandria, 46, 77, 83, 86
Emanation, 99, 119
Epictetus, 3, 18
Epicurus, 150–1
Eriugena, John Scottus, 69ff., 115–20, 122–5, 128–9
Eros, 160, 187ff., 221ff.
Esse. See "Being"
Essence, 89ff., 99, 114, 122

Eternity, 45ff., 98
Eucatastrophe, 204
Eudorus of Alexandria, 22
Eusebius of Caesarea, 66
Eustathius of Thessalonica, 5
Eustratius of Nicaea, 85
Evrard, E., 58
Exemplarism, 110ff. *See* "Demiurge"
Existence. *See* "Being"

Fabro, C., 179
Faith, 31–2, 198ff.
Faseolo, G., 173
Festugière, A. J. P., 34
Ficino, M., 157–68, 170ff., 174, 178, 183–4
Flodr, M., 179
Folliet, G., 34
Forms or Ideas, 22, 47, 49, 51, 76ff., 99ff.,
    109ff., 206ff.

Gadamer, H. G., 136ff.
Galileo Galilei, 176, 182
Gandillac, M. de, 136ff.
George of Trebizond, 145–6, 157, 174
Georgios Scholarios, 85
German Idealists, 189
Gersh, S., 66, 137
Gilbert of Poitiers, 130
Gilson, E., 41, 132
Giorgio, F., 184
Gnosticism, 17–18, 20, 165
God, 20ff., 24ff., 46ff., 91ff., 101ff., 109ff.,
    129ff., 147ff., 173ff., 187ff., 193ff.,
    214ff., 229ff.
God the Father, 19–20, 26ff., 72, 110, 197ff.
God the Son, 20, 25ff., 72, 110, 130, 197ff.
Gods, 103ff., 147, 160ff.
Godfrey of Fontaines, 174
Good, The, 21, 99ff., 110ff., 216ff., 225, 228
Grace, 37
Gregory of Nazianzen, 39–40
Gregory of Nyssa, 39, 154, 157, 230
Gregory Palamas, 121
Grimani, D., 175
Gudeman, A., 58

Hadot, P., 25, 29, 34–5
Harnack, A., 35
Hathaway, R. H., 65
Hegel, 136ff., 189
Heidegger, M., 205, 210
Henad, 73ff., 100, 106, 218
Henry Bate of Malines, 170
Henry of Ghent, 124, 174
Henry, P., 34–5
Hermeticism, 180
Hermias of Alexandria, 6–8, 15ff., 68
Hierarchy, 20ff., 103ff., 161ff., 173ff. *See*
    "Being"

Hierocles of Alexandria, 68–9
Hilduin, 90
Hinduism, 121
Hippolytus of Rome, 13
Holy Spirit, 20ff., 26ff., 72, 110, 197ff., 222
Homer, 3ff.
Honecker, M., 144

Iamblichus, 23ff., 65, 69, 71, 74, 84, 157, 172
Ignatius of Antioch, 66
Immanence/transcendence, 105, 133ff.
Immaterialism, 37ff.
Incarnation, The, 25ff., 38, 41, 165, 190ff., 204,
    220ff., 229ff.
Intellect (*Nous*), 22ff., 30, 56ff., 67, 79, 99ff.,
    111ff., 129, 136, 170ff.
Irenaeus, 39
Isidorus, 46
Italos, J., 85

James of Viterbo, 170
Javelli, G. C., 175
Jerome, Saint, 19–20
Jewish Platonists, 207, 211
Jews, 229
John of Scythopolis, 66ff.
Jones, H., 188
Julian the Apostate, 69
Justinian, 19–20, 50

Kannicht, R., 73
Kant, 152, 157, 189, 225
Kingdom of Heaven, 15, 227
Klibansky, R., 146, 164
Knowledge, 78ff., 192ff., 207ff.
Koch, H., 65
Koch, J., 132

Language as icon, 217ff.
Leibnitz, 154
Lessing, 157
Lewis, C. S., 203ff.
Life. *See* "Being"
Logos, 7, 16–17, 26ff., 39, 113ff., 222
Lossky, V., 136ff.
Lucian of Samosata, 15
Lucretius, 36, 152, 158

Macrobius, 133
Madruzzo, C., 181–2
Manichaeism, 204
Marcel, R., 162
Marcellus of Ancyra, 28
Marinus, 64
Marrou, H. I., 34
Martello, B., 162
Matter, 9, 22, 47ff., 107, 173ff.
Maximus of Ephesus, 69

Maximus of Turin, 14
Maximus of Tyre, 9
Mazzoni, J., 176
Medici, Cosimo de', 145, 157, 159
Medici, Lorenzo de', 159, 162–3, 167
Medici, Pietro de', 159
Messiah, 227
Methodius of Olympus, 13
Middle Platonism, 9, 15ff., 22ff., 79
Milton, J., 198
Moerbeke, William of, 54, 61, 72, 134, 145, 159, 170, 171
Moses Maimonides, 149
Moule, C. F. D., 220
Movement, 47ff.
Murdoch, I., 218
Murray, G., 119
Myth, 3ff., 217ff.

Naasenes, 17
Nag Hammadi Treatise II, 6, 17
Names (divine), 67ff.
Negative theology, 40, 146ff., 199, 216ff.
Neopythagoreanism, 180
Nicaea, Council of, 32
Nicene Creed, The, 29, 226
Nicholas of Cusa, 128, 143ff.
Nifo, A., 171ff., 175ff.
Nominalism, 77ff., 125–6, 152
Non-being, 95, 173ff.
Nous. See "Intellect"
Numenius, 9, 15–17, 22–23, 165

Ockham, William of, 125, 152
Olympiodorus, 23, 46, 55, 61, 77, 83
O'Meara, D. J., 28
One, The, 29, 40, 99ff., 111ff., 129, 132ff., 188
Opifex. See "Demiurge"
Origen, 16, 19ff., 39, 59, 65, 73, 162, 166, 229
Orpheus, Pseudo, 159
Orsini, R., 167
Otherworldliness, 26, 37, 41, 209ff.
Ousia, 30, 80ff., 91ff., 99
Ovid, 161, 179

Paracelsus, 191ff.
Parmenides, 97
Participation, 98ff., 174ff., 209
Passeri, M., 173
Patrizi, F., 184
Paul, Saint, 22, 65, 67, 71, 148, 162. *See* "Bible"
Paul of Venice, 170, 174
Pégis, A., 126
Pendasio, F., 173
Pépin, J., 34
Peter, Saint, 67
Petrarch, 146, 164
Phantasia, 56

Philo of Alexandria, 79
Philoponus, J., 45ff., 54ff., 77, 80ff.
Philosophia perennis, 214
Photius, 85
Piccolomini, F., 173
Pico de la Mirandola, G., 157, 163, 178, 180ff.
Plato, 5–8, 37, 45, 59, 61, 62, 69, 70–1, 78–9, 102–3, 110–1, 114, 137, 145ff., 157ff., 170ff., 179ff., 198, 204, 212, 214, 218, 228ff.
Plethon, G., 85, 145, 158
Plotinus, 5, 7, 15, 26, 29, 35ff., 51, 65, 73, 79, 99ff., 104, 111ff., 137, 157ff., 170ff., 174, 176, 180, 198, 207, 213, 228ff.
Plutarch of Athens, 55, 57, 69
Plutarch of Chaeronea, 4, 70
Pneuma, 20
Pneumatics, 21
Pomponazzi, P., 175, 178
Porphyry, 8ff., 16, 23, 25ff., 35ff., 60, 79ff., 85, 99, 160ff., 173
Posidonius, 79
Power-Wisdom-Love, 162, 198ff.
Predication, 130ff.
Predominence, 30
Prime Mover, 48ff., 155
Priscianus Lydus, 55
Proclus, 5, 7, 14ff., 20ff., 45–6, 55, 64ff., 90, 97ff., 133, 144ff., 171ff., 213, 218
Providence, 37, 45, 61, 91, 167
Psellus, M., 23, 86
Psychology. *See* "Soul," "Intellect"
Puech, Ch. H., 34
Pythagoreans, 4

Quint, J., 134

Rahner, H., 16
Rationes aeternae, 114ff.
Realism, 77ff., 97ff.
Redemption, 26, 165, 221
Resurrection, 36, 60
Roques, R., 65
Roscelin, 77
Rufinus, 19–20

Sabellianism, 28
Saffrey, H. D., 46
Salvation, 16, 25ff., 38ff.
Savonarola, 162
Sccpticism, 183, 190ff., 215ff.
Schelling, 189
Schleiermacher, F., 137ff.
Scholasticism, 121ff., 163–4, 173ff.
Scotus, John Duns, 175
Seneca, 3
Shakti, 121
Sheldon-Williams, I. P., 73–4
Siger of Brabant, 174

Simon the Mage, 17
Simplicianus, 24
Simplicius, 46, 50ff., 55–6, 80, 169ff.
Smith, W. C., 219
Socrates, 6ff., 68ff., 161ff., 207
Sophonias, 54
Soul, 4ff., 22, 25ff., 56ff., 99ff., 160ff., 170ff., 198, 209ff., 229ff.
Spinoza, 125
Stead, C., 217
Steel, C., 74
Stephanus of Alexandria, 46, 54ff., 77
Steuco, A., 184
Subordinationism, 20, 28ff.
Substance. *See "Ousia"*
Suicide, 46
Synesius of Cyrene, 35, 45
Syrianus, 21ff., 62, 68ff., 71, 158, 228
Swineshead, R., 174ff.

Theiler, W., 35, 71–2
Themistius, 46, 170ff.
Theurgy, 68ff.
Thierry of Chartres, 120, 149
Tigerstadt, A. N., 183
Time, 48ff., 95ff., 228
Tolkein, J. R., 203ff.
Transcendence. *See* "Immanence"
Travesari, A., 146
Triad, 71, 99ff., 161, 188ff., 221
Trinity, 19ff., 25ff., 129ff., 135ff., 152, 162, 165, 189ff., 218, 221, 230
Trombetta, A., 175

Trouillard, J., 213ff.
Truth, 129, 131ff., 187ff., 209ff.

Ulysses, 3ff.
Unity, 105, 129ff.
Universals, 75ff., 102ff.
Urs von Balthasar, H., 66

Vancourt, R., 58
Vanneste, J., 65
Varro, 36
Vernia, N., 170ff.
Victorinus, M., 24ff., 40
Vimercato, F., 173
Vio, T. de, 175
Virgil, 14, 161

Walker, D. P., 180
Westerink, L. G., 61, 69
Whittaker, T., 74
Wieland, W., 52
Wiles, M., 218
William of Conches, 137
Williams, C., 203ff.
Word, The, 25ff., 113ff., 130, 153, 156. *See* "God"

Zabarella, J., 179
Zerbo, G., 175
Zeus, 69, 160
Zimarra, M., 175ff.
Zohar, 207
Zoroaster, 158, 161, 167